Practical Trial Handbook

California

A Concise and Practical Guide on the Rules of
Evidence, Courtroom Procedure, and Trial Skills &
Strategies

Judge Mark S. Curry (Ret.)

Acknowledgements

Thank you to my wife for her superb editing and to Judge Horst for his inspiration and support. I also wish to acknowledge the citizens of the State of California and the Placer County Superior Court for allowing me the opportunity and honor to serve as a judge.

Introduction

For 36 years I have worked in the courtroom, initially as a prosecutor for 22 years, then as a Superior Court judge in Northern California until my recent retirement. As a prosecutor, I tried many cases, including 24 murder trials to a verdict. As a trial court judge, I have presided over hundreds of jury or court trials, from complex murder and civil cases to half-day civil or family law bench trials. As a result, I have had the opportunity to observe many lawyers trying their cases, ranging in skill from the extraordinary to the incompetent. I have witnessed seemingly strong cases lost due to poor lawyering and marginal cases won due to exceptional skills. I have seen what works and what does not work in the courtroom.

One of my observations over time has been that some lawyers show up for trial unprepared. Not in the sense of not knowing the substantive issues or law, but rather unprepared regarding their trial skills and lack of knowledge of basic rules of evidence and procedure. One reason I believe this to be true is that most lawyers do not try cases on a consistent basis and can get a little rusty, so to speak. Months, if not years, can pass by between trials, and some attorneys may only try one or two cases over the span of their entire career. Furthermore, attorneys who do try cases often, such as prosecutors and criminal defense attorneys, do not have the time to focus on improving their trial skills and knowledge because of their heavy caseloads. Another observation is that even experienced trial lawyers tend to repeat the same mistakes because that is how they first learned the skill.

More than five years ago, I began contemplating a handbook that would set forth and explain the rules of evidence, trial procedure, and basic trial tactics and strategies that every trial lawyer should know in order to competently try any type of case in any jurisdiction. A treatise that would capture the nuts and bolts of a trial and/or a contested evidentiary hearing, from beginning to end. I realized, however, that there are already many professionally written treaties available covering nearly every aspect of trial practice, so I wanted my handbook to be more practical, concise, and a little less formal than the others; a handbook law students and less experienced trial lawyers could use as a learning tool and the more experienced as a refresher.

The result is the *Practical Trial Handbook* which I believe has accomplished my objectives. In this handbook the evidentiary rules and procedures related to nearly every aspect of a court or bench trial are explained and described, from the motion in limine to the final argument and everything in between. In addition, the handbook describes basic trial tactics and strategies lawyers must know, such as how to introduce evidence, cross-examine a witness, or deliver a persuasive closing argument. Specific areas of discussion and explanation include pre-trial procedures, jury selection, opening statements, foundational requirements for evidence, direct and cross-examination, strategies for impeachment, expert witnesses, trial objections, courtroom presentation, hearsay and other exclusionary rules, and closing argument. The handbook is designed to cover the rules, procedures, and strategies common to nearly every type of trial or contested evidentiary hearing, regardless of the substantive law. Thus, whether you practice in criminal, civil, juvenile, family, or probate, etc., if you have to try a case to a jury or the court, this handbook should be helpful.

Perhaps most importantly, the handbook also contains more than 150 "Trial Tips," practical, real-world advice on trying a case that cannot be learned in the classroom nor found in the more formal trial treatises. The tips provide not only basic "how to" advice, but also give suggestions on trial tactics or strategies which have proven to be successful. These informal and wide-ranging "Trial Tips" can be found throughout the handbook for nearly every stage of a trial and, in my opinion, are what sets this handbook apart from the others.

In order to cover all the applicable rules of evidence, courtroom procedures, and trial tactics in one handbook of less than 300 pages, it was necessary to distill information and to provide in some areas merely an overview of potentially very complicated areas of the law, e.g., the hearsay rule. Thus, one could argue that perhaps the handbook is too basic and too generic. For example, the rules of evidence discussed are commonly cited and some of the trial strategies and tactics mentioned are well known. However, having observed many lawyers litigating their cases, I have found that the most effective and successful are those who understand the fundamentals and simply stick to the basics.

In this regard, the handbook is not meant to be an exhaustive, highly-refined legal treatise on evidence or trial practice. There are plenty of well-written and researched resources out there to consult for specific trial issues or more complex areas of law. In addition, the suggestions and comments in this book concerning what judges do or may prefer, or what tactics or strategies to use, are strictly my own opinions and suggestions. They are not a reflection of how other judges may run their courtrooms or apply the law, nor should counsel feel compelled to follow, or even use, any trial tactic or procedure recommended. And, of course, I am not giving any form of legal advice. Lastly, keep in mind that the law and the rules cited are meant only to provide you with the basic legal principles and should not be a substitute for your own independent legal research to confirm the current law applicable in your jurisdiction.

There are two editions: The *Practical Trial Handbook* references the Federal Rules of Evidence (FRE) citing Federal authority with California case law and citations for comparison. The *Practical Trial Handbook California* focuses on the California Rules of Evidence, with reference to the Federal Rules of Evidence that are contained at the end of the book. Other than those differences, however, the two handbooks cover essentially the same material.

In closing, there is no substitute for trial experience. However, I am confident that if you learn the fundamentals and develop good basic trial skills as discussed in this book, you are well underway to becoming an accomplished and successful trial lawyer. Good luck. Mark Curry

CONTENTS

1. STRATEGIES FOR SUCCESS

Before delving into the nuts and bolts of a trial, it might be worthwhile to briefly consider the question of what makes a *good* trial lawyer. In every legal community there are always certain attorneys who develop the reputation of being such a lawyer. They gain this reputation not only because they are successful in trial, but also because of how they handle themselves and present their cases. As a judge who has seen many trial lawyers come and go over the years, it is easy to spot the good ones. The question becomes, therefore, what is it that these attorneys do or know that less successful attorneys do not?

Upon reflection, I have come to my own conclusions regarding this question. I have observed that many successful trial lawyers tend to employ some of the same strategies or have certain traits in common. Although difficult to quantify, I have nonetheless attempted to distill these common denominators into general categories. These traits or characteristics may seem obvious, but if you are lacking in any one of them, your trial effectiveness is diminished, perhaps significantly. Keep in mind, however, that being "effective" in the courtroom does not necessarily equate to winning or losing; rather, it means only that the lawyer has mastered the skill of presenting a case well. The by-product of becoming an effective trial lawyer is that you will then improve your chances of success.

Persona

To begin with, there is no one specific type of person that makes a good trial lawyer. However, there are some general characteristics I have noticed that successful litigators tend to share. First, you must like the courtroom environment, meaning, you are not bothered by working in a very public setting or by public speaking. Some people are very excellent attorneys, but simply prefer not to do much in the courtroom because it does not suit their personality. Secondly, in the courtroom, you cannot be a wallflower because trying a case does require a certain amount of assertiveness. If you try many cases, you will undoubtedly come across attorneys who are overly aggressive, to the point of being overbearing. They will interrupt, object to everything, and generally make the courtroom environment unpleasant. As opposing counsel, you must be able to stand up to these types of attorneys and make yourself known. On the other hand, you do *not* have to be one of those overbearing, over-aggressive attorneys to be successful. In fact, just the opposite is true. Those types of attorneys are often less successful in the courtroom because of their antics and behavior, which is a turn-off not only to the jurors, but also the court. Lastly, to be a good trial lawyer you must be a good communicator, because much of trial work is speaking and talking. On the other hand, you do not have to be Clarence Darrow. In fact, many successful trial lawyers have speech impediments that does not diminish their effectiveness in the slightest.

Case Evaluation

Successful trial lawyers know how to accurately evaluate the "worth" or strength of a case long before trial. They can objectively analyze the strengths and weaknesses of the evidence and predict how the case may unfold at trial. If you start out with a case that is problematic from the inception, not even the most experienced trial lawyer may be able to save it, and the result is likely to be a substantial loss of time and money. Thus, one common reason for an unexpected result at trial is simply that the case should never have been tried in the first place. Successful trial lawyers, therefore, are those who know which cases to try and which cases to settle, or not pursue at all.

Trial Tip: Run the facts past a colleague or disinterested third party for a more unbiased opinion. Put the case away for a few days; then take a second look.

Preparation

The best lawyers are generally the most prepared and organized. This may seem patently obvious, but surprisingly, I have observed more than a few trials where counsel seemed ill-prepared. There are many things that need to be done in preparation for a trial, and how to prepare for any particular type of trial is beyond the scope of this handbook. However, the first step is to find and follow a checklist to help keep you organized. (See e.g., Cal. Prac. Guide Civ. Trials & Evd. ¶ 1:2 [Trial Preparation Checklist]) For the trial itself, one of the most important steps in preparation is to have a detailed outline for each witness covering the expected testimony for direct as well as cross-examination. Commonly, the witness's prior statements, such as deposition testimony, are used to create the outline that lists the relevant facts and evidence to be elicited. Preparing these outlines in advance will give you a roadmap to follow. The witness outlines are also helpful when planning for the opening statement and/or the closing argument. The bottom line is that planning and preparation are key to success. You cannot "wing" a trial and expect good results.

Juror (Court) Appreciation

Seasoned trial lawyers appreciate their audience. This requires an awareness that it is the opinion of those twelve people sitting only a few feet away in the jury box that matters the most. In the case of a bench trial, obviously, it is the judge who must be impressed with your performance. Some attorneys do not fully appreciate this concept. They seem to pay attention to the jurors only during jury selection and then totally ignore them once the evidence begins. There can sometimes develop a disconnect between what the lawyer thinks he or she is proving versus how the jury (or court) perceives the evidence. On too many occasions I have observed lawyers bickering and quibbling between themselves over inconsequential matters or feverishly attempting to prove or disprove uncontested matters, while in the meantime, the jurors (and the court) have checked out. Had the attorneys bothered to look over at the jury, they would have seen eyes that are either glazed over, staring at the ceiling, looking at watches, or even closed in sleep. Experienced trial lawyers, on the other hand, appreciate their audience. They monitor the mood and attentiveness of the jurors and the judge. They design and present their case with the jurors specifically in mind. They think about the case and the evidence from the jurors' perspective. Lastly, if it is a bench trial, do not assume the court knows all when it comes to the law or is supremely capable of digesting complex facts without difficulty. Judges sometimes have a lot on their plate, so make your presentation easy for them to follow too.

Brevity

Successful trial lawyers know another secret: Sometimes, less is more in the courtroom. The most effective courtroom presentations are generally those that are concise and to the point. There is a tendency for some attorneys, even experienced, to over-try their cases. They enter too much evidence, call too many witnesses, and present too much detail. Like nervous travelers packing luggage until it is bursting, they over-pack with unnecessary information. Less-experienced trial lawyers find it hard to pack light because they lack the confidence and worry they will be perceived as not being thorough enough. Consequently, they throw everything but the kitchen sink at the jury, which dilutes the strength of the important points they make. Jurors have limited attention spans and poor long-term recall. Successful trial lawyers look for ways to pare down a case to make it lean and mean and can overcome the temptation to over-try it.

> **Trial Tip:** Jurors are impressed with attorneys who seem prepared and get to the point. The slowness and repetition of a trial are common juror complaints. In your opening statement, and even your closing argument, explain how you have streamlined and shortened it for their benefit. They will be appreciative.

Self-Awareness

Experienced lawyers are aware they are also on trial. The minute jurors first enter the courtroom, they immediately begin to size up the attorneys and form impressions. Judges do this too. It is only human nature. They are curious. They will check out appearances and dress, some more critically than others. They will observe the attorneys' mannerisms, how well they speak, and whether they act professional or seem unprepared. They will note whether an attorney is polite or rude and how they treat witnesses, opposing counsel, and the court. Some jurors will be skeptical and distrustful of attorneys. To one degree or another, every juror will quickly form an initial impression of an attorney or the case, which may carry through the entire trial even if it is erroneous. There is also a tendency for some lawyers to pander or over-ingratiate themselves to jurors, especially during jury selection. Perhaps a little of this might be helpful to improve the jurors' impression or image of the lawyer, but often it feels contrived and insincere. Jurors are intuitive. If they sense you are play acting, you lose credibility. Successful trial lawyers gain the trust of the jury (and the court) by acting professional and down to earth.

Trial Tip: Attorney personality conflicts at trial can affect impartiality. Don't be tempted to stoop to the level of an attorney who is rude or unprofessional. If you stay calm and professional in the face of adversity, the jurors (and the court) will take note.

Presentation

Lastly, and perhaps most importantly, effective trial lawyers know how to choreograph their presentation to make it as impactful and memorable as possible. Even if you have the facts and law on your side, if you do not present your case in a clear, concise, and interesting format, your chances of success can be greatly diminished. The problem is that in this modern era of the internet, social media, and overdramatized court shows, people are accustomed to a high degree of sensory stimulation, mostly visual, in a short period. Their only previous experience with a courtroom may be drawn from Hollywood, and they expect to be entertained. Real-life trials, however, are not nearly as exciting and *much* slower. Holding the juror's (and the court's) attention throughout trial is a real problem.

Thus, good trial lawyers design their presentation to capture and hold the jurors' attention. They employ a little Psychology 101 to help the jurors remember by incorporating stimuli and memory aids, such as demonstrative evidence, and making their presentation professional. They attempt to make their case entertaining even when the subject matter is dry.

Trial Tip: Do a little research (online) regarding the problems associated with human memory and retention, especially for jurors. There are some studies out there on the topic. Using strategies and tactics to make your case more interesting and memorable will pay dividends.

2. PRE-TRIAL PROCEDURES & EVIDENCE

After weeks, months, or even years of preparation, the day finally arrives when you walk through the courtroom doors with your brief case in hand and a box of evidence, ready for trial. It might be your first trial or it might be your 100th, but there is still a sense of excitement and nervousness. This is the courtroom where the case will be tried. However, before the first witness is called, there is still important work to be done and the success or failure of your case could hinge upon how this pre-trial stage proceeds. Some lawyers overlook the importance of this phase, and consequently, risk starting at a disadvantage right from the very beginning.

Trial Brief

A "trial brief" should be considered for nearly every type of trial. The brief should have been written well before trial and filed with the court prior to trial or on the first day, depending on the local court rules. Typically, the court will review the trial briefs in chambers, often prior to even meeting with the parties for the first time. Thus, it is a golden opportunity to educate the court about your theories and facts prior to the commencement of the trial. Because the judge may be making important decisions and rulings that affect your case, you want the court to be fully conversant with every aspect of your case.

> **Trial Tip:** The trial brief should be concise and easy to follow. The judge's initial impressions matter, especially when it comes to the motions. If the judge is unclear or confused about any aspect of your case, you are already at a disadvantage.

The "trial brief" should be just that—"brief." It should contain a concise statement of the facts and legal theories. Do not write a novel. Keep it relatively short and to the point. A trial brief that exceeds five or six typed pages usually contains too much information, unless the case is complex. A well-written trial brief will generally contain: 1) A brief description of the parties and procedural history; 2) a summary of the causes of action, claims, defenses, and damages requested; 3) a summary of the facts and contested issues at trial; and 4) a summary of the relevant law pertaining to each cause of action, if needed. If there is a particularly thorny legal issue, you might also consider filing a separate "pocket brief"—written points and authorities that sets forth the relevant law in a page or two. However, most judges typically do not like reading page after page of obviously cut-and-pasted boilerplate law. Generally, the trial brief is distinct from a motion in limine and filed separately. Check your local rules.

Conference with the Court

Generally, one of the first procedural things to happen on the first day of trail is the judge will conference with the parties. If all parties have counsel, typically the conference occurs in the judge's chambers and it is often informal with no court reporter present. If one or more of the parties is pro per, many courts prefer to hold the conference in the courtroom. Some court rules require such a pre-trial conference. (See e.g., FRCP 16(e); CA Rule of Ct. 3.670).

The primary purpose of the conference is to learn about the court's particular procedures and to talk scheduling. At the conference, the judge may request that counsel summarize the case to get an overview. Hopefully, by this point, the judge will have read the trial briefs and thus be familiar with the issues. Keep in mind, however, that although you have lived with the case for a year or more and are intimately aware of all its nuances, the judge is just now learning about it. The judge may also not be well versed in the contested areas of law. Every judge has his or her own idiosyncrasies or procedures for trial, so the pre-trial conference is the time to ask questions. Some courts may even issue written trial policies and procedures to follow.

Some judges may only discuss matters peripherally, preferring that any substantive issues should be discussed on the record and in the courtroom. Other judges, however, may allow the parties to delve into the facts and contested issues in chambers in a more informal setting. Be aware that some judges might even begin making rulings and decisions about the case, just based on what counsel is relating in chambers. The following are topics typically covered at the pre-trial conference:

- *Trial scheduling* – Establishing a detailed trial schedule generally benefits everyone. As any experienced trial lawyer knows, witness scheduling can be a real headache, especially for experts such as doctors who often have scheduling conflicts. Experienced judges will push the lawyers to come up with *realistic* time estimates and will be cautious about underestimating the length. The pre-trial conference is the time to alert the court to any scheduling problems. The more planning and thought that goes into the scheduling at this early stage, the more efficiently a trial normally proceeds. If there are witness scheduling conflicts, consider conferring with opposing counsel about taking certain witnesses out of order. Most judges will not care, if the parties agree.

- *Jury Selection Procedures* – Every court will have its own rules and procedures for jury selection. Issues to consider include the form and substance of a questionnaire, the selection process, e.g., "six-pack" or struck jury, attorney voir dire and time limits, and procedures for making a challenge for cause and/or exercising a peremptory challenge to strike a juror. (See Jury Selection, infra, at p. 29.)

- *Settlement* – Discussion regarding possible last-minute settlement might be raised by the court. Many cases do settle on the eve of trial, especially if the court is willing to help with negotiations. However, some ethical guidelines may prevent the trial court from conducting extensive settlement negotiations, unless the parties stipulate that it will not prevent the court from presiding over the trial if settlement fails. (*Roth v. Parker* (1997) 57 Cal.App.4th 542, 549.)

- *Motions in Limine* – If the parties have filed motions in limine, determine the court's preference for hearing the motions and whether an evidentiary hearing may be required outside the presence of the jurors? Confirm you have received all motions filed by your opponent. In some jurisdictions, the court may have already ruled on some evidentiary motions prior to trial. (See Motions in Limine, infra, at p. 13.).

- *Stipulations* – Any stipulations or agreements between the parties should be addressed and solidified. Stipulations of uncontested fact or admissibility is a good method to streamline and shorten a trial. Often, pre-trial motions are resolved by stipulation. Knowing this, experienced judges often direct the parties to meet and confer on this issue if they have not.

Trial Tip: The use of stipulations at trial can be a real timesaver. This usually benefits all parties. The key is to work out the stipulations with opposing counsel prior to trial *and* to express them in *writing* to avoid any possible miscommunication.

- *Courtroom Procedure and Etiquette* – Every court will have its own set of courtroom rules and procedures, both formal and informal. In addition, every judge has his or her own idiosyncrasies about how things should be handled. The courtroom staff is a good resource. Familiarize yourself with the following procedures: marking and handling of exhibits; the court's preferences for examining witnesses, e.g., from counsel table, standing, or behind a podium; entering the well and/or approaching witnesses; objections and sidebar conferences; the use of courtroom AV equipment; and will the case be reported?

- *Court Reporter* – Whether the trial will be reported or not should be considered. If the trial is not reported, counsel should be aware that the lack of a reporter's transcript may make an appeal exceedingly difficult, if not impossible. For example, if the court makes a ruling, the appellate court will presume the trial court applied the correct standards of law. (*State Farm Fire & Casualty Co. v. Pietak* (2001) 90 Cal.App.4th 600, 610.) Moreover, it is the appellant's responsibility to provide an adequate record demonstrating error and prejudice from the error. (*Aguilar v. Avis Rent A Car System, Inc.* (1999) 21 Cal.4th 121, 132; *Denham v. Superior Court* (1970) 2 Cal.3d 557, 564.)

- *Instructions* – The court's procedures or preferences regarding the jury instructions/verdict forms should be discussed. Many judges prefer that jury instructions are provided to the court by counsel as early as possible. In fact, California C.C.P. § 607a, requires that counsel *shall* deliver to the court and opposing counsel all proposed jury instructions before the first witness is sworn in. "In a civil case, each of the parties must propose complete and comprehensive instructions in accordance with his theory of the litigation; if the parties do not do so, the court has no duty to instruct on its own motion. Neither a trial court nor a reviewing court in a civil action is obligated to seek out theories plaintiff might have advanced, or to articulate for him that which he has left unspoken." (*Metcalf v. County of San Joaquin Supreme Court of California* (2008) 42 Cal.4th 1121, 1131.)

Procedures for Exhibits and Evidence

Before the trial starts in earnest, it is important to familiarize yourself with the rules and procedures regarding exhibits and evidence. The pre-trial conference is a good time to learn. In the typical trial, on the first day the parties show up at the courtroom with their boxes and/or binders of "evidence," materials they plan to use. Obviously, depending on the type of case, the are many different forms of "evidence" that might be admitted. The more common include documents, reports, records, photographs, recordings (video and/or audio), diagrams, maps, and more tangible items, such as crime scene evidence. Many courts and jurisdictions have rules and procedures regarding how to handle items of evidence and the pre-trial conference is a good time to learn those procedures.

Trial Tip: The courtroom clerk and the bailiff should be your best friends. They know the court's idiosyncrasies and procedures. In addition, at some point you may need a small "favor," e.g., a copy or to get in the courtroom early to set up. If you're rude or condescending, the copy shop is down the street and wait for the proper time.

Marked for Identification

Generally, any proffered item of evidence will need to be "*marked for identification*" as an exhibit. Typically, the court clerk is responsible for marking, documenting, and maintaining the courtroom exhibits. Many courts require that all proffered evidence should be "pre-marked" at the beginning of the trial to avoid interruption once the trial begins. Thus, on the first day of trial, the parties bring their proposed evidence to the courtroom and submit it to the court clerk for marking. If there are only a few items of evidence, the process is relatively simple and uncomplicated. The clerk will log the item, give it an exhibit number, and attach a sticker or other marking to the exhibit. (See below.) The clerk generally maintains an exhibit list with a description of each item and the corresponding exhibit number. This list will be used later by the court and counsel when the court is requested to officially "admit" the items as evidence.

Exhibit Sticker/Tag

Courts have different methods for marking the exhibits. For example, some courts have plaintiff's exhibits marked with a number and defendant's exhibits marked with a letter. Other courts use sequential numbers, regardless of which party is submitting, but assign certain numbers by party, e.g., plaintiff's exhibits are 1-99, and defendant's 100-199. Some courts have the exhibits marked sequentially, regardless of which party is proffering them. During the trial and testimony, the evidence item will generally be referred to by the assigned exhibit number or letter.

Counsel: "Sir, showing you what has been marked for identification as item
        number 14, do you recognize this?"

Documents can be challenging if a party is seeking to admit a large number. Rather than mark each individual page, the court often directs that certain documents should be secured together in some fashion, i.e., stapled or in a binder, and marked as one exhibit. For example, a 25-page contract would only receive one exhibit number.

Trial Tip: Prepared attorneys come to court with their exhibits organized, separated, and even pre-marked, if they know the court's marking system. Clerks appreciate these attorneys, compared to those who show up with a mass of disorganized exhibits and expect the clerk to figure it out. Check the court's local rules regarding exhibits beforehand.

Exchange or Review of Exhibits

It is obviously important that by the first day of trial you are familiar with the opposing parties proposed evidence, including their witnesses and the substance of their testimony. With today's modern discovery statutes, the days of surprise evidence or witnesses at trial are over, or at least they should be. Nonetheless, a relatively common motion in limine is a request to exclude evidence or issue sanctions on the bases that a party failed to comply with a discovery requirement. Thus, one of your objectives during the pre-trial stage is to confirm that you do, in fact, have all the discovery and that there will not be any surprises during trial that could potentially prejudice your case.

In this regard, you should be familiar with the actual evidence and exhibits the opposing party will seek to admit. Some judges will direct the parties to meet and confer to review and/or exchange exhibit lists. Keep in mind that judges prefer to have all known objections and issues litigated *before* the jury arrives and some tend to get grumpy when objections are made during testimony that could have been raised in limine. On the other hand, there could be valid tactical reasons a party may hold back on marking or disclosing some exhibits or evidence that might be used only for *impeachment* or cross-examination.

Trial Tip: Before testimony begins, you should have a pretty good idea what evidence your *opponent* plans to introduce. Consider making a request to view any evidence your opponent intends to show the jury during the opening statement. Some courts may require it.

Motion to Admit

Generally, before an item of evidence is formally "admitted" or "received" as evidence, the proponent must make a formal motion to "admit" it. The timing of when the motion is made can vary, depending on the jurisdiction and the court's preferences. If there are only a few exhibits to be admitted, some courts may permit the motion as soon as the foundational elements have been established, often while the jury is present. However, other judges may prefer that the motion be made after the entirety of the witness's testimony is complete, including cross-examination, but before the witness departs the courtroom. If there are numerous exhibits to be admitted, constantly interrupting the testimony to hear and rule on each motion can be disruptive and time consuming. It is a process the jury does not need to see, particularly if there are objections. In this circumstance, some courts direct that the formal motions to admit evidence should occur towards the end of the party's case and outside the presence of the jury. The judge may permit the proponent party to lay the foundation and then "publish" it to the jury, even before the item is technically admitted or received as evidence. This is particularly true if there is no real dispute regarding admissibility. To keep the trial moving forward, the court may also permit a party to rest their case, "subject to" the court's formal ruling on the admission of the exhibits. Later, at a convenient time, the court will convene outside the presence of the jury to rule on the motions, using the clerk's exhibit sheet as a guide.

> **Trial Tip:**. If there is a particular exhibit where the admissibility is highly contested, it might be wise to request permission from the court to make the motion to admit it before the witness departs the courtroom in case additional testimony is required.

Objection Required

When a motion to admit evidence is made, the court will inquire of the opposing party whether there is an "objection." Obviously, if there is no objection, the court will admit the evidence. If there is an objection, it must be timely and specific. Stating, "I submit it," is tantamount to no objection. If you do object, you must state specifically the basis for your objection, e.g., relevance, lack of authentication, etc., otherwise, the court may summarily overrule your objection, even though there might have been some deficiency. (See Trial Objections, infra, at p. 210.) Generally, there is no sua sponte duty of the court to determine relevance and admissibility in the absence of an objection. (*United States v. Multi— Management, Inc.,* 743 F.2d 1359, 1364 (9th Cir.1984); *People v. Griggs* (2003) 110 Cal.App.4th 1137, 1139.) Even incompetent evidence can be admitted if there is no objection. (*People v. Panah* (2005) 35 Cal.4th 395, 476; CA Evid. Code § 353.)

Steps to Admit Evidence

1. ***Item Marked for Identification*** – Each item of evidence is marked for identification with a reference number or letter, generally at the beginning of the trial.

2. ***Opposing Counsel Preview*** – Generally, the opposing party has the right to inspect an exhibit or an item of evidence *before* it is presented to the witness or jury, e.g., a document or a photograph. (See also discussion re: production of writing used to refresh memory, Evid. Code § 771, at p. 71-72.) The purpose of allowing the inspection is to avoid surprise and to give the opposing party an opportunity to object. Some attorneys like to make a record of this process.

Counsel: "May the record reflect I have shown counsel a copy of the contract, exhibit 14." [Exhibit then shown to witness]

3. ***Permission to Approach*** – If a witness must handle or examine an exhibit while on the witness stand, many judges require, and it is good court etiquette, to request permission from the court to approach the witness and/or enter the well.

Counsel: "Your Honor, permission to approach the witness?" … or …"Your Honor, may I approach the witness?"

4. ***Witness Identifies/Authenticates the Exhibit*** – The proponent establishes or lays the proper foundation required for admissibility. This typically requires a witness to explain, describe, or "authenticate" the exhibit. (See Authentication, infra, at p. 154 et seq.)

Counsel: "I'm handing you what has been marked for identification as exhibit 14. Do you recognize what is depicted in this photograph?"
Witness: "Yes, it's a picture of the intersection where the accident happened."
Counsel: "Does the photograph accurately and fairly depict the intersection as it appeared on the morning of the accident?"
Witness: "Yes, it does."

5. ***Motion to Admit*** – Before an item of evidence is officially "admitted" or "received" as evidence, there must be a formal motion. In some jurisdictions, counsel will "offer" to have an item admitted.

Counsel: "Your Honor, I move to have exhibit 14 admitted"…or… "I move to admit exhibit 14 into evidence"…or…"Your Honor, I would offer exhibit 14."

Stipulation to Admission

Evidence is often admitted by agreement or stipulation. A stipulation saves time and generally benefits both parties to help streamline and shorten the trial. Often, these stipulations relate to evidence that is uncontroverted. The pre-trial conference is a good time to discuss with opposing counsel and the court any proposed stipulations. Courts typically do not get involved with stipulations regarding evidence and will usually accept them *if* the parties are not stipulating to masses of extraneous and irrelevant materials. In a bench trial, the court might be more wary regarding what exactly the parties are "stipulating" to, as the court will be required to review all the "evidence." Some experienced judges try to avoid the scenario whereby the parties "stipulate" to the admission of voluminous amounts of "evidence," typically in the form or documents, and expect the court to sort through it without much direction or explanation by the parties. This can be particularly true if one or more of the parties is in pro per and simply hands over a stack of disorganized paperwork as evidence, without objection.

Trial Tip: Before you spend a lot of time (and money) preparing a motion, reach out to opposing counsel and determine whether a stipulation is possible. Quite often, the attorneys are able to reach agreement on many issues beforehand. Reduce the stipulations to writing and submit them to the court at the pre-trial conference. Most judges will accept it. It can be a real time saver.

Exhibits - Making a Good Record

Whenever handling exhibits or evidence in the courtroom, be conscious of creating a good record. If the trial is being reported or recorded, it means that at some time in the future someone else may read the "cold" record, perhaps on appeal or even during jury "read back" in the deliberation room. Witness gestures, mannerisms, and emotion are not captured on paper. For example, when a witness points to a location on a photograph or a diagram and testifies that something happened "over there" or "right here," the written record is useless. The trial lawyer's role in this regard is to create a good record by describing the courtroom action not captured by the court reporter. For example, if the witness points or gestures, describe for the record what is occurring. "Your Honor, may the record reflect the witness is pointing to the right side of his head, just above the ear." By the same token, when you refer to an exhibit, make sure you clearly indicate "for the record" the exhibit number and what is occurring. "Let the record reflect I am showing the witness item number 14." In addition, when a witness points to or identifies a certain location on a diagram or a photograph, consider having the witness mark on the exhibit somehow, for example, with a colored Sharpie pen to identify the location referred to. However, it is important to plan regarding how you are going to instruct the witness to mark to avoid a confusing jumble of scribbles or marks.

Counsel: "Referring you to exhibit 14, using this red pen, can you please make an X where you were standing on the sidewalk when you saw the accident occur in the intersection? [Witness marks on exhibit.] Can you write your initials next to that mark, please? [Witness places initials.] Let the record reflect she has placed an X with her initials M.J. on the southwest corner of the intersection near the mailbox. Is that correct?"
Witness: "Yes."

Trial Tip: Making a descriptive record of courtroom action is the hallmark of an experienced attorney.

The Motion In Limine

The motion in limine ("at the start") is an important procedural tool for the trial lawyer. How the court rules on a motion can, and often does, affect the course of the trial. Typically, prior to trial or at the beginning, depending upon local rules, a party will file a motion objecting to some form of evidence and requesting the court to exclude it from consideration at trial. Some attorneys will file a motion requesting the court admit evidence based on the assumption there might be an objection and wanting to get the issue resolved. This is not a bad idea if you need some certainty regarding admissibility and the opposing party is equivocal or has indicated they will object. Some motions in limine are also requests for the court to issue certain orders related to the trial, for example, a motion to exclude witnesses from the courtroom. (Discussed infra.) In some trials, there may be only a few or no motions, while in other cases, such as complex criminal or civil matters, there could be literally dozens from each party. Generally, the motion is in writing, but oral motions are not uncommon for relatively minor issues.

Purpose

Motions in limine are a commonly used tool of trial advocacy and management in both criminal and civil cases. Such motions are generally brought at the beginning of trial, although they may also be brought during trial when evidentiary issues are anticipated by the parties. In either event, they are argued by the parties, either orally or in writing or both, and ruled upon by the trial judge. The usual purpose of motions in limine is to preclude the presentation of evidence deemed inadmissible and prejudicial by the moving party. A typical order in limine excludes the challenged evidence and directs counsel, parties, and witnesses not to refer to the excluded matters during trial. In other words, motions in limine are typically motions addressing issues related to whether certain evidence should be admitted during trial. (*Mansur v Ford Motor Company* (2011) 197 Cal.App.4th 1365, 1386.) "The advantage of such motions is to avoid the obviously futile attempt to '*unring the bell*' in the event a motion to strike is granted in the proceedings before the jury." (*Blanks v. Shaw* (2009) 171 Cal.App.4th 336, 375; *Amtower v. Photon Dynamics, Inc.* (2008) 158 Cal.App.4th 1582, 1593.) Motions in limine permit more careful consideration of evidentiary issues than would take place in the heat of battle during trial. They minimize sidebar conferences and disruptions during trial, allowing for an uninterrupted flow of evidence. Finally, by resolving potentially critical issues at the outset, they enhance the efficiency of trials and promote settlements. (*Kelly v. New West Federal Savings* (1999) 49 Cal.App.4th 659, 669.)

Some jurisdictions have court rules concerning when the motions must be filed and served on opposing counsel. When counsel waits to file their motions until the first day of trial, it may cause a delay because the court is probably going to need time to review and consider the motions before any hearing.

> **Trial Tip:** The importance of a well-written motion in limine cannot be overemphasized. It must be concise, clear, and easy to read. The judge needs to understand the issues and the law. Too often, motions are poorly written, confusing, or too lengthy.

Format and Affidavits

Every jurisdiction will have its own rules regarding the format of the motion. (See e.g., FPCP Rule 7 (b)(1)) For example, in some jurisdictions, motions are submitted and ruled on before the first day of trial while in other jurisdictions, the motions must be filed and served on the opposing party a certain number of days before trial. It is generally preferable that each substantive motion have its own pleading and be appropriately labeled, for example, "Motion to Exclude Evidence of Insurance Coverage." Less important requests, for example, to exclude witnesses from the courtroom, might be consolidated on one pleading with other minor issues. If there is a particularly complex legal issue, consider filing a separate "pocket brief," which is essentially a few pages of points and authorities on the relevant law for the court to review beforehand.

The motion should have an introduction with your request, a summary of the facts, and the applicable law with argument as to why the court should grant your request. However, keep it relatively short and concise. Avoid citing pages of obviously cut-and-paste boiler-plate law, which the judge will probably skim over anyway. In support of the motion, it is generally permissible to attach affidavits, declarations, or exhibits; however, local rules may address the type of materials that can be attached or a page limit. The key is not to overwhelm the court with a treatise for each motion.

Court is "Gatekeeper"

"Evidence" is anything presented to the senses and offered to prove the existence or nonexistence of a fact. (Black's Law Dictionary (11th ed. 2019)) In the trial setting, before evidence can be considered by the trier of fact it must be "admitted" by the court. In a typical trial, one party will propose to introduce some form of evidence and the opposing party will either object or not object to its introduction. As the "Gatekeeper," the court is obligated to rule on the admissibility of evidence. (*Daubert v. Merrell Dow Pharmaceuticals, Inc.*, 509 U.S. 579, 589, 113 S.Ct. 2786, 125 L.Ed.2d 469; *Sargon Enterprises, Inc. v. University of Southern California* (2012) 55 Cal.4th 747, 772.) However, there is generally no sua sponte duty of the court to determine relevance and admissibility in the absence of an objection. (*United States v. Multi—Management, Inc.*, 743 F.2d 1359, 1364 (9th Cir.1984); *People v. Griggs* (2003) 110 Cal.App.4th 1137, 1139.) Even incompetent evidence can be admitted if there is no objection. (*People v. Panah* (2005) 35 Cal.4th 395, 476; CA Evid. Code § 353.) This rule is especially important for an appeal because appellate issues are often deemed forfeited due to the failure to lodge a proper objection in the trial court.

To determine the admissibility of nearly every form of evidence, the court is required to answer certain "preliminary questions." These same questions are also what the trial lawyer should consider when contemplating introducing some evidence or deciding whether to object to your opponent's proffered evidence. FRE Rule 104 (below) sets forth the basic guidelines and procedures the court will follow when determining the admissibility of evidence. Generally, for nearly all forms of evidence, there are four fundamental questions the court must consider: (1) Is the evidence relevant? (2) Is the evidence properly authenticated? (3) Does admission of the evidence violate a rule prohibiting admission, e.g., the Hearsay Rule or Best Evidence Rule? and (4) Is the probative value substantially outweighed by its prejudicial effect? (CA Evid. Code § 352; FRE Rule 403.)

Generally, the proponent of evidence has the burden to "lay the foundation" and establish the requirements for admissibility; however, the standard the court applies is relatively low. The court simply examines all the evidence in the case and decides whether the jury could reasonably find the conditional fact ... by a *preponderance of the evidence.*" (*Daubert*, supra; *Huddleston v. United States*, 485 U.S. 681, 690, 108 S.Ct. 1496, 99 L.Ed.2d 771 (1988); *U.S. v. Evans,* 728 F.3d 953, 962 (9th Cir. 2013); *People v. Cottone* (2013) 57 Cal.4th 269, 283.) In its role as the "Gatekeeper," it is important to note that the court is only making "preliminary" findings. Thus, if there is a conflict in the evidence or if the admissibility hinges on the credibility of a witness, the court will generally allow the evidence to be admitted and permit the jury to give it the appropriate "weight." In this situation, it is often said the issue goes to "weight rather than admissibility." (See e.g., Kennedy *v. Collagen Corp.*, 161 F.3d 1226, 1231 (9th Cir. 1998).)

Trial Tip: If there are numerous motions in limine, confer with opposing counsel and recommend to the court an order in which they should be heard. Often, how the court rules on one motion can affect the outcome of other motions or helps promote settlement.

Motion Hearing

Generally, at some time prior to the opening statements, the court will hold a hearing outside the presence of jury to rule on the motions. As mentioned, in some complex trials, there can be dozens of motions to consider, and hopefully during the trial conference, the parties and the court have discussed the order in which to hear the motions. The outcome of some motions might be contingent on how the court rules on others.

During the hearing, the judge will typically indicate that he or she has read the briefs and may invite oral argument. If the issue is important and contested, counsel should refrain from stating merely "submit it," without any argument, unless the other side is conceding, or you are confident the judge has already decided. At a minimum, a short summary of the main points and the law should be recited. When an attorney responds "Submit it," without argument, the court may interpret this to mean the attorney does not have much faith in his or her own position. On the other hand, while judges may like to hear *some* oral argument, most judges do not desire a complete rehash or restatement of what was previously stated in the written motion. Keep it short, concise, and to the point. During argument, you will find that some judges listen passively while others engage the attorneys with questions or concerns. Following argument, the court may rule summarily from the bench or take the issue "under submission" and rule later.

Offer of Proof

For the court to rule on a motion and to preserve the issue for an appeal, it may be necessary to make an "offer of proof" in conjunction with your motion in limine. The offer of proof must address the "substance, purpose, and relevance of the excluded evidence" (Evid. Code § 354, subd. (a)). It should describe, in detail, the evidence the proponent seeks to admit, its relevance, and admissibility. Essentially, it is providing the court with a preview of what the evidence (or testimony) would be, if allowed. The offer of proof can be in written form or oral. An offer of proof is in lieu of having an evidentiary hearing with live witnesses. It is important to note that the appellate court will rely on the "offer of proof" to determine whether the trial court's decision was correct. Thus, the "offer of proof" should be on the record and complete. To qualify as an adequate offer of proof, the proponent must first describe the evidence and what it tends to show, and second, identify the grounds for admitting the evidence. *(Phillips v. Hillcrest Med. Ctr.,* 244 F.3d 790, 802 (10th Cir.2001); Polys, 941 F.2d at 1407; see also *People v. Whitt* (1990) 51 Cal.3d 620, 648.) The offer of proof must "set forth the actual evidence to be produced and not merely the facts or issues to be addressed and argued." (*In re Mark C.* (1992) 7 Cal.App.4th 433, 444.) The trial court may reject a general or vague offer of proof that does not specify the testimony to be offered by the proposed witness. (See *Gutierrez v. Cassiar Min. Corp.* (1998) 64 Cal.App.4th 148, 161-162; *Semsch v. Henry Mayo Newhall Memorial Hospital* (1985) 171 Cal.App.3d 162, 168.)

Trial Tip: Make sure any "offer of proof" is complete. If the court rules against you, confirm that it is not necessary that you object again during testimony. Request to have a "standing" or "continuing" objection.

Preserving Objection

If an objection to exclude evidence is overruled and the evidence permitted, it is generally not required to object again later during the trial to the same evidence for the same reason; however, it is wise to confirm this *on the record* with the court. Make it clear that you have a "standing" or "continuing" objection to the introduction of the evidence. (See Trial Objections, infra at p. 229.) By doing so, you are trying to avoid any possible argument later on appeal that the issue was forfeited because there was no timely objection at the time the evidence was presented. A motion in limine to exclude evidence is normally sufficient to preserve an issue for review without the necessity for the defendant to renew an objection at the time the evidence was offered. (*Summers v. A.L. Gilbert Co.* (1999) 69 Cal.App.4th 1155, 1184; *People v. Morris* (1991) 53 Cal.3d 152, 190, disapproved on other grounds in *People v. Stansbury* (1995) 9 Cal.4th 824.) However, if the evidence presented during trial is substantially different from that presented at the hearing on the motion in limine or included in an offer of proof, it is incumbent on the party who made the motion to renew the objection to the evidence. (*People v. Champion* (1995) 9 Cal.4th 879, 925 [when there are variations between an offer of proof and the evidence adduced at trial, defendant must bring them to the attention of the court]; *People v. Morris*, supra, 53 Cal.3d at p. 190 ["Events in the trial may change the context in which the evidence is offered to an extent that a renewed objection is necessary to satisfy the language and purpose of Evidence Code section 353"].

The Evidentiary (402) Hearing

In many cases, the judge will be able to resolve the motions simply based on the party's written motion, an offer of proof, and perhaps some oral argument. However, in some circumstances, the court may find it necessary to have an evidentiary hearing with live testimony, outside the presence of the jury. (CA Evid. Code § 402; FRE 104 (c).) The request for such an evidentiary hearing should be incorporated into a written motion. At this hearing, testimony and evidence can be received. The value of the hearing is that it permits the court to hear evidence and to make rulings outside the presence of the jury. However, the trial court is *not* mandated to hold the evidentiary hearing unless the issue involves the admissibility of the defendant's admission or confession. (Evid. Code 402(b); *People v. Hoyos* (2007) 41 Cal.4th 872, 897.) A hearing is appropriate whenever testimony is needed to lay the foundation for the admissibility or exclusion of evidence. However, issues regarding a witness's credibility are properly left to the jury and are not a proper subject of a hearing. (*People v. Smith* (2007) 40 Cal.4th 483, 515.) Requesting the court to hold an evidentiary hearing should be considered for highly contested issues, such as an objection to the admissibility of expert testimony. In Federal court, an evidentiary hearing to determine the admissibility of expert testimony is called a "Daubert" hearing. (See *Daubert v. Merrell Dow Pharms., Inc., 509* U.S. 579, 592–93 (1993).)

A 402 hearing might also be requested or authorized by the court to determine the relevance or prejudice of evidence. However, rather than authorize an evidentiary hearing with live testimony, which takes time and scheduling, the court may opt to accept an "offer of proof" by the parties concerning the disputed evidence. Rather than hold a hearing, however, "the court may admit conditionally the proffered evidence under this section, subject to evidence of the preliminary fact being supplied later in the course of the trial." (Evid. Code § 403, subd. (b).)

COMMON MOTIONS IN LIMINE

There are numerous different types and forms of motions that can be applicable in a trial, obviously depending upon the nature of the case. Some can be extraordinarily complex and require several days of hearings to determine. The law pertaining to all the possible motions is vast and beyond the scope of this handbook, however, there are several which are so common and can apply to nearly every type of trial that a review of them here is worthwhile.

Relevance

The "relevance" of evidence is an issue that crops up in nearly every trial, either during testimony or in a motion in limine. The trial court has wide discretion in determining the relevance of evidence under the statutory standard. (*People v. Kelly* (1992) 1 Cal.4th 495, 523.) A failure to make a timely and specific objection forfeits the issue. Even incompetent evidence can be admitted if there is no objection. (*People v. Panah* (2005) 35 Cal.4th 395, 476; See Trial Objections, infra at p. 220.)

Evid. Code § 210. Relevant evidence   (FRE Rule 401)

"Relevant evidence" means evidence, including evidence relevant to the credibility of a witness or hearsay declarant, having any tendency in reason to prove or disprove any disputed fact that is of consequence to the determination of the action.

Evid. Code § 350. Only relevant evidence admissible (FRE Rule 402)

No evidence is admissible except relevant evidence

Evid. Code § 351. Admissibility of relevant evidence.   (FRE Rule 402)

Except as otherwise provided by statute, all relevant evidence is admissible.

Whether evidence is "relevant" is a highly fact-intensive determination based on logic and the nature of the contested issues. When evidence leads only to speculative inferences, however, it is irrelevant. (*People v. Kraft* (2000) 23 Cal.4th 978, 1035.) It is important to keep in mind that the "relevance" of evidence is considered in the context of what is *at issue*. For example, it is not uncommon in a personal injury case involving a motor vehicle accident where the plaintiff suffered injury that the defendant will concede liability, making the only issue one of damages. In other words, the defendant is not denying she was negligent and caused the accident but disputes the degree of injury and/or the amount of damages claimed by the plaintiff. In this situation, the defendant might make a motion in limine to exclude evidence of the facts and circumstances surrounding the accident on the ground that it is irrelevant to the *contested* issue of damages. The defendant may not want the jury to know just how recklessly she was driving and/or see photographs of the wrecked cars, as it has no relevance to whether the plaintiff's medical treatment was necessary and costs reasonable.

> **Trial Tip:** Judges really don't like surprise motions made mid-trial that cause interruption and delay, especially when the issue was known and could have been litigated in limine. Furthermore, a motion in limine is a good offensive tactic to head-off potentially inadmissible or irrelevant evidence before testimony begins.

Undue Prejudice ("352")

Even if evidence is relevant, in almost every jurisdiction, the court retains the authority to exclude it on the basis that the evidence is unduly prejudicial, confusing, or a waste of time. This is a quite common motion in limine and, without question, the single most powerful weapon in the trial lawyer's arsenal. This is because the court has wide discretion to exclude relevant evidence based on a very subjective balancing of factors. Evidence Code § 352 (below), sets forth the court's authority and duties in this regard. Federal Rule 403 is similar. All trial lawyers should know this (or similar) section well because it is so commonly invoked in a variety of evidentiary scenarios during a trial. (See Trial Objections, infra, at p. 242.)

> **Evid. Code § 352 Discretion of court to exclude evidence (FRE Rule 403)**
>
> The court in its discretion may exclude evidence if its probative value is substantially outweighed by the probability that its admission will (a) necessitate undue consumption of time or (b) create substantial danger of undue prejudice, of confusing the issues, or of misleading the jury.

Section 352 provides the judge with the broad authority and discretion to exclude virtually any type of evidence, and the court's ruling will be upheld on appeal absent a clear showing of an abuse of discretion, meaning the trial court has engaged in an "arbitrary determination, capricious disposition, or whimsical thinking." (*People v. Mullens* (2004) 119 Cal.App.4th 648, 658; *Thompson v. County of Los Angeles* (2006) 142 Cal.App.4th 154, 168.)

"Evidence is not prejudicial, as that term is used in a section 352 context, merely because it undermines the opponent's position or shores up that of the proponent. The ability to do so is what makes evidence relevant." (*Vorse v. Sarasy* (1997) 53 Cal.App.4th 998, 1008.) "The prejudice which ... section 352 is designed to avoid is not the prejudice or damage to a defense that naturally flows from relevant, highly-probative evidence. Rather, the statute uses the word in its etymological sense of 'prejudging' a person or cause on the basis of extraneous factors." (*People v. Zapien* (1993) 4 Cal.4th 929, 958.)

"Evidence should be excluded as unduly prejudicial when it is of such nature as to inflame the emotions of the jury, motivating them to use the information, not to logically evaluate the point upon which it is relevant, but to reward or punish one side because of the jurors' emotional reaction. In such a circumstance, the evidence is unduly prejudicial because of the substantial likelihood the jury will use it for an illegitimate purpose." (*Vorse v. Sarasy*, supra, at p. 1009.) In other words, evidence is unduly prejudicial when it has very little effect on the issues, but uniquely tends to evoke an emotional bias against one party and thus poses an intolerable risk to the fairness of the proceedings. (*People v. Karis* (1988) 46 Cal.3d 612, 638; *Ajaxo Inc. v. E *Trade Group Inc.* (2005) 135 Cal.App.4th 21, 45; *Piscitelli v. Salesian Society* (2008) 166 Cal.App.4th 1, 11; *People v. Waidla* (2000) 22 Cal.4th 690, 724 ["Evidence is substantially more prejudicial than probative if, broadly stated, it poses an intolerable risk to the fairness of the proceedings or the reliability of the outcome."].)

When the motion is made, in essence, the court is required to perform a weighing analysis, by contrasting the relevance versus the prejudicial effect. The trial court should state on the record that it has conducted such an analysis and the factors considered. However, the California Supreme Court has repeatedly reaffirmed that "when ruling on a section 352 motion, a trial court need not expressly weigh prejudice against probative value, or even expressly state that it has done so. All that is required is that the record demonstrate the trial court understood and fulfilled its responsibilities under section 352." (*People v. Williams* (1997) 16 Cal.4th 153, 213.)

Trial Tip: The "352" (FRE 403) motion is one of the most powerful pre-trial motions at your disposal because it *requires* the court to conduct a weighing analysis. Not only can the court exclude evidence, but it can also fashion orders to *limit* evidence. In that event, your motion should provide the court with suggestions regarding how to limit or curtail such evidence. Also, consider requesting the court to give a limiting instruction to the jury.

Undue Consumption of Time and Cumulative Evidence

The court also has the authority under section 352 to exclude evidence that is cumulative, redundant, time consuming, or likely to confuse the issues. It is within the discretion of the trial court to exclude impeachment evidence as cumulative when there is already evidence of the witness's lack of credibility. (*People v. Burgener* (1986) 41 Cal.3d 505, 525.) In a classic formulation, the California Supreme Court has said that section 352 empowers courts to prevent trials from "degenerating into nitpicking wars of attrition over collateral credibility issues." (*People v. Wheeler* (1992) 4 Cal.4th 284, 296; see also *People v. Sapp* (2003) 31 Cal.4th 240, 289 [quoting Wheeler].)

> **Trial Tip:** Some judges may invoke "352" on its own motion to curtail or limit testimony. This generally occurs when the questioning veers off into marginally relevant areas or becomes extended and repetitive. All judges are concerned about their trials becoming protracted and running past the predicted time estimate.

Bifurcation or Severance

It is not uncommon in trials that there are certain issues, charges, allegations, or causes of actions that one party requests to be tried separately. In this circumstance, a motion to "bifurcate" is commonly brought and heard in limine. (C.C.P. § 598; C.C.P. § 1048(b).) For example, in a criminal trial, the defense may move to bifurcate the issue regarding prior convictions or allegations. If there are two or more defendants charged, a motion to sever one or more for trial may be appropriate under the Aranda/Bruton line of cases. (*People v. Aranda* (1965) 63 Cal.2d 518 (Aranda); *Bruton v. United States* (1968) 391 U.S. 123 (Bruton).) If the court grants the motion, the trial is typically divided into two separate hearings where certain issues are litigated in the first phase and other issues in the second, using the same jury. Part two of a bifurcated trial generally follows the same procedures of part one, with additional opening statements, presentation of evidence, further instruction by the court, and closing argument. The main purpose of bifurcating a trial is to prevent the jury from receiving potentially prejudicial evidence in the first phase. For example, in a civil trial, the issue of punitive damages is often bifurcated, meaning the jury determines liability first, then punitive damages in the second phase. The court may also order bifurcated the equitable issues to be tried by the court and the legal issues to be tried before the jury. (See *Arntz Contracting Co. v. St. Paul Fire & Marine Ins. Co* (1996) 47 Cal.App.4th 464, 487 [court's finding on equitable issues may affect jury findings]; See infra, p. 29, re: legal versus equitable claims.)

Expert Testimony

The admissibility of expert testimony is often litigated in limine. The issue could be whether the expert is qualified to make an opinion, the nature of that opinion, or the scope of the opinion. (See Experts Witness, infra at p. 197 et seq.) Upon request, the court may order a "402" evidentiary hearing outside the presence of the jury to allow the court to hear the expert testimony before it goes to the jury. In addition, if the expert is relying upon scientific evidence, the court may need to determine if the Kelly/Frye doctrine is applicable. (*People v. Kelly* (1976) 17 Cal.3d 24,; *Daubert v. Merrell Dow Pharmaceuticals, Inc., 509 U.S. 579, 113 S.Ct. 2786, 125 L.Ed.2d 469 (1993).*)

One issue not uncommon in civil cases is whether the expert's opinion(s) were revealed in a prior deposition. A party's expert may not offer testimony at trial that exceeds the scope of his deposition testimony if the opposing party has no notice or expectation that the expert will offer the new testimony, or if notice of the new testimony comes at a time when deposing the expert is unreasonably difficult. (*Eastbay v. Clark* (2009) 171 Cal.App. 4th, 772, 780.) However, like any other witness, the fact that an expert's testimony at trial differs from his deposition testimony goes to the expert's credibility; it does not, without some further evidence of prejudice to the opposing party, serve as ground for exclusion. (*Eastbay*, supra, at p. 781.) The fact that experts, disclosed and deposed prior to trial, give contradictory testimony at trial is not grounds to exclude their testimony. Such 'surprises' go to the weight, not the admissibility. (Ibid; Code of Civ. Proc., § 2025.620, subd. (a) ["Any party may use a deposition for the purpose of contradicting or impeaching the testimony of the deponent as a witness..."]; accord, *Williams v. Volkswagenwerk Aktiengesellschaft* (1986) 180 Cal.App.3d 1244, at p. 1258 [trial court did not abuse its discretion by allowing expert to give an opinion that differed from the one offered at his deposition]; see infra, Experts, p. 197.)

Deposition Issues

The admissibility of deposition testimony is sometimes litigated in limine. One party may wish to introduce all or portions of a witness's deposition testimony. Code of Civil Procedure section 2025.620 permits the introduction of "any part or all" of a deposition of *a party* by the adverse party for "any purpose." In addition, if a witness (not just a party) lives more than 150 miles from the courthouse, the deposition testimony may also be admissible under certain circumstances. (§ 2025.620(c).) Typically, the deposition testimony is introduced when one party literally reads it into the record. If a deposition was audio or video recorded with proper notice, the proponent may also be permitted to play the recorded depositions at trial under certain circumstances. (See C.C.P. § 2025.620(d); 2025.340(m) [requiring advance notice of intent to use recording at trial].)

However, issues can arise regarding whether the procedural and notice requirements were properly followed. In addition, the deposition testimony admitted must still comply with the rules of evidence as though the deponent were then present and testifying as a witness. (§2025.620.) In other words, irrelevant or inadmissible deposition testimony, e.g., inadmissible hearsay, cannot be admitted within the deposition testimony. (*In re Automobile Antitrust Cases I and II* (2016) 1 Cal.App. 5th 127, 143 [error to admit deposition testimony that contained hearsay].) There could also be issues of whether a proper objection was made at the deposition and the effect of that objection. One party may claim there was a waiver. However, C.C.P. section 2025.460(c) states: "Objections to the competency of the deponent, or to the relevancy, materiality, or admissibility at trial of the testimony or of the materials produced, are unnecessary and are not waived by failure to make them before or during the deposition."

Determining the admissibility of deposition testimony can create challenges. The court may need to review the proposed deposition testimony and rule upon a party's objection(s) to portions of that deposition testimony, for example, if the deponent stated inadmissible hearsay. If the court sustains an objection, the deposition transcripts may need to be edited or that portion not read to the jury. This can be time consuming if the deposition testimony is lengthy and replete with improper questioning and/or inadmissible evidence. For this reason, some judges require the parties to "lodge" the certified deposition transcripts with the clerk.

> **Trial Tip:** Inadmissible evidence is often elicited during depositions. Although an objection is made at the time, the witness is generally permitted to answer. At trial, whenever a party seeks to introduce all or part of deposition testimony, opposing counsel must be vigilant that it complies with the rules of evidence. If not, an objection should be raised in limine to give the court time to rule.

Hearsay

Hearsay is an issue that crops up with surprising regularity at trial and one that still confounds some attorneys. Some object when a statement is obviously not "hearsay," while others fail to object when damaging hearsay is elicited. Typically, the issue is raised in a motion limine when the hearsay issue is known beforehand and significant, for example, the introduction of records purportedly containing hearsay. Probably the most common issue during testimony is whether the statement is being offered for its truth or whether there is some relevant non-hearsay purpose. The second most common issue is whether an exception applies. For the trial lawyer, it is important to have a good understanding of the rule and its exceptions. (See Hearsay, p. 182 et seq.) It that regard, it can be helpful to have a cheat-sheet with the rule and exceptions available for quick reference during trial.

Discovery Issues

An all-too-common motion in limine relates to discovery issues whereby typically one party complains the other has not complied with a pre-trial discovery requirement. A failure to comply with a discovery statute can have the consequence of sanctions, exclusion, or in extreme cases, dismissal. The rules and procedures for pre-trial discovery in civil and criminal cases can be complex and beyond the scope of this handbook. There are often strict notice requirements and time limitations. For example, expert witnesses in civil cases must be disclosed prior to trial in most jurisdictions. In California, however, the identity of *non*-expert witnesses intended to be called at trial is entitled to a qualified work product privilege and cannot be compelled without a showing that denial of such discovery "will unfairly prejudice the party seeking discovery or will result in an injustice." Moreover, disclosure of a witness's anticipated testimony at trial "clearly calls for production of a writing reflecting the attorney's impressions, conclusions and opinions and thus falls within the absolute work product privilege." (*Snyder v. Superior* (2007) 157 Cal.App.4th 1530, 1536.)

In California, discovery in criminal cases for both prosecution and defense is controlled by statute. (See Penal Code § 1054 et. seq.) In addition, the prosecution must disclose to the defense any evidence that is "favorable" to the accused and "material" on the issue of guilt or punishment. (*Brady v. Maryland*, (1963) 373 U.S. 83, 83 S.Ct. 1194, 10 L.Ed.2d 215. *United States v. Agurs* (1976) 427 U.S. 97, 107, 96 S.Ct. 2392, 49 L.Ed.2d 342.)

Witness Exclusion

It is common that one or more parties will move to exclude witnesses from the courtroom. For obvious reasons, it is generally not a good idea for a witness to watch and listen to other witnesses giving testimony. The exclusion of witnesses from the courtroom is a matter within the trial court's discretion. (Evid. Code § 777; FRE 615) The purpose is to prevent tailored testimony and aid in the detection of less than candid testimony. However, the court may permit expert witnesses who may base their opinion upon what they hear in court. (*People v. Valdez* (1986) 177 Cal.App.3d 680, 687.) Further, upon request, the trial court can order witnesses not to converse with each other until they are examined. If the case involves the possibility of witness collusion, you would be wise to file the motion, just to be safe.

Trial Tip: If the court grants your motion to exclude some evidence, request the court to direct opposing counsel to inform their witnesses of the court's ruling to avoid accidental disclosure.

Judicial Notice

A relatively common motion is a request by a party for the court to take judicial notice of some fact or information. The value of this procedure is that if the court does take "judicial notice" of some fact or information, that fact is deemed proved. The court is required to instruct the jury to accept the noticed information as fact. (Evid. Code § 457.) Thus, judicial notice can be a particularly useful method of introducing evidence without having to call witnesses. One of the more common requests is for the court to take judicial notice of court records, e.g., court decisions from related cases. The Evidence Code divides judicial notice into mandatory and discretionary.

Section 451 sets forth the matters that the court "shall" take judicial notice of, which include: The decisional, constitutional, and public statutory laws of this state and of the United States, rules and procedures of court, the true signification of all English words and phrases and of all legal expressions, and "facts and propositions of generalized knowledge that are so universally known that they cannot reasonably be the subject of dispute." Facts "universally known" could include dates, locations, historical events, and well-known scientific principles.

Section 452 sets forth matters the court "may" take judicial notice of, including: "The decisional, constitutional, and statutory law of any state of the

United States, regulations, official acts of government, court records, foreign laws, facts and propositions that are of such *common knowledge* within the territorial jurisdiction of the court that they cannot reasonably be the subject of dispute, and facts and propositions that are not reasonably subject to dispute and are capable of immediate and accurate determination by resort to sources of reasonably indisputable accuracy." (Evid. Code § 452(h)) Subdivision (h) is intended to cover facts which are not reasonably subject to dispute and are easily verified. These include, for example, facts which are widely accepted as established by experts and specialists in the natural, physical, and social sciences that can be verified by reference to treatises, encyclopedias, almanacs, and the like or by persons learned in the subject matter. (*People v. Jones* (1997) 15 Cal.4th 119, 171, fn. 17, overruled on other grounds in *People v. Hill* (1998) 17 Cal.4th 800, 823, fn. 1.)

Trustworthiness and Hearsay Issues

Evidence Code section 454 directs the trial court to consider whether the source of the information is trustworthy. The analysis may depend upon whether the information sought to be noticed contains hearsay. A court cannot take judicial notice of hearsay allegations as being true just because they are part of a court record or file. (*Sosinsky v. Grant* (1992) 6 Cal.App.4th 1548, 1562-1569.) While courts are free to take judicial notice of the existence of each document in a court file, including the truth of results reached, they may not take judicial notice of the truth of hearsay statements in decisions and court files. Courts may not take judicial notice of allegations in affidavits, declarations, and probation reports in court records because such matters are reasonably subject to dispute and therefore require formal proof. (*Lockley v. Law Office of Cantrell, Green, Pekich, Cruz & McCort* (2001) 91 Cal.App.4th 875, 882; *Kilroy v. State* (2004) 119 Cal.App. 4th 140, 145.)

> **Trial Tip:** Requesting the court to take judicial notice of public records or court filings can be a time saver. If the court does take judicial notice, consider how those facts get transmitted to the jury. Consider contacting opposing counsel prior to trial regarding whether a stipulation is possible to save even more time. Be aware that a request for juridical notice generally requires prior notice to the opposing party.

Insurance

A motion to exclude evidence of insurance coverage is relatively common. (See Evid. Code § 1155 (below).) One or more of the parties may have had insurance coverage and it is not uncommon that counsel for one or more of the parties is retained by an insurance company to defend the suit. Generally, it is the defendant who is most concerned about evidence of liability insurance, worried that the jurors may find it easier to award damages if they know the tab is being picked up by the insurance company and not necessarily the defendant in court.

> **Evid. Code § 1155 Liability insurance**
>
> Evidence that a person was, at the time a harm was suffered by another, insured wholly or partially against loss arising from liability for that harm is inadmissible to prove negligence or other wrongdoing.

However, the principle is subject to the exception that insurance evidence may properly be allowed when the evidence is introduced for other purposes. (See *Staples v. Hoefke* (1987) 189 Cal.App.3d 1397, 1410-1411.) "The fact of insurance ... may be relevant on an issue other than the quality of the insured's conduct, and therefore may be introduced under the doctrine of limited admissibility, with a limiting instruction, where its probative value outweighs the possible prejudice from its admission." (1 Witkin, Cal. Evidence (4th ed. 2000) § 134, p. 484.) For example, the fact of insurance may be admissible as tending to prove ownership of a vehicle or employment of a person covered by the policy. (See *Perry v. Paladini, Inc.* (1928) 89 Cal.App. 275, 285 [ownership]; *Mullanix v. Basich,* supra, 67 Cal.App.2d at p. 682 [employment].)

Settlement Offers

In most civil cases, prior to trial there are settlement discussions and offers to settle. A motion to exclude any reference to settlement or offers is common and often uncontested.

> **Evid. Code § 1152 Offers to compromise**
>
> Evidence that a person has, in compromise ... furnished or offered or promised to furnish money or any other thing ... to another who has sustained ... loss or damage, as well as any conduct or statements made in negotiation thereof, is inadmissible to prove his or her liability for the loss or damage or any part of it.
>
> **Evid. Code § 1154 Offer to discount a claim**
>
> Evidence that a person has ... offered ... to accept a sum of money or any other thing ... in satisfaction of a claim, as well as any conduct or statements made in negotiation thereof, is inadmissible to prove the invalidity of the claim or any part of it.

Both provisions are based on public policy in favor of the settlement of disputes without litigation and are intended to promote candor in settlement negotiations: "The rule prevents parties from being deterred from making offers of settlement and facilitates the type of candid discussion that may lead to settlement." (*Zhou v. Unisource Worldwide* (2007) 157 Cal.App.4th 1471; *Carney v. Santa Cruz Women Against Rape* (1990) 221 Cal.App.3d 1009, 1023; see *Caira v. Offner* (2005) 126 Cal.App.4th 12, 32.)

Trial Tip: When arguing a motion, avoid citing *In re down-the-hall*, by referring the judge to how other judges have ruled on similar issues. If there is some custom or habit normally followed in your jurisdiction, approach the subject delicately. In that same vein, if you feel the court has erred, it is not inappropriate to request the court to reconsider, but do so respectfully.

Character Evidence

The admissibility of "character evidence" is a relatively common issue at trial and generally raised in a motion in limine. (See discussion re: Character Evidence, infra, at p. 244.) The general rule is that character evidence is inadmissible when offered to prove his or her conduct on a specified occasion. However, as with other evidentiary rules, there are exceptions. The exceptions generally fall into *two* distinct categories related to the purpose of the character evidence. It can be admissible if it is related to a witness's character for truthfulness or untruthfulness, *or* it can be admissible as a form of circumstantial evidence to prove a party acted in conformity with that character trait. The later form is generally at issue when a party seeks to introduce some prior act or behavior of the opposing party to prove the current allegation. For example, in a criminal case, the prosecution may seek to introduce evidence that the defendant committed a prior similar uncharged robbery to prove he committed the charged robbery. The use of character evidence as it relates to the truthfulness or untruthfulness of a witness and impeachment, is discussed more fully, infra, at p.125, Impeachment of Character.

Know Your Deadlines

In every jurisdiction, in addition to discovery statutes, there are also procedural rules and deadlines relating to trial that counsel *must* be aware of. Often, the local court rules have very specific deadlines related to the trial. Unfortunately, the failure of a party to comply with these deadlines is an all too common occurrence. It can and does result sometimes in the exclusion of evidence, sanctions, or even dismissal. Some of the more common trial-related rules with specific deadlines relate to:

- Payment of jury fees
- Disclosure of expert witnesses
- Discovery cutoff
- Judicial notice
- Production/discovery of documents
- Disclosure of trial exhibits
- Filing/exchange of witness lists
- Filing of trial briefs
- Filing of motions in limine
- Submission of jury instructions

3. JURY SELECTION

The process of jury selection can seem intimidating, even to the experienced trial lawyer. It typically begins when a "panel" or group of prospective jurors somberly arrive at the courtroom. From this group, 12 (or less, if using a less-than-12 people-sized jury) will be chosen to hear the case, plus an alternate or two. The overarching goal of the jury selection process is to find jurors who can impartially and fairly judge the case. However, your goal, as the trial lawyer, is also to seat jurors who will be the most favorable and receptive towards your case. Conversely, this means attempting to identify and weed out jurors that, in your opinion, are least likely to look upon your case in a favorable light. It really is a predictive process where you will be trying to forecast the mindset of 12 random people. A very tall order.

Attorneys generally have no say in how the jurors are randomly summoned to the courthouse or seated in the jury box. However, after that point, the attorneys do have some input into how the jurors are educated and given the opportunity to shape the complexion of the jury by using their right to "challenge" certain jurors. Although there have been many fine books published on the topic of how to pick the perfect jury, and some attorneys even opt to hire a "jury consultant," the truth is, there are no hard and fast rules. In the end, the process of jury selection and your opportunity to shape it, boils down to collecting enough data and information about each juror to make the best possible educated guess. It requires a lot of attorney intuition and knowledge of human behavior, which generally cannot be reduced to a law book. However, if you understand the basic procedures and follow some basic guidelines, as discussed below, you stand a good chance of selecting the best possible jury for your case.

Trial Tip: Your task begins with simple observation the moment a juror is called forward to be seated. Pay careful attention to the juror's appearance, mannerisms, and attire, which are all important clues about their persona. What is the juror reading, a comic book or *The Wall Street Journal*?

Right to a Jury: Legal v. Equitable Claims

The right to a jury trial in civil cases is guaranteed by the Federal and California Constitutions. (U.S. CONST. amend. VII; Cal.Const., art. I, s. 16 ["Trial by jury is an inviolate right and shall be secured to all, but in a civil cause three-fourths of the jury may render a verdict."]) "The American tradition of trial by jury, considered in connection with either criminal or civil proceedings, necessarily contemplates an impartial jury drawn from a cross-section of the community." (*Thiel v. Southern Pac. Co.* (1946) 328 U.S. 217, 220.)

Although the right to a jury trial is guaranteed by the Constitution, not all actions are entitled to trial by jury, for example, family law proceedings or juvenile trials. Generally, only matters of *law* are entitled to a jury, while actions in *equity* are not. Legal matters include tortious acts, such as negligence, fraud, or breach of contract. Equitable matters are typically requests for declaratory, injunctive relief; specific performance; or quiet title. "A jury trial, as a general proposition ... is a matter of right in a civil action at law, but not in equity. In determining whether the action was one triable by a jury at common law, the court is not bound by the form of the action but rather by the nature of the rights involved and the facts of the particular case—the gist of the action." (*Nwosu v. Uba* (2002) 122 Cal.App.4th 1229, 1237-1238; *People v. One 1941 Chevrolet Coupe* (1951) 37 Cal.2d 283, 299; see also *Walton v. Walton* (1995) 31 Cal.App.4th 277, 291 ["gist" of the action is ordinarily determined by the mode of relief to be afforded, though the prayer for relief is not conclusive."].)

In practice, it is not uncommon that a complaint will allege both legal and equitable matters, such as negligence and breach of contract (legal) and a request to quiet title or declaratory relief (equitable). The legal and equitable causes of actions are often interrelated and based upon the same underlying facts. Because equitable claims are heard by the court and legal issues by the jury, the procedural question can arise as to whether the claims should be bifurcated, and if so, which goes first?

When plaintiff's claims consist of a "mixed bag" of equitable and legal claims, the equitable claims are properly tried first by the court. (*Nwosu*, supra, at p. 1237.) A principal rationale for this approach has been explained as follows: "When an action involves both legal and equitable issues, the equitable issues, ordinarily, are tried first, for this may obviate the necessity for a subsequent trial of the legal issues." (Ibid.) Numerous cases with a mixture of legal and equitable claims have identified this same principle—that a trial of equitable issues first may promote judicial economy." (Ibid.) Counsel should be aware that "the court may decide the equitable issues first, and this decision may result in factual and legal findings that effectively dispose of the legal claims." (*Nwosu*, supra, at p. 1244 [court's ruling regarding claims for specific performance and quiet title disposed of claim for fraud].)

Basic Procedure

Although the process of jury selection is similar in most jurisdictions, every jurisdiction and court will have its own rules and procedures. Typically, a group or "panel" of prospective jurors are randomly summoned from the local community, screened for hardship, and directed to the courtroom. The process is designed to be random. In the old days, when the jurors arrived at the courtroom, the names of the prospective jurors were put into a drum, spun, and then drawn randomly by the clerk, one by one, akin to a lottery. As each name was called, that juror was seated in the jury box in the order drawn. The juror designated as, "Juror

Number One," is often seated in the upper, left-hand corner of the jury box; however, that may depend on the courtroom layout. The clerk would continue this process until the jury "box" was filled. If additional jurors were needed, the clerk would draw those names randomly from the drum as well. Modernly, the process is essentially the same except instead of using an old drum, the computer is used to generate a *random juror list*. The clerk uses this random list to call forth the jurors, one by one, and they are guided to the appropriate seat by the bailiff. (See CCP § 232(a); C.C.P § 222(b) ["When the jury commissioner has provided the court with a listing of the trial jury panel in random order, the court shall seat prospective jurors for voir dire in the order provided by the panel list"].) "To help facilitate the jury selection process, the judge in civil trials should provide the parties with both the alphabetical list and the list of prospective jurors in the order in which they will be called." (C.C.P. § 222.5.)

Hardship Screening

At some point prior to the commencement of voir dire, the jury panel is screened for "hardship." A juror can be excused from serving on the grounds of an "undue hardship." (C.C.P. § 204) In some jurisdictions, the jury commissioner or the court clerk determine the basic hardships and qualifications, e.g., convicted of a felony or not a citizen. (See *People v. Basuta* (2001) 94 Cal.App.4th 370 [approving of jury commissioner determining hardships, if record kept].)

California Rules of Court, rule 860(b), defines general principles governing the granting of excuses. Subdivision (c) of rule 860 requires the juror seeking to be excused to state facts specifying the hardship and why the hardship cannot be avoided by a deferral of service. Subdivision (d) of rule 860 provides in detail the basis on which a hardship excuse may be granted. Such excuses may be granted if the prospective juror has no reasonably available means of transportation, service would require excessive travel, the prospective juror has impairments that would make service potentially harmful, the juror is immediately needed for the protection of public health and safety, or the juror must care for a person who requires his/her personal attention. The subdivision also states that an extreme financial burden is a basis to be excused and gives four factors, including the expected length of service, for determining whether the claimed hardship is sufficient.

The attorneys are generally not involved in this hardship process, nor do they provide input; however, a party can object if the court is improperly excusing jurors. (*People v. Mickey* (1991) 54 C3d 612, 665.) Typically, the judge will conduct a brief voir dire with each juror claiming a hardship. Extreme financial hardship is by far the most common. Many jurisdictions provide minimal or no compensation to jurors for their service. Consequently, for longer trials, low-wage earners and self-employed persons tend to get excused more often simply because they cannot afford it. Conversely, retired persons and those who have government or other jobs where the employers will compensate the employee for jury service (usually larger corporations), tend to get seated more often for the longer trials. Keep this in mind when you are thinking about what type of jury you prefer.

Trial Tip: Staying organized is half the battle during jury selection. Use a seating chart (below) and develop a system to keep notes for each prospective juror. With so many prospective jurors coming and going, it is important that you keep track of the names, positions, and juror information. Some attorneys use 'sticky notes" with the juror's name and info attached to the chart at the appropriate position. It can then be moved if the juror moves.

As the jurors are being called forward and seated, note on the chart where each juror is being seated and cross-check the name on the random list. (Note: The chart below includes the six "six-pack" jurors waiting to replace any excused from the twelve.)

1	2	3	4	5	6
7	8	9	10	11	12
13	14	15	16	17	18

PLAINTIFF	PLAINTIFF	Defendant	Defendant	Joint	Court	Court
01	11	01	11	21	01	11
02	12	02	12	22	02	12
03	13	03	13	23	03	13
04	14	04	14	24	04	14
05	15	05	15	25	05	15
06	16	06	16	26	06	16
07	17	07	17	27	07	17
08	18	08	18	28	08	18
09	19	09	19	29	09	19
10	20	10	20	30	10	20

Jury Seating Chart

"Six-Pack" Method

Every court will have its own method of jury selection. However, the "six-pack" method, also referred to as the "jury box" method, is a common one. (See *People v. Avila* (2006) 38 Cal.4th 491, 537.) From the random list, twelve prospective jurors are directed to fill the jury box, beginning with juror "Number One." Once the box is full, six more prospective jurors are also called from the random list and seated in chairs usually in front of the jury box. Some judges refer to these six as the "on deck" jurors, using a baseball metaphor. Thus, there are now eighteen prospective jurors ready for voir dire. Jurors whose names were not called remain seated in the audience and observe the process.

These eighteen jurors are examined by the court and counsel, if permitted. Any one of the eighteen can be removed by the court "for cause," as discussed infra. If a juror is removed "for cause," a prospective replacement juror is called from the *audience* to fill that position and the other jurors in the box remain where they are seated. When the time comes for the peremptory challenges ("strikes"), those challenges are made only regarding the twelve in the jury box. If one of the twelve jurors in the box is excused via a peremptory challenge, that juror is replaced by one of the six "on deck" jurors. When this occurs, the jurors literally change seats, meaning, the spare "on deck" juror takes the empty seat and the jury box is always full. If the court follows a procedure whereby the jurors do not actually change seats, it can get confusing, so it is especially important to keep track of which juror is replacing the juror removed for a challenge, so that there is no confusion regarding who are the twelve jurors at any given time.

If it happens that the six "on deck" jurors are used up, meaning, they have all been seated in the jury box to fill vacancies, then six more prospective "on deck" jurors are chosen from the audience who will then need to be examined and "qualified," meaning, a determination there is no "cause" to remove them. Once the parties complete their peremptory challenges, either by exhausting their allotted number or by "passing," the twelve remaining jurors in the jury box are sworn. The court will also generally use this same process to select the alternate jurors. The advantage of the six-pack method is that it allows eighteen jurors to questioned at one time and permits the parties to know the quality of the upcoming replacement "on deck" jurors.

Other Methods

The "six-pack" or "jury box" method is only one of several methods used and trial courts are generally accorded discretion regarding the specific process. For example, some courts use the "struck jury" system where a group of potential jurors are first examined and challenged for cause by both sides, excused jurors are replaced on the panel, and the examination of replacements continues until a panel of qualified jurors is presented. The size of the panel at this time is 12 plus the number of alternates and peremptory strikes allowed all parties. The parties then proceed to exercise their peremptories in some order which will result in all exhausting their strikes at approximately the same time. (See *U.S. v. Esparza-Gonzalez* 422 F. 3d. 897, 902 (9th Cir. 2005))

Trial Tip: Devising a system to keep track of all the juror information is critical. Some attorneys use a notepad with each page devoted to a specific juror. Others make notes on the jury chart itself. It is important to make notes/comments for each juror and have them available and organized for future use. Don't be one of those attorneys who gets the juror's information or name confused, which happens.

Juror Questionnaire

At some point early in the process, the prospective jurors are generally provided with a questionnaire to complete. Many courts have a standardized one-page questionnaire that might vary somewhat depending upon whether it is a civil or criminal case. The questionnaire typically requests biographical information, such as the juror's marital and family status, past and present occupations, and education, etc. In civil cases, it may also request information regarding whether the juror has any experience with the court system; for example, formerly or presently a plaintiff or a defendant in a lawsuit. In criminal cases, it may inquire whether the juror has ever been a "victim" of crime, is associated with law enforcement, or has other familiarity with the criminal justice system. Copies of the questionnaire are normally distributed to the attorneys and the court at about the time the jurors are seated. Thus, for example, if the court is using the six-pack or similar method, by the time the 18 jurors are seated and ready for voir dire, each attorney and the court should have a copy of each juror's questionnaire before them. The questionnaire is important because it contains some of the first bits of information about each juror that you will use to make your decision. (See California Standards of Judicial Administration, Standard 3.25 ["The examination of prospective jurors in a civil case may be oral, by written questionnaire, or by both methods, and should include all questions necessary to ensure the selection of a fair and impartial jury."].) The written questionnaire serves as an alternative to oral voir dire and is thus considered part of the voir dire process, generally. (*Bellas v. Superior Court of Alameda County* (2000) 85 Cal.App. 4th 636, fn. 2.)

Attorney Drafted Questionnaire

The standard one-page juror questionnaire provides trial attorneys with only basic information. Some courts may permit the attorneys to prepare and draft their own questionnaire. "Upon request, the court may approve a more in-depth questionnaire prepared by the attorneys." (CCP § 205(d)). A more in-depth questionnaire should be considered for use in complex or high-profile cases. An attorney-crafted questionnaire has the advantage of asking questions specifically designed and tailored to fit the type of the case. However, if the court does permit an attorney questionnaire, some planning is required to determine how the questionnaires will be copied and distributed. In some murder trials, for example, questionnaires can be as large as 15 or 20 pages, which creates logistical issues regarding copying and distribution. In addition, counsel and the court will generally need time to review them. Often, the court will recess the proceedings a day or two to permit review. One further advantage of using an attorney-created questionnaire is that it allows the questionnaires to be maintained in accordance with the random list. This gives counsel the advantage during the review process of knowing the quality (or not) of the upcoming jurors, which is valuable information when contemplating whether to exercise a peremptory challenge.

Trial Tip: The responses on the questionnaire itself may reveal a juror with an obvious bias or a clear reason why he or she should be removed "for cause." To save time and to avoid poisoning the well, so to speak, meet and confer with opposing counsel and the court to see if a stipulation can be reached to excuse the juror without further hearing. If the cause is obvious, the court will generally agree.

Confidentiality of Juror Information

Note that although the court can seal "personal juror identifying information" (Code Civil Proc.§ 237(a)(2)), the *content* of juror questionnaires is publicly accessible, unless: 1) the reason for ordering them sealed outweighs the presumption of open access to records of judicial proceeding; 2) the limitation on access is tailored as narrowly as possible; and 3) the trial court's findings are articulated with enough specificity. (*Bellas v. Superior Court of Alameda County* (2000) 85 Cal.App.4th 636, 645.) Venire panels should be "advised in unambiguous language at the time questionnaires are distributed that they will become public records accessible to anyone and, as an alternative to writing in sensitive personal data, jurors can respond to questions asked on the questionnaire on the record in chambers with counsel present." (*Bellas*, supra at p. 652; *Copley Press, Inc. v. Superior Court* (1991) 228 Cal.App.3d 77.)

Court Introductions

Once all the prospective jurors are in place, the court will normally begin with introductory remarks, which generally includes describing for the jurors the nature of the lawsuit, permitting the parties to introduce themselves, and providing the jurors with some preliminary instruction, such as the "separation" admonishment, to wit: not to discuss the case with others, no independent research or investigation, no contact with the parties or witnesses, and to remain fair and impartial. In addition, if the parties have provided the court with a neutral "statement of the case," the court will generally read it to the prospective jurors about this time.

Trial Tip: Confer with opposing counsel to see whether a neutral "*statement of the case*" can be worked out. It might entail a summary of the uncontested facts and a description of what is at issue. When the jurors understand the substance of the case from the beginning, it makes it easier to discuss with them biases or prejudices they may have regarding this particular type of case.

Mini Opening Statement by Counsel

A relatively new rule in California authorizes the use of introductory statements by counsel at the *beginning* of the voir dire process. This might be considered in lieu of the statement of the case. Rule of Court 4.202 states: "Prior to the examination of prospective jurors, the trial judge may, in his or her discretion, permit brief opening statements by counsel to the panel." The legislative comments on the rule explain, "This statement is not a substitute for opening statements. Its purpose is to place voir dire questions in context and to generate interest in the case so that prospective jurors will be less inclined to claim marginal hardships." (See also C.C.P. 222.5.)

Court Voir Dire

The court typically begins the interrogation process. "To select a fair and impartial jury in civil jury trials, the trial judge shall examine the prospective jurors." (C.C.P. § 222.5.) "The responsibility for securing a fair and impartial jury has been placed on the trial judge, who is charged with the duty of examining prospective jurors. He/she must also permit reasonable examination of prospective jurors by counsel. The grand objective of the examination is to elicit information from prospective jurors, which permits the exercise of challenges for cause in order to arrive at a fair and impartial jury. But the specific methods to achieve this objective have not been prescribed, and several different procedures are feasible." (*Rousseau v. West Coast House Movers* (1967) 256 Cal.App.2d 878, 883.) The identification of juror bias is a factual finding concerning the juror's state of mind that is decidedly within the province of the trial judge. (*Wainwright v. Witt*, 469 U.S. 412, 428, 105 S.Ct. 844, 83 L.Ed.2d 841 (1985).) The trial court's determination on juror bias is entitled to the presumption of correctness because it "involves credibility findings whose basis cannot be easily discerned from an appellate record." (Id. at 429.)

To select a fair and impartial jury, the judge must conduct an initial examination of the prospective jurors orally, or by written questionnaire, or by both methods. (CA Rule of Ct. 4.201.) The California Standards of Judicial Administration, Standard 3.25, suggests specific questions or topics to be covered by the judge, which include the length of the trial, general background information, knowledge of the parties or the case, familiarity with lawsuits, and other suggested questions depending on the nature of the case. Many of the topics listed in the Judicial Standards are often covered in the standard civil jury questionnaire. Although the Standards of Judicial Administration provide the court guidance, it is not required that they follow precisely. "In examining prospective jurors in civil cases, the judge should *consider* the policies and recommendations in standard 3.25 of the Standards of Judicial Administration." (CA Rule of Ct. 3.1540, emphasis added.) Failure to use the recommended language may be a factor to be considered in determining whether a voir dire was adequate, but the entire voir dire must be considered in making that judgment. (*People v. Holt* (1997) 15 Cal. 4th 619, 661.) The trial court also has discretion to summarize the evidence with no limitations on its content or timing so long as it is "accurate, temperate, nonargumentative, and scrupulously fair." (*People v. Sorrels* (2012) 208 Cal.App. 4th 1155, 1165.) In addition, CA Rule of Ct. 3.1540(c) provides that on completion of the court's initial examination, the trial judge must permit counsel for each party that so requests to submit additional questions that the judge will put to the jurors.

> **Trial Tip:** If there is a sensitive topic or issue in the trial, draft some questions for the jurors and inquire whether the court will broach the subject first during its voir dire. When the judge discusses an issue, the jurors may attach more importance to it.

Every judge will have his or her own style and method for voir dire. Some are very thorough while others are more generic. A more common method is to voir dire the prospective eighteen jurors as a group. For example, the court may explain the basic duties of a trial juror and inquire, by a show of hands, whether any juror would be unable to perform that function. If a juror raises a hand, the court will follow up with additional questions. The thoroughness of the questioning by the court may also depend on whether a lengthy juror questionnaire was used. The jury questionnaire is considered part of the voir dire process. (*Bellas v. Superior Court of Alameda County* (2000) 85 Cal.App. 4th 636, fn. 2.)

In Federal Court, it is not required that the court conduct an oral examination. The use of a written questionnaire can suffice. Although voir dire ordinarily contemplates seeing the jurors and hearing them speak ... any court-supervised examination of prospective jurors is reasonably understood to be part of voir dire. District courts routinely employ questionnaires to facilitate voir dire in a number of circumstances." (*U.S. v. Quinones*, 511 F.3d 289, 299 (2d Cir. 2007).)

It is common that during the court's voir dire, facts surface that would justify a juror's excusal "for cause." (Discussed below.) This occurs most often when the juror openly states a bias or some other obvious reason why the juror cannot impartially hear the case. The court can excuse the juror "for cause" without the agreement of counsel. (*People v. Merced* (2001) 94 CA 4th 1024, 1028.)

> **Trial Tip:** During the court's voir dire, the best thing you can do is to listen carefully and to observe. Your first impression is usually the correct one. Take notes, particularly regarding issues you may want to address later during your voir dire, if permitted.

Pre-Instruction

In some cases, counsel should consider requesting the court to pre-instruct the jurors on relevant principles of law, including perhaps specific definitions and/or the elements of a cause of action or a defense in controversy. If the parties stipulate, some judges will accede. Knowing the specific contested issues and legal principles involved may in some cases assist counsel during the selection process. However, if the legal principles are complex or if the parties disagree over the meanings, permitting the attorneys to discuss specific principles of law during voir dire can lead to confusion and result in the undue consumption of time. Many judges, on their own motion, will curtail voir dire that begins to stray from the basic concepts of law or delves into the specific facts of the case.

Attorney Voir Dire

Attorney voir dire generally commences following the court's. In most jurisdictions, the attorneys are permitted to conduct their own voir dire. In California, it is a right. (C.C.P. § 222.5.) However, in Federal Court, it is discretionary and the judge typically conducts most of the voir dire. The court may conduct the voir dire itself and permit parties to submit additional questions at its discretion. (Federal Rules of Civil Procedure Rule 47(a).) "There is no constitutional right for counsel to conduct voir dire." (United States v. Torres, 191 F.3d 799 (7th Cir.1999), cert. denied, 528 U.S. 1180, 120 S.Ct. 1218, 145 L.Ed.2d 1118 (2000).)

Eventually, the time will come when the juror's attention will be focused on you. This may be the first time you have spoken much with the jurors present. Some attorneys prefer to conduct their examination while seated at counsel table next to their client, while others like to use a podium. It can be difficult sometimes for attorneys to know exactly how to conduct the examination. In that regard, perhaps the most important concern at the outset is not to make yourself look incompetent or foolish by asking questions that are unclear, confusing, or even insulting. However, some attorneys step in it right from the beginning by asking questions or making comments that are unintelligent or offensive. With experience every trial lawyer will develop his or her own style and format. As a guide, however, below are three general areas of inquiry you may wish to consider. How much time you devote to each area will, of course, depend on the particular case and the issues involved.

1. Juror Background

In order to get a good feel for any particular juror, perhaps the most important thing you can do is simply learn as much background information as possible. It goes without saying that a person's attitudes and biases are mainly formed by past life experiences.

Learning background information is accomplished by reviewing the juror's questionnaire *and* by oral questioning. The answers in the written questionnaire may give you a clue of where to direct your questions. In the public setting of a courtroom, however, people are often reluctant to open up and may not make their issues readily apparent. Conversely, those who immediately proclaim they cannot be fair sometimes just have an agenda to get off jury duty. If a juror does volunteer that he or she has a bias or a prejudice, even for a legitimate reason, that revelation will generally occur during the court's voir dire and the judge will often excuse that juror "for cause," before attorney voir dire begins.

The task for the trial attorney now is to search for more subtle issues. Some jurors, with past life experiences that might bias most people, will opt to remain silent and not volunteer anything, not because they have an agenda, but because they believe they can overcome the experience and will not let it affect their judgment. In addition, they may be shy and not want to talk about it with anyone. Some jurors may feel the entire process is an unnecessary invasion of their privacy. For others, it can be embarrassing and even humiliating for them to discuss, in a courtroom full of strangers, a skeleton in the closet or something that causes an emotional reaction.

> **Trial Tip:** Be on guard for the "sleeper." A juror who has serious issues, but who stays quiet during voir dire. Jurors who write practically nothing in their questionnaire and seem reluctant to volunteer anything should be a concern. You generally do not want a juror who is an unknown quantity or an outlier. Conversely, watch for the juror who seems a little too eager and overly chatty.

The best method to tease out information is generally by asking very specific questions. First, look for clues in the questionnaire, then follow up with more questions. For example, if the juror has noted in the questionnaire that she was previously involved in a lawsuit, don't merely ask, "Is there anything about that situation that will affect your impartiality in this case?" Instead, follow up by asking more specific questions about that prior case. What type of case was it? Was she the plaintiff or defendant? Were there injuries? Was there a settlement or a trial? Was she happy, upset, or dissatisfied with the result of that case? How did she feel about the attorneys handling the case? Open-ended questions force the witness to provide more information.

The key is to get the juror to open up a little. Some jurors will be open and talkative, while others will be reserved and quiet. Subtle clues about biases can be detected simply by the tone of voice or body language, *if* you are paying attention. This is where the attorney's ability to read people comes into play. Even if a juror has nothing remarkable in her background, requesting that she briefly expand on her current occupation, hobbies, or pastimes can help you get a bead on the juror. Hidden biases can sometimes be discovered simply by asking the right question.

> **Trial Tip:** Don't rely solely on the answers written in the questionnaire. Jurors will often rush through it or answer without really thinking. Frequently, the oral questioning reveals information that was inadvertently (or purposefully) omitted from the questionnaire or the question was misunderstood.

2. Willingness to Follow and Apply the Law

Another important objective of voir dire is to ensure that all jurors will be able to follow and apply the law. This might include the burdens of proof or the obligation not to be swayed by irrelevant or sympathetic evidence. Subject to limitation, either party is entitled to ask prospective jurors questions specific enough to determine if those jurors harbor bias that would cause them not to follow an instruction on the issues presented in the case. (*People v. Coffman and Marlow* (2004) 34 Cal.4th 1, 47.) While attorneys are not permitted to "indoctrinate" the jury or have them commit to a particular viewpoint or position, it is appropriate to cover the basic concepts of law involved in the trial and confirm every juror will follow the law. (*People v. Abilez* (2007) 41 Cal.4th 472, 492-493.) "Even if a juror has proclaimed his general willingness to follow the law and instructions, the rule (no indoctrination) should not prohibit further reasonable questioning calculated to elicit a juror's admission of actual unwillingness to apply a particular rule of law pertinent to the impending trial. Any overt resistance of that kind and degree would form the basis for a challenge for cause on grounds of actual bias." (*People v. Balderas* (1985) 41 Cal.3d 144, 184.)

For example, in a wrongful death case where there will be emotional testimony that a person has died, it may be appropriate to alert the jurors of this fact and inquire whether the jurors can follow and apply the rule that requires them to base their decision on facts and evidence and not sympathy. In this situation, counsel may wish to get assurances from each juror that he or she will be able to follow the law and to separate emotion from fact, despite evidence that someone died. By the same token, seeking assurances that all jurors will be able to award damages if the case is proven is also appropriate.

> **Trial Tip:** If there is particularly troubling or upsetting evidence in the case, e.g., graphic photographs of injuries, it is better to get that out during voir dire to see whether there are any jurors who will not be able to stomach it or may react very emotionally.

3. Negative Information

A third possible objective is to reveal negative information or facts related to your case. The purpose of doing this is not to indoctrinate the jury, but to see whether any jurors would be biased or prejudiced against the case merely because these facts exist. It is appropriate to expose the jurors to some of the issues or concepts involved to ensure there are no biases. (*People v. Soltero* (1978) 81 Cal.App.3d 423, 428.) Every case will typically have a weakness. During the jury selection process, you may wish to alert the jury of its existence in order to determine whether it would cause any juror to automatically shut down and not fulfill their obligation to look objectively at all the facts and evidence. In other words, would the prejudicial evidence make it impossible for them to remain impartial? Revealing unfavorable facts at the outset will also make it much less of a surprise when the evidence is introduced during the trial; for example, evidence of drug use or something the jurors might find offensive. The question for the jurors is whether they will be able to look past these negative facts and base their decision on the relevant facts and the law. Jurors tend to have more faith in cases in which a party does not attempt to hide or sugarcoat the truth. For example, counsel might state, "In this case, it will be undisputed that my client caused the accident and had been drinking that evening. The issue will be one of damages. Would you be able to fairly and objectively determine the damages, even if you know my client acted in that way?"

Trial Tip: One strategy for voir dire is to begin with general concepts addressed to the group en masse, where jurors can raise a hand if they have a response, similar to being in a classroom. Thereafter, move to individual jurors for more specific questions, usually related to something they wrote in their questionnaire. Some attorneys like to speak with each juror to develop a rapport. However, if the court has set time limits, *gauge the time* accordingly. Some attorneys inadvertently run short and never get through all the jurors.

"Improper" Questions

Although section 222.5 permits "liberal and probing" questions, the scope and subject matter of attorney voir dire is not unlimited. Section 222.5 states, in relevant part, "The trial judge should permit counsel to conduct voir dire examination without requiring prior submission of the questions unless a particular counsel engages in improper questioning. For purposes of this section, an "improper question" is any question that, as its dominant purpose, attempts to precondition the prospective jurors to a particular result, indoctrinate the jury, or question the prospective jurors concerning the pleadings or the applicable law." Further, The California Standards of Judicial Administration, Standard 3.25, attempts to set forth what are not appropriate questions for voir dire. Section (f) reads:

> "When any counsel examines the prospective jurors, the trial judge should not permit counsel to attempt to precondition the prospective jurors to a particular result or allow counsel to comment on the personal lives and families of the parties or their attorneys. Nor should the trial judge allow counsel to question the jurors concerning the pleadings, the applicable law, the meaning of particular words and phrases, or the comfort of the jurors, except in unusual circumstances, where, in the trial judge's sound discretion, such questions become necessary to insure the selection of a fair and impartial jury."

"The trial judge should not permit counsel to precondition the prospective jurors to a particular result or allow counsel to comment on the personal lives and families of the parties or their attorneys." (Standards of Judicial Administration, Standard 4.30(c).) The law is clear that it is not a proper object of voir dire to obtain a juror's advisory opinion based on a preview of the evidence. Rather, a proper inquiry must be directed to whether, without knowing the specifics of the case, the juror has an 'open mind' on the issues presented." (*People v. Butler* (2009) 46 Cal.4th 847, 859-860.) Questions designed to educate the jury panel as to particular facts, compel jurors to vote a particular way, prejudice the jurors for or against a party, argue the case, indoctrinate the jury, or instruct the jury in matters of law, are not appropriate questions for "cause." (*People v. Abilez* (2007) 41 Cal.4th 472, 492-493; *People v. Soltero* (1978) 81 Cal.App.3d 423, 428; *People v. Ashmus* (1991) 54 Cal.3d 932, 959; *People v. Burgener* (2003) 29 Cal.4th 833, 865.) Counsel has no right to ask specific questions that invite prospective jurors to prejudge the evidence (*People v. Cash* (2002) 28 Cal.4th 703, 721-722.) However, to facilitate the intelligent exercise of both peremptory challenges and those for cause, parties may inform prospective jurors of the general facts of the case. (*People v. Ervin* (2000) 22 Cal.4th 48, 70; *People v. Kirkpatrick* (1994*) 7 Cal.4th 988, 1004-1005.) Subject to limitation, either party is entitled to ask prospective jurors questions specific enough to determine if those jurors harbor bias that would cause them not to follow an instruction on the issues presented in the case. (*People v. Coffman and Marlow* (2004) 34 Cal.4th 1, 47.)

Counsel can also run afoul of these limitations when they attempt to ingratiate themselves with the jury by providing irrelevant or personal information, e.g., family or past occupations, or by talking about the specific facts of the present case. For example, Counsel can say: "My client is going to testify that she did not run the red light. Do you think you can keep an open mind and impartially listen to her testimony?" [Improper because counsel is attempting to indoctrinate the jury to the facts of her case.] Or: "In this case, it will be contested who ran the red light. Do you think you can fairly and impartially consider all the evidence in that regard?" [Proper because it is generally okay to apprise the jurors of the contested issues to see if any biases exist regarding an issue.]

Time Limits

Many judges wisely place time limits on attorney voir dire. However, C.C.P. § 222.5 states, in relevant part: "Specific unreasonable or arbitrary time limits shall not be imposed in any case. The trial judge shall not establish a blanket policy of a time limit for voir dire." Before counsel begins voir dire, it is important that counsel know the time limitations imposed and keep track of the time. This should have been a topic discussed at the pre-trial conference.

Objection During Voir Dire

During attorney voir dire, the questions must be fair and properly framed. The standard witness objections of "leading," "compound," or "vague and ambiguous" are applicable during voir dire too. A trial court has wide latitude to place reasonable limits on voir dire and to decide the questions to be asked. (*People v. Jackson* (2016) 1 Cal. 5th 269, 359.)

In practice, the most common sin of the trial lawyer during voir dire is probably to weave specific facts about the case into a question in order to see how the prospective juror reacts. However, it is improper to request a juror to prejudge the evidence. For example, "My client is going to testify that she did not cause the accident because the plaintiff's vehicle was speeding. Do you think you can keep an open mind and impartially listen to her testimony?" versus "In this case, it will be contested as to who ran the red light. Do you think you can keep an open mind and impartially listen to her testimony?"

Trial Tip: Consider devising a simple grading system for each prospective juror, for example, a 1 - 5 scale where a "1" means an automatic kick, "2" is a probable kick, and a "5" is the perfect juror. Don't waste time on "1's" or "2's." Focus on the "3s" and "4s." Also, because the selection process is part intuition, no need to take copious notes.

Challenge for Cause - "Actual" or "Implied" Bias

Following the completion of the attorney voir dire, the court will next hear any motion to challenge a juror "for cause." Most judges will permit the motion to be made at the sidebar or in chambers where the parties can argue for or against whether cause has been established, out of juror earshot. For obvious reasons, counsel would prefer not to make the motion in the presence of that juror in the event the court denies the challenge. The defense makes the first challenge. (C.C.P. § 226.) If there is no challenge for cause, then the proper response is, "Pass for Cause, Your Honor."

The parties are allowed an unlimited number of challenges for cause. (C.C.P. § 226; *People v. Black* (2014) 58 Cal.4th 912, 916.) The moving party must convince the court that the prospective juror should be removed "for cause," as described in the provisions of Code of Civil Procedure Section 225, which ordinarily means an *"actual bias"* or *"implied bias."* An "actual bias" occurs when there is the "existence of a state of mind on the part of the juror in reference to the case, or to any of the parties, which will prevent the juror from acting with entire impartiality, and without prejudice to the substantial rights of any party." (§225(b)(1)(C). An "implied bias" is recognized as a matter of law when certain circumstances occur, for example, when the juror is related or closely connected to a party. (C.C.P. § 229.) An implied bias is shown when the juror has "an unqualified opinion or belief as to the merits of the action founded upon knowledge of its material facts or of some of them" or "the existence of a state of mind in the juror evincing enmity against, or bias towards, either party." (§ 229(e),(f).) Whether actual or implied, the standard for both is essentially that the juror is patently biased or prejudiced. The Federal standards are similar.

In practice, the parties will often "stipulate" that a particular juror should be excused for "cause." Typically, this is a juror with obvious issues, e.g., an admission of a strong bias in the questionnaire due to some prior knowledge or circumstance. The court does not have to accept the stipulation, but most judges will if the cause is obvious, and proceeding with further examination of this juror would simply be a waste of time. Of course, the attorneys would like to stipulate for "cause" to avoid using a precious preemptory challenge.

Tactical Issues

In practice, if there is a particular juror one party would prefer not to hear the case, counsel will attempt to establish "cause" during the interrogation to save a preemptory challenge. The use of leading questions is often used by counsel to make the showing. For example, "So, Mrs. Wright, in light of your prior experience, where you were a defendant in a personal injury case, it sounds like you would have trouble remaining impartial in this case, correct?"

However, the questions must be fair and properly framed. The standard witness objections of "leading," "compound," or "vague and ambiguous" are applicable during voir dire too. A trial court has wide latitude to place reasonable limits on voir dire and to decide the questions to be asked. (*People v. Jackson* (2016) 1 Cal. 5th 269, 359.) The trial court has discretion to channel the voir dire examination of the jurors within reasonable bounds and in a manner designed to expedite the jury selection process. (*People v. Wright* (1990) 52 Cal.3d 367, 419.) In addition, even when a juror has indicated a possible bias, opposing counsel generally will have the opportunity to "rehabilitate" the juror. Of course, opposing counsel would like the other party to use a preemptory challenge. Some jurors will flip-flop by making inconsistent statements depending on which counsel is doing the questioning.

To successfully challenge a juror for cause, counsel must be able to articulate *on the record* how the prospective juror harbors either an actual or implied bias. As a practical matter, counsel will not have to state specifically whether it is "implied" or "actual," but it is helpful to know the buzz words. When making the challenge, explain what it is about the juror that makes counsel feel the juror is biased. Generally, it is something the prospective juror has said during oral interrogation and/or written in the questionnaire, but not necessarily. Sometimes a juror's attitude and body language can demonstrate bias, despite the fact the juror steadfastly maintains he or she can be fair and impartial. Cite for the record your observations, e.g., body language and mannerisms.

Once the motion is made, the court must then decide whether to grant or deny the motion. Assessing the qualifications of jurors challenged for cause is a matter falling within the broad discretion of the trial court. (*People v. Bonilla* (2007) 41 Cal.4th 313, 339.) The trial court must determine whether the prospective juror will be "unable to faithfully and impartially apply the law in the case." A juror will often give conflicting or confusing answers regarding his or her impartiality or capacity to serve, and the trial court must weigh the juror's responses in deciding whether to remove the juror for cause. The trial court's resolution of these factual matters is binding on the appellate court if supported by substantial evidence. (Id.) Where equivocal or conflicting responses are elicited regarding a prospective juror's ability to follow the law, the trial court's determination as to his true state of mind is binding on an appellate court. (*Bonilla*, supra, accord, *People v. Moon* (2005) 37 Cal.4th 1, 14, 32 Cal.Rptr.3d 894, 117 P.3d 591.) Generally, the mere fact that a juror has a certain background or differing opinions will not constitute "cause" if the juror is willing to follow the law. (*People v. Danks* (2004) 32 Cal.4th 269, 302-303.)

> **Trial Tip:** The court's dismissal of a juror "for cause" saves you a preemptory challenge. Thus, if the juror has shown *any* arguable bias against your case, consider making the motion. You have nothing to lose if the court denies it, except you have tipped your hand to opposing counsel.

Denial of Challenge – Review

It is important to note that even if the court wrongly denies your motion to excuse a juror "for cause," to preserve your right to appeal the ruling, a party must: (1) exercise a peremptory challenge to remove the juror in question, (2) use all of his or her peremptory challenges, and (3) communicate to the court dissatisfaction with the jury selected. (*People v. Crittenden* (1994) 9 Cal.4th 83, 121; *Burns v. 20th Century Ins. Co.*, (1992) 9 Cal.App.4th 1666, 1672-1673 [forfeiture by failure to exhaust peremptories renders moot failure to exclude all insureds of defendant insurer].) However, if during the trial the juror's bias caused the juror to vote a certain way, it may be grounds for a later motion for a new trial based on juror misconduct, if it can be proved. (See infra, Juror Misconduct, at p. 256.)

No Challenge for Cause

If a party does *not* wish to issue a challenge for cause, the appropriate response is, "Pass for cause, Your Honor." This means you are satisfied that none of the prospective jurors (18 if you are using the six-pack method) has an actual or implied bias. Once the court has ruled on any challenges or the parties have "passed for cause," the prospective jurors are said to be "qualified."

Peremptory Challenge

After the parties have either "passed for cause" or the court has ruled on any challenges for cause, the next step is when the parties may exercise their preemptory challenges. (C.C.P. § 226.) This is when you can potentially affect the makeup of the jury because a party can excuse a juror for any reason and without having to provide any explanation. "Jurors may be excused based on 'hunches' and even 'arbitrary' exclusion is permissible, so long as the reasons are not based on impermissible group bias." (*People v. Box* (2000) 23 Cal.4th 1153, fn. 6; see also infra, re: Batson/Wheeler.) "The central function of the right of peremptory challenge, or "strike" in some jurisdiction, is to enable a litigant to remove a certain number of potential jurors who are not challengeable for cause, but in whom the litigant perceives bias or hostility." (Id) "The function of the [peremptory] challenge is not only to eliminate extremes of partiality on both sides, but to assure the parties that the jurors before whom they try the case will decide on the basis of the evidence placed before them, and not otherwise." (*Swain v. Alabama,* 380 U.S. 202, 212, 85 S.Ct. 824, 831, 13 L.Ed.2d 759 (1965), overruled on other grounds by *Batson v. Kentucky,* 476 U.S. 79, 106 S.Ct. 1712, 90 L.Ed.2d 69 (1986).)

Order of Using

"Peremptory challenges shall be taken or passed by the sides alternately, commencing with the plaintiff or people; and each party shall be entitled to have the panel full before exercising any peremptory challenge. When each side passes consecutively, the jury shall then be sworn, unless the court, for good cause, shall otherwise order. The number of peremptory challenges remaining with a side shall not be diminished by any passing of a peremptory challenge." (C.C.P. § 231(d)(e).)

> **Trial Tip:** Some attorneys feel compelled to use challenges just because they can. However, sometimes, the final 12 chosen look as good as, or even worse than the first 12. On the other hand, some attorneys will bravely pass on the first 12 without using a single challenge.

The Numbers

Every jurisdiction permits the parties to exercise a certain number of peremptory challenges. C.C.P. § 231 reads, in part:

> (c) In civil cases, each party shall be entitled to six peremptory challenges. If there are more than two parties, the court shall, for the purpose of allotting peremptory challenges, divide the parties into two or more sides according to their respective interests in the issues. Each side shall be entitled to eight peremptory challenges. If there are several parties on a side, the court shall divide the challenges among them as nearly equally as possible. If there are more than two sides, the court shall grant such additional peremptory challenges to a side as the interests of justice may require, provided that the peremptory challenges of one side shall not exceed the aggregate number of peremptory challenges of all other sides. If any party on a side does not use his or her full share of peremptory challenges, the unused challenges may be used by the other party or parties on the same side.

> (d) Peremptory challenges shall be taken or passed by the sides alternately, commencing with the plaintiff or people, and each party shall be entitled to have the panel full before exercising any peremptory challenge. When each side passes consecutively, the jury shall then be sworn, unless the court, for good cause, shall otherwise order. The number of peremptory challenges remaining with a side shall not be diminished by any passing of a peremptory challenge.

> (e) If all the parties on both sides pass consecutively, the jury shall then be sworn,

unless the court, for good cause, shall otherwise order. The number of peremptory challenges remaining with a side shall not be diminished by any passing of a peremptory challenge.

In Federal Court, in a civil case, "each party shall be entitled to three peremptory challenges. Several defendants or several plaintiffs may be considered as a single party for the purposes of making challenges, or the court may allow additional peremptory challenges and permit them to be exercised separately or jointly." (Federal Rules of Civil Procedure Rule 47; 28 U.S.C.A. § 1870.)

In criminal cases in California, each party has 10 preemptory challenges for misdemeanors, 10 for felonies without a life sentence possibility, and 20 for cases with a possible life sentence or the death penalty. (C.C.P. § 231.)

Making the Decision

When the court indicates that the parties may begin exercising their peremptory challenges, the process can go rather quickly so it will be very helpful if you and your client have already given it some thought. In addition, it is imperative that you have the jury chart in front of you and remain organized. Recall that when using the "six pack" method, the challenges are made only against any of the 12 in the jury box. When a juror in the box is excused, then the next qualified juror from the additional "on deck" six, takes the removed juror's place.

In most jurisdictions, the plaintiff or prosecution goes first, followed by the defense, and the challenges then alternate. For example, California's procedure is codified: "Peremptory challenges shall be taken or passed by the sides alternately, commencing with the plaintiff or people; and each party shall be entitled to have the panel full before exercising any peremptory challenge. When each side passes consecutively, the jury shall then be sworn, unless the court, for good cause, shall otherwise order. The number of peremptory challenges remaining with a side shall not be diminished by any passing of a peremptory challenge." (C.C.P. § 231(d)(e).)

Which jurors to excuse, if any, using your preemptory challenges is really where attorney intuition, common sense, and some strategy come into play. Obviously, how many challenges you have at your disposal is a major factor. As discussed above, in some criminal prosecutions, it is not uncommon that each side can have as many as 20. To assist in making the decision, it can be very helpful if you have scored or graded the quality of each juror during the entire voir dire process based upon the characteristics you are looking for. Each case is obviously different, and you may have a certain type of juror that you prefer. Some lawyers attempt to draw conclusions based on stereotypical categories; for example, that teachers are too empathetic, engineers too analytical, and former military too conservative. Others draw distinctions between women versus men, educated versus non-educated, young versus old, and leaders versus followers. Some try to predict who will be the foreperson.

Despite the attorney's best guesses, however, it has been my observation that often these generalities and stereotypes do not hold true. In the end, there is no magic formula, but there are a few tips that may help you rank the jurors and decide correctly. First, be observant. Without asking a single question, you can derive a lot about the juror's persona simply by the power of observation. Take a good hard *look* at each juror. How is the juror dressed? Unkempt or disheveled looking individuals should always raise a red flag. Is the juror paying attention, responsive to questions, and engaged, or does the juror appear irritated, distracted, or uninterested? Does the juror appear to be interacting with the other jurors, or does the juror look like a loner? Does the juror appear unusually timid or assertive? Also, *listen* to the juror talk. The manner and style of speech can be very indicative concerning education, intellect, and background. Train yourself to be observant, because the subtle clues you garner from simple observation may be all you need to make the decision.

Second, consider the juror's background, including employment and educational history. Long periods of unexplained unemployment may require further inquiry. Look for jurors who have shown responsibility and who seem grounded. One important quality is the ability to get along with other people and to work in a group setting. In a criminal case the jurors are required to arrive at a *unanimous* decision, while in a civil case a majority must agree. Jurors who are very opinionated or loners, for lack of a better word, should be a concern. During voir dire, some attorneys ask questions specifically designed to determine if the juror can work well with others.

Lastly, after you have watched, listened, and asked a few questions, chances are that by now you have developed a pretty good *feel* for each juror. Try not to get too hung up on attempting to psychoanalyze or overthink it. Either you like the juror or you do not. If you have to talk yourself into a particular juror, then you are probably making the wrong decision. Generally, your gut feeling is the right call and you should not second-guess yourself. By this stage, you should have already been thinking about the complexion of the jury as a whole and which particular jurors must go. How and when to exercise a challenge can involve some strategy with these considerations in mind:

- **Jurors you must excuse**: Using your grading system, you will have ranked or scored the jurors in the box. Typically, there will be one or two that you know for sure you *have* to excuse based on their answers, background, or even a feeling you had about them. For example, a juror who had a bad experience with a case similar to the current case, but claims he or she can be fair nonetheless.

- **On the fence:** There may also be one or two more jurors where you have a question mark next to their names and that you graded a three or a four. In other words, you are on the fence about them. Whether to challenge these jurors may, in turn, depend on the remaining factors.

- **Quality of upcoming jurors**: Consider the quality (or not) of the upcoming replacement jurors if one of the 12 is excused. Presumably, you will have also ranked these prospective jurors too. The question is, does the replacement juror(s) look any better or worse than the one you are thinking of replacing or any better than the 12 already in the box? If all the replacement jurors look good, get rid of one or two of the questionable ones.

- **Opponent's options and challenges**: During this process, it is also helpful to strategize a bit by trying to predict your opponent's next move. Commonly, there will be one or more jurors in the box who you are fairly certain your *opponent* will excuse—jurors who, from your opponent's perspective, tend to favor your case. Sometimes it will be obvious, for example, where opposing counsel made a motion to challenge the juror for cause that was denied. Essentially, you are attempting to predict which jurors your opponent will challenge. If you are very confident that your opponent will, in fact, exercise a challenge on one or more of these jurors, then as a tactical matter, you could initially "pass" before exercising any of yours. Tactically, it can be advantageous to have more challenges left than your opponent, especially if the replacement jurors all look good to you. In other words, if your opponent exercised two challenges and you passed each time, then you are somewhat in the driver's seat. If your opponent runs short, you can then "pack" the jury box with the favorable jurors. However, keep in mind that if you "pass" and your opponent passes, then you are stuck with those 12 jurors.

- **Feel of the jury**: This final factor is highly subjective and relates back to your overall impression of how the jury looks and feels as a group. Experienced trial lawyers know that sometimes the right combination of people just has a better "feel" than another combination. There is no scientific explanation for this other than plain ol' attorney intuition.

Trial Tip: In the end, go with your initial gut reaction. If you have to talk yourself into keeping a particular juror, then you are probably making a mistake.

Alternate Jurors

In nearly every jury trial, the court will probably require at least one alternate juror. Generally, the alternate jurors are chosen after the 12 jurors in the box have been sworn. The alternates are generally selected from prospective jurors who have been examined and "qualified." They are usually the next jurors in order off the random list. In most jurisdictions, the court will allow one peremptory challenge per party for each alternate. For example, if the court directs that there will be two alternate jurors, each party will have two peremptory challenges and will use them alternately.

Improper Use of Challenge

Although the parties are permitted to exercise peremptory challenges without stating a reason, it is impermissible to remove a juror based on racial discrimination or other improper motive. If the motion is granted, the entire venire is excused and jury selection begins anew. (See *People v. Gutierrez* (2017) 2 Cal.5th 1150; *Batson v. Kentucky* (1986) 476 U.S. 79; *People v. Wheeler* (1978) 22 Cal.3d 258 (collectively Batson/Wheeler).) The rules apply in civil cases. (*Holley v. J & S Sweeping Co.* (1983) 143 Cal.App.3d 588, 590.)

The three-step inquiry governing Wheeler/Batson claims is well established. (*People v. Lomax* (2010) 49 Cal.4th 530, at p. 569.) First, the trial court must determine whether the defendant has made a prima facie showing that the prosecutor exercised a peremptory challenge based on race. Second, if the showing is made, the burden shifts to the prosecutor to demonstrate that the challenges were exercised for a race-neutral reason. Third, the court determines whether the defendant has proven purposeful discrimination. The ultimate burden of persuasion regarding racial motivation rests with, and never shifts from, the opponent of the strike. The three-step procedure also applies to state constitutional claims." *(People v. Lenix* (2008) 44 Cal.4th 602, 612-613.) If a race-neutral explanation is tendered, the trial court must then decide whether the opponent of the strike has proved purposeful racial discrimination. (*Johnson v. California* (2005) 545 U.S. 162, 168, 125 S.Ct. 2410, 162 L.Ed.2d 129 (Johnson).) To prevail, the defendant must show that "it was more likely than not that the challenge was improperly motivated." (Id. at p. 170, 125 S.Ct. 2410.)The defendant need not prove that all of the prosecutor's race-neutral reasons were pretextual, or even that the racial motivation was "determinative." (*Snyder v. Louisiana*, 552 U.S. at 485, 128 S.Ct. 1203 (citing *606 *Hunter v. Underwood*, 471 U.S. 222, 228, 105 S.Ct. 1916, 85 L.Ed.2d 222 (1985)). Instead, to prove a *Batson* violation, the defendant must demonstrate that "race was a substantial motivating factor" in the prosecutor's use of the peremptory strike. (*Cook v. LaMarque*, 593 F.3d 810, 815 (9th Cir. 2010).)

The use of a peremptory challenge on the basis of *gender* is also prohibited *(J.E.B. v. Alabama*, 511 U.S. 127, 129, 114 S.Ct. 1419, 128 L.Ed.2d 89 (1994) ["Gender, like race, is an unconstitutional proxy for juror competence and impartiality."] Likewise, the exclusion of jurors based on *sexual orientation* is also improper and subject to a *Batson* challenge. (See *SmithKline Beecham Corp. v. Abbott Labs*. (9th Cir. 2014) 740 F.3d 471, 484; *In re Marriage Cases* (2008) 43 Cal.4th 757, 840-844, [sexual orientation is a suspect classification for purposes of California's equal protection clause]; *People v. Douglas (2018)* 22 Cal.App.5th 1162, 1169.) Lastly, a *Batson* challenge applies with equal force to civil actions. (*Edmonson v. Leesville Concrete Co., Inc.,* 500 U.S. 614, 111 S. Ct. 2077, 114 L. Ed. 2d 660 (1991).)

4. OPENING STATEMENT

The opening statement is arguably one of the most important phases of a trial for the obvious reason that the minds of the jurors are the freshest and most receptive to new information. By this stage, the jurors are probably aware of the general nature of the case, but the specific details and facts have yet to be revealed. There is a sense of anticipation in the air for the jurors as they settle in with their notebooks following one or more days of monotonous jury selection. How the jurors will perceive and think about your case for the remainder of the trial may depend upon how clearly and persuasively you present the opening statement.

> **Trial Tip:** The juror's initial impression of the evidence following the opening statement is critical. Whether right or wrong, their initial impressions may last throughout the entire trial. Do *not* shortchange the opening statement, even in a court trial.

Purpose and Importance

"An opening statement has a narrow purpose and scope. It is to state what evidence will be presented, to make it easier for the jurors to understand what is to follow, and to relate parts of the evidence and testimony to the whole; it is not an occasion for argument. To make statements which will not or cannot be supported by proof is, if it relates to significant elements of the case, professional misconduct. Moreover, it is fundamentally unfair to an opposing party to allow an attorney, with the standing and prestige inherent in being an officer of the court, to present to the jury statements not susceptible of proof but intended to influence the jury in reaching a verdict" (*U.S. v.Dintz* 424 U.S. 600, 612, 96 S.Ct. 1075, 1082 (1976) [Justice Burger concurring opinion].) The purpose of an opening statement is not only to advise the jury of the evidence the party intends to introduce, but also "'to prepare the minds of the jury to follow the evidence and to more readily discern its materiality, force, and effect." (*People v. Harris* (1989) 47 Cal.3d 1047, 1080.)

Opening statements are said to provide the jury with a "road map" of what a party expects the evidence to prove. It may properly show how the evidence and all of the reasonable inferences that may be drawn from that evidence relate to the theory of the case. (*People v. Millwee* (1998) 18 Cal.4th 96, 137.) The opening statement is based on evidence the party anticipates presenting. (*People v. Boyette* (2002) 29 Cal.4th 381, 446-447; see also *People v. Dennis* (1998)17 Cal. 4th 468, 518.) It is generally improper during the opening statement to comment on your opponent's evidence or lack thereof. On the other hand, the purpose of the opening statement is to describe what the evidence will show, and if the evidence will demonstrate a failure of proof or credibility issues related to witnesses in the opposing party's case, the court may allow it over objection, especially in the defense opening of a criminal case.

Despite the importance of the opening statement, some trial lawyers squander this golden opportunity. Anxious to start the trial or due to unpreparedness, they shortchange it by rushing through it, skimming over the evidence, or worse yet, making it confusing right from the beginning. Therefore, it is critical that, by the time you conclude your statement, all jurors know and fully understand the important facts and your theories. If even one juror is left confused or unclear, you have done yourself a great disservice. Some studies have shown that as many as 80 percent of jurors make up their minds after the opening statement. (See *From O.J. to McVeigh: The Use of Argument in the Opening Statement*, Perrin, 48 Emory L.J. 107, 130-131 (1999) [citing studies re: juror retention]; see also Paula Hannaford et al., The Timing of Opinion Formation by Jurors in Civil Cases: An Empirical Examination, 67 Tenn. L. Rev. 627 (2000) (citing Donald E. Vinson, Jury Trials: The Psychology of Winning Strategy 171 (1986)).)

Laying it all out there in the opening is important; but, on the other hand, there may be valid tactical reasons why you may not want to commit to a particular factual scenario or a theory in the opening statement. If you are on the defending side, it may be because you want to see how your opponent's case rolls out before committing. By the same token, if you are still not 100 percent sure regarding what evidence you plan to present, e.g., whether to call an expert witness, you certainly do not want to represent facts that you later decide not to prove up or that might not turn out the way you had anticipated. On the whole, however, it is generally best to get your facts and theories out there early so the jury can be thinking about them as the trial unfolds, especially if you are the defendant and have to wait for the plaintiff to finish their case before presenting your evidence.

Trial Tip: Before you get to the specific details of the evidence, explain what happened from your client's perspective, from beginning to end and without interruption, in no more than 10 minutes or so. Some attorneys like to immediately recite a short dramatic prologue, but be cautious that it doesn't seem melodramatic. You lose credibility if the jurors get the sense you are play acting.

A Campfire Tale – A Narrative

Crafting a good opening statement takes preparation and forethought. Because this will be the first time the jurors really get to hear the facts, the objective is to make the opening as captivating and as interesting as possible. In that regard, people like to hear an interesting story, especially if told well by a good storyteller. As such, trial lawyers should take heed from the theater or a good novel in which first the stage is set and the actors introduced before the plot thickens. Therefore, before you begin describing what happened, take a few minutes at the beginning to describe the scene or location involved and some background information about the "actors." Once the stage is set, so to speak, relate the story of what happened in a chronological, story-like narrative fashion from beginning to end, as you might when telling a neighbor or a friend about something exciting that happened recently. It is important at this stage not to digress or to skip around; keep it flowing. "Nothing prevents the statement from being presented in a story-like manner that holds the attention of lay jurors and ties the facts and governing law together in an understandable way..." (*People v. Farnam* (2002) 28 Cal.4th 107, 159.) It may be presented in a dramatic manner that is calculated to hold the jury's attention. (*People v. Dennis* (1998) 17 Cal.4th 468, 518.)

Like a campfire tale, the narrative portion of the opening statement should tell a story such that all jurors can envision in their minds what occurred as you are describing it. For instance, in a robbery case, following a description of where the robbery occurred and some background on the victim and possibly even the defendant, recount how the robbery unfolded, blow-by-blow, without interruption. The same principal is true for a civil personal injury case. Tell the story from the plaintiff's perspective of how she came to be driving that day, a detailed account of the accident, and the trauma and treatment she received as a result of the accident, all in chronological order.

> **Trial Tip:** An opening statement should generally not take more than an hour, even for complex cases. For shorter trials, it may be considerably shorter. The key is that at the conclusion, the jurors should understand the big picture and the contested issues. If the opening is too long or if too much information and detail is given, it might overload and confuse them right from the beginning.

Use of Exhibits

The use of demonstrative or other courtroom evidence during the opening statement is important. Photographs, videos, maps, diagrams, or charts used in conjunction with your oral statement are very powerful, especially if you choreograph them to synch with your descriptions. For example, the moment you describe the actual collision, a picture of the wrecked cars appears on the courtroom monitors, followed by images of your client's injuries at the hospital when you get to that portion of the story. The use of PowerPoint slides to highlight the proposed evidence and forthcoming testimony is another very effective way to reinforce what you are saying. Jurors tend to retain information better when they hear *and* see it simultaneously.

Procedurally, any exhibits you plan to use during the opening statement should have been pre-marked by the clerk *and* shown to opposing counsel beforehand. "It is well settled that the use of photographs and tape recordings, intended later to be admitted in evidence, as visual or auditory aids, is appropriate during opening statements." (*People v. Wash* (1993) 6 Cal. 4th 215, 256; *People v. Fauber* (1992) 2 Cal.4th 792, 827; see *People v. Green*, supra, 47 Cal.2d at p. 215 [upholding use of photographs of murder victim during opening statement].) Note: Caution should be exercised when using exhibits during the opening statement that might not be later admitted as evidence. This could result in a possible mistrial.

> **Trial Tip:** During the pre-trial conference, discuss with the court the procedures regarding the use of exhibits during the opening statement. For opposing counsel, request to preview any exhibits your opponent plans to use during the opening statement to facilitate an objection outside the presence of the jury.

Define the Issues

After the jury has heard the "story" and, therefore, understands the big picture, go back and define the case by explaining in more detail the cause of actions, your theories or defense, and how they will apply to this case. This might also be a good time to reveal any weaknesses or unfavorable evidence; for example, "My client does not dispute that she caused the accident, but what she does dispute is the extent of the plaintiff's claimed injuries." Also, consider delineating for the jurors what precise issues they will be called on to decide, which may help them to sort out in their own minds what is relevant as the trial progresses. Generally, the more enlightened the juror, the better.

Tell it Again

Once you have told the general story one time through in the narrative format and defined the issues, consider going back to the facts a second time to fill in the details. Explain in more detail how you are going to prove your case, for instance, the names of the witnesses and the expected testimony. Some attorneys give a brief description of each witness's anticipated testimony, in particular, an important one, such as an expert. This will obviously take more time than the first rendition, but now the jurors will have a greater appreciation for the details and *how* you plan to prove your case. The net effect is that the jurors will have heard the case *twice*, once told like a campfire tale in a more narrative style and a second time in a more clinical, detailed, and explanatory manner.

Overstating the Case

Although you certainly want to sound confident in your case, use caution to not overstate it, or worse yet, misstate the evidence. If you inform the jury that you will introduce some evidence or prove a fact, you must be fairly confident that you can live up to that promise. Promising something during the opening statement and then not being able to deliver it during the trial only gives the opposing party good fodder for their closing argument, and rightly so. It could also conceivably result in a mistrial if the evidence represented was prejudicial to the opposing party, e.g., describing the opinion of an expert witness that did not testify. If there is any doubt about whether a certain fact or facts will be proved, the better tactic is to make your opening statement a little more general.

Concede Bad Facts

As you should have already done during jury selection, the opening statement is also a good opportunity to steal your opponent's thunder by revealing unfavorable facts; for example, that your client had been drinking or used foul language. Jurors have much more tolerance for parties who atone for their sins, rather than deny or minimize them. Similarly, conceding uncontested issues, such as that your client ran the red light and contests only damages, is generally also a good tactic, but do so cautiously. Once you have conceded an issue or a fact during the opening statement, it will be very difficult, if not impossible, to later argue the opposite during the closing argument if the evidence did not pan out as anticipated.

> **Trial Tip:** Listen carefully to your opponent's opening statement and take notes. If representations are made during the opening that are not proven, it may give you good fodder for the closing argument.

Reserve or Waive?

Depending upon the nature of the case and your jurisdiction, you may have the right to waive or reserve your opening until the close of your opponent's case. Generally, this relates to the defendant party. In certain situations, there may be valid tactical reasons why reserving might be appropriate. Most often, the reason is to wait and see how the plaintiff's evidence rolls out before committing to a certain theory or defense, or perhaps to move for a non-suit when the plaintiff rests. However, it is generally not a good idea to wait. If the jurors only hear one side of the story, they may get the wrong impression for days, if not weeks, until it is your turn. Furthermore, by not making an opening statement immediately, some jurors may think it is because you have a weak case. The same holds true if you give only a very short or abbreviated opening. On a similar note, some attorneys will waive opening in a bench trial; however, do not assume the court knows your facts and theories, unless you laid it out well in your trial brief. Some judges may give you feedback regarding whether the court would appreciate an opening or not. If in doubt, the better tactic is to give the court at least a good overview.

Limitations and Objections

Although the purpose of the opening statement is "'to prepare the minds of the jury to follow the evidence and to more readily discern its materiality, force, and effect" (*Harris*, supra), there are restrictions. One of the main limitations is that *argumentative* statements are prohibited. (3 Witkin, Cal. Evid. 5th (2012) Presentation, § 36, p. 84.) An opening statement gives counsel the opportunity to explain the case to the jury and to outline the proof. "It is not an occasion for argument." (*United States v. Dinitz,* 424 U.S. 600, 612, 96 S.Ct. 1075, 1082, 47 L.Ed.2d 267 (1976).) However, where exactly to draw the line between argument and explaining the "force and effect" of the evidence is sometimes difficult to determine. The attorneys can explain facts and draw inferences from them, but statements regarding the importance of the case, or explaining concepts of law or how the jury should apply the facts to the law, is generally considered "argument." (*Williams v. Goodman* (1963) 214 CA2d 856, 869.) It is also improper for counsel to state his or her personal opinions or beliefs. (*Hawk v. Sup.Ct. (People)* (1974) 42 CA3d 108, 119.) For example:

Counsel: "This is one of the worst cases I have ever seen, and when all the evidence is concluded, let your conscience be your guide and you will undoubtedly find the plaintiff was negligent." [An objection for "improper argument" would likely be sustained.]

In practice, attorneys often attempt to weave in a little argument here and there, particularly towards the end, often without objection. Some attorneys attempt to get away with some argument by prefacing their statement with, "The evidence will show...," but then add argument, e.g., "...that the plaintiff's case is meritless." Some judges may also curtail statements where counsel attempts to predict the opponent's evidence or theories and then comments upon the inherent weaknesses in the opponent's case. Some judges require the opening statement to remain confined principally to the evidence that party intends to prove or establish during his or her case. The other side may do likewise. This way, the jury gets the contrasting viewpoints.

On the other hand, it would seem permissible for counsel to explain what counsel anticipates to be the overall nature of the evidence and any deficiencies, which might include the opponent's evidence. For example, in a trial involving the contested issue of who caused a traffic accident, it would be permissible to state that the eyewitnesses the opponent intends to call are mistaken or biased, and recite the facts that will support that conclusion, e.g., the witness had been drinking. Likewise, comment upon evidence expected to be revealed during cross-examination is generally permitted, especially if the witness has been deposed and the answer known. (See *Wright v. United States* 508 A.2d 915, 921 (D.C. Cir. 1986).)

Lastly, all statements made by counsel during the opening statement must be in "good faith," meaning generally not reciting facts or evidence counsel knows is false, cannot be proved, or is inadmissible. (See ABA Model Rule: "A lawyer shall not … in trial, allude to any matter that the lawyer does not reasonably believe is relevant or that will not be supported by admissible evidence …" [ABA Model Rule 3.4(e) (emphasis added); see also ABA Code of Prof. Resp. DR 7-106(C)(1)-(4).] Importantly, however, just because the evidence did not ultimately turn out the way counsel predicted it would in the opening statement does not necessarily mean counsel acted in "bad faith." That is just the nature of a trial.

Objection and Request for Admonition

If misconduct does occur during the opening statement, there *must* be a timely objection immediately when the infraction occurs *and* a request for a curative admonition. A failure to comply with these two requirements can forfeit the issue on appeal. (*People v. Earp* (1999) 20 Cal. 4th 826, 858; *People v. Dykes* (2009) 46 Cal. 4th 731, 761 [failure to object forfeits issue on appeal]; see infra, Trial Objections, at p. 214.) "A party is foreclosed from complaining on appeal of misconduct during arguments to the jury where his counsel sat silently back during the arguments, allowed the alleged improprieties to accumulate without objection, and simply made a motion for a mistrial at the conclusion of the argument." (*Brokopp v. Ford Motor Co.* (1977) 71 Cal.App. 3d. 841, 860.)

In some cases, a party will contend that the opponent's opening statement "opened the door" to otherwise inadmissible evidence. However, California and other state courts have held that, because an opening statement has no evidentiary value, it does not open the door to otherwise inadmissible evidence. The "open the door" argument is a "popular fallacy." (*Rufo v. Simpson* (2001) 86 Cal.App.4th 573, 600; *Winfred D. v. Michelin North America, Inc.* (2008) 165 Cal.App.4th 1011 [error to admit evidence of extra-marital affairs].))

> **Trial Tip:** Straying into "argument" is probably one of the most common areas of misconduct during the opening statement. However, it is often a matter of degree. An impassioned opening merely outlining the facts is probably acceptable. On the other hand, explaining theories, how the law applies, or denigrating the opposing party's case leans towards argument.

5. WITNESS TESTIMONY

"Testimony" occurs when a witness is placed under oath or affirmation and questioned by the parties. It lies at the very heart of nearly every trial and its origins are rooted in history. In most cases, the testimony occurs live in the courtroom and from the witness "stand," where the witness is on full display. However, testimony may have also occurred prior to trial, such as during a deposition or a prior court hearing. Regardless of how the "testimony" occurs, for it to be admissible as evidence in a trial, it must adhere to certain rules and criteria. This chapter explains the *general* requirements for nearly all forms of testimony, while the subsequent chapters discuss the rules, procedures, and some strategies for how testimony is taken depending upon which party is doing the questioning.

Oath or Affirmation

In order for a witness's statement to be considered admissible testimony, it is generally required that it be taken under oath or affirmation. "Every witness before testifying shall take an oath or make an affirmation or declaration in the form provided by law, except that a child under the age of 10 or a dependent person with a substantial cognitive impairment, in the court's discretion, may be required only to promise to tell the truth." (CA Evid. Code § 710)

Control by Court

In Federal Court and virtually all other jurisdictions, the court is the "Gatekeeper" of evidence and authorized to exercise "reasonable control" over the mode and order of examining witnesses and presenting evidence. (CA Evid. Code § 765 (below))

CA Evid. Code § 765. Court to control mode of interrogation (FRE Rule 611)

(a) The court shall exercise reasonable control over the mode of interrogation of a witness so as to make interrogation as rapid, as distinct, and as effective for the ascertainment of the truth, as may be, and to protect the witness from undue harassment or embarrassment.

(b) With a witness under the age of 14 or a dependent person with a substantial cognitive impairment, the court shall take special care to protect him or her from undue harassment or embarrassment, and to restrict the unnecessary repetition of questions. The court shall also take special care to ensure that questions are stated in a form which is appropriate to the age or cognitive level of the witness. The court may, in the interests of justice, on objection by a party, forbid the asking of a question which is in a form that is not reasonably likely to be understood by a person of the age or cognitive level of the witness.

Under section 765 the court is given wide latitude over the mode and order of the testimony. For example, if the court feels an attorney is harassing or unnecessarily berating or being rude to a witness, the court can, and often does, intervene sua sponte to cut it off and/or admonish counsel. Further, if the court feels the questioning is becoming repetitive and unproductive, the court can, and often does, admonish counsel to wrap it up. As a trial lawyer, therefore, you need to be aware of the court's authority over testimony, and in the right circumstance do not be hesitant to request the court to make some order different than the normal procedure, for example; precluding a party from using leading questions during cross-examination for a child or a witness with cognitive impairment.

Trial Tip: If the court has to admonish regarding your tone or questions, it will obviously not look good to the jurors. Jurors tend to have the most respect for attorneys who remain calm and collected in the face of adversity, as opposed to those who get frustrated and act unprofessional.

Competence of Witness

The witness must have the ability to capacity to perceive, recollect, and communicate truthfully. A person is disqualified as a witness only if he or she is incapable of expressing himself or herself understandably concerning the testimonial matter, or is "incapable of understanding the duty of a witness to tell the truth " (*People v. Anderson* (2001) 25 Cal. 4th 543, 572.)

CA Evid. Code § 700. General rule as to competency (FRE Rule 601)

Except as otherwise provided by statute, every person, irrespective of age, is qualified to be a witness and no person is disqualified to testify to any matter.

CA Evid. Code § 701. Disqualification of witness

(a) A person is disqualified to be a witness if he or she is:
 (1) Incapable of expressing himself or herself concerning the matter so as to be understood, either directly or through interpretation by one who can understand him; or
 (2) Incapable of understanding the duty of a witness to tell the truth.

(b) In any proceeding held outside the presence of a jury, the court may reserve challenges to the competency of a witness until the conclusion of the direct examination of that witness.

Generally, the issue regarding a witness's competence or capacity to testify is brought to the court's attention in a motion in limine by a party moving to exclude the testimony on that basis. The burden of proof is on the party who objects to the proffered witness. (*Anderson*, supra.) The two most common grounds put forward are either: 1) the witness is too young, or 2) the witness suffers from some mental or cognitive impairment making the witness incapable of perceiving, recollecting, and communicate truthfully. "It follows that if the proposed witness was suffering from some insane delusion or other mental defect that deprived him of the ability to perceive the event about which it was proposed that he testify, he was incompetent to testify about that event." (*Anderson*, supra, at. 572).

The hearing on the issue of competence is generally conducted outside the presence of the jury. In the case of a child witness, the court might itself voir dire the child to determine whether the child understands the nature of the proceedings and the duty to tell the truth. The court might also inquire whether the child can distinguish between the truth and a lie. In the case of a witness with an alleged cognitive or mental impairment, the inquiry is similar. The court might also consider psychiatric evidence regarding the witness's mental state or psychiatric diagnosis.

In most cases, the court will exclude the testimony for lack of "competence" only if the witness has virtually no comprehension or understanding of why they are in court or the duty to tell the truth. For example, in *People v. Dennis* (1998) 17 Cal.4th 468, 525–526, a witness, who was four-years-old at time of murder and eight when she testified, was found competent to testify. The court held, "If there is evidence that the witness has those capacities, the determination whether she in fact perceived and does recollect is left to the trier of fact." (*Id.* a p.526.) Thus, if there is some evidence to support competency, the issue becomes more one of weight, rather than admissibility. The believability of the witness is *not* a competence issue

Personal Knowledge

Whether a witness has "personal knowledge" is a relatively common issue at trial. To testify, a *non-expert* witness must have personal knowledge of the subject matter of the testimony, namely, "a present recollection of an impression derived from the exercise of the witness's own senses." The witness must also have the capacity to perceive and recollect. (*People v. Lewis* (2001) 26 Cal.4th 334, 356; Evid. Code § 702; FRE § 602.)

Evid. Code § 702 Personal knowledge of witness (FRE Rule 602)

(a) Subject to Section 801 [expert witnesses], the testimony of a witness concerning a particular matter is inadmissible unless he has personal knowledge of the matter. Against the objection of a party, such personal knowledge must be shown before the witness may testify concerning the matter.

(b) A witness' personal knowledge of a matter may be shown by any otherwise admissible evidence, including his own testimony.

The proponent of the testimony has the burden of establishing the preliminary fact of personal knowledge. (CA Evid. Code § 403(a)(2).) The issue of personal knowledge commonly arises when it is not clear from the testimony whether the witness actually perceived something. Often, the witness will make conclusory statements, such as, "The minivan ran the red light," without any preceding clarification of how the witness knows the information. Also, in some circumstances, the witness may seem certain, giving rise to the question of whether the witness saw what happened.

Counsel: "Then what happened?" (on direct)
Witness: "Oh, the minivan ran the red light."
Counsel: "How do you know that?"
Witness: (A) "That's what the officer told me."
      (B) "That's what I figured must have happened from the way the
            cars were positioned in the intersection afterwards."
      (C) "That's what I think I happened from what I saw, but it was
            dark and I was across the street."
      (D) "That's what I remember happening, but I was totally drunk."

In the above example, answer (A) is based on hearsay, and thus, the witness lacks personal knowledge. Answer (B) is based on speculation and conjecture, and therefore, lacks personal knowledge. However, what about answers (C) and (D)? Clearly, the accuracy and reliability of the testimony is highly suspect in both answers.

Trial Tip: : Be alert when a witness does not state specifically whether she actually *saw* something happen. Some people will testify on direct examination as though they were present and saw what occurred, yet when cross examined, it turns out the witness lacks the requisite personal knowledge—for example, where the witness later puts "two and two together" to come up with the conclusion; the beauty of cross-examination.

Weight versus Admissibility

The proponent of testimony has the burden to establish that a witness has the requisite "personal knowledge." Generally, this is established with the witness's own testimony demonstrating that the witness actually perceived the matters in question. When there is an objection, the court's duty as the Gatekeeper is to make a "preliminary finding" of personal knowledge before admitting the evidence. (FRE Rule 104) However, the court may exclude testimony for lack of personal knowledge *only* if no jury could reasonably find that the witness has such knowledge. Thus, a witness challenged for lack of personal knowledge must be allowed to testify if there is evidence from which a rational trier of fact could find that the witness accurately perceived and recollected the testimonial events. Once that threshold is passed, it is for the jury to decide whether the witness's perceptions and recollections are credible. (*People v. Cortez* (2016) 63 Cal.4th 101, 124; See also *U.S. v Garcia* 291 F. 3d. 127, 140, 2nd Cir (2002).) In other words, if there is conflicting evidence whether a witness does or does not have personal knowledge, the issue is one of weight, rather than admissibility. Thus, in example (C) and (D) above, although the witness's observations might be highly suspect or inaccurate, the court would probably overrule the objection and allow the jury to determine whether the witness actually saw the accident and if so, how accurately.

In practice, if there is an objection and it is not clear how the witness knows the information, in many cases, the proponent can cure the deficiency by simply backing up a few steps and having the witness explain more thoroughly the basis for the information. In addition, it is common that a witness will testify that she "thought" something was observed, or use words such as "pretty sure," "I think so," or "probably." The witness may seem unsure of what she observed. However, this is generally not considered a lack of personal knowledge. Uncertainty of recollection goes to the weight and not the admissibility of a witness's testimony. (*People v. Lewis* (2001) 26 Cal.4th 334, 356-357.) The fact that the witness was drunk or might be lying goes to weight. If there is evidence that the witness has the capacity to perceive and to recollect, the determination whether he or she in fact perceived and does recollect is left to the trier of fact. (*Lewis*, supra, at p. 357.) Furthermore, the fact that a witness has made inconsistent and exaggerated statements does not indicate an inability to perceive or recollect. Nor does a witness's mental defect or insane delusions necessarily reflect that the witness lacks the capacity to perceive or recollect. A witness's uncertainty about his or her recollection of events does not preclude admitting his or her testimony. (*People v. Avery* (1950) 35 Cal.2d 487, 492, 218 P.2d 527.)

Trial Tip: If a witness lacks personal knowledge, it is usually because the witness's testimony is based on speculation or hearsay. Cross-examination may flesh it out, and if it turns out the witness did lack personal knowledge, a motion to strike the testimony would follow.

Witness Answers

Testimony is generally taken using a question and answer format. (*People v. Kronemyer* (1987) 189 Cal.App.3d 314, 353.) The proponent of the witness typically begins questioning with direct examination, followed by cross-examination, then perhaps by further re-direct examination, and possibly even re-cross-examination. The procedures and rules related to all forms of examination are discussed in greater detail, infra, at p. 77 et seq. [direct examination] and p. 93 et seq. [cross-examination]. In some jurisdictions such as California, the jurors may submit written questions for the witness, previewed by the court and counsel. If approved, the court itself relates the juror's question to the witness and the witness responds (See Cal. Rules of Court, Rule 2.1033 ["A trial judge should allow jurors to submit written questions directed to witnesses. An opportunity must be given to counsel to object to such questions out of the presence of the jury."] Because the court has discretion to control all aspects of witness examination, the court can vary these rules depending on the circumstances.

Unless the court specifically determines there is some legal bar to the witness's testimony, such as a *privilege* (See Privilege, infra at p. 192.), a witness *must* answer the questions put to him or her by the examiner, regardless of whether the witness wants to answer. Even if the question is improper or requests inadmissible evidence, if there is no objection, the witness must still answer. Generally, the court has no sua sponte duty to intervene if no one objects and many courts take a hands-off approach and let the attorneys try their cases. There might be valid tactical reasons why a party is not objecting. On the other hand, if the court felt an injustice was occurring, for example, where the evidence is clearly inadmissible and prejudicial to a defendant in a criminal case, the court could intervene and essentially interpose its own objection and prohibit the testimony. Some judges might call a time-out and meet with counsel outside the presence of the jury to inquire further why there is no objection.

However, as discussed, if there is no an objection and no legal bar to the testimony, the witness must answer and a failure or a refusal to respond, may result in the court ordering the person to answer. If the witness continues to refuse, it is considered *contempt of court* in most jurisdictions and subjects the witness to criminal and/or civil penalties. In some jurisdictions, the court has the authority to jail or fine the witness until the witness relents. One further possible consequence of a witness's refusal to testify is that the court might find the witness is "unavailable," which may be relevant when determining whether a hearsay exception is applicable, as some require unavailability.

Nonresponsive Answers

Regardless of whether it is direct examination or cross-examination, the failure to respond appropriately to a question is objectionable. (See Trial Objections, infra, at p. 221.) In California, the rule is codified: "A witness must give responsive answers to questions, and answers that are not responsive shall be stricken on motion of any party." (CA Evid. Code § 766.) The FRE do not have a similar specific statutory rule, but the rule is nonetheless applied in nearly every jurisdiction. Generally, even the *proponent* of the witness can object and move to strike the answer of their own witness, if unresponsive. (See *U.S. v. Shillingstad* 632 F. 3d. 1031, 1036, 8th Dist. (2011).) The unresponsive answer and objection is quite common in trial.

Counsel: "Did you apply your brakes as you approached the intersection?"
Witness: "I saw the minivan run the red light. It was the other driver's fault."

Opp. Counsel: "Objection, Your Honor, nonresponsive. Move to strike."
Court: "Sustained. The answer is stricken."

The failure of a witness to answer correctly is often simply related to the witness's inattentiveness or nervousness, and not necessarily a deliberate attempt to avoid the question. Anxious to get the story out, they launch into a statement as though they didn't even hear the question. If the witness is friendly, the easy fix is to re-ask the question, with perhaps a gentle admonition to listen more carefully to the question.

Counsel: "Thank you. But the question was, did you apply your brakes as you approached the intersection? Yes or no?"

Trial Tip: If it is *your* witness that does not appropriately answer, but instead nervously rambles on without an objection, take control and stop the witness. Holding up your hand to indicate "stop," with a gentle interruption, often works well. Then, repeat the question with the admonition to listen more carefully and just answer the question. As the proponent, you want to avoid the argument that your witness somehow "opened the door" to evidence not relevant or otherwise inadmissible.

A witness's unresponsive answer can also be more deliberate, particularly during *cross-examination*. A common scenario is when the witness answers the question, but then adds more gratuitous information than requested. This is when counsel must use witness control techniques to force the witness to only answer the questions asked. (See Cross-Examination (witness control), infra, at p. 94.)

Counsel: "You didn't apply your brakes as you approached the intersection, did you?"
Witness: "No, but the minivan ran the light, it wasn't my fault."
Counsel: "Objection, Your Honor, unresponsive. Move to strike the answer following her answer, 'No.'"
Court: "Motion granted. That last portion of the answer is stricken."

Trial Tip: One key to avoiding an unresponsive answer is to ensure that your question is narrowly framed. If the question is too broad, vague, or general, the witness will likely respond in a similar fashion.

Narrative Responses
As discussed, courtroom testimony generally proceeds in a question and answer format. The examiner asks a specific question to which the witness is

expected to respond appropriately. Witnesses are not permitted to simply say whatever they want in "narrative" form without any guidance from the examiner. This can be difficult for some witnesses because in the real world, when asked to relate something, people are used to explaining and describing it in their own words, and not in short segments. In the courtroom, however, elicitation of facts is more of a step-by-step process. The purpose of the rule is to keep the testimony focused on the contested issues and to avoid the possible introduction of prejudicial information. Thus, if the examiner's question requests a narrative answer or if the answer itself is in a narrative format, then the objection "Narrative" would be applicable. (See Trial Objections, infra, at p. 240.)

Counsel: "What happened?"
Opp. Counsel: "Objection, Your Honor, calls for narrative."

In this circumstance, the court might sustain the objection because counsel's question provides no guidance to the witness whatsoever concerning how to answer. The question invites the witness to say practically anything in any order. Furthermore, the question is also objectionable because it is "vague." The easy fix is simply to reframe the question by giving the witness some context of what you're asking for.

Counsel: "Tell us what happened, moments after the cars collided."

Although a narrative response is objectionable, it is also *not* required that the witness answer only in small bits and pieces. This chopped up form of examination is unnatural and has been criticized by legal scholars. "Enlightened judges rarely curb the use of questions calling for *short* narrative responses, except in criminal trials when it poses the risk of exposing the jury to constitutionally inadmissible testimony." (1 McCormick On Evid. § 5 (7th ed.)[emphasis added].) As the proponent of the witness during the direct examination, you would generally like the witness to explain or describe an event in more than just a sentence or two before the next question to make it interesting and to bring the story to life.(See strategies for direct examination, infra, at p.68.) In practice, most courts tend to sustain a "narrative" objection only when the witness's answer becomes long-winded and begins to stray off topic.

Lay Opinion

During testimony, a lay (non-expert) witness can give an opinion, to an extent. Technically, an opinion is simply one person's subjective viewpoint or belief about something. As such, its admissibility seems to run in conflict with the requirement that a witness must have "personal knowledge." However, lay opinion testimony is actually an important component of a witness's testimony and is common. The rule regulating its admissibility is set forth in Evid. Code § 800 (below).

Evid. Code § 800 Lay witnesses; opinion testimony (FRE Rule 701)

If a witness is not testifying as an expert, his testimony in the form of an opinion is limited to such an opinion as is permitted by law, including but not limited to an opinion that is:

    (a) Rationally based on the perception of the witness; and

    (b) Helpful to a clear understanding of his testimony." (FRE 701 [similar])

Lay opinion is important because there are some things in life that simply cannot be described adequately without some subjective interpretation. The use of opinion permits a witness to descriptively and colorfully explain or narrate something. For example, witnesses are often requested to describe how a person acted or appeared. In response, the witness might describe a person as being mad, angry, sad, upset, happy, hysterical, drunk, or even crazy. When asked to describe a condition, the witness might opine about a distance or the lighting conditions. A witness might testify that a car was traveling fast, slow, or out of control. The law recognizes that some opinion is an important component of human communication.

Counsel: "Can you describe the defendant's demeanor at that time."
Witness: "He was drunk and in a rage."

"Lay opinions are permitted where the concrete observations on which the opinion is based cannot otherwise be conveyed." (*People v. Hinton* (2006) 37 Cal.4th 839, 889.) The opinion rule for non-experts merely requires that witnesses express themselves at the lowest possible level of abstraction. Whenever feasible, "concluding" should be left to the jury; however, when the details observed, even though recalled, are "too complex or too subtle" for concrete description by the witness, he may state his general impression. Thus, for example, a lay witness may express an opinion that a person was "drunk," that people engaged in a discussion were "angry," that an impact was strong enough to jar a passenger from a seat, or that someone appeared to be "trying to break up a fight." (*People v. DeHoyos* (2013) 57 Cal.4th 79, 130-131; *People v. Chapple* (2006) 138 Cal.App.4th 540, 547.) Lay opinion with regard to alcohol and drug intoxication and sobriety is admissible if "rationally based on the perception of the witness." (*People v. Williams* (1988) 44 Cal.3d 883, 914.) Thus, a witness is generally permitted to opine that a person appeared drunk, intoxicated, or high. "Love, hatred, sorrow, joy, and various other mental and moral operations, find outward expression, as clear to the observer as any fact coming to his observation, but he can only give expression to the fact by giving what to him is the ultimate fact, and which, for want of a more accurate expression, we call opinion…" (*Holland v. Zollner* (1894) 102 Cal. 633.)

Although lay opinion describing a complex human emotion or condition is admissible, a lay witness generally may *not* give an opinion about another person's state of mind, but may testify about objective behavior and describe behavior as being consistent with a state of mind. (*People v. Chatman* (2006) 38 Cal.4th 344, 397.) For example, a witness's testimony that a person looked angry and enraged is proper. However, that same witness's opinion that a person meant to kill the victim would be excluded because it speculates about the person's intent, e.g., "He meant to run the light."

Trial Tip: Witness testimony that is descriptive and incorporates the emotions or reactions of people helps bring the story to life. For example, that someone was "angry," "upset," "hysterical," "crying," "sad," "happy,'" etc. This is all appropriate lay opinion.

Lay versus Expert Opinion

The admissibility of lay opinion often turns upon whether the opinion is one which an "expert" should give, rather than a "lay" person. Matters that go beyond common experience and require scientific knowledge may not properly be the subject of lay opinion testimony. (*People v. DeHoyos* (2013) 57 Cal.4th 79, 129.) For example, a witness can estimate distances and conditions at the scene of a traffic collision, however, would be precluded from opining about the cause of the accident. (See *Osborne v. Todd Farm Service* (2016) 247 Cal.App.4th 43, 52 [exclusion of the plaintiff's lay opinion about origin of hay bale involved in her fall based upon its color and other characteristics properly excluded where "her opinions about the appearance of hay bales [lacked] any rational basis"]; *Jambazian v. Borden* (1994) 25 Cal.App.4th 836, 848-849 [rejecting the argument that "a lay witness may render a medical opinion as to whether a patient has a condition which requires particular advice be given as to the risks of a surgery."].) Similarly, a lay witness generally may not give an opinion about another person's specific state of mind, but may testify about objective behavior and describe behavior as being consistent with a state of mind. (*People v. Chatman* (2006) 38 Cal.4th 344, 397.) For example, testimony that a driver meant to run the stop light or wasn't paying attention, reflect the driver's mental state and would be prohibited. Conclusionary opinions that are normally reserved for the court or the jury are also improper; for example, an opinion that a person violated the law, was negligent, or breached a contract. However, an opinion regarding the truthfulness or untruthfulness of another witness is permitted in some circumstances. (See Impeachment of Character, infra, at p. 125.)

Speculation or Conjecture

A witness cannot speculate or guess. This rule is closely related to the rule regarding lay opinion and personal knowledge. Generally, the witness's answer becomes objectionable when the testimony is based on an assumption not borne out by the facts. "An issue of fact can only be created by a conflict of evidence. It is not created by speculation, conjecture, imagination or guess work." (*Brown v. Ransweiler* (2009) 171 Cal.App.4th 516, 525.) Courts have found lay witness testimony unhelpful and thus inadmissible if it is mere speculation, an opinion of law, or if it usurps the jury's function. (*Nationwide Transp. Fin. v. Cass Info. Sys., Inc.*, 523 F.3d 1051, 1060–61 (9th Cir.2008) (lay witnesses may not tell the finder of fact what result to reach); *United States v. Freeman*, 498 F.3d 893, 905 (9th Cir.2007) (speculative testimony was inadmissible); *United States v. Crawford*, 239 F.3d 1086, 1090 (9th Cir.2001) (legal conclusions are inadmissible when presented as lay testimony). "The prohibition against an examiner's question that calls for an answer based on speculation and conjecture is also founded on the concept of relevancy. Such testimony is irrelevant, because it does not have a tendency in reason to prove or disprove the disputed issue on which the testimony is proffered." (*People v. Rodriguez* (2014) 58 Cal.4th 587, 631.) "An examiner's question asking a lay witness to testify to facts that the witness has not personally observed, or to state an opinion not based on his or her own observations, calls for speculation and conjecture by the witness and is prohibited…" (Ibid.)

Witness: "I think the other driver intended to run the traffic light"… "I could have stopped in time had I seen the other driver coming"… "her brakes were obviously working fine…"

In each of these examples, the witness is making assumptions and opinions based on guesswork. Thus, an objection would be appropriate. (See also Trial Objections, infra, at p. 234.)

Counsel: "Objection, Your Honor, speculation and conjecture."

An objection may also be appropriate to the form of a question that requests a witness to speculate.

Counsel: "Could the other car have stopped in time, in your opinion?"
Opp. Counsel: "Objection, Your Honor. Calls for speculation."

Counsel: "Officer, did you feel that my client was being honest?"
Opp. Counsel: "Objection, Your Honor. Calls for speculation."

In the above, the questions require the witness to speculate and the objections would likely be sustained. In addition, whether or not the witness feels the other vehicle could have stopped in time or that the plaintiff was honest probably has no *relevance*. Lastly, keep in the mind that the rule prohibiting testimony based on speculation and conjecture also applies to expert witnesses. Expert testimony must be "properly grounded, well-reasoned, and not speculative." (*United States v. Hermanek*, 289 F.3d 1076, 1094 (9th Cir.2002) (See Experts, infra, at p. 197.)

> **Trial Tip:** The difference between proper lay opinion and improper speculation is often one of degree and is dependent, in large part, on how the question is framed. Keep this in mind when preparing your testimony outline.

Witness Memory Issues - Strategies to Overcome

All witnesses, other than experts, are required to testify from their memory. However, because a trial typically occurs months, it not years, after the event or circumstance they are trying to remember, most witnesses have trouble remembering to one degree or another. You will find that some witnesses have excellent memory, while others can hardly remember what they did that same morning. Many factors can affect memory, including the passage of time and the witness's mental state both at the time and currently. Regardless, whether you are the proponent or the cross-examiner, you should expect memory issues and be prepared to deal with them accordingly when they occur.

Leading Questions to Refresh Memory

It is common that a witness will have difficulty recalling minor details, for example, a date, time, or a street name. Usually, these foundational facts are uncontested by the parties. During examination, is it generally important to get to past them quickly and on to spend more time on the substantive testimony Therefore, an easy method to help the witness is simply by using a leading question. In fact, leading questions are generally permitted to help revive a witness's memory. (See FRE 611(c) [leading questions permitted "as necessary to develop the witness's testimony"; *People v. Collins* (2010) 49 Cal.4th 175, 210; *Rush v. Illinois* Cent. R. Co. 399 F.3d 705, 717, (6th Cir. 2005).) Trained to believe that every leading question is improper, many inexperienced lawyers do no use enough leading questions to set up the basic foundational facts, causing the testimony to become unnecessarily protracted. If the witness has trouble remembering some uncontested detail or fact, use a leading question.

Witness: "Let me see, I think the accident happened on a Monday or Tuesday, in June. It's been awhile."
Counsel: " Does Monday, June 22nd, at about three o'clock, sound familiar?"
Witness: "Oh, yes. That's that right."

Counsel: "The accident occurred at the intersection of Lincoln Way and Maple Street, didn't it?" [When witness has difficulty remembering street names.]

Trial Tip: One of *the* most effective methods to avoid or minimize witness failure of recollection, is to prepare by allowing them to review their prior statements prior to testimony. Interrupting the flow of testimony to repeatedly "refresh recollection" is time consuming and distracting for the jurors.

Refresh Recollection

When a witness is having trouble remembering more significant facts or information, the next step is to attempt to refresh the witness's recollection. This is accomplished rather simply by permitting the witness to review a writing to see whether it helps jog the witness's memory. Often, this review occurs right there on the witness stand and necessarily causes a pause in the testimony. Typically, when the witness indicates he or she is having trouble recalling, counsel will approach the witness and request the witness to review a writing. The witness will then read the document(s) quietly to him or herself. After the witness has reviewed the writing, questioning resumes assuming the writing has helped to revive the witness's memory.

"Present recollection refreshed involves the use of a writing which has no purpose other than to refresh the memory of a witness. It is basic evidence law that a witness's recollection may be properly refreshed by writings and papers which are not in themselves admissible in evidence." (*Frio v. Superior Court* (1988) 203 Cal.App.3d 1480, 1492; *Taylor v. Maddox*, 366 F.3d 992, 1011 (9th Cir.2004).) As stated by Justice Learned Hand, "Anything may in fact revive a memory: a song, a scent, a photograph, an allusion, even a past statement known to be false." Indeed, even inadmissible evidence may be used to refresh a witness's recollection. (3 Wigmore on Evidence §§ 758-765 (3d ed.), ..." (quoting *United States v. Baratta*, 397 F.2d 215, 222 (2d Cir.1968). cert. denied, 393 U.S. 939, 89 S.Ct. 293)

"The best practice is for the trial court to have the witness silently read the writing and then to state whether the writing has refreshed his or her recollection." (*Rush v Illinois Cent R.Co.*, 399 F. 3d. 705, 716 (6th Cir. 2005).) As the writing itself is not evidence, the witness, nor counsel, should read out loud from the writing. (See *People v. Friend* (2009) 47 Cal.4th 1, 40 [approving of this procedure]) A witness may not testify directly from a writing. (*U.S. v. Carey*, 589 F. 3d. 187, 190, (5th Cir. 2009).) Refreshment does not depend upon the source of the writing, the identity of the writing's author, or the truth of the writing's contents, for "it is hornbook law that any writing may be used to refresh the recollection of a witness." However, caution must be exercised to insure that the document is actually being used for purposes of refreshing and not for purposes of putting words in the mouth of the witness," (*Carey*, supra, at p. 190-191; *Esperti v. United States*, 406 F.2d 148, 150 (5th Cir.1969).)

Counsel: "As you approached the intersection, how many other vehicles were ahead of you in your lane?"

Witness: "Um, three, or two, I think. I'm not sure, it's been two years."

Counsel: "That day, while you were still at the scene, were you interviewed by a police officer regarding what happened?"

Witness: "Yes."

Counsel: "Did you attempt to be as accurate and as truthful as you could when you spoke with the officer?"

Witness: "Yes."

Counsel: "Would reviewing your statement to the officer help refresh your memory?"

Witness: "Yes. It might."

Counsel: "Your Honor, may I approach the witness? ... Counsel, [referring to opposing counsel] I'm referring the witness to page 134 of discovery ... Mrs. Jones, would you please take a moment and review it quietly to yourself to see whether it helps you remember how many cars were ahead of you?" [Witness reviews statement quietly to herself]

Counsel: "Did reading that help you to remember?"

Witness: "Oh yes. There was only one car ahead of me at the time."

In the above, the witness read the statement she made to the police officer two years earlier which helped her to remember. Once the witness's memory has been refreshed, testimony continues from memory. In some cases, a witness's memory may need to be "refreshed" several times throughout the testimony. It is important to note that more than just documents can be used to refresh memory. A "writing" can include other forms of communication, such as a photograph or a recording. If it is a recording, however, keep in mind that it is generally not permitted to play the recording in open court such that the jury can hear it, although that might be permitted for impeachment.

Trial Tip: If you note that your witness has made a mistake, request that the witness fresh his or her memory with a writing to correct the mistake. Don't let it hang out there for opposing counsel to pounce on during cross-examination.

Production and Introduction of Writing

California Evid. Code § 771 (below) relates to the adverse party's options when a witness has used a writing to refresh his or her recollection. Every trial lawyer should be aware of this section and the options it allows.

> **Evid. Code § 771 Production of writing used to refresh memory (FRE Rule 612)**
>
> (a) Subject to subdivision (c), if a witness, either while testifying or prior thereto, uses a writing to refresh his memory with respect to any matter about which he testifies, such writing must be produced at the hearing at the request of an adverse party and, unless the writing is so produced, the testimony of the witness concerning such matter shall be stricken.
>
> (b) If the writing is produced at the hearing, the adverse party may, if he chooses, inspect the writing, cross-examine the witness concerning it, and introduce in evidence such portion of it as may be pertinent to the testimony of the witness.
>
> (c) Production of the writing is excused, and the testimony of the witness shall not be stricken, if the writing:
>
> (1) Is not in the possession or control of the witness or the party who produced his testimony concerning the matter; and
>
> (2) Was not reasonably procurable by such party through the use of the court's process or other available means.

Typically, the "writing" is a copy of the witness's prior statement(s), such as a report, deposition testimony, or declaration. However, it could also be a photograph if the witness is having trouble remembering accurately, for example, the layout of an intersection. As the opposing party, it is important to be aware of your right to inspect and introduce the writing. Most courts require that before a writing is shown to the witness to refresh memory, that opposing counsel is given the opportunity to review it. At a minimum, the examining party should refer opposing counsel to a particular page number from discovery or a volume and page number from a deposition transcript. The point is, you should be fully aware of what the witness is being asked to review. This is particularly true if the witness brought the writing with him or her to court and has it on the witness stand. Police officers and experts often show up to court with their own copies of reports and documents. However, it is not uncommon that a witness may have documents that the parties are not familiar with, for example, an amended report or something previously undiscovered.

An important aspect of section 771 is that it can apply to writings or materials used to "refresh recollection" *prior* to the trial. Thus, for example, if while preparing to testify, the witness reviewed some private notes she had jotted down shortly after the accident, opposing counsel can make a motion that they should be produced for inspection, if she did not bring them to court with her. Opposing counsel would also have the right to cross-examine her about those notes and even introduce them as evidence. Sometimes, lay witnesses do record their memories in some fashion, often without counsel's knowledge, for example, a diary or a journal. A failure to produce the writing could result in the court striking the testimony or perhaps even a mistrial.

Section 771 can also apply to experts, who commonly review many reports and documents prior to testimony. If the expert witness used them to "refresh" his memory, he or she may be required to produce them upon demand. The issue can become thorny, however, when it is claimed that the materials reviewed by the expert prior to trial are privileged, e.g., attorney-client, or work product. (See *People v. Smith* (2007) 40 Cal. 4th 483 [771 requirement for production prevails over psychotherapist-patient privilege]; see also *Sullivan v. Superior Court* (1972) 29 Cal.App. 3d 64.) *Sporck v. Peil*, 759 F.2d 312, (3rd Dist 1985).) If there is a claim the writing is privileged or work product, the court may then need to conduct an in camera review of the writing to determine its admissibility.

Past Recollection Recorded

When a witness is struggling with more significant memory issues, another easy and reliable method of getting the facts into evidence is Past Recollection Recorded (or Recollection Recorded in Federal Court), which is an exception to the Hearsay Rule. The beauty of this rule is that by laying some basic foundational requirements, the actual hearsay statement, prepared close in time to the event, can be read straight into the record without distortion. It eliminates the awkward procedure of repeatedly refreshing memory, as described above. The doctrine of past recollection recorded "was developed to allow a witness to use his previously recorded memorandum on the stand as part of his testimony when his recollection was insufficient. Upon laying the proper foundation to assure trustworthiness, the writing could be read into evidence." (Witkin, Cal.Evidence (2d ed.) supra, at p. 512; *Sherrell v Kelso*, (1981) 116 Cal.App.3d Supp. 2; *Frio v. Superior Court* (1988) 203 Cal.App.3d 1480, 1492.)

Evid. Code § 1237 Past Recollection Recorded (FRE Rule 803(5))

(a) Evidence of a statement previously made by a witness is not made inadmissible by the hearsay rule if the statement would have been admissible if made by him while testifying, the statement concerns a matter as to which the witness has insufficient present recollection to enable him to testify fully and accurately, and the statement is contained in a writing which:

(1) Was made at a time when the fact recorded in the writing actually occurred or was fresh in the witness' memory;
(2) Was made (i) by the witness himself or under his direction or (ii) by some other person for the purpose of recording the witness' statement at the time it was made;
(3) Is offered after the witness testifies that the statement he made was a true statement of such fact; and
(4) Is offered after the writing is authenticated as an accurate record of the statement.

(b) The writing may be read into evidence, but the writing itself may not be received in evidence unless offered by an adverse party.

"The motive behind section 1237 is to allow previously recorded statements into evidence where the trustworthiness of the contents of those statements is attested to by the maker, subject to the test of cross-examination..." (*People v. Simmons* (1981) 123 Cal.App.3d 677 at p. 682.) The difference between recollection refreshed and past recollection recorded is that in recollection refreshed the witness relates his or her own refreshed recollection of an event. In past recollection recorded, the witness has inadequate present recollection and merely reads into evidence a writing which itself contains the facts. (*Frio v. Superior Court,* supra.) FRE Rule 803(5) is similar. A document may be read to a jury under the rule as past recorded recollection if: (1) the witness once had knowledge about the matters in the document; (2) the witness now has insufficient recollection to testify fully and accurately; and (3) the record was made at a time when the matter was fresh in the witness' memory and reflected the witness' knowledge correctly. (*U.S. v. Porter* 986 F.2d 1014, 1016 (6th Cir. 1993).)

Full and Accurate Memory

Almost all witnesses will have some trouble remembering to one degree or another, so it is generally not difficult to establish that the witness does *not* have a "full and accurate" recollection. If the witness remembers the major points but has forgotten the finer details, as most witnesses will, then the witness is unable to describe the event "fully and accurately". A witness need not demonstrate no memory; a partial failure to recall will suffice. (*Frio,* supra.) No "magic words" are required to establish incomplete memory. (*People v. Miller* (1996) 46 Cal.App.4th 412, fn. 5 [overruled on other grounds].)

Fresh in Memory

The writing must have been made at the time or while the event was still fresh in the witness's mind. Typically, the statement was made relatively soon after the event. However, there is no specific time required between the event and when the statement was recorded. (*People v. Cowan* (2010) 50 Cal. 4th 401, 465.) For example, if the witness testifies the event was still fresh in her mind when she testified at a deposition six months after the accident, that might be sufficient. The facts must still be "reasonably fresh" in the witness's memory. (*People v. Miller,* supra [recorded statement made at least three weeks after recorded events occurred was admissible under Evid. Code § 1237].) In *People v. Cowan,* supra, the court upheld a three-month delay between a conversation and when it was recorded, holding, "Defendant points to no authority for the proposition that such a lapse of time between the events recorded and the time of the recording renders a past statement inadmissible under Evidence Code section 1237, and we are aware of none." Indeed, federal courts have admitted statements made after even greater lapses of time under the federal counterpart to section 1237, Federal Rule of Evidence 803(5).21 (*United States v. Patterson* (9th Cir.1982) 678 F.2d 774, 778-779 [ten months]; *United States v. Williams* (6th Cir.1978) 571 F.2d 344, 348-350 [six months]; These courts reasoned that district courts should have the flexibility to consider all pertinent circumstances in determining whether the matter was fresh in the witness's memory when the statement was made. (*United States v. Patterson*, supra, 678 F.2d at p. 779.)

True Statement

The witness must testify the statement made was true. (Evid. Code 1237(a)(3).) Typically, the witness is simply asked whether she told the truth in the prior statement. However, what if the witness does not remember making the statement? In *People v. Cummings* (1993: 4 Cal.4th 1233, 1293-1294), the court held that testimony that the statement made was true is sufficient even if the witness does not remember precisely what was said. In *Cummings,* an informant could not remember a statement to police due to detoxification and drug-related problems but did testify the statements were true. The court upheld admission of the statement as Past Recollection Recorded. Contrast *People v. Simmons* (1981: 123 Cal.App.3d 677, 682-683), finding no Past Recollection Recorded where the witness had amnesia and could not recall any of the events in his statement, making it, or any circumstances surrounding the statement. He testified only that he had no reason to lie when he made the statement. In *Parker v. Reda*, 327 F. 3d 211, 213, a police officer witness had no memory of the event or writing a memorandum which described the event. However, his testimony that he recognized the memorandum as a document he wrote at the time and that it accurately reflected his knowledge, was found sufficient. (See also *United States v. Marshall* 532 F.2d 1279, 1285-86 (9th Cir. 1976) [holding that chemist's report was admissible as past recollection recorded because "although the chemist had no independent recollection of the results of the tests he performed, his analyzed evidence report, which was both acknowledged by him to be accurate and prepared contemporaneously with the conducting of the relevant tests"].)

Counsel: "After the collision, were you able to get a good look at the suspect vehicle before it left the scene?"
Witness: "Yes."
Counsel: "Can you describe what you remember about it?"
Witness: "It was a blue pick-up truck. Ford, I think."
Counsel: "Did you see the license plate?"
Witness: "I did, but I can't remember it now. It's been over two years."
Counsel: "Are you having trouble recalling the specifics of the truck?"
Witness: "Yes."
Counsel: "Okay. Now, after the accident, did you write down what happened?"
Witness: "Yes. I wrote the license plate and a description on a scrap of paper from my glove box."
Counsel: "When did you do that?"
Witness: "A few minutes later."
Counsel: "Was the accident still fresh in your mind?"
Witness: "Yes."

Counsel: "Did you try to be as accurate and as truthful as you could when you wrote it down?"

Witness: "Yes."

Counsel: "Showing you what has been marked as exhibit 14, do you recognize this document?"

Witness: "Yes. This is that paper. That's my handwriting."

Counsel: "Your Honor, may the witness read her notes into the record as recorded recollection?"

In the above, opposing counsel would first have the right to inspect the writing beforehand and provided an opportunity to object if, for example, it also set forth other inadmissible evidence, such as her husband's recollections. Opposing counsel would also have the opportunity to cross-examine the witness and move to have the actual writing admitted as evidence, if that would be helpful.

Witness Did not Make the Writing

The witness is sometimes not the person who prepared the writing; for example, where the witness made a statement to a police officer at the scene and the officer recorded the statement in a police report. The writing can be prepared by "some *other person* for the purpose of recording the witness's statement at the time it was made." (Evid. Code § 1237(a)(2).) If you establish that the witness does not have a full and accurate memory *and* made a truthful account of the event to another who recorded it, you will then call that "other person" to testify (commonly a police officer) concerning the accuracy of the recording. (See *Sherrell v Kelso*, (1981) 116 Cal.App.3d Supp. 2 [police officer who investigated traffic collision permitted to read into record witness statements recorded in police report].) Where the statement was recorded by someone other than the declarant, accuracy may be established through the testimony of the person who recorded the statement. FRE Rule 805(5) requires that the statement "was made *or adopted* by the witness." (emphasis added); See also *U.S. v. Mornan*, F.3d 372, 377, (3rd Cir. 2005); Therefore, in the above, the witness would confirm that while the incident was still fresh in her mind she truthfully told an officer what she observed, expecting him to record it. Thereafter, the officer who recorded the statement in the report would testify as to the accuracy of the recordation and then read the witness' statement into the record.

Trial Tip: Recollection recorded is where you go when a witness's memory cannot be adequately refreshed. It is an easy and effective method to get more accurate facts into evidence and often under-utilized by counsel.

6. DIRECT EXAMINATION

The direct examination is the time when the witness should be center stage and permitted to tell his or her own story without much interruption. This is typically accomplished by counsel asking the witness more open-ended questions and permitting the witness to answer in a narrative format. The attorney's role is to guide or "direct" the witness, step by step, through the testimony to make it as informative and as memorable as possible. However, sometimes it is easier said than done, and the ability of the trial attorney to conduct *good* direct examination is a trial skill that is often overlooked.

The main difficulty is that many witnesses are not good storytellers or historians. Other than perhaps experts, you generally do not get to pick your witnesses, and they come in all varieties, from the highly intelligent to the uneducated and illiterate. Some will possess a natural ability to express themselves clearly and will have excellent recall, while others will have a poor memory, poor communication skills, and possibly even mental health or substance abuse issues. Yet, regardless of their varied backgrounds and levels of intellect, all witnesses are required to sit in the same chair and answer the questions you put to them during the direct examination.

The effectiveness of direct examination is dependent, in large part, on the skill of the examiner and the degree of preparation. However, some attorneys tend to take it for granted. They do not prepare properly, use few notes, and simply ask the witness, "What happened next?" or "Then what happened?" over and over again. Worse yet, they can make a relatively straightforward issue confusing and muddled simply by demonstrating poor examination technique. For example, one of the more common deficiencies is when counsel's questions do not follow a logical sequence, but instead, tend to skip around or "digress" repeatedly, making it difficult for the jury to track. Good examiners, on the other hand, know how to "direct" their witness by eliciting testimony that moves from point A to point B in a logical and linear fashion. They also know how to use aids and props, e.g., diagrams and photographs, to enhance the oral word of the witness.

> **Trial Tip:** Some lawyers tend to take direct examination for granted and do not prepare adequately. Good direct requires planning and preparation.

Preparation

The preparation for direct examination should begin long before trial. The first step is to assimilate and organize all witnesses' prior statements, which can include, deposition testimony, statements to the police, declarations, pleadings, interviews, and preliminary hearing testimony in criminal cases. Important passages in each statement should be highlighted and tabbed for quick reference. Even when the witness is "friendly," witnesses often forget, become confused, or get flustered. Having the witness's prior statements at your fingertips and organized is helpful because it may become necessary to quickly refresh the witness's recollection, lay the foundation for past recollection recorded, or perhaps even impeach the witness with an inconsistency.

Testimony Outline

For the direct examination, it is generally not necessary to literally write out each question, although some lawyers do, but a written, detailed outline for each witness is important. During preparation, begin by preparing a list of the important facts or key points you wish to establish from the witness's testimony. Making a list of five or ten points will help you to design the examination. Next, create a detailed written outline with bullet points and sub-points to be covered during the questioning. When drafting the outline, consider reviewing the applicable jury instruction for the elements or defenses of the applicable cause of actions to make sure you are hitting all the key areas. The outline should follow the order in which you intend to proceed for the examination. Generally, chronological is easiest for the jury to follow, where you start at the beginning of a sequence of events and move the witness through it in a step-by-step manner.

During the trial, as you move through the testimony you can use your outline to check off the areas covered. Even for minor witnesses, the use of an outline is helpful because nothing is worse than realizing, after the witness has left the stand and been excused, that you forgot to ask something important because you did not have it written down.

> **Trial Tip:** It is not uncommon that counsel forget or neglect to ask a witness a certain question and then have to re-call that witness. The use of a good written outline helps to prevent that.

Witness Preparation

Prior to testifying, every witness should be properly prepared. That advice may seem obvious, but far too often, important witnesses testify with little or no apparent pre-trial preparation. The most important aspect of preparation is to permit the witness to review thoroughly all his or her prior statements and to explain the courtroom procedures for testimony. Because a trial typically occurs many months, if not years, after the event, nearly every witness will need to be "refreshed" prior to testifying. If the witness hits the stand cold with minimal or no review, the result is generally a failure of recollection or mistakes. The constant interruption of the testimony to "refresh recollection" is distracting and annoying to the jurors and it makes testimony harder to follow. Furthermore, forgetful witnesses are not very impressive to a jury, and they can come across as being deceitful or uncooperative when they are just having trouble remembering.

Shortly before trial, consider having a conference with the important witnesses, including your own client, to allow them the opportunity to review their prior statements, which in civil cases is most often their deposition testimony, but it might also include statements to investigators or declarations in the pleadings. Consider permitting the witness to take the statements home to review at his or her leisure. The point is, before the witness hits the stand, you want the witness to be completely up to speed on *every* statement he or she has ever made concerning the contested trial issues.

Additionally, keep in mind when preparing a witness that whatever materials the witness reviews and whatever the witness is told prior to testifying is fair game for cross-examination. Thus, it is prudent to remind the witness to listen carefully to the questions and to answer them truthfully. Admonitions to remain calm and suggestions of proper attire are also appropriate. In addition, be careful not to suggest to the witness what to say or to inform the witness what other witnesses may have said. Consider meeting with each witness separately to avoid any possibility or suggestion that the witnesses have exchanged stories. If you are concerned about a claim that you "coached" the witness, consider recording your interaction or having a third person present.

Some attorneys are reluctant to meet a witness in person prior to trial, concerned that such a meeting could be cast as suspicious or improper by opposing counsel. Generally, however, the *benefit* of having a witness properly prepared and fresh on the facts far outweighs the possible negative implications of meeting with a witness. Jurors are impressed with a witness who seems on top of the facts and can answer questions without hesitation or without refreshing. Jurors are typically not bothered by the fact that an attorney met with a witness before the trial to review the testimony. They expect it. On the other hand, there may be valid tactical reasons why you may not wish to meet with a witness or to have the witness review prior statements prior to trial. For example, if you believe the witness is going to recant or is hostile, then it might be a better tactic to subpoena the witness straight to the courtroom with no preparation in advance. Or, if you sense the witness is hostile—unsympathetic to your case—you might consider providing the witness with a copy of the statements shortly before testimony. When a hostile witness has received and reviewed his or her prior statement(s) and knows the prior statements are documented, it tends to help prevent the witness from claiming on the stand that he or she did not make the statements or cannot remember.

Trial Tip: Perhaps one of the most important aspects of witness preparation is to have the witness review all prior statements, e.g., deposition testimony, shortly before testimony. Too often, witnesses are called to the stand "cold" without any preparation which generally results in the witness having difficulty remembering. Counsel then has to repeatedly refresh recollection. The jury (or court) may interpret this as a lack of credibility.

Attorney Witness Concerns

While it is perfectly appropriate for counsel to meet with and to prepare a witness prior to trial, counsel should take precautions not to inadvertently become a potential witness yourself. The "advocate-witness rule" prohibits an attorney from acting both as an advocate and a witness in the same proceeding unless certain circumstances apply. (See *Kennedy v. Eldridge* (2011) 201 Cal.App.4th 1197, 1208; Rule 3.7 ABA Model Rules.) The problem arises most often when a witness relates something important to counsel and there was no one else present to overhear or otherwise record the statement. This can happen inadvertently during trial, for example, a witness may seek to talk with you in the hallway during a break or after court. Some witnesses may wish to speak with you "off the record." The concern is obviously that the witness might tell you something that could potentially make you a witness; for example, confide that they did not tell the truth or are withholding important information. Prosecutors in criminal cases must be particularly alert for this scenario given their ethical obligation to reveal any exonerating evidence. (*Brady v. Maryland* (1963) 373 U.S. 83, 83 S.Ct. 1194, 10 L.Ed.2d 215.)

Trial Tip: Avoid making yourself a witness by always meeting with witnesses, and possibly even your own client, in the presence of a third party.

General Rule – No Leading Questions

The general rule is that leading questions are *not* permitted during the direct examination, except under *special circumstances* where the interest of justice otherwise requires. (Evid. Code § 767; *People v. Kronemyer* (1987) 189 Cal.App.3d 314, 353; see also FRE 611(c)[similar].) "A leading question is a question that suggests to the witness the answer that the examining party desires." (Evid. Code § 764; *People v Pearson* (2013 56 Cal.4th 393, 426; *People v. Williams* (1997) 16 Cal.4th 635, 672) "A question calling for a 'yes' or 'no' answer is a leading question only if, under the circumstances, it is obvious that the examiner is suggesting that the witness answer the question one way only, whether it be 'yes' or 'no.' When the danger of false suggestion is present, leading questions should be prohibited; when it is absent, leading questions should be allowed." (*Williams*, at p. 672.) One treatise on evidence offers this explanation on leading questions: "A question may be leading because of its form, but often the mere form of a question does not indicate whether it is leading. The question which contains a phrase like 'did he not?' is obviously and invariably leading, but almost any other type of question may be leading or not, dependent upon the content and context ... The whole issue is whether an ordinary man would get the impression that the questioner desired one answer rather than another. The form of a question, or previous questioning, may indicate the desire, but the most important circumstance for consideration is the extent of the particularity of the question itself." (1 McCormick on Evidence, supra, § 6, pp. 17-18.)

In practice, the improper use of leading questions during direct examination most often occurs when it is obvious that counsel really wants the witness to answer a certain way related to a contested issue. Of course, the best case is to object *before* the witness answers, but if the witness does answer, then a motion to strike should be appropriate. One reason to object at the first instance is to keep opposing counsel from repeating the bad behavior. If the opposing party knows you will object, it helps to set keep them in line, so to speak. (See Trial Objections, infra, at p. 218.)

[Direct examination]
Counsel: "The light was green as you entered the intersection, wasn't it?" *or*
"Isn't it true, the light was green as you entered the intersection?"
Opp. Counsel: "Objection, Your Honor, leading.

Trial Tip: During direct examination, the focus should be on the witness and *not* on counsel. For this reason, consider remaining seated at the counsel table or using a podium. It can be distracting if you move around or pace.

Leading Questions during Direct Examination

Despite the general rule prohibiting the use of leading questions during direct examination, in reality, they are actually an important component of direct examination. In fact, some lawyers do not use enough leading questions. In California, leading questions are permitted for "special circumstances where the interest of justice otherwise requires." (CA Evid. Code § 767; *People v. Kronemyer* (1987) 189 Cal.App.3d 314, 353.) In Federal Court, FRE Rule 611(c) provides: "Leading questions should not be used on direct examination *except* as necessary to develop the witness's testimony."

The object is not to waste a lot of time on uncontested matters. One of the most important exceptions is that leading questions are permitted to establish *preliminary matters*. "It is proper to ask leading questions when they are designed to more quickly reach the testimony material to the issues." (*People v. Augustin* (2003) 112 Cal.App.4th 444, 449.) Leading questions may be asked on direct examination if there is little danger of improper suggestion and where such questions are necessary to obtain relevant evidence. (*People v. Williams* (2013) 56 Cal.4th 165, 192.) "The rule against asking leading questions...does not apply stringently in non-controversial matters, or when it is legitimate to employ some suggestion to refresh a witness's memory, or when an expert witness is being interrogated or when exhibits are being identified." (*People v. Campbell* (1965) 233 Cal.App.2d 38, 44.)

There is, of course, a degree of tolerance for leading questions under certain circumstances. Because it is so case-specific, the trial judge is best situated to strike a practical and fair balance and is afforded extensive discretion over the phrasing of questions. (See *U.S. v. Hansen* 434 F. 3d 92, 105 (1st Cir. 2006).)

As a practical matter, therefore, must courts will allow some degree of leading questions for uncontested facts to keep the case moving forward. Leading questions *should* be used to establish foundational facts and information, such as locations, dates, background information, photographs, and documents. The use of leading questions will help you get quickly past the non-controversial, preliminary matters in order to get to the main issue. Once the preliminary foundational matters have been covered, then slow the pace down with more open-ended, non-leading questions as you get to the contested issue.

Counsel: "On January 1, 2016, you lived at 101 Maple Street in the City of Auburn, correct?"

Counsel: "On the afternoon of March 14, 2015, at about 2:30 p.m., you were driving westbound on Maple Street approaching the intersection of Lincoln, weren't you?"

Counsel: "Exhibit 12 is a photograph of the intersection as it appeared the day of the accident, is that correct?" [May or may not be suggestive depending upon whether the depiction of the intersection is in controversy. If there is no dispute over the authenticity and accuracy of the photograph – overruled.]

> **Trial Tip:** Inexperienced lawyers tend to not use enough leading questions during direct for uncontested issues. Inexperienced lawyers also object routinely to questions that are technically leading, but related to uncontested matters.

Refreshing Memory with Leading Questions

As discussed previously, witnesses frequently forget minor details or other uncontroverted information, such as dates, times, locations, and even prior statements. The attorney's role is to help refresh their *memory*. Leading questions are permitted to help stimulate or revive a witness's memory. (*People v. Collins* (2010) 49 Cal.4th 175, 210 [use of leading questions to revive witness of prior statement upheld]; *People v. Williams* (1997) 16 Cal.4th 635, 672.)

Adverse Party

In civil trials, it is common that one party may call another to testify, which is generally permitted. Contrast this to a criminal case where, under the Fifth Amendment, the prosecution is prohibited from calling the defendant to the stand. When one party calls another to testify, the party calling the witness may wish to use leading questions. In this circumstance, the party calling the witness may request permission from the court to treat the witness as an "adverse witness" under Evidence Code section 776.

Evid. Code 776 Examination of adverse party (FRE Rule 611(c))

(a) A party to the record of any civil action, or a person identified with such a party, may be called and examined as if under cross-examination by any adverse party at any time during the presentation of evidence by the party calling the witness.

Section 776(b) deals with the situation where "witnesses" are called by a party who are not adverse to that party. In this situation, the rules of redirect apply, meaning no leading questions. However, Evidence Code section 773(b) states: "The cross-examination of a witness by any party whose interest is not adverse to the party calling him is subject to the same rules that are applicable to the direct examination." This relates to cases with multiple parties and determines who can and cannot use leading questions.

Hostile Witnesses

From time to time, you are going to come across a truly hostile witness—a witness who is being deliberately evasive and combative. For these witnesses, it can be like pulling teeth just to get the basic narrative. They will answer in one-syllable words, feign memory loss, or simply not answer the question at all. Obviously, just because you must call the witness to establish your case does not guarantee their friendliness or cooperation. One method of dealing with this is to request permission from the court to treat the witness as "hostile," such that leading questions can be used, if necessary.

The use of leading questions on direct examination is permitted when a party is faced with a hostile witness. (*People v. Spain* (1984) 154 Cal .App.3d 845, 853; CA Evid. Code 767.) Witnesses may be shown to be hostile, for example, because of their relationship with the defendant or because their demeanor on the stand indicates they are inclined to favor the defense as much as possible (*People v. Grey* (1972) 23 Cal.App.3d 456, 464), or "inclined to tell as little as they actually know of the matter as possible." (*People v. Bliss* (1919) 41 Cal.App. 65, 71.) Assessment of the circumstances revealing the witness's hostility is uniquely within the realm of the trial court, and therefore the use of leading questions on direct examination is committed to the sound discretion of the trial court. (*Spain*, at p. 853.) FRE 611(c) is similar.

You cannot pick and choose your witnesses, and sometimes an important witness to your case will be truly "hostile" —a witness who will be deliberately evasive and combative. Typically, even prior to trial, you will have a pretty good idea about a witness's predicted demeanor on the stand; for example, the witness has been avoiding service or has made it known that he or she will not cooperate.

Even once you get these types of witnesses on the stand, it can be like pulling teeth just to get the basic story. They will answer in one-syllable words, feign memory loss, or simply not answer the question at all.

In this situation, prior to testimony and outside the presence of the jury, let the court know the situation and make a request to treat the witness as "hostile" under section 776 (FRE Rule 611) in order to allow leading questions, if necessary. Some judges may deny the request initially in order to assess the testimony as it plays out to see if the witness is truly hostile. "Assessment of the circumstances revealing the witness's hostility is uniquely within the realm of the trial court, and therefore the use of leading questions on direct examination is committed to the sound discretion of the trial court." (*People v. Spain* (1984) 154 Cal App.3d 845, 853.) Rule 611(c) has significantly enlarged the class of witnesses presumed hostile, and therefore subject to interrogation by leading questions *without* further showing of actual hostility. (*Haney v. Mizell Memorial Hosp.* 744 F.2d 1467, 1478 (11th Cir. 1984).)

Trial Tip: Even if the witness is "hostile" or "adverse", tactically, you may still want to use non-leading questions to draw out more narrative, fuller answers. On the other hand, for the truly hostile witness, where you know you're not going to get any straight answers, leading questions might be appropriate. Further, consider requesting the court to limit cross-examination to non-leading questions only.

Other Circumstances for Leading Questions

There can be other circumstances where leading questions might be permitted, depending on the type of the witness and the circumstances. The court has wide discretion. For example, a child or a witness with a disability where communication is difficult for some reason. (See *e.g., People v. Augustin* (2003) 112 Cal.App.4th 444, 449 [leading questions permitted for witness suffering from cerebral palsy]; see also *Mead v. Mead* (1919) 41 Cal.App. 280 [leading questions appropriate for feeble 83-year-old man suffering from deafness and paralysis].)

Direct Examination – A Format

Preparation and planning for how to present a witness's testimony is important. You cannot just call a witness to the stand cold and expect good results. As mentioned previously, during direct examination, the witness should be center stage where you, the examiner, remain in the background to guide the witness. By the time your witness hits the stand, the witness should be fully prepared by having reviewed prior statements and being informed of the ground rules regarding testimony. In addition, you should have in front of you as a guide the outline you prepared of the witness's testimony. To conduct the actual examination, you should have a strategy or a plan, such as the following:

Witness Introduction and Warmup

The first series of questions are directed towards allowing the witness the opportunity to introduce him or herself to the jury and to warm up. Witnesses are often nervous and anxious, so a few easy softball questions at the very beginning helps the witness relax and get over the stage fright.

Counsel: "Good afternoon, Mrs. Smith, can you tell the jurors a little about yourself—where you live and what you do?" … "Have you ever testified before? Nervous?" etc.

Most courts will permit some general background information, e.g., occupation, family status, education, etc. It is important for the jurors to get a feel for who the witness is. If there are family members or other interested parties in the courtroom, it might also be a good idea for the witness to identify those people so the jurors know who is who. The object is to humanize the witness. However, there are limits. For example, it is generally impermissible to ask a witness to describe something extraordinary or remarkable for the simple purpose of making the witness look good. "Please tell us about your military honors " … or …"Didn't you once save a child from a burning building?" The court has the authority to limit this type of collateral information. (CA Evid. Code § 352.) In addition, this type of specific background or "character" evidence likely violates Evidence Code section 787, prohibiting specific instances of conduct to support or attack the credibility of a witness. (See Impeachment of Character, infra, at p. 125.)

In practice, how much witness background information to elicit is a tactical decision which may depend upon the importance of the witness and whether the witness's credibility will be questioned. However, about five to ten minutes' worth of general background testimony is usually all that is needed for the jurors to get a pretty good impression. On the other hand, it is also important to get to the main subject matter as soon as possible while the jurors are still fresh. Spending too much time on background may detract from what is important. A word of caution: If you do opt to have a witness provide a more thorough and in-depth accounting of him or herself, be wary that the witness's testimony does not inadvertently reveal something unflattering or "open the door" to something previously unknown, e.g., the witness has a criminal record. The cardinal rule for cross-examination, namely, do not ask a question that you do not know the answer to, applies equally to your own witnesses on direct examination. You really do not want any unforeseen little bombshells to prejudice your case.

Trial Tip: How much background information of the witness to elicit is a tactical decision and may depend upon how contested the testimony will be. If there is an issue regarding a witness's background, the best time to litigate that is in a pre-trial motion in limine, e.g., bad character you wish to exclude.

Set the Stage

After the witness has been introduced and before getting to the main event, the next step is to *set the stage*. You would like the jurors to be able to visualize in their minds what the witness is talking about before the key testimony. This might include describing the other key players in the lawsuit or the scene of the event. For example, in a traffic collision case, have the witness describe her car and the intersection using photographs or diagrams before describing the actual accident. If the witness is not a good witness/narrator, consider using a third party, e.g., a police officer or an investigator, to set the stage *before* the witness testifies. Setting the scene also means describing the mood or other existing conditions. If you launch right in to having the witness describe the accident before the jurors fully understand the layout of the intersection, it will only lead to confusion. Once the stage is set, so to speak, the witness's testimony should flow smoother and with fewer interruptions.

> **Trial Tip:** One of the more common mistakes made during direct examination is not following a simple, logical, step-by-step, progression. Repeatedly stopping and starting, or skipping around from topic to topic or out of order, only serves to confuse the jurors and makes the testimony less forceful. The story must flow in a linear fashion.

Direct the Witness

For substantive areas of testimony, you are going to essentially present the story *two times* via the witness. The first time through, you are going to let the story flow, so to speak, from beginning to end. Of course, you will be asking questions along the way, but you want to keep it moving. Once the witness has covered the basic narrative, e.g., describing the accident in a narrative fashion, then you go back and clean up the details or have the witness confirm the most crucial facts. Try not to interrupt the witness too much during the first rendition. Wait to ask detailed questions after the basic story is out there.

During the examination, remember your role is to guide the witness, namely, direct the witness to the specific area where you would like to start and finish their explanation. If your question is too broad, e.g., "What happened?" the witness will not know where to start or how much detail to provide. Give the witness some direction.

Counsel: "When you entered the intersection, what did you see?"
　　　　versus
　　　"What happened next?"

In addition, as mentioned above, the use of leading questions to establish preliminary facts is helpful to get the witness to the main event more quickly.

Counsel: "You were traveling Eastbound on Elm Street just before the accident, correct?"

Witnesses are nervous and will forget or gloss over important points. In that circumstance, it may be necessary to guide the witness back to the particular area of focus. Like frames in a movie, back the witness up a few steps.

Counsel: "Taking you back to the moment right before the accident, can you describe what you saw the blue car do?"

It is also common for witnesses to talk too fast or to race through the narrative. This is when you need to take more control, and if necessary, interrupt the witness to remind him or her to *slow down.* Ask questions designed to keep the witness in check and proceed more slowly. If necessary go back and have the witness repeat the answer more slowly.

Witness: "And when I got to the intersection, that's when I saw the car run the red light, and then the man jumped out and started running, and that other guy, he also jumped out and ran after him."
Counsel: "Okay. Thank you. Now let's take it a little more slowly and step-by-step. when you first reached the intersection, at that moment, what was the first thing you saw?"
Witness: "I saw the car run the red light and then..."
Counsel: "Okay, let me interrupt you there. When you saw the car run the red light, in what direction was it traveling?"

Other witnesses are shy, nervous, or reluctant, and getting them to answer questions fully, or at all, is sometimes like pulling teeth. Some witnesses are quiet and soft-spoken which means *you* will need to ask them politely to speak up or to use the court microphone. For reluctant witnesses, use leading questions to get them right to the topic, followed by very short and specific questions to give the witness no room to avoid answering.

Counsel: "You were involved in a traffic accident on the afternoon of March 3rd, at the intersection of Elm and Lincoln, correct?"
Counsel: "You were driving your red Honda minivan, correct?"
Counsel: "Describe for us what happened, what you *saw* happen, the moment before your car entered into the intersection."

Trial Tip: As the witness is testifying, periodically check the jury to see if they seem to be following along. The jurors' faces and body language are clues. Some jurors may sit there passively even though they did not hear or understand the answer. When in doubt, re-ask the question or in a slightly different way.

Use of Exhibits

The use of exhibits or "demonstrative" evidence to enhance the direct examination is important. "A picture is worth a thousand words" is an expression every trial lawyer should embrace. A diagram, map, or photograph in conjunction with live testimony is much more impactful than mere words. (See Non-Testimonial Evidence, infra, at p. 154.) However, the key to success is forethought and preparation. Like a well-choreographed stage show, the more you plan, the better the production. Good trial lawyers move seamlessly through the direct examination by using exhibits to highlight and illustrate the testimony. When the presentation is well choreographed, even boring topics can seem more interesting.

Witness: "I was about to enter the intersection, when I saw the minivan coming from my right side and directly into my path."

Counsel: "I would like to direct your attention to the aerial photograph of the intersection upon the screen, Exhibit 43, can you see it?"

Witness: "Yes."

Counsel: "Does it appear to fairly and accurately depict the intersection where the accident happened?"

Witness: "Yes, it does."

Counsel: "Using this laser pointer, can you first point to the location where your vehicle was located when you first saw the minivan?"

Witness: "My car was right here." [witness using pointer to indicate location.]

Counsel: "For the record, on Exhibit 43, the witness is pointing to bottom of the intersection, where the words Elm Street are printed on the exhibit. Is that correct?"

Witness: "Yes."

Instead of using a laser pointer, the witness could also be requested to actually mark on the exhibit with a colored marker or something similar.

Counsel: "Using this blue marker, on the exhibit, can you put an X with your initials to indicate the location where your vehicle was located when you first saw the minivan?"

Trial Tip: Whenever requesting a witness to mark on an exhibit, be sure you have given thought regarding how to instruct the witness. Some attorneys have the witness make an "X", place their initials, a number, or even hand draw a rectangle or other symbol to represent what they are describing, e.g., a vehicle. *However*, be wary of witness markings turning into a bunch of confusing scribbles, which happens. Nothing prohibits counsel from making the marks at the witness's direction to keep it clearer.

Revisit Important Areas

Once the witness has described the event from beginning to end, hopefully without too much interruption, now is the time to go back and revisit important areas with more specific questions. In every witness's testimony there is a defining moment where something very important or material to the case is stated, an area you would like to emphasize or highlight. Like frames in a movie, direct the witness back to the key moment and then have the witness describe it *slowly*, frame by frame. Being able to focus and redirect the witness on direct examination to specific topics is a skill that requires very precise, simple questions. This is the time to flesh out extreme detail, if needed.

Counsel: "I'd like to go back to the moment, just seconds before your vehicle entered into the intersection. Can you describe what you saw at that moment?"

Witness: "Ahead of me, I saw the blue mini-van run the red light and cross into the intersection right in front of me."

Counsel: "Then what happened?"

Witness: "My car broadsided the minivan, before I could brake."

Concluding Questions

After you are satisfied that you have adequately established all the facts and information from the witness you had been planning for, a good tactic is to go back one final time for a recap of the most important points of the testimony.

Counsel: "Just to be clear, is there any doubt in your mind that it was the minivan that ran the red light?"

Witness: "None whatsoever."

Counsel: "Thank you. No further questions, Your Honor."

In the above, arguably, having the witness restate an answer could raise the objection "Asked and Answered." (See Trial Objections, infra at p. 225.) If the witness's credibility is at issue or if clarification is needed, most judges will allow some leeway. However, if the witness is simply repeating the same answer over and over again and the court gets the impression it is for effect only, an "asked and answered" objection will likely be sustained. Ultimately, you would like to wrap up the witness's direct examination with a brief re-affirmation of the central contested issue, leaving no doubt in the minds of the jurors.

Redirect Examination

Following cross-examination, counsel is permitted "redirect" examination. However, redirect is limited to the scope of the cross-examination. (Evid. Code § 774; FRE Rule 611(b).) During cross-examination, questions were asked and answers given that may have raised questions or created confusion in the minds of the jurors. Because the witness may have responded to leading questions with only a "yes" or "no," the witness may not have been able to fully explain an answer or something that may have been taken out of context. For example, if only a portion of a witness's previous statement was referred to, it may be necessary to introduce the entirety of the statement to put everything in context. (Evid. Code § 356, infra at p. 146; see also witness rehabilitation, infra, at p. 137.)

Once cross-examination is concluded, use redirect to go back and clear up any confusion or questions raised. In addition, consider requesting that your witness confirm, one more time, the substance of the direct testimony, namely, that it was the defendant's car that ran the light.

Counsel: "During cross-examination, counsel asked you questions about a statement you made to a police officer shortly after the accident wherein you purportedly said that you were not sure which car ran the light. Do you remember those questions?"

Witness: "Yes."

Counsel: "How long did you speak with that first officer while at the scene?"

Witness: "Very brief, a minute or less."

Counsel: "After speaking to the first officer, did you then later provide a more detailed statement to another second officer?"

Witness: "Oh yes, he asked a lot of questions."

Counsel: "Did you tell that second officer that it was the minivan that ran the light?"

Witness: "Yes, several times."

Counsel: "Why did you tell the first officer that you were not sure which car ran the light?"

Witness. "I was in shock. I really didn't know what he was asking."

Trial Tip: It is generally not a good idea to hold back on establishing all the relevant facts during the initial direct examination. However, there could be a situation where there are some facts, generally unfavorable, that you would rather not bring out during the initial direct examination, but may possibly cover during *re-direct*, depending on whether opposing counsel goes into it during cross. For example, if the witness was not cross-examined about her poor eyesight, then why bring it out?

Misrecollection and Mistakes

For every trial lawyer, there will inevitably be that awkward moment when your star witness just said something during your direct examination that you know is inaccurate or different from the witness's earlier statement. Often, the discrepancy is merely due to forgetfulness or inadvertence. However, you cannot let the answer stand without correcting the record. In effect, you must impeach your own witness. (Evid. Code § 785; *People v. Osorio* (2008) 165 Cal.App.4th 603, 615 ["The credibility of a witness may be attacked or supported by any party, including the party calling him."].) The best method is simply to refresh the witness's recollection by permitting the witness to review the prior writing, even if mid-testimony. (Refresh recollection, supra.) You can simply interrupt the testimony and request that the witness review his or her prior statement.

Witness: "I was traveling about thirty-five miles per hour when the accident occurred."

Counsel: "Could you have been traveling slower than that speed?"

Witness: "Oh, no. I'm pretty certain it was about thirty-five."

Counsel: "Now, you spoke to a police officer right after the accident, did you not?"

Witness: "Yes."

Counsel: "Were the facts fresh in your mind at the time? In other words, did you remember clearly what had happened?"

Witness: "Yes."

Counsel: "Mr. Williams, I'm going to have you read for a moment the statement you gave to the officer that afternoon to see if that helps refresh your memory regarding how fast you were going." (Witness reviews his statement.)

Counsel: "Does that help?"

Witness: "Yes, yes it does. I remember I was going twenty-five miles per hour. Not thirty-five. I was mistaken. It's been over two years. The details are a little fuzzy now."

Counsel: "Did you make a truthful statement to the officer that day?"

Witness: "Of course."

Counsel: "Did you attempt to be as accurate as possible when you described what had happened and your speed?"

Witness: "Yes."

Counsel: "How fast did you tell the officer you were traveling right before the accident?"

Witness: "Twenty-five."

Note: This last question might draw a *hearsay objection* because technically it is an out-of-court statement being offered for the truth of the matter. However, if opposing counsel were to now attack the witness's credibility, the accident-day statement might be admissible as a Prior Consistent Statement. (Evid. Code 1236, discussed infra at p. 148.) If the witness were to stick to his thirty-five m.p.h. trial estimate, then it may be admissible as a prior inconsistent statement. (Evid. Code § 1235, discussed infra at p. 131.)

Trial Tip: If, during direct examination, you observe that your witness has made a mistake or an error of some type, don't let it just hang out there for cross-examination. Go back and correct the record, so to speak, even if it means impeaching your own witness. Better to steal your opponent's thunder and permit the witness to explain it, even if it's some bad facts. Later, during argument, you can point out how the witnessed owned up to it.

Recalling the Witness

A witness is generally under court order, usually in the form of a subpoena, to attend trial. Once the witness has completed his or her testimony, the court may inquire of counsel whether the witness is "excused," which means the witness is released from the legal requirement of further attendance. Some courts may permit the witness to remain *subject to recall*," if requested by a party. This means the witness remains under court jurisdiction and must return to court for further testimony at some point later in the trial, if needed. Whether a witness has been "excused" or left "subject to recall" can make a procedural difference; for example, whether the witness has been given the opportunity to explain an inconsistency. (See Inconsistent Statement, infra, at p. 129.)

Trial Tip: If there is any possibility the witness may be needed again at some point later during the trial, if it is an option, request the witness remain "subject to recall."

It is not uncommon that after direct and cross-examination have been completed and the witness is excused, that a party will request permission from the court to "recall" that witness. This might occur because new, unanticipated issues have arisen that require further additional testimony. Unfortunately, another reason it happens is due to counsel's oversight where certain questions or issues were inadvertently not covered during the original examination. Of course, forgetting to ask a key witness an important question is not very impressive either to the court or the jury. The right to recall a witness is not automatic and, in most jurisdictions is within the sound discretion of the trial court. (*United States v. Coleman*, 805 F.2d 474, 482 (3d Cir.1986); *United States v. Erickson*, 75 F.3d 470 (9th Cir.1996); see also CA Evidence Code § 778 ["After a witness has been excused from giving further testimony in the action, he cannot be recalled without leave of the court. Leave may be granted or withheld in the court's discretion."]) In practice, if the witness is needed to rebut other evidence and the additional testimony will not consume much time or prejudice the other party, the court will generally grant the request.

7. CROSS-EXAMINATION

Cross-examination is arguably one of the most difficult trial skills to master due to the unpredictability of testimony and difficult witnesses. In the courtroom, you never really know how the testimony will roll out until it does. There are frequently unexpected little surprises and twists that come to light. Witnesses forget things, go off script, embellish, and lie. Some are quiet and timid, while others are hostile and angry. In addition, the witness's trial testimony can differ from out-of-court statements, requiring the examiner to "impeach" the witness with the inconsistencies. One of the hardest skills to master related to cross-examination is the ability to control the witness—to force the witness to answer only the question asked without elaboration or gratuitous comment. It is this dynamic nature of witness testimony that can make cross-examination interesting, to say the least. It requires you to truly think on your feet and to quickly adapt the questioning in light of the changing testimony.

Over time, courts have acknowledged the importance of cross-examination, in that it permits "not only of testing the recollection and sifting the conscience of the witness, but of compelling him to stand face to face with the jury in order that they may look at him, and judge by his demeanor upon the stand and the manner in which he gives his testimony whether he is worthy of belief." (*California v. Green* (1970) 399 U.S. 149, 158, 90 S.Ct. 1930; *People v. Roldan* (2012) 205 Cal.App.4th 969, 978.) "The purpose of the cross-examination is to sift his testimony and weaken its force, in short, to discredit the direct testimony. Thus, not only the presumable bias of the witness for the opponent's cause, but also his sense of reluctance to become the instrument of his own discrediting, deprive him of any inclination to accept the cross-examiner's suggestions unless the truth forces him to." (*People v. Spain* (1984) 154 Cal.App.3d 845, 853.) "Cross-examination has two purposes: its chief purpose is to test the credibility, knowledge and recollection of the witness; the other purpose is to elicit additional evidence." (*Fost v. Superior Court* (App. 1 Dist. 2000) 80 Cal.App.4th 724, 733.)

Perils of

Cross-examination involves the questioning of your adversary's witnesses, who will generally have nothing good to say about your case and who are often biased and uncooperative. If done well, cross-examination can undermine a witness's credibility and win cases. On the other hand, if done poorly, it has the potential to backfire and do more harm than good.

The perils of cross-examination were quite aptly stated by John Henry Wigmore, the original author of the leading American text on evidence, who lamented, "Cross-examination is the greatest legal engine ever invented for the discovery of truth. You can do anything with a bayonet except sit on it. A lawyer can do anything with cross-examination if he is skillful enough not to impale his own cause upon it." Another famous trial lawyer wrote, "Cross is not a fishing expedition in which you uncover new surprises at the trial. In cross-examination, as in fishing, nothing is more ungainly than a fisherman pulled into the water by his catch." (Louis Nizer, *My Life in Court*, 1961, p. 79.)

The takeaway from these admonitions is that trial lawyers should always approach cross-examination with caution. However, for those who prepare properly and employ some basic strategies and tactics, cross-examination can be a powerful and persuasive courtroom tool.

Organization and Preparation

Like many other aspects of a trial, preparation is the key to successful cross-examination. With the modern rules of discovery and civil procedure, before the first day of trial arrives you should know who your opponent's witnesses are and the general substance of their testimony. The day of "surprise" witnesses are long gone. The trial lawyer's first task, therefore, is to obtain and organize the prior statements of each witness you intend to cross-examine. This includes deposition testimony, interrogatories, declarations, interviews, pleadings, and prior testimony. Important passages should be tabbed and/or highlighted for easy and quick reference. For important witnesses, a more detailed summary or outline of the witness's statement(s), with notes of where specific important passages are located, is important. For lengthy depositions, an index may be necessary. Before you can develop a strategy for cross-examination, you must first know the full *content* of all the witness's statements. Being organized is half the battle.

> **Trial Tip:** Having the witness's prior statements at your fingertips and organized is important for cross-examination. If a witness deviates from an earlier statement, the trial attorney must be able to quickly find that passage to confront the witness with the inconsistency.

Plan of Attack

Once the materials are organized, the next most important task is to develop a strategy and plan of attack, a short list of defined specific objectives to be accomplished by the examination. No cross-examination should ever begin unless there is a reason or an objective. Inexperienced or unprepared lawyers tend to launch into cross-examination without a plan or clear objective. They feel compelled to cross-examine a witness regarding nearly every fact related during direct examination, thereby giving the witness yet another opportunity to retell their version of the facts a second time. This mode of questioning essentially allows the witness to "ring the bell" one more time, or worse, permits the witness to expand on the direct testimony. When questioning is done in this manner, whatever helpful facts are established during cross-examination are lost because so much extraneous or unhelpful information is elicited, as the witness basically repeats the damaging direct testimony. Good cross-examiners, on the other hand, focus their questions only on a specific area or topic with the objective of establishing facts helpful *only* to the examiner's case. When the examiner achieves those objectives, the questioning ceases.

There are two basic objectives of cross-examination: (1) to undermine (impeach) the credibility of the witness and/or (2) to highlight facts which are either helpful to your case or damaging to your opponent's case. If neither of these two basic purposes can be achieved from the examination, then counsel should consider asking *no* questions.

Nearly every witness will have at least some weakness. Consider where those weaknesses lie and come up with a strategy. It might be something minor, such as the witness is related to a party, and exposing that relationship might show a bias. Or, it might be something major, such as the witness is lying. Create a laundry list of the weaknesses and the objectives you hope to accomplish before formulating the actual questions to ask. Having a well-defined set of objectives before you begin the examination will help you properly frame the questions and stay on task.

Furthermore, if one of your objectives is to cause the witness to break down and admit to a lie or even acknowledge a mistake, forget about it. It almost never happens. There will be no *Perry Mason* moment in a real courtroom. This is because no matter how compelling the evidence is to the contrary, people simply do not like to admit they are wrong, especially in a courtroom full of people. When backed into a corner and confronted with a mistake, inconsistency, or inaccuracy, most witnesses will merely attempt to explain it away by providing further explanation or elaboration.

Trial Tip: Prepare a written outline of questions to be covered during cross-examination. Trying to cross-examine on the fly is very difficult and often backfires. Every case should be prepared and tried with the closing argument in mind, including cross-examination.

Logical Progression

There must be some logic to the order of examination. During preparation, while thinking about your objectives, consider how to design the examination to get from point A to point B. Where to start and where to end? The primary consideration is always an examination the jurors can follow. If the examination skips around from topic to topic, or does not follow some logical path, the effectiveness is lost, as are the jurors.

One effective method of cross-examination is to start general and then work towards the specific. This permits the examiner to first lock in the witness regarding the uncontroverted foundational facts, and then move slowly inward towards the area of controversy. For example, first establish the nature of the relationship between a witness and a party, e.g., husband and wife, before moving towards questions that suggest the witness is biased because of that fact. In essence, the examiner surrounds the witness with a wall of foundational facts to prevent or foreclose any potential avenues of escape, such as a denial or an excuse.

Counsel: "You are nearsighted, aren't you?"

Counsel: "In fact, prior to the accident, you had been to an optometrist about your eyesight, hadn't you?"

Counsel: "The eye doctor prescribed glasses or contacts to wear, didn't he?"

Counsel: "Isn't it true that without your glasses, it's difficult for you to see very well when it's dark?"

The above questions first establish the condition of the witness's eyes *generally*, before any specific questions regarding whether her eyesight affected her ability to see on the night of the accident.

Counsel: "Now, when the accident occurred it was dark out, wasn't it?"

Counsel: "And at the time of the accident you were not wearing your glasses, were you?"

Counsel: "So, that made it difficult to see well, didn't it?"

In the above, even if the witness denies the last statement and claims she could see just fine, the earlier foundational facts established cast doubt on her credibility.

> **Trial Tip:** An effective tactic for cross is to begin at the weakest or most vulnerable point of the testimony, e.g., an inconsistency or other damaging evidence. In other words, come out swinging. This often causes the witness to tighten up and to react defensively. Close the examination similarly.

Short and Concise

Once you have identified your objectives, the next task is to formulate the questions. The best cross-examination is concise and surgical. Get in, elicit the facts you are after, and get out. Cross-examining a witness for hours or days concerning inconsequential points or details will only serve to dilute the strength of the facts established that are helpful to your case.

Experience has shown that often cross-examination is too long. Generally, in every trial there are only two or three key contested issues, and sometimes even fewer. Often the parties will agree on almost every issue with the exception of one or two. These contested issues or facts are where the cross-examination has to be focused. If you waste too much time covering uncontested ground, the importance of what you are trying to establish will be lost on the jury or the court. Remember that when examining any witness you are also up against the game clock, which is the jurors' limited attention span. Use your time wisely.

One of the preeminent experts on cross-examination techniques, the late professor of law, Irving Younger, described the concise nature of cross-examination this way: "I like to imagine that the juror has in his or her head a cup that can contain information. When we start the cross-examination we are pouring information into the cup. But, it's a small cup and it fills up quickly. And once it's filled up, nothing more will go in. So anything more that you try to do is a waste. But it's worse than that! If you try to put more into the cup that is already filled, guess what? It tips over and it spills out, so that it's empty, and they remember nothing." Professor Younger's point is that every question asked during cross-examination should mean something. Too many lawyers flounder around by asking meaningless questions or covering the same ground covered during direct.

Trial Tip: A rehash of direct testimony is *not* good cross-examination.

Leading Questions

During direct examination, the witness was permitted to essentially relate facts or information in a narrative format. During cross-examination, however, you are going to focus the jury on only selected portions of that story and only certain facts that you desire to highlight. You, and not the witness, are in control of the direction and content of the examination. Leading questions are the primary tool the trial lawyer will use to accomplish this task. A question is "leading" if it "suggests to the witness the answer the examining party requires." (*People v. Williams* (1997) 16 Cal.4th 635, at p. 672.) Below are the fundamental qualities of good cross-examination:

1. ***Short, simple, and concise*** – Each question must be short and concise, requiring the witness to admit or deny only *one* statement of fact at a time. Use simple words and phrases. Long, drawn out questions, even if followed with a tag line, not only invite confusion, but are also susceptible to objection by opposing counsel as "compound" or "vague." Worse yet, such a question may permit the witness to make a lengthy explanation. Keep it simple.

2. ***Witness affirms or denies*** – The object is to force the witness to either confirm or deny the statement of fact or information propounded by the examiner. Typically, the question requires the witness to answer with a "yes" or "no." The most common method is to use a simple "tag line" at the end or at the beginning of the facts stated.

a. (Beginning) "*Isn't it true*, the light was red when you approached the intersection?"

b. (End) "The light was red when you approached the intersection, *wasn't it?*" or "…isn't that true?" or "…*correct?*" or "…*right?*"

c. (Agreement with Statement) "*Would you agree* that by the time you looked up, the light was yellow?"

d. Avoid tag lines that create confusion or create double negatives. Example: "…Is it not true, that the light was red as you approached the intersection?"

Without a Tag Line

Sometimes, the use of the same or similar tag lines repeated over and over becomes distracting and even annoying to the jury. Some trial lawyers are good at propounding the statement of fact without the use of a tag line just by using voice inflection. A good technique is to mix it up a little. Example:

Counsel: "As you approached the intersection, you had your cell phone in your lap?"
Witness: "Yes."
Counsel: "You knew someone had just sent you a text, correct?"
Witness: "Yeah."
Counsel: "You were curious who was texting?"
Witness: "Well, yeah, I guess, but I didn't check."
Counsel: "Thank you, but the question was whether you were curious. You were wondering who it was that had just texted you, isn't that true?"
Witness: "Yes."

Trial Tip: The most common technical problem associated with poor cross-examination is that the question is too long. Generally, the shorter the statement of fact, the better.

Examples of simple, concise leading questions:
"You owned a cell phone at the time of the accident, correct?"
"And, you used your cell phone to send and receive text messages, right?"
"In fact, that's mainly how you communicated with your daughter, via text message, isn't that true?"
"Isn't it true, that at the time of the accident, the cell phone was with you in the car?"
"It was on your lap, wasn't it?"

"You were on your way to pick up your daughter, weren't you?"

"And running late, correct?"

"She was supposed to have texted you, but she hadn't?"

"So, as you were driving, you were waiting for her text, right?"

Examples of poorly worded leading questions:

"You were running late, which is why you had your cell on your lap, so
  you could see her text while you were driving, correct?"

    [Vague and ambiguous (confusing)]

"Why did you have your cell phone on your lap?"

  [Gives the witness carte blanche to explain. No tag line. Includes the "why?"
  word, a cardinal sin for cross.]

"Is it not true that you had your cell phone with you in the car that day, correct?"

    [Confusing. Double negative.]

"As you were driving, you had the cell phone on your lap, waiting for your
  daughter to text you and you looked down briefly to see if she had texted, correct?"

    [Compound question in that it sets forth three different factual propositions.]

Trial Tip: Good cross-examination first locks the witness down on uncontested facts to prevent an avenue of escape, and then moves on to the contested facts or issues.

Stick to the Plan – Save it for Closing

An important objective of cross-examination is to draw out facts and circumstances that undermine the witness's credibility, for example, facts that show the witness is biased. However, rather than confront or accuse the witness of being biased while on the stand, a better strategy might be to subtly establish the foundational facts and then later during argument, draw the ultimate conclusions for the jury; namely, that the witness should be discredited, and here's why. If you are too direct, the witness may attempt to explain it away and steal your thunder. During argument, if you call out the witness as a liar or biased, the witness is not there to talk back, so to speak. Similarly, when establishing an inconsistent statement, you may want to lay the groundwork for the inconsistency by showing what the witness said on a prior occasion versus now. However, rather than directly confront the witness with the inconsistency on the stand, which allows the witness an opportunity to explain it away, save that accusation for argument.

A mistake some lawyers make occurs when they initially score some good points during cross-examination, such as eliciting facts that suggest the witness has a bias, but then rather than ending the questioning when the point is made, they go for the *coup de grâce*. They ask one question too many, thereby permitting the witness the opportunity to explain it all away. The annals of courtroom testimony are replete with examples where attorneys should have ended their cross-examination after achieving their objectives, but instead yielded to the temptation to keep going. The end result of too many questions is often an unanticipated answer or the ringing of the proverbial bell just one more time. Resist the temptation to keep asking questions hoping for an admission or concession.

Another peril of continuing to press is the possibility of an unintended or unforeseen answer. This situation occurs most often when counsel ventures into uncharted waters and asks a witness to explain something when the answer in unknown. "Don't ask a question that you don't know the answer to" is the maxim taught in every law school trial advocacy class in America, but it is surprising how frequently trial lawyers still continue to violate this basic rule and get burned. This is where examiners impale themselves with their own swords, as forewarned by Professor Wigmore.

> **Trial Tip:** Stick to your planned objectives, and when you achieve them, sit down. Nearly every trial lawyer has experienced that awful moment when he or she asked one question too many and the witness gave an unexpected and damaging answer. Don't be tempted to go for the *coup de grâce.*

Use of Non-leading Questions

Although the general rule is to use only leading questions during cross-examination, as with any rule there are always exceptions. There can be circumstances where it might be helpful to flesh out factual details using more open-ended non-leading questions. Generally, this occurs when the questions concern less contested matters. For example, questions related to distances, positions, or locations might be explored by simply asking the witness to "explain" or provide more detail, without the use of leading questions. Similarly, open-ended questions requesting the witness to explain or clarify something from the direct testimony might be fine, as long as you are confident the answer will not hurt you.

> **Trial Tip:** Open-ended (non-leading) questions can be helpful during cross to quickly resolve less controverted matters.

The Devil is in the Detail

The use of open-ended, non-leading questions can also be *very* effective when the examiner believes the witness's testimony is patently false. Pointed questions requesting a witness to explain or provide greater detail can, in many instances, demonstrate the falsity of the testimony. It requires the lie to become more complex, which in turn can cause difficulty for the witness to create facts on the spot. Details can also highlight inconsistencies or incredulous scenarios. "The devil is in the detail" is an adage experienced trial lawyers know well. Some witnesses will lie by incorporating as much truth as possible and lie only where necessary. Requiring the witness to provide extreme detail on the fabricated portions of the story is where inconsistencies and falsities can be revealed.

For example, in the murder trial of *People vs. Mariet T. Ford*, a former college football star was accused of murdering his pregnant wife and son. Ford testified in his own defense and provided a factually complicated alibi. The prosecutor (the author) initially used leading questions during cross-examination to pin Ford down on damaging facts, such as his extramarital affairs. However, concerning his actions in the home on the morning of the murders, the prosecutor asked many open-ended questions requiring him to provide much detail. It was the incredulity of his complex and detailed story that ultimately convicted him.

Trial Tip: The use of open-ended questions during cross, which requests a witness to provide specific detail, can be very effective when the story is a patent lie. Further detail will only serve to entangle the witness in a web of lies.

What *Not* to Ask

Staying in control is critical during cross-examination. Unless you are willing to turn that control over to the witness, there are certain words or phrases that a cross-examiner should generally *never* use when questioning about contested issues. Two words that give a witness virtual carte blanche are, "Why?" and "How?" If you ask a witness to explain "why" or "how" something happened, you have just permitted the witness to say virtually anything. Other similar words or phrases are just as bad, for example, "what happened" ... "explain" ... "tell us" ... "please describe"..."clarify." All these words permit the witness to answer at will. For the same reason, avoid questions that call for the witness to give an opinion or to explain what they were thinking. The bottom line is to avoid any question that permits the witness to provide a lengthy explanation. This is why the use of tight, well-crafted leading questions is so important. However, it is sometimes easier said than done. Even the most veteran trial lawyers have experienced that helpless feeling at least once in their career when a witness has launched into a rambling diatribe of damaging testimony because counsel asked the question that permitted the answer. In this situation, all the trial lawyer can do is to sit there helplessly and think to him or herself, "*Why* did I ask that question?!"

Counsel: "You were interviewed by a police officer while at the scene of the accident, were you not?"

Witness: "Yes."

Counsel: "And the officer asked you questions about what had happened, isn't that true?"

Witness: "Yes."

Counsel: "And you answered his questions truthfully, correct?"

Witness: "Yes, the best I could."

Counsel: "Then why didn't you tell the officer that you had the green light, as you have testified today in court?"

Witness: "Well, I tried to, but he wouldn't listen. He was in a hurry. He said he had to go to another accident quickly and so he just scribbled a few notes and left. I mean, I told him everything that happened, but apparently, he didn't bother to write it down because he was too busy."

In this situation, the cross-examiner lost control by permitting the witness to explain away an apparent discrepancy.

Trial Tip: "Why?" or a similar question, will derail your cross-examination and permit the witness to respond at will with testimony which is usually not helpful to your case.

"No Questions, Your Honor."

If testimony during direct examination was largely irrelevant or inconsequential to the contested issues, what better method to telegraph that fact to the jury than to announce with a shrug, "No questions, Your Honor." However, for less experienced lawyers, it can be hard to let any witness go by without at least one question. Some trial lawyers feel compelled to cross-examine concerning immaterial or uncontested matters, which thereby permits the witness the opportunity to basically go back over the useless material once again. In the meantime, the jurors are watching. If you cross-examine a witness concerning irrelevant information, some jurors may think it *must* be important because *you* appeared to think it was! If the testimony does no harm, consider "No questions." Later, during your closing argument, you can explain to the jury the lack of importance of the witness's testimony and why you chose not to ask any questions. In the end, the jurors will appreciate that you are no nonsense, and it bolsters your credibility.

Trial Tip: "No questions, Your Honor," signals to the jury your view that the testimony has no importance to the contested issue. However, some lawyers have trouble saying those words.

Use of Exhibits

The strategic use of exhibits, such as photographs or diagrams, during cross-examination can be very effective to establish a fact or to clarify a point. For example, requesting that an eyewitness to an accident mark on an aerial photograph of the intersection where he or she was located at the time of the accident may reveal the witness was not as close as described. Many witnesses are poor judges of distances and pictures may help clarify this. However, the effective use of exhibits takes some pre-planning. Good trial lawyers will have considered beforehand the best time to produce the exhibit, how the exhibit will be displayed, and how the witness will be instructed to mark on the exhibit.

Counsel: "Showing you Exhibit 47, do you recognize this as a photograph of the intersection of Lincoln Way and Maple Street?"

Witness: "Yes."

Counsel: "Do you see where you were standing just before the accident occurred?"

Witness: "Yes, I was right over there [indicating], standing on the sidewalk."

Counsel: "You're pointing to the top right-hand portion of the photograph, at the sidewalk on the north side of the street, is that correct?"

Witness: "Yes."

Counsel: "Using this blue marker, I'm going to mark on exhibit forty-seven your initials, GH1, right here on the sidewalk. Did I accurately mark where you were standing when the accident occurred?"

Witness: "Yes."

Counsel: "Okay. Thank you. You testified that moments before the accident, you looked up and saw a blue car traveling north on Lincoln, is that correct?"

Witness: "Yes."

Counsel: "Referring to Exhibit 47 again, can you point to where you first saw the blue car, the location of the car when you first saw it?"

Witness: "It was coming down Lincoln Way right here [indicating] and then passed into the intersection."

Counsel: "You pointed on the photograph to Lincoln Way just before the limit line for the intersection. Is that correct?"

Witness: "Yes."

Counsel: "That's where you first saw the blue car?"

Witness: "Yes."

Counsel: "Okay, using the blue marker, I'm going to put the initials BC for blue car, where you indicated. Did I mark it correctly?"

Witness: "Yes."

In the above, notice that the examiner is the one doing the actual marking, which helps to keep the markings clear and simple. There is no requirement that the witness must do the actual marking so long as the witness confirms the markings are correctly placed. Also, note that the examiner is stating out loud where the witness was pointing. This makes a good record.

> **Trial Tip:** If, during direct-examination, the witness makes an estimate of distance you believe to be inaccurate, consider using an aerial/satellite photograph to have the witness show specifically where things were located. Witnesses frequently misjudge distances. Demonstrating that a witness was actually 150 feet away, rather than 50, as the witness estimated, may cast doubt on reliability.

Witness Control Techniques

To maintain witness control during cross-examination requires that the witness must answer only the specific question you propound and *not* provide any other information or comment. However, this is often easier said than done. Some witnesses are openly combative, hostile, and noncompliant, while others will refuse to be pinned down by dodging and weaving their way around each question. One of the most common issues encountered is when the witness will respond, but then attempt to add further explanation or embellishment beyond what was requested. The leading question, which requires only a "yes" or "no" type response, is designed to prevent this, but many witnesses are adept at trying to get around it.

Counsel: "The light was red as you approached the intersection, wasn't it?"
Witness: "Well, yes, but I knew it was going to turn green. I think there was something wrong with the light."

Counsel: "As you approached the intersection, your cell phone was on your lap, wasn't it?"
Witness: "Yeah, but I wasn't texting, if that's what your implying."

Counsel: "Doctor, isn't it true that the plaintiff had a preexisting injury to her lower back from a previous fall?"
Witness: "That preexisting injury was seven years ago and not the cause of the pain she is now experiencing."

Counsel: "After the accident, you talked with your sister about the case, didn't you?"
Witness: "My sister has nothing to do with this."

In each example, either the witness answered the question, but then added more information than requested, or simply did not answer the question at all, but provided unrequested information. When this happens, control is lost. When these scenarios occur, which they will, to maintain control you must take some decisive action.

> **Trial Tip:** Like training a new puppy, it is important to react and scold at the *first* instance of noncompliance. An immediate reaction often tends to make the witness more compliant and sends the message that you're not going to let them get away with it.

Repeat and Admonish

The very *first* time the witness misbehaves, you need to react as soon as the infraction occurs. Whether it is an admonition or a repeating of the question, the witness needs to know the rules. This helps set the tone and lets the witness know who is in charge. Do not wait and let the witness get away with it for five minutes before you finally decide to do something. Begin your training of the witness with the least show of force, so to speak, and then ratchet it up from there.

When the witness does not answer the question or attempts to add further information, the first tactic is simply to interrupt and/or to repeat the question with an admonishment. If the witness's answer is unresponsive or begins to go beyond the question posed, it may be necessary to interrupt the witness. Simply raising a hand as a signal to "stop," with an admonition to listen to the question, is often effective. For example, "Thank you, you've answered the question" or "Let me stop you right there, you've answered the question." At this stage, it generally pays to be polite and courteous, even if you feel the witness is deliberately attempting to embellish.

Counsel might also admonish the witness to just answer the question. "Thank you, but that wasn't the question. The question was…" or "Please listen to the question: The light was red when you entered the intersection, yes or no?" Some judges may not like the attorneys admonishing a witness, but most will permit it *if* the attorney is being courteous *and* the witness is clearly not answering the questions.

Counsel: "Now, that morning, before the accident, you were waiting for your daughter to text you about whether she needed a ride home, weren't you?"
Witness: "She never did."
Counsel: [repeat and admonish] "Thank you, but the question was, before the accident, you were waiting for your daughter to text you about whether she needed a ride home. Yes or No? Please just answer the question."
Witness: "She was supposed to, but she never did."
Counsel: "Is that a yes?"
Witness: "Yes."

In the above, the examiner was polite, but firm. If necessary, repeat the exact question two or three times, until the witness finally relents with a 'yes' or 'no.' In the meantime, the court and jurors are observing this and the witness's credibility rating is going downhill.

> **Trial Tip:** Some attorneys maintain good witness control merely by the tone of their voice and the simple act of raising a hand to signal the witness to stop. "Let me stop you right there, the question was...." Remain polite, but firm. Again, the witness needs to know you are in charge.

Objection with Motion to Strike

If the witness persists in either not responding to the question or adding more than requested, the next tactic is to make a formal objection to the court: *"Objection, Your Honor, nonresponsive, move to strike."* (See Nonresponsive Answers, supra, at p. 63, 236.) It is appropriate for the questioner to object to unresponsive answers and move to strike unresponsive testimony. (*In re Rosoto* (1974) 10 C.3d 939, 949.) A formal objection, followed by the court's ruling, often startles the witness, and they will generally become more compliant afterwards. In addition, when the judge weighs in and sustains the objection, striking the answer, it signals to the jury that even the judge feels the witness is being uncooperative.

Counsel: "You had your cell phone in your hand as you approached the intersection, isn't that true?"
Witness: "As I said, I wasn't texting."
Counsel: "Objection, Your Honor, the answer is *nonresponsive*. Move to strike."
Court: "Sustained. The answer is stricken."
Counsel: "The question was, you had your cell phone in your hand as you approached the intersection. Yes or no?"
Witness: "Yes, but I wasn't texting."
Counsel: "Objection, unresponsive, and I would move to have the answer stricken after her response 'Yes.'"
Court: "Granted."

Request the Court for Assistance

Every once in a while, you are going to encounter a particularly difficult witness; a witness who is combative and noncompliant in response to nearly every question. In this circumstance, after repeated admonishments, consider turning to the court for assistance. Surprisingly, many trial lawyers seem reluctant or unsure of this procedure.

Counsel: "Objection, Your Honor, unresponsive and move to strike the answer. May the court admonish the witness to only answer the questions?"

If it is true that the witness is being difficult and not responding, typically the judge will turn towards the witness with an admonishment to listen carefully and to answer only the questions posed. If the witness persists, the court might even take a more stern approach and make a specific order to answer appropriately. This generally destroys whatever credibility the witness may have had beforehand.

Caution: The most important aspect of this process is to ensure that your question is properly framed to require only a "yes" or "no" answer. If, in the court's opinion, the question cannot be answered with a simple "yes" or "no," the court may overrule the objection and permit the witness to answer. Again, this is why the question must be simple and short. Some judges are more apt to sustain unresponsive objections than others. Some judges may take a more hands-off approach. Get a feel for the court's temperament and attitude regarding leading questions. In any event, when a witness is being truly hostile and non-compliant and you remain professional, the jury gets it and you have made your point. During argument, remind them of the witness's attitude and how it demonstrated the witness's obvious bias.

Trial Tip: Be confident your question is properly framed such that it requires only a "yes" or "no" answer. If the question is compound, poorly worded, or simply cannot be answered with a simple "yes" or "no," the court will likely overrule your objection and motion to strike and permit the witness to answer, making *you* look like the bad guy.

Questions or Comments back to Counsel

Occasionally you will run into the particularly difficult witness who will talk back or make gratuitous comments. The witness might respond to a question by asking counsel a question: "Why are you asking me that, anyway!?" or "Is that answer good enough for you!?" The key here is to remain calm and not be tempted to respond to a question or comment by the witness. The first tactic is simply to ignore the comment and to calmly proceed on with the questioning. However, if it gets bad enough, do not hesitate to ask the court for assistance. Responding to a hostile witness only invites further conflict and looks unprofessional to the jury. Remember, the jurors are observing both the witness's attitude and yours.

Counsel: "The light was red as you approached the intersection, wasn't it?"

Witness: "Are you suggesting that I ran the red light, counsel? You know that's not true!"

Counsel: "Objection, unresponsive. I move to strike. And, Your Honor, I would request the court admonish the witness to just answer the questions."

Demeanor and Tone

Cross-examining difficult witnesses can be exasperating and frustrating work, and you may naturally feel irritated and annoyed as your blood pressure rises. Some witnesses may deliberately attempt to push your buttons. However, remember the jury (and the court) has been watching the entire spectacle. They see what is going on and how the witness is being uncooperative and evasive. In this respect, your cross-examination has succeeded, even if no real factual points were established. However, some attorneys stoop to the witness's level by also becoming rude or condescending, which only hurts your credibility in the eyes of the jury. If you remain cool, calm, and collected, even in the face of an uncooperative witness, your credibility is enhanced. The jurors expect you to remain professional. Becoming angry, losing your temper, or making insulting comments only means you have lost control.

How you conduct the examination is also important. The cadence of your questions, the tone of your voice, and the forcefulness of your questions will naturally depend upon the type of witness and the issues. For example, how you cross-examine an 80-year-old woman with memory issues will be completely different than a convicted felon spinning a lie. If you call out the 80-year-old as a liar, it may offend the jury. Likewise, cross-examining sympathetic witnesses, such as a person severely injured in a car crash, can be challenging, especially when their testimony is critical and requires extensive questioning. This is when you want to be careful not to offend the jurors. However, you can still ask probing and important questions without offending the jurors if you use the appropriate demeanor and tone. For example, consider whether it is wise to imply a witness is lying versus mistaken. Jurors can more easily accept mistakes than lies, unless the evidence is irrefutable, especially if the witness is sympathetic.

> **Trial Tip:** Taking notes during direct testimony to use for cross-examination is important. Some trial lawyers divide a sheet of legal paper down the middle, taking rough notes of the direct testimony on one side and penciling out potential areas of cross on the other. On the other hand, you don't want to be writing copious, verbatim notes with your head down and risk missing something important the witness just said.

Scope of Cross-Examination

"Cross-examination is the examination of a witness by a party other than the direct examiner upon a matter that is within the scope of the direct examination of the witness." (CA Evid. Code § 761.) "A witness examined by one party may be cross-examined upon any matter within the scope of the direct examination by each other party to the action in such order as the court directs." (CA Evid. Code §

773(a).) "The cross-examination of a witness by any party whose interest is not adverse to the party calling him is subject to the same rules that are applicable to the direct examination." (CA Evid. Code § 773(b).) "Cross-examination should not go beyond the subject matter of the direct examination and matters affecting the witness's credibility. The court may allow inquiry into additional matters as if on direct examination." (FRE Rule 611(b).) Cross-examination may embrace any matter germane to direct examination, qualifying or destroying it, or tending to elucidate, modify, explain, contradict or rebut testimony given by the witness. (*United States v. Hiland,* 909 F.2d 1114, 1132–33 (8th Cir.1990) (quoting *Roberts v. Hollocher,* 664 F.2d 200, 203 (8th Cir.1981))."); *U.S. v. Lara,* 181 F.3d 183, 199 (1st Cir. 1999).) In practice, if you feel the questioning is going beyond your direct examination, an objection should be considered. (See Trial Objections, "Beyond the Scope," infra, at p. 242.)

Counsel: "Objection, Your Honor, beyond the scope of direct."

This might occur when the examiner seems to be headed towards facts or circumstances not raised in the direct examination and seemingly unconnected or unrelated to the contested issues. However, if during direct examination, you purposefully tried to avoid asking the witness about something unfavorable concerning credibility, hoping to avoid cross-examination on the topic by opposing counsel, most judges are going to side with the opposing party and allow it. On the other hand, if the questioning is related to a "collateral matter," the court might also invoke Rule 352 and limit the questioning. (See Collateral Matters on Impeachment, infra, at p. 128.)

Is The Door Open?

It is not uncommon that a witness on direct examination will say something that opposing counsel may feel has "opened the door," thereby permitting further cross-examination on that topic. If mentioned on direct examination, most courts will permit wide latitude about the subject matter on cross. However, if the subject matter was objectionable and opposing counsel did not object, hoping to cross-examine about collateral matter, the court may sustain an objection. "By allowing objectionable evidence to go in without objection, the non-objecting party gains no right to the admission of related or additional otherwise inadmissible testimony. The so-called 'open the door' or 'open the gates' argument is a popular fallacy." (*People v. Gambos* (1970) 5 Cal.App.3d 187, 192; *People v. Morrison* (2011) 199 Cal.App.4th 158, fn. 4.) The notion that such a rule opened the door exists has been labeled a popular fallacy and rejected by courts and commentators alike. (*People v. Morrison* (2011) 199 Cal.App.4th 158, fn. 4.)

The court in *Valadez v. Watkins Motor Lines, Inc* 758 F.3d 975, 981 (8th Cir. 2014), summarized the rule: "The doctrine of opening the door allows a party to explore otherwise inadmissible evidence on cross-examination when the opposing party has made unfair prejudicial use of related evidence on direct examination. In theory, the admission of inadmissible evidence allows the injured party to cure the problem and clear up the false impression or to clarify or complete an issue opened up by opposing counsel. But the door is not opened to all similar, inadmissible evidence. Rather, the evidence introduced in response must rebut something that had been elicited....The doctrine of opening the door cannot 'be subverted into a rule for injection of prejudice." (*Valadez v. Watkins Motor Lines, Inc* 758 F.3d 975, 981 8th Cir. 2014; See also *United States v. Durham*, 868 F.2d 1010, 1012 (8th Cir.1989).)

Are Witnesses Lying?

Some lawyers like to ask a witness to opine whether other witnesses are lying or mistaken. However, generally this type of question requires the witness to speculate. "A witness with no personal knowledge of the facts may not make an opinion that another person is lying. Such opinions are of little assistance in deciding the credibility of testimony by percipient witnesses who do have personal knowledge. There is a difference between asking a witness whether, in his opinion, another is lying and asking that witness whether he knows of a reason why another would be motivated to lie. It is also improper on cross to ask if other witnesses were lying or "everybody is lying except you?" as it calls for speculations." (*People v. Zambrano* (2004) 124 Cal.App.4th 228, 238.) However, in *People v. Chatman* (2006) 38 Cal.4th 344, the court held it was permissible to ask the defendant whether he knew of facts that would show a witness's testimony might be inaccurate or mistaken, or whether he knew of any bias, interest, or motive for a witness to be untruthful. Because the defendant put his own veracity in issue, the cross-examination was a legitimate inquiry to clarify the defendant's position. The questions sought to elicit testimony that would properly assist the trier of fact in ascertaining whom to believe. (*Chatman*, supra, at p. 383.)

In practice, most judges would likely not permit one witness to speculate about the truthfulness or untruthfulness of another witness or party, as the opinion is clearly speculation and also probably not relevant. And yet, this type of testimony occurs with some regularity.

Counsel: "Officer, did you have any reason to believe my client was not telling you the truth?"… "Officer, did the defendant's story make sense to you?"… "Did you believe the witness?"

Trial Tip: At the risk of being repetitious, the most effective cross-examination follows a pre-determined strategy, uses short, concise questions, and maintains witness control. The most common mistakes are poorly worded questions, rehashing the direct testimony without purpose, and losing control of the witness.

---

8. IMPEACHMENT

Impeachment is the process of establishing certain facts or circumstances that may tend to cast doubt upon the credibility or believability of a witness's testimony. It is virtually anything that might cause the jury (or the court) to question whether the witness is mistaken, exaggerating, or untruthful. In *Davis v. Alaska* (1974) 415 U.S. 308, 316, 94 S.Ct. 1105, the Supreme Court observed: "Cross-examination is the principal means by which the believability of a witness and the truth of his testimony are tested. Subject always to the broad discretion of a trial judge to preclude repetitive and unduly harassing interrogation, the cross-examiner is not only permitted to delve into the witness's story to test the witness's perceptions and memory, but the cross-examiner has traditionally been allowed to *impeach*, e.g., discredit, the witness."

In the previous chapter, the mechanics and strategies for cross-examination were discussed. This chapter and the subsequent chapter on Inconsistent Statements will discuss various strategies and common areas for witness "impeachment." Cross-examination is the primary tool you will use to carry out the intended impeachment. However, successful impeachment does not necessarily mean that in every case it will be shown the witness is a bald-faced liar. Rather, more commonly, it means the elicitation of subtle facts and circumstances that may tend to show the witness has a bias, is exaggerating, mistaken, or merely misremembers an event. The role of the trial lawyer during trial, therefore, is to skillfully expose for the jury and/or the court all the circumstances that *may* affect a witness's credibility—to plant the seed of doubt.

> **Trial Tip:** If there's nothing relevant to impeach a witness with, "No questions, Your Honor," may be the response.

Your Own Witness

Generally you will be attempting to "impeach" your opponent's witnesses; however, on occasion you may need to impeach a witness you called in your case-in-chief. You do not get to pick and choose your witnesses and, therefore, it is not uncommon that the party calling the witness may need to discredit or impeach that witness for some reason. For example, if you believe your witness now misremembers an event, yet provided a more accurate prior statement, you may want to "impeach" the witness with that inconsistency to show the earlier statement is more reliable. In some instances, just to prove your case, you may need to call a witness or two that you know will be "hostile" and/or uncooperative, for example, the adverse party in a civil trial or recanting witness/victim in a criminal case. CA Evid. Code Rule § 785 (below) makes it clear that any party may attack the credibility of any witness, regardless of which party actually calls the witness to the stand.

> **CA Evid. Code § 785. Parties may attack or support credibility (FRE Rule 607)**
>
> The credibility of a witness may be attacked or supported by any party, including the party calling him.

What and Where to Attack

The first step towards successful impeachment is to identify the area(s) of potential impeachment *before* cross-examination begins. In some cases, you may have weeks or months to prepare prior to trial. In other cases, you may only have minutes. Regardless, nearly every witness, to one degree or another, will have some weakness or vulnerability. Some will have many serious and obvious credibility issues, while others will have practically none. The task for the trial lawyers is to identity what they are and expose them.

When considering a strategy for impeachment of any witness, a good starting point is to review California Evidence Code section 780 (below), which sets forth a pretty good laundry-list of factors related to witness credibility. In fact, these criteria are also incorporated into a jury instruction. (See CALCRIM 226.)

> **Evid. Code § 780 Testimony; proof of truthfulness; consideration**
>
> Except as otherwise provided by statute, the court or jury may consider in determining the credibility of a witness any matter that has any tendency in reason to prove or disprove the truthfulness of his testimony at the hearing, including but not limited to any of the following:
>
> (a) His demeanor while testifying and the manner in which he testifies.
> (b) The character of his testimony.
> (c) The extent of his capacity to perceive, to recollect, or to communicate any matter about which he testifies.
> (d) The extent of his opportunity to perceive any matter about which he testifies.
> (e) His character for honesty or veracity or their opposites.
> (f) The existence or nonexistence of a bias, interest, or other motive.
> (g) A statement previously made by him that is consistent with his testimony at the hearing.
> (h) A statement made by him that is inconsistent with any part of his testimony at the hearing.
> (i) The existence or nonexistence of any fact testified to by him
> (j) His attitude toward the action in which he testifies or toward the giving of testimony.
> (k) His admission of untruthfulness.

> **Trial Tip:** For each material witness, prepare a list of potential areas of impeachment *before* creating an outline for cross-examination.

To help with your preparation and for the sake of discussion here, these section 780 factors (above) can be further divided into four categories: (1) Perception and Memory, (2) Bias and Motive, (3) Inconsistent Statements, and (4) Character.

Perception and Memory

Other than perhaps "expert" witnesses, people are summoned to court and expected to remember and describe something they perceived in the past with at least one of their five senses. It could have been an accident they witnessed or a conversation they overheard. Because the event they are describing occurred in the past, the witness is relying on memory to relate what happened. Given that human beings are not recording machines, it is plain to see that courtroom testimony has the potential of becoming totally distorted from reality because errors can happen anywhere along the continuum between the initial perception to the later recitation in the courtroom. Memory research has demonstrated that memory is complex and frequently inaccurate. First, the initial observation or perception may have been inaccurate due to distances, weather conditions, lighting, or the witness's physical or mental state at the time, e.g., the witness was intoxicated. Secondly, there could be issues regarding the witness's ability and mental capacity to accurately remember and describe what happened. The mere passage of time can erode memory. Some people naturally have good recall, while others can hardly remember what they ate for breakfast that day. In addition, the witness's own biases or prejudices can color perception, including what the witness has been told or learned after the fact. Lastly, witnesses must also have the ability to communicate (testify) and express themselves clearly in order for the memory to have much meaning. Thus, as can be seen, there are many subtle and complex human and social factors that can affect the quality and credibility of testimony when it comes to perception and memory. The attorney's role during cross-examination is to expose for the jury (or the court) any of these potential flaws to get them at least thinking about these credibility issues.

> **Trial Tip:** Highlight for the jury any fact or circumstance that may tend to show the witness may have misperceived the event. In this instance, the object is not to call out the witness as a liar, but rather to raise the possibility of an innocent mistake or misrecollection. Therefore, the tone of cross-examination should be less confrontational.

Mental State

The mental state of a witness at the time of the event is almost always relevant concerning the accuracy and reliability of testimony. Was the witness under stress, excited, fearful, tired, sleepy, inattentive, or perhaps even mentally unstable? A witness may be cross-examined about her mental condition or emotional stability to the extent it may affect her powers of perception, memory or recollection, or communication. (*People v. Herring* (1993) 20 Cal.App.4th 1066, 1072.) Studies have shown that stress and excitement can affect perception and memory. In criminal cases, the defense is permitted to call an expert witness to explain the problems associated with witness identification, and there is a jury instruction listing factors the jury may consider. (See *People v. McDonald* (1984) 37 Cal.3d 351, 377; CALCRIM 315.) It can be as simple as showing the witness was tired or exhausted, and thus not paying attention.

Counsel: "You work at the hospital as a nurse?"
Witness: "Yes."
Counsel: "And you were on your way home from work when the accident
            happened, correct?"
Witness: "That's right."
Counsel: "You had just finished a twelve-hour night shift, is that correct?"
Witness: "Yes."
Counsel: "You had been up all-night working?"
Witness: "Yes."
Counsel: "In fact, you had been up for more than twenty-four hours without
            sleep before the accident, isn't that true."
Witness: "Yes."
Counsel: "It is fair to say you were pretty tired that night?"
Witness: "Yes."

In the above, these simple questions suggest that perhaps the witness was not as attentive as usual due to fatigue. In addition, if there was evidence the witness was hysterical or emotional at the scene, several questions about her emotional state at that time may help establish that it affected her ability to be objective.

Some witnesses may have mental health issues that could possibly affect perception or memory, for example, a person with dementia. However, this is an area where counsel should proceed cautiously because many people suffer from mental health issues that have no effect on their credibility. Counsel might be wise to raise this issue to the court, outside the presence of the jury, before examination begins. "A witness may be cross-examined on mental instability, if such illness affects the witness's ability to perceive, recall, or describe the events in question." (*People v. Gurule* (2002) 28 Cal.4th 557, 591-592; *People v. Herring* (2005) 36 Cal.4th 96, 116-117.) However, "…it is a fact of modern life that many people experience emotional problems, undergo therapy, and take medications for their conditions. A person's credibility is not in question merely because he or she is receiving treatment for a mental health problem." (*People v. Anderson* (2001) 25 Cal.4th 543, 579; see also *U.S. v. Jimenez*, 256 F.3d 330, 343 (5th Cir. 2001), for a summary of cases permitting or excluding evidence of mental illness related to witness impeachment.)

Drugs and/or Alcohol Use

Alcohol and/or drugs at the time of the event is almost always relevant to memory and perception. Some witnesses may even come to court while under the influence. Cross-examination about the amount and nature of the drugs or alcohol ingested can make for good impeachment, e.g., how much was used and when. However, evidence of habitual narcotics use is not admissible to impeach perception or memory unless there is expert testimony on the probable affect of such use on those faculties. (*People v. Wilson* (2014) 44 Cal.4th 758, 794.)

Counsel: "After you left work that evening and prior to the accident, you stopped at the Short Stop bar for a drink, didn't you?"

Witness: "Just a few."

Counsel: "You were there for about an hour, correct?"

Witness: "About that."

Counsel: "And you had three to four beers during that time, didn't you?"

Witness: "I'm not sure."

Counsel: "Well, at your deposition, prior to trial, do you remember testifying that you had at least three or maybe four beers? Does that help refresh your recollection?"

Witness: "Yeah. I guess so."

Counsel: "And, shortly after you finished your last beer, you hit the road, didn't you?"

Witness: "Yes."

Counsel: "And the accident happened just a few minutes after you left, isn't that true?"

Witness: "Yes."

Counsel: "Now, were you feeling the effects of the beers at the time of the accident?"

Witness: "Oh, no. Not at all."

Counsel: "Nothing?"

Witness: "Nope."

Counsel: "You're sober now, aren't you?"

Witness: "Of course."

Counsel: "So, is it your testimony that after three or four beers, you were as sober then, as you are today?"

Witness: "Yep."

In the above, the examiner could have stopped before asking the ultimate question of whether the witness felt the effects. If the examiner already knew or guessed beforehand the answer would be "no," then it was a tactical decision whether to proceed with more open-ended questions. However, the claim to have been completely sober, in light of having consumed three or four beers, may itself have cast some doubt on the testimony.

Memory

The ability of the witness to accurately recall is obviously important. The examiner's objective here is to highlight the possibility that the witness's memory is flawed. The mere passage of time is one of the most common reasons why people forget or make mistakes. One method to highlight forgetfulness is to ask the witness to recall certain facts and details that are n*ot* in controversy, for example, what the witness did the day before or the day after. Typically, the witness will be unable to remember smaller details, which may show the witness's memory is hazy or confused. In effect, you are testing the witness's memory right in front of the jury regarding something the witness would not have been expecting.

Counsel: "This accident happened nearly two years ago, correct?"
Witness: "Correct."
Counsel: "Do you remember what you were doing earlier that day, a couple hours before the accident, for example?"
Witness: "I think I went to the grocery store."
Counsel: "Do you remember what you bought?"
Witness: "Hmm, I'm not sure."
Counsel: "Do you remember what day of the week the accident happened?"
Witness: "It could have been a Thursday…or it might have been Tuesday, I'm not sure."
Counsel: "Do you remember what you were wearing?"
Witness: "No."

If the witness's memory is generally hazy and vague concerning some of the details, but surprisingly clear when it comes to those facts helpful only to one party's position, it may indicate the witness is not being truthful. Design your cross to highlight this apparent anomaly. In addition, pay close attention to the witness's *earliest* statement, e.g., a statement to a police officer at the scene of the accident. Contrast that statement to what the witness said at her deposition and now at trial. If there are any differences, the inconsistencies *must* be highlighted. This may tend to show, at the very least, that the witness's memory has been evolving and changing. The fact that a witness's story has changed over time is potentially a very damaging impeachment.

Trial Tip: Demonstrating that the witness's memory has changed or evolved over time, even for innocent reasons, e.g., the passage of time, is a good strategy for impeachment.

Counsel: "You testified earlier today that as you made the left-hand turn in the intersection, you had your turn signal on, correct?"
Witness: "That's correct."
Counsel: "And you're certain you put the signal on before starting the turn?"

Witness: "Positive."

Counsel: "Now, right after the accident, you spoke to a police officer about what happened, correct?"

Witness: "Yes."

Counsel: "And, he asked you to tell him what happened, correct?"

Witness: "Yes."

Counsel: "You tried to be as accurate and as truthful with him as you could, I assume?"

Witness: "Yes, but I was very upset."

Counsel: "It was just a few minutes after the accident when he talked with you, wasn't it?"

Witness: "Yes, I guess so."

Counsel: "Do you remember telling the officer at that time that you weren't sure if put your turn signal on?"

Witness: "No, I don't remember saying that."

Counsel: "Would reviewing your statement to the police officer perhaps refresh your memory?"

Witness: "It might."

[Counsel "refreshes" the witness's memory with the writing by permitting her to review her statement. See Recollection Refreshed, supra, at p. 70.]

Counsel: "Does reading that help to you remember what you told the officer?"

Witness: "Yes. Kind of."

Counsel: "That day, you told the officer that you weren't sure whether you signaled, didn't you?"

Witness: "I guess I did. Yes."

In the above circumstance, counsel is not necessarily attempting to paint the witness as a liar, but rather, merely pointing out that the passage of time has eroded or clouded her memory. The fact that she was not certain at the scene of the accident, but now more certain in court, demonstrates her memory has been altered.

Trial Tip: Your demeanor and tone with the witness is important. Jurors may be put off if you attack a witness as a liar, when it's only innocent misrecollection, especially if the witness is sympathetic.

Information Received Prior to Testimony

When there is some traumatic event, such as a traffic accident or a crime, followed by a lawsuit or a prosecution, it is only natural that witnesses and participants will talk freely about it with people they know, such as family members, friends, colleagues, and other witnesses. More modernly, people now also post information on the internet about such things for the world to see. However, exchanging information or listening to gossip or inaccurate information can sometimes color and perhaps even change a person's memory of an event. For example, if at the time of an accident a witness is not sure whether her light was green, but later discusses with other witnesses their memories of the accident, it may create, in essence, a collective memory. The witness may use another person's memories to help validate her own belief regarding whether she, in fact, had the green light. Later, when she testifies, the witness may appear certain even though immediately following the accident, before she spoke with anyone, she was uncertain. Again, the cross-examiner is not necessarily trying to show collusion between witnesses, but how all the information received by the witness has affected memory and perception. On the other hand, the fact that a witness has talked with other witnesses or parties prior to trial may also show a more sinister motive—suggesting an effort to "get their stories straight."

Trial Tip: Questioning a witness regarding what information the witness has received or learned prior to testimony can be a good strategy. Who has the witness talked with, when did they talk, and what was discussed? Has the witness reviewed any reports, records, or researched anything about the case? (Remember your right to demand inspection and/or introduce a writing used to refresh recollection. EC 771, supra, at p. 72.)

As mentioned, it is not uncommon for witnesses to have exchanged or compared stories with other witnesses, interested parties, or family members. Furthermore, the witness may have reviewed related materials, such as police reports, medical records, or even the deposition transcripts of other witnesses. The witness may even have "Googled" issues related to the trial. Lastly, the witness may have discussed the matter and their testimony with an attorney, particularly if the witness is a party. While it may be improper to question the witness regarding what was said during the meeting due to the attorney/client privilege, the fact that the witness has consulted with an attorney may shed some light on the witness's embroilment in the controversy. In some cases, however, there could be an argument that the witness has waived the privilege depending on the witness's testimony during the direct examination. (See *U.S. v. Bilzerian* 926 F.2d 1285, 1292 (2nd Cir. 1991) ["The attorney-client privilege cannot at once be used as a shield and a sword."].)

Witness: "I'm certain I had the green light."
Counsel: "Now, your daughter was with you in the car when the accident happened, correct?"
Witness: "Yes."
Counsel: "And immediately after the accident, you and your daughter talked about what happened, didn't you."

Witness: "Well, yes."

Counsel: "And since the accident, you have discussed with her what happened, haven't you?"

Witness: "Occasionally."

Counsel: "Now, isn't it true that while at the scene of the accident, you told an officer that you thought the light was green, but you weren't sure?"

Witness: "I think I was in shock."

Counsel: "You don't deny making that statement at that time, do you?"

Witness: "No."

Counsel: "And prior to today, you've reviewed the police reports and the statements of what other witnesses claimed to have seen, haven't you?"

Witness: "Yes."

Counsel: "And you talked to your daughter about what she remembered, haven't you?"

Witness: "Maybe, a little."

Counsel: "When was the last time you talked with her about the case?"

Witness: "A few weeks ago."

In the above, the witness appears to have had some uncertainty at the time of the accident, but now at trial, after speaking with her daughter and reading what other witness's reported, she is more certain. Point made.

Furthermore, despite the fact that it can be perfectly normal for people to have discussed with others a memorable event or to have done some on-line research, when asked on the witness stand whether they have *ever* discussed the case with anyone or researched anything, surprisingly, many witnesses will deny it. Even family members will deny having ever talked about the facts of the case with other family members, even though it seems implausible. Some witnesses seem to think that it is improper or forbidden for them to have talked with anyone about the case before trial and the witness is overly concerned about how it might look, especially when the cross-examiner's tone suggests it is something nefarious. However, a total denial often looks even more suspicious.

Counsel: "The plaintiff in this case is your sister, correct?"

Witness: "Yes."

Counsel: "Prior to coming to court today, have you and your sister ever talked about your testimony?"

Witness: "Not really."

Counsel: "Did she tell you what to say?"

Witness: "No."

Counsel: "Have you discussed with her any facts about the case?"

Witness: "No, we don't talk about it."

Note: Asking any witness what was said during a conversation can be risky because the examiner is essentially flying in the dark. The witness could respond with an answer you do not like.

Memory Getting Better?

Every trial lawyer will encounter a witness whose memory seems to improve at trial. The witness will miraculously recall specific details of things helpful to the case, but then get vague and fuzzy when questioned about unhelpful details. In this circumstance, the goal is to highlight for the jury the fact that the witness apparently has selective memory. One method is to contrast what they claim to remember now versus what was remembered previously and how they differ.

Counsel: "On direct examination you testified that you now specifically
    remember that you braked before entering the intersection, is that
    correct?"

Witness: "Yes."

Counsel: "However, isn't it true that at your deposition, about nine months ago, you
    testified that you didn't remember whether you braked before
    entering the intersection?"

Witness: "Well, I've been giving it a lot of thought since then and it's coming back
    to me in bits and pieces."

Counsel: "So, you testified at the deposition that you didn't remember if you
    applied the brakes, correct?"

Witness: "Yes."

Counsel: "You also didn't mention that fact to the police officer on the day
    of the accident, did you?"

Witness: "No. He didn't ask."

Counsel: "So, now it seems your memory has improved, at least since the
    deposition?"

Witness: "Well, I've been giving it a lot of thought lately."

In the above, you may also wish to explore a motive for why the witness's memory seems to be improving. The witness might also be questioned about her specific memory of other details to see if it has improved there too. Chances are that it has not.

> **Trial Tip:** Selective memory, where the witness can recall specific helpful facts, but has a hard time recalling unhelpful facts, is not uncommon. Highlighting this fact will undermine the witness's credibility.

Physical/Environmental Conditions

Any physical or environmental impediment or condition that could have affected the witness's ability to accurately perceive the event can be a fertile area for impeachment. Depending on the circumstances, cross-examination concerning the time of day, lighting conditions, weather conditions, distances, and spatial relationships might be relevant. Was the witness's line of sight impeded by any obstacle? The use of aerial photographs or scene photographs can help to clarify. Consider requesting that the witness refer to common distances the jurors can relate to, for instance, the distance to the back of the courtroom or in relation to the length of a football field. Lastly, consider whether the witness may have had some physical limitations that may have affected perception, such as poor vision or hearing.

Trial Tip: Many witnesses are poor at estimating distances. During direct examination, it may appear as though the witness was relatively close to the event and had a clear view. However, during cross-examination, with the use of photographs or diagrams, it is often revealed the witness was actually much farther away than represented.

Counsel: "Can you estimate the distance in feet or yards from your front porch, where you saw the accident, to the intersection where it occurred?"

Witness: "I don't know how many feet, but it was right there. I could see it clearly. No more than 50 feet, I would say."

Counsel: "Was it farther or closer than the back of this courtroom?"

Witness: "I would say about the same."

Counsel: "For the record, the back of the courtroom is sixty feet, according to the court's measurements."

[Note: Usually the judge or the bailiff has a chart with the distances in the courtroom pre-measured.]

Counsel: "Now, would you mind pointing out on Exhibit 34, an aerial photograph of the intersection and surrounding houses, where your house is? Can you please use this blue pen to mark which one is your house? You can just put your initials."

Witness: "Right here. You can even see my porch."

Counsel: "Let the record reflect the witness has drawn her initials in blue on the porch at the house labeled 7450 Maple Street, on Exhibit 34. Is that correct, Mrs. Jones?"

Witness: "That's right."

Counsel: "So, that's the porch where you were standing when you saw the minivan run the red light, correct?"

Witness: "Yes."

Counsel: "That evening, it was dark, wasn't it?"

Witness: "Yes."

Counsel: "And there are no streetlights in the intersection, are there?"

Witness: "I'm not sure. Maybe. I don't know."

In the above, because the witness has marked on the aerial photo the precise location of where her porch is located, it should be easy for an investigator to accurately measure the distances and perhaps even take some additional photographs showing the vantage point and/or perspective the witness would have had from the porch. The chances are good that the distances, when measured, are much greater than the witness estimated. For example, it would be impressive to a jury if, rather than 50 feet, the actual distance was closer to 150 feet.

> **Trial Tip:** The use of photographs or to-scale diagrams during cross to pin down locations and features works well. Note that Google Earth satellite imagery can provide very accurate distance measurements, which the court might take judicial notice of. (See infra, at p. 168.)

Bias or Motive

Demonstrating that a witness has a bias or a motive to shade the truth or to lie is good impeachment. "A more particular attack on the witness' credibility is effected by means of cross-examination directed toward revealing possible biases, prejudices, or ulterior motives of the witness as they may relate directly to issues or personalities in the case at hand. The partiality of a witness is subject to exploration at trial, and is always relevant as discrediting the witness and affecting the weight of his testimony." (3A J. Wigmore, Evidence s 940, p. 775 (Chadbourn rev. 1970). "We have recognized that the exposure of a witness' motivation in testifying is a proper and important function of the constitutionally protected right of cross-examination." (*Davis v. Alaska*, 415 U.S. 308, 94 S.Ct. 1105, 39 L.Ed.2d 347 (1974).) Evidence offered to show a bias, a prejudice, or a motive to fabricate is evidence of a state of mind that shows a motive for untruthfulness. (*People v. Carpenter* (1999) 21 Cal.4th 1016,1054.)

Relationships and Affiliations

The relationship and/or affiliation between a party and a witness is one of the strongest indicators of a possible bias. The cross-examiner's task is to artfully highlight the relationship that may indicate a bias without directly accusing them of it, if possible. Rarely will a witness admit to having bias or to favoring a party. Rather, when confronted directly, many witnesses will only dig in deeper and may even embellish or attempt to shore up their testimony. An effective tactic is to begin by generally establishing the surrounding circumstances, such as the relationships, alliances, or other connections between the witnesses or the parties. For example, pointing out that witnesses are family members, friends, or coworkers may suggest they have an affinity towards one party to such a degree that they have lost their objectivity or might be willing to lie. Sometimes, merely asking the right questions causes the witness to react defensively and to become difficult, which helps make your point.

Counsel: "Now, you're best friends with the plaintiff, correct?"
Witness: "Yes."

Counsel: "Known her for almost twenty years, right?"
Witness: "True."
Counsel: "You even went to visit her at the hospital after the accident, didn't you?"
Witness: "Yes."
Counsel: "She asked you to come to court today and testify on her behalf?"
Witness: "As a character witness, yes."
Counsel: "You would like to help her, wouldn't you?"
Witness: "Yes, but I would never lie."
Counsel: "Did the two of you discuss your testimony before coming to court today?"
Witness: "Never. Not at all."
Counsel: "Not even once?"
Witness: "No."

Pressure to Conform

Some witnesses are called to testify for a particular purpose and may feel pressure to conform their testimony one way or the other. For example, expert witnesses who are being paid will naturally feel pressure to maintain a certain position. Consequently, you will almost never see an expert witness change an opinion on the stand in such a way that would be harmful to the party who hired him or her. Doctors, police officers, and government employees may likewise be reluctant to change a position, even if shown it is wrong due to pride, reputation, or employment consequences. Once again, the role of the examiner is to merely highlight factors which may show bias and then revisit those factors later during argument.

Financial Motive

Many witnesses hit the stand with something to be gained or lost by their testimony, *money* being the primary motivating factor. Pointing out a financial incentive is obviously important. Will the witness receive any form of monetary compensation as a result of the outcome of the trial *or* receiv4 some form of monetary compensation related to their testimony, e.g., an expert witness? For impeachment, eliciting facts designed to show how the witness stands to gain financially may suggest a bias or motive to fabricate, shade the truth, or not be totally impartial. Evidence that a trial witness has a financial incentive in the outcome of the trial is "classic evidence of bias, which is routinely permitted on cross-examination." (*Crowe v. Bolduc*, 334 F.3d 124, 132 (1st Cir.2003).)

For example, in civil cases, some medical providers (such as chiropractors) may not demand immediate payment from the plaintiff, but instead require a lien for payment based on any settlement or jury award. In essence, for payment, the provider is counting on the prospect that the plaintiff will prevail. In addition, because the provider gets paid for each visit or consultation, there could be an incentive for the provider to require unnecessary treatments to pad the bill. Pointing out these circumstances may cause jurors to become a little more skeptical.

Furthermore, sometimes the financial incentive may not be readily apparent without a few probing questions.

> **Trial Tip:** Any financial incentive of the witness should be fully explored. For professional witnesses in particular, e.g., an expert, the method and expectation of payment is not always readily apparent. Whether the witness has made a business of testifying is also important.

Counsel: "Doctor, you've been hired by the plaintiff in this case, correct?"
Witness: "Yes."
Counsel: "Now, you have a consulting business, in addition to your regular practice, isn't that right?"
Witness: "Yes."
Counsel: "And, the majority of your consulting work is for plaintiff's attorneys?"
Witness: "I'm always willing to work for any side. I just analyze the facts and give an opinion based on the evidence, regardless of who hires me."
Counsel: "Well, isn't it true that you mainly do work for plaintiff's attorneys?"
Witness: "Yes, to some extent."
Counsel: "What percentage of your business is with plaintiff's attorneys versus defense counsel?"
Witness: "Well, let's see, I would estimate about ten percent or less for defense."
Counsel: "Only ten percent *or less*?"
Witness: "Yes."
Counsel: "When was the last time you did any work for a defense firm?"
Witness: "It's been a few years."
Counsel: "In fact, you've previously done work for plaintiff's counsel in *this* case, haven't you."
Witness: "Yes."
Counsel: "And, you get paid not only for the evaluation, but you also charge an hourly rate for your court time, isn't that true?"
Witness: "Yes."
Counsel: "For instance, in this case, you are receiving $900 per hour as you sit here this afternoon and testify, correct?"
Witness: "That's right."
Counsel: "How much have you charged in total related to this case?"
Witness: "About $8,000."
Counsel: "Not including your fees for today's testimony, correct?"
Witness: "That's right."

> **Trial Tip:** Often merely cross-examining a witness concerning a possible motive or bias causes them to become defensive, and sometimes, even hostile. Even though you may not have proven much, the witness's attitude helps to make the point, warranting comment during your argument.

Impeachment of Character

In general, "character evidence" can be admissible for two similar, but distinct, reasons, each having their own requirements for admissibility. First, it can be admissible as a form of circumstantial evidence to prove that a party acted in conformity with that character. For instance, in a criminal case, the prosecution may seek to introduce evidence that the defendant committed a prior robbery in order to help prove he committed the charged robbery. The rules related to character evidence for this purpose are discussed infra, Character Evidence, at p.   .)

The second reason for admissibility, and the topic of discussion here, relates to a witness's character for truthfulness or untruthfulness The theory is that there is something about the person's character, past or present, that bears upon whether the witness's trial testimony is truthful, for example, if the witness is a proven liar or a convicted felon. In that circumstance, the adverse party may seek to impeach the witness with that character trait in order to undermine the witness's credibility.

Character evidence admitted to prove conduct falls under the provisions of CA Evidence Code § 1101 et seq., and is more fully explained infra, at p. 244. The admissibility of character evidence as it relates to the credibility of witnesses is governed by Evidence Code sections 786 thru 790 (below).

CA Evid.Code § 785 Parties may attack or support credibility (FRE Rule 404)
The credibility of a witness may be attacked or supported by any party, including the party calling him.

CA Evid.Code § 786 Character evidence generally
Evidence of traits of his character other than honesty or veracity, or their opposites, is inadmissible to attack or support the credibility of a witness.

CA Evid.Code § 787 Specific instances of conduct (FRE Rules 404/405)
Subject to Section 788 (felony convictions) , evidence of specific instances of his conduct relevant only as tending to prove a trait of his character is inadmissible to attack or support the credibility of a witness.

CA Evid.Code § 788 Prior felony conviction
For the purpose of attacking the credibility of a witness, it may be shown by the examination of the witness or by the record of the judgment that he has been convicted of a felony...(with exceptions)

CA Evid.Code § 789 Religious belief
Evidence of his religious belief or lack thereof is inadmissible to attack or support the credibility of a witness.

CA Evid.Code § 790 Good character of witness
Evidence of the good character of a witness is inadmissible to support his credibility unless evidence of his bad character has been admitted for the purpose of attacking his credibility.

Section 786 limits character-credibility evidence to honesty and veracity and their opposites because those are the only four traits relevant to that issue. Except for prior felony convictions, section 787 prohibits the admission of evidence of specific instances of a witness's conduct to attack his credibility when its only relevance is to establish a trait of his character. (*Piscitelli v. The Salesian Society* (2008) 166 Cal.App.4th 1, 7-8, 82 Cal.Rptr.3d 139, fn. omitted.) In civil cases, the rule remains that wrongful acts or instances of untruthfulness cannot be used to prove bad character of the witness for honesty or veracity (§ 787; *Hernandez v. Paicius* (2003) 109 Cal.App.4th 452, 460), except where there has been a felony conviction. (§ 788.) Thus, the parties are permitted to introduce character evidence relevant to truthfulness in the form of opinion or reputation evidence. For example, the defendant could call someone who knows the plaintiff to testify that the plaintiff has a poor reputation in the community for truthfulness. Evidence Code § 1324 states: "Evidence of a person's general reputation with reference to his character or a trait of his character at a relevant time in the community in which he then resided or in a group with which he then habitually associated is not made inadmissible by the hearsay rule." Of course, the court always retains discretion to limit or exclude under 352.

Good Character Prohibited Unless Attacked

"Evidence of the good character of a witness is inadmissible to support his credibility unless evidence of his bad character has been admitted for the purpose of attacking credibility." (Evid. Code § 790; *People v. Taylor* (1986) 180 Cal.App.3d 622, 629-630.) Character evidence to rehabilitate credibility is limited to evidence of the witness's honesty or veracity, and "evidence of traits of his character other than honesty or veracity, or their opposites, is inadmissible to attack or support the credibility of a witness." (Evid. Code § 786.) The Law Revision Commission's comment to Evidence Code section 786 explains: "Section 786 limits evidence relating to the character of a witness to the character traits necessarily involved in a proper determination of credibility. Other character traits are not sufficiently probative of a witness's honesty or veracity to warrant their consideration on the issue of credibility." (Cal. Law Revision Com. com., 29B pt. 2 West's Ann. Evid. Code (1995 ed.) foll. § 786, p. 644.) For example, if the witness's credibility is attacked with evidence suggesting the plaintiff is a dishonest businessman, evidence of honest business relationships would be permitted to rebut. It is important to keep in mind that all such character evidence must be relevant to honesty and veracity. Sometimes, however, the proffered character evidence may have only marginal relevance to this issue and the court may wisely opt to limit such evidence under § .352.

Criminal Cases - Inapplicable

However, it is important to note that sections 786, 787, and 790, do <u>not</u> apply to criminal cases in California. These code sections were effectively repealed by the 1982 passage of the Truth in Evidence amendment to the California Constitution, section 28, subdivision (d), which states, in part, "Relevant evidence shall not be excluded in any criminal proceeding." (See *People v. Harris* (1989) 47 Cal. 3d. 1047, 1081; *People v. Stern* (2003) 111 Cal.App. 4th 283, 297.) Thus, the only limiting factor regarding a witness's character for honesty or veracity, or their opposites, in a criminal case in California is relevance and the court's discretion to exclude evidence under Evidence Code section 352, discussed supra, at p. 17.)

In addition, note that in a criminal case, the defendant can introduce character evidence in the form of opinion and reputation, if relevant to the charged offense. (Discussed infra, Defendant's Character, infra at p. 248.)

Felony Convictions

Prior felony convictions constitute relevant impeachment evidence. Section 788 provides: "For the purpose of attacking the credibility of a witness, it may be shown by the examination of the witness or by the record of the judgment that he has been convicted of a felony" except in specified circumstances such as a pardon or dismissal. In enacting the statute, the Legislature rejected restricting impeachment evidence to convictions involving dishonesty or a false statement. (*Robbins v. Wong (*1994) 27 Cal.App.4th 261, 270.) Because of "the diminished level of prejudice attendant to felony impeachment in civil proceedings," the requirement that a prior conviction involve moral turpitude is the threshold showing for relevancy only in a criminal case—not a civil case. The only limitation on this form of impeachment evidence in a civil case is that the trial court, upon proper objection, is required "to perform the weighing function prescribed by section 352." (Id. at p. 274.) This means the trial court must "balance probative value against potential prejudicial effect." (Id. at p. 264.) In so doing, the trial court may utilize the restrictions set forth in criminal cases "to formulate guidelines for the judicial weighing of probative value against prejudicial effect under section 352." The factors the court may consider are: (1) whether the prior conviction reflects adversely on an individual's honesty or veracity; (2) the nearness or remoteness in time of a prior conviction; (3) whether the prior conviction is for the same or substantially similar conduct to the charged offense; and (4) what the effect will be if the defendant does not testify out of fear of being prejudiced because of the impeachment by prior convictions. (*People v. Beagle* (1972) 6 Cal.3d 441, 453.) In practice, the impeachment of a witness with a felony conviction occurs when the witness is asked to confirm there was a conviction for the specified offense. Once the witness admits the conviction, no further details concerning the underlying facts may be elicited.

Counsel: "Mrs. Jones, in 2009, you were convicted of committing the crime
        of welfare fraud, were you not?"

Witness: "Yes."

Counsel: "And that was a felony conviction, correct?"

Witness: "Yes."

Limitations on Impeachment – "Collateral Matters"

The court has broad discretion to exercise reasonable control over the mode and order of examining witnesses, including the scope of cross-examination. While the court allows "wide latitude" for cross-examination and impeachment, there are limits when it comes to "collateral matters." Typically, the situation arises when a party seeks to impeach a witness with some tangential (collateral) fact or conduct that is unfavorable. For example, if the witness testifies he has been a loving and caring husband or a financially prudent person, the opposing party might seek to impeach the witness with evidence of an extra-marital affair or a prior bankruptcy. If there is an objection, the court will need to determine its relevance and admissibility under Evidence Code section 352. (FRE Rule 403) A matter is collateral if it "could not have been introduced into evidence for any purpose other than contradiction." (*United States v. Jarrett*, 705 F.2d 198, 207 (7th Cir.1983).) A trial court has discretion to exclude impeachment evidence if it is collateral, irrelevant, cumulative, confusing, or misleading. (*People v. Price* (1991) 1 Cal.4th 324, 412.) "A collateral matter has been defined as 'one that has no relevancy to prove or disprove any issue in the action.'" (*People v. Rodriguez* (1999) 20 Cal.4th 1, 9.) "A party cannot "cross-examine a witness upon collateral matters for the purpose of eliciting something to be contradicted." (*People v. Mayfield* (1997) 14 Cal.4th 668, 748.) In *Winfred D. v. Michelin North America, Inc.* (2008) 165 Cal.App.4th 1011, the court ruled it was error to admit evidence of the plaintiff's extra-marital affairs as relevant to his credibility, even though during his deposition he lied about them. The court explained the analysis involves "the strength of the relationship between the evidence and inferences derived therefrom and the issue upon which the evidence is offered, and whether such evidence tends to prove a main issue or a collateral matter. If proffered evidence affords strong inferences on a main issue in a case, its probative value is substantial. If the evidence affords only weak inferences of fact on a major issue, its probative value is obviously weak or slight. Also, if such evidence tends to prove some collateral, disputed issue, such as impeachment of a witness on a collateral matter, its probative value is less than that of evidence offering substantial proof of a main issue." (Id.at p. 1032.)

In practice, the extent to which the court permits impeachment on issues that are arguably on the fringe of relevance is highly dependent on the case. It is often argued that the door was opened by the witness's testimony. (Supra at p. 109.) The recency, materiality, and whether the witness is a party or a relatively minor player, are all factors the court may consider in making the determination.

Trial Tip: The issue of whether cross-examination should be allowed regarding a "collateral issue" often arises when a party/witness volunteers some information that was not requested. The opposing party then seeks to impeach the witness with evidence inconsistent with the witness's testimony. One way to avoid this is to admonish the witness prior to trial to just answer the questions and not volunteer anything.

9. INCONSISTENT STATEMENT

"The witness who has told one story aforetime and another today has opened the gates to all the vistas of truth which the common law practice of cross-examination and re-examination was invented to explore. The reasons for the change of face, whether forgetfulness, carelessness, pity, terror, or greed, may be explored by the two questioners in the presence of the trier of fact, under oath, casting light on which is the true story and which the false. It is hard to escape the view that evidence of a prior inconsistent statement, when declarant is on the stand to explain it, if he can, has in high degree the safeguards of examined testimony." (*People v. Zapien* (1993) 4 Cal.4th 929, at p. 953, quoting 2 McCormick on Evidence (4th ed. 1992, Hearsay Rule, § 251, p. 120, fn. omitted).)

In a trial, demonstrating that the witness's story is changing, or has changed, is one of the most powerful means of impeachment because it can cast doubt on the witness's entire testimony, depending upon the degree of inconsistency. Thus, it is deserved of its own chapter. In most cases, a witness or a party will have made some previous statement(s) concerning the issue at hand. For instance, the witness may have made an oral statement to a police officer at the scene of an accident, prepared a written statement of some kind, or gave testimony at a deposition or a prior hearing. The question for you, the cross-examiner, is whether any of the prior statements differ in any way from the trial testimony?

Witness statements change or vary for a variety of reasons. The most obvious is when the witness is lying and molding the testimony to fit whatever theory is being advanced. More commonly, however, the witness's story changes due to other factors, such as a failure of recollection, inadvertence, bias, or the passage of time. Regardless of the reason, the fact that the statement has changed, even to a small degree, can affect the juror's overall confidence in the testimony. A witness can seem very credible during direct examination, but when it is shown through cross-examination that the witness has previously said something different, the juror's impression of the witness may change dramatically. Thus, for the trial lawyer, it is important to know the fundamentals of how to effectively "impeach" a witness with a prior inconsistent statement, a task often easier said than done.

> **Trial Tip:** Detecting inconsistencies in a witness's testimony is critical and requires preparation. Once an inconsistency has been identified, the next important task is to determine how to effectively use that inconsistency to impeach the witness. Reviewing and organizing a witness's prior statements is key.

Detection of Inconsistency

Before a witness can be impeached with an inconsistency, counsel must first be able to *detect* there is one and respond to it quickly, as courtroom testimony can flow quickly. Some inconsistencies will be glaring, such as when the trial testimony is diametrically opposed to an earlier statement. However, more often, inconsistencies are less glaring. For example, at the scene of a traffic collision, the witness might have stated to an investigator that she "thought" her light was green, but was not positive. Two years later at trial, however, that same witness may seem much more confident and testify that she is 100 percent certain the light was green. This apparent contradiction, although somewhat minor, could be a crucial factor the jury would consider when deciding the case. Subtle differences in wording can be important in some cases.

The key to successful impeachment is to first recognize that the witness' story has changed to some degree and then be able to effectively impeach the witness with the apparent contradiction. Because an inconsistency may not always be obvious, during the examination, counsel must be vigilant and have a means to compare what the witness is saying now on the stand to what the witness has said in the past. The problem is, however, the witness may have made numerous prior statements, possibly encapsulated within hundreds of pages of deposition transcript, making it difficult to spot. Some attorneys miss inconsistencies simply because they were not listening carefully or fully versed in all the witness's prior statements. To be prepared, at a minimum, the witness's prior statements should be summarized or available for immediate review in the courtroom. Experienced trial lawyers will have key witness statements summarized and organized by subject matter, highlighting important quotes or passages, with reference to specific volumes and page numbers of the transcripts for quick reference.

[On cross]
Counsel: "Is it your testimony today that you are *positive* you had the green light as you entered the intersection?"
 Witness: "Yes. I know it was green."
Counsel: "You're positive?"
Witness: "Yes."
Counsel: "Now, do you remember testifying at your deposition about a year ago?"
Witness: "Yes."
Counsel: "And, at the deposition, you were sworn to tell the truth and asked questions, just like today, correct?"
Witness: "Yes."
Counsel   "And, you answered the questions as truthfully as you could, correct?"
Witness: "Yes."
Counsel: "Now, at your deposition, do you recall being asked by one of the attorneys how sure you were that the light was green?"
Witness: "I don't recall that exact question. The deposition was a year ago."
Counsel: "Well, do you recall saying the following, and I quote, 'I'm pretty sure it was green, but I can't be positive.' Unquote. Do you recall giving that answer at the deposition?"
Witness: "Not really."

Counsel: "Would you like to review the transcript of your testimony to see if that helps to refresh your recollection? May I show it to you?"

Witness: "Sure, I guess."

Counsel: "Your Honor, may I approach the witness? … And, counsel (referring to opposing counsel) I intend to show the witness page 157, lines 1-28, of her January 21, 2019 deposition."

Court: "You may approach."

Counsel: "Can you please read to yourself this one page of your deposition testimony and please look up when you're finished."

[Note: Counsel is "Refreshing Recollection" with the deposition transcript, as discussed supra.]

Counsel: "Does reading that help you remember your testimony from the deposition?"

Witness: "Yes, I guess so."

Counsel: "So, at your deposition, when asked how sure you were sure that the light was green, your response was, 'I'm pretty sure it was green, but I can't be positive,' correct?"

Witness: "Yes."

Hearsay Exception

In California, an inconsistent statement is an exception to the hearsay rule, meaning the prior statement is admissible not only to impeach the witness, but also for the truth of the facts asserted in the prior statement. This is important because theoretically the jury can disregard the courtroom testimony and base its decision solely upon an out-of-court inconsistent statement by the same witness.

Evid. Code § 1235 Inconsistent statements (FRE Rule 801(d)(1).)

Evidence of a statement made by a witness is not made inadmissible by the hearsay rule if the statement is inconsistent with his testimony at the hearing and is offered in compliance with Section 770.

Evid. Code § 770 Evidence of inconsistent statement of witness; exclusion; exceptions

Unless the interests of justice otherwise require, extrinsic evidence of a statement made by a witness that is inconsistent with any part of his testimony at the hearing shall be excluded unless:
(a) The witness was so examined while testifying as to give him an opportunity to explain or to deny the statement; or
(b) The witness has not been excused from giving further testimony in the action.

A statement by a witness that is inconsistent with his or her trial testimony is admissible to establish the truth of the matter asserted in the statement under the conditions set forth in Evidence Code sections 1235 and 770. (*People v. Cowan*

(2010) 50 Cal.4th 401, 463.) "The 'fundamental requirement' of section 1235 is that the statement in fact be inconsistent with the witness's trial testimony." (Ibid.) Thus, for example, if the witness testifies at trial that the light was green when she entered the intersection, but gave a statement to the officer at the scene that it was red, if the jury believes that her statement to the police officer is more credible, it can consider the earlier statement for the truth, namely, the light was red. Note that in Federal Court, whether an inconsistent statement is hearsay depends upon the status of the witness. (FRE 801(d).) Generally, a prior statement is admitted for the non-hearsay purpose of determining the witness's credibility. (*U.S. v. Dietrich*, 854 F.2d 1056, 26 Fed. R. Evid. Serv. 1193 (7th Cir. 1988).)

In California, before evidence of an inconsistent statement is admissible, one of the two exceptions in section 770 must apply. Section (a) is the most common form of impeachment where the witness is confronted with the inconsistency and given the opportunity to explain or deny it while on stand.

As discussed above, because an inconsistent statement is an exception to the hearsay rule, the jury can consider the witness's out-of-court statement for the truth, i.e., that she really did not see anything, even though she testified under oath to the contrary. In addition, although under section 770(a) the witness must be given an opportunity to explain or deny the inconsistency, there is nothing which requires the cross-examiner to provide that opportunity. Typically, that opportunity is provided during redirect by opposing counsel, who can go back and permit the witness to explain why she made the statement. However, the damage is done.

Another tactic of impeachment is *not* to directly confront the witness with the inconsistency and not agree to excuse the witness by requesting the court to order the witness "subject to recall." (§770(b).) After the witness has left the stand, the inconsistent statement is then introduced, e.g., through the testimony of the officer who took the witness's statement. The advantage of doing it this way is that the witness was not initially given any opportunity to explain her answer because no one asked her about it. There may be tactical reasons why you do not want to reveal during your cross-examination that you are in possession of an inconsistent statement. The legislative comments to the section explain, "Among other things, Section 770 will permit more effective cross-examination and impeachment of several collusive witnesses, since there need be no disclosure of prior inconsistency before all such witnesses have been examined." In effect, because the witness was not excused, section 770(b) puts the onus on the proponent to recall the witness to provide an explanation if they want her explanation.

Trial Tip: Even though you may have the witness's 250-page deposition transcript in front of you during cross, if you are unable to quickly find the passage that you feel is inconsistent, the opportunity will be lost. The court and jury will quickly lose patience if you have to repeatedly state, "May I have a moment, Your Honor?" as you frantically look for the passage in the transcript that you know exists, but can't readily locate.

"Opportunity to Explain or Deny"

In some circumstances, there could be an issue regarding whether a witness was given an opportunity to explain or deny an inconsistency, assuming the witness was excused. The problem occurs when the witness was not specifically asked about the inconsistent statement but was questioned more tangentially about related subject matter. The rule is that the witness must be given a "realistic opportunity" to explain or deny the alleged inconsistent statement, which includes reference to more than one of the following: 1) the people involved in the conversation, 2) its time and place, or 3) the specific statements that were made during it. *(People v. Garcia* (1990) 224 Cal.App.3d 297, 300.) For example, in *Bossi v. State of California* (1981) 119 Cal.App.3d 313, the court concluded that handing a witness the 60-page transcript of a deposition taken of him eighteen months earlier and asking him, "Now, at that time and place, were all of these questions asked and all of these answers given?" was an insufficient foundational question for admission of statements contained in the deposition transcript because it did not afford the witness a realistic opportunity to explain or deny any specific statement contained therein. *(Bossi,* supra, 119 Cal.App.3d at p. 325.) Therefore, to introduce an inconsistent statement, the witness must be directed specifically to the inconsistent passage or phrase in the deposition testimony.

Is There an Inconsistency?

In some cases, when a witness is confronted on the stand with an apparent inconsistency, the witness will claim either that he does not remember making the prior statement and/or he cannot remember the event itself. This is particularly common in criminal cases with hostile witnesses. Some witnesses will have "selective" memory, where they will clearly remember facts favorable to the side the witness is aligned and have trouble remembering unfavorable facts. In the situation where a witness claims to have trouble remembering, a you may wish to introduce the witness's prior statement on the theory that it is inconsistent.

Counsel: "Did you witness the accident?"

Witness: "I did, but I don't remember much now. It was a long time ago."

Counsel: "Well, do you recall speaking with an officer that day at the accident scene?"

Witness: "Not really. I mean, I was in shock."

Counsel: "Ok. Specifically, do you recall saying to an officer, quote, I saw the minivan run the red light without stopping, unquote? Did you make that statemen to an officer?"

Witness: "Like I said, I was in shock. I don't know."

Counsel: "Any recollection at all of making that particular statement?"

Witness: "No. I don't remember saying that. Like I said, I hardly can remember anything from that day."

In the above, counsel for plaintiff would really like to get the witness's prior statement into evidence to help prove that the defendant's minivan did run a red light and cause the accident. Generally, however, the testimony of a witness that he or she does not remember an event is not inconsistent with that witness's prior statement describing the event. (*People v. Green* (1971) 3 Cal.3d 981, 988.) However, when a witness's claim of lack of memory amounts to deliberate evasion, inconsistency is *implied*. (Id. at pp. 988–989) As long as there is a reasonable basis in the record for concluding that the witness's 'I don't remember' statements are evasive and untruthful, admission of his or her prior statements is proper. (*People v. Ledesma* *(2006)* 39 Cal.4th 641,711.) Inconsistency in effect, rather than contradiction in express terms, is the test for admitting a witness' prior statement. A witness's deliberate evasion of questioning can constitute an implied denial that amounts to inconsistency, rendering a prior statement admissible. Normally, the question of evasiveness arises when a witness claims memory loss about the subject of the questioning. Answering questions in a deliberately nonresponsive manner, however, also can rise to the level of evasion. (*People v Cowan* (2010) 50 Cal.4th 401, 465) Federal law is generally in accord. (See *U.S. v. Mornan*, 413 F.3d 372, 379 (3rd Cir. 2005) citing 5–801 Weinstein's Federal Evidence § 801.21[2][b]; see also *United States v. Bigham*, 812 F.2d 943, 946–47 (5th Cir.1987) [prior grand jury testimony is admissible where the witness "was obviously an evasive and reluctant witness, and the trial judge reasonably could have concluded that his loss of memory was feigned"]; *United States v. Williams*, 737 F.2d 594, 608 (7th Cir.1984) [in the context of a recalcitrant witness, lack of memory is inconsistent with detailed grand jury testimony]; *United States v. Thompson*, 708 F.2d 1294, 1302 (8th Cir.1983) ["The district court should have considerable discretion to determine whether evasive answers are inconsistent with statements previously given."]; see also *United States v. Owens*, 484 U.S. 554, 565, 108 S.Ct. 838, 98 L.Ed.2d 951 (1988) ["It would seem strange ... to assert that a witness can avoid introduction of testimony from a prior proceeding ... by simply asserting lack of memory of the facts to which the prior testimony related."].)

Furthermore, when a witness "selectively" answers some questions, but remains silent as to others, the entire prior statement can be inconsistent under the circumstances where in-court testimony, as well as his refusal to answer questions, are materially inconsistent with his statement. (*People v. Homick* (2012) 55 Cal.4th 816, 861; see also *In re Deon D.* (1989) 208 Cal.App.3d 953, 959.) A witness's prior silence regarding critical facts may also constitute a prior inconsistent statement where "failure to mention those matters ... conflict[s] with that which is later recalled. Where the belatedly recollected facts merely augment that which was originally described, the prior silence is often simply too ambiguous to have any probative force...." (*United States v. Leonardi*, 623 F.2d 746, 756 (2d Cir.) (citation omitted), cert. denied, 447 U.S. 928, 100 S.Ct. 3027, 65 L.Ed.2d 1123 (1980). See, e.g., *United States v. Ayotte*, 741 F.2d 865, 870-71 (6th Cir.), cert. denied, 469 U.S. 1076, 105 S.Ct. 574, 83 L.Ed.2d 514 (1984). At the same time, "statements need not be diametrically opposed to be inconsistent." (*United States v. Agajanian*, 852

F.2d 56, 58 (2d Cir.1988) (quotations omitted).)

In the above hypo, if the court were to find that the witness' purported lack of memory is feigned, then inconsistency is "implied" and the prior statement can be admissible. For example, if the witness is the defendant or someone aligned with the defendant, the witness may have a motive to feign lack of memory. In that circumstance, the plaintiff would call the officer who took the witness's statement and that officer would relate the relevant portion to the jury. However, what if the court were to find the witness's lack of recall was genuine? Due to shock or whatever, the witness was being honest, for example, an elderly person with memory issues or the accident happened many years ago. How does the plaintiff get the witness's prior statement into evidence, if the defendant objects on the grounds of hearsay? As discussed previously, you still have options: 1) You could attempt to "refresh" the witness's recollection by permitting the witness to review the witness's entire statement to see if it helps to jog his memory. (See Refresh Recollection, supra at p. 75.) 2) If the witness's memory cannot be "refreshed," you can attempt to establish the foundational requirements for Past Recollection. Recall that Past Recollection Recorded is an exception to the Hearsay Rule too.

Inconsistent Writings

The use of writings during cross-examination is common. Evidence code sections 768 and 769 (below) provide some guidance regarding how writings and documents can be strategically used during cross-examination.

Evid. Code § 768. Writings (FRE Rule 613(a))

(a) In examining a witness concerning a writing, it is not necessary to show, read, or disclose to him any part of the writing.
(b) If a writing is shown to a witness, all parties to the action must be given an opportunity to inspect it before any question concerning it may be asked of the witness.

Evid. Code § 769. Inconsistent statement or conduct (FRE Rule 613(b))

In examining a witness concerning a statement or other conduct by him that is inconsistent with any part of his testimony at the hearing, it is not necessary to disclose to him any information concerning the statement or other conduct.

One circumstance where the rules regarding the use of a writing to impeach could apply in a more modern setting is when a witness has sent a text message, email, or posted some electronic message that is contrary to their testimony or which shows a bias. Emails, text messages, and other forms of electronic communication can create a good written record and quite often they are introduced at trial. Many times, the electronic messages were not meant to be made public and can be very damning to a party in a court action. For example, people sometimes carelessly post things on Facebook that they would not ordinarily say in public. If the posts are inconsistent with trial testimony or reflect a bias or prejudice about the case, it could fall into the hands of the opposing party and be used against them when they testify.

Tactically, the cross-examiner may not wish to reveal possession of the emails or texts (a writing) until after he has at least cemented the witness into a story that will demonstrate the witness is lying. In other words, the cross-examiner hopes the witness will hang himself, so to speak. The cross-examiner might ask the witness whether he or she has ever made certain statements, in general. Under § 768, there is no requirement the examiner disclose that the statements came from emails, texts, or the witness's Facebook page. The witness is in real trouble if she initially denies ever making such statements, but then is forced to admit it when confronted, towards the end of cross-examination, with the electronic messages she posted. Under § 768(b), however, once the counsel discloses the existence of the messages and confronts the witness with them, opposing counsel is then permitted to inspect them before questioning.

As mentioned previously, the cross-examiner might also elect not to confront the witness with the damning emails or text messages, but rather introduce them later, after the witness has left the stand, assuming the witness was left "subject to recall" and counsel can lay the appropriate foundation to authenticate them. (See Authentication of Writings, supra, at p. 154.) This tactic might be wise if the opposing party is unaware you have such powerful impeachment evidence and you do not want to tip your hand too early.

Trial Tip: When to reveal and confront a witness with an inconsistency is sometimes a tactical decision. To avoid witness collusion, you may not want to tip your hand immediately. Do not agree to "excuse" the witness.

Impeachment with Deposition Testimony

Because witnesses are often deposed prior to trial in civil cases, impeaching a witness with an inconsistency from the deposition is common. Generally, the parties will have possession of the deposition transcripts, which some attorneys "lodge" with the court at the beginning. As discussed above, the key to successful impeachment with deposition testimony is that counsel has thoroughly reviewed and summarized the deposition testimony beforehand. The process for impeachment is generally the same as for other witnesses, namely, counsel first confirms the trial testimony, establishes that the witness was under oath at the deposition, then confronts the witness with the prior deposition testimony, normally by referring to a specific quote from the deposition transcript. "Any party may use a deposition for the purpose of contradicting or impeaching the testimony of the deponent as a witness, or for any other purpose permitted by the Evidence Code." (CCP § 2025.620(a).)

Counsel: "You testified at a deposition about a year ago, didn't you?"

 Witness: "Yes."

Counsel: "You understood at the deposition that you were under oath, just like you are today, correct?"

Witness: "Yes."

Counsel: "And at the deposition, you were asked questions about the traffic accident and what happened, weren't you?"

Witness: "Yes."

Counsel: "Referring to page 32, lines 14-28 of her July 28th deposition."
(To opposing counsel)

Counsel: "Do you recall testifying at the deposition, when asked whether the light was green, that your answer was, quote, 'I'm pretty sure I had the green light, but not 100 percent certain,' unquote? Do you recall making that statement at the deposition?"

If the witness admits to making the statement, the inconsistency is established. However, if the witness denies making it or cannot remember, you can attempt to refresh the witness's memory by having her review a couple pages of the deposition testimony to see if that helps. Or you could request permission from the court to mark the pages referenced as an exhibit and move to have it admitted.

If the witness is a "party," Code of Civil Procedure section 2025.620 permits the introduction of "any part or all" of a deposition of a party by the adverse party for "any purpose." No inconsistency is required. Generally, counsel will notify the court and opposing counsel of the specific page and line number from the witness's deposition transcript and then literally read that portion into the record. No questions need to be asked of the witness. However, the portions of the deposition testimony admitted by any party must still comply with the rules of evidence as though the deponent were then present and testifying as a witness. (§2025.620.) In other words, irrelevant or inadmissible deposition testimony, e.g., inadmissible hearsay, cannot be introduced. (*In re Automobile Antitrust Cases I and II* (2016) 1 Cal.App. 5th 127, 143 [error to admit deposition testimony that contained hearsay].)

Impeachment of Hearsay

In the circumstance where a hearsay statement is admitted under one of the exceptions; for example, a spontaneous statement under section 1240 (See Appendix at p. 261.), the opponent can impeach that hearsay statement with an inconsistency under Evidence Code section 1202 (below). Evidence Code section 1202 deals with the impeachment of a declarant whose hearsay statement is in evidence, as distinguished from the impeachment of a witness who has testified. It clarifies two points. First, evidence to impeach a hearsay declarant is not to be excluded on the ground that it is collateral. Second, the rule applying to the impeachment of a witness—that a witness may be impeached by an inconsistent statement only if he or she is provided with an opportunity to explain or deny it—

does not apply to a hearsay declarant. (*People v. Blacksher* (2011) 52 Cal.4th 769, 806, fn. 22.)

CA Evid. Code § 1202. Credibility of hearsay declarant (FRE Rule 806)

Evidence of a statement or other conduct by a declarant that is inconsistent with a statement by such declarant received in evidence as hearsay evidence is not inadmissible for the purpose of attacking the credibility of the declarant though he is not given and has not had an opportunity to explain or to deny such inconsistent statement or other conduct. Any other evidence offered to attack or support the credibility of the declarant is admissible if it would have been admissible had the declarant been a witness at the hearing. For the purposes of this section, the deponent of a deposition taken in the action in which it is offered shall be deemed to be a hearsay declarant.

Strategies for Impeachment with Inconsistency

As discussed above, if you have an inconsistent statement of a witness, there are some tactical considerations regarding how best to exploit it. Keep in CA Evid. Code § 768, which requires that "when examining a witness about the witness's prior statement, a party need not show it or disclose its contents to the witness. But the party must, on request, show it or disclose its contents to an adverse party's attorney." FRE Rule 613 is similar.

A common strategy to impeach a witness with an inconsistency is to establish all the preliminary facts necessary to close every avenue of escape, so to speak. Generally, the first task is to get the witness to either admit or deny making it. When confronted with an apparent inconsistency, most witnesses will have predictable responses. For example, the witness might claim he or she never made the statement. Period. "That's a lie! I never said that." If a witness flatly denies making the prior statement, then evidence of a purported prior statement by witness is clearly inconsistent and admissible, assuming the proponent can *authenticate* the prior statement, meaning, prove the witness made it. The witness may claim he or she does not remember making the statement. As discussed above, if the court finds the witness is deliberately evasive, then inconsistency is implied and the prior statement is admissible. Lastly, the witness may admit that he or she made the statement, but claim that he or she was misquoted, that words were taken out of context, or that the statement was inaccurately reported. If the witness admits to making the entire statement, but has an explanation, then technically, the prior statement is not inconsistent. The witness can simply explain what he or she meant to say. However, if the issue is whether the witness's prior statement is accurate, then the recorder of the statement, e.g., a police officer, would be called to rebut the allegations by the witness and to introduce the prior inconsistent statement.

In practice, some lawyers try to avoid having the witness see or review the actual statement, at least until all the preliminary facts have been established.

However, as required section 768, once you start confronting the witness about the statement, upon request, opposing counsel is entitled to see it. Of course, if you are the proponent of the witness and opposing counsel begins questioning your witness about an apparent statement that you are not familiar with, you should make the request to review it.

> **Trial Tip:** In today's modern era of electronic communication, parties and other witnesses commonly use the internet to communicate. Internet posts, tweets, text messages, and emails have become very common forms of evidence at trial, often to the detriment of a party. Much of this electronic communication is available in the public domain and worth investigating pre-trial.

Steps to Establish an Inconsistency – The Three C's

Once you have identified an inconsistency, the next question is what to do about it. Although there are different methods, depending on the nature of the case, below are three basic steps to establish an inconsistency:

In this hypo, during direct examination, the witness/defendant testified she is certain the traffic light was green as she entered the intersection.

1. *Confirm and Lock-in Testimony* – Confirm and lock in the witness's trial testimony *and* the circumstances of the prior statement. The purpose is to prevent or head off the witness from later having an excuse or an explanation.

Counsel: "You testified on direct examination, that you are now certain the light was green when you crossed over the limit line into the intersection, is that correct?"
Witness: "Yes."
Counsel: "You are sure?"
Witness: "Oh, yes."

In the above, by confirming the portion of the courtroom testimony you plan to impeach with, you prevent the witness from later claiming that that's not what she meant, or was misunderstood or confused.

Counsel: "Now, shortly after the accident, you spoke with an officer at the scene didn't you?"
Witness: "Yes."
Counsel: "And, that was only a few minutes after the accident, correct?"
Witness: "I think so."
Counsel: "The officer asked you questions about what happened, didn't he?"

Witness: "Yes."
Counsel: "And you told him, correct? You explained what happened, right?"
Witness: "Yes."
Counsel: "I presume you were truthful?"
Witness: "Of course."

The object here is to confirm the circumstances of the prior statement to again head off any possible excuse, e.g., "I didn't understand what he was asking" or "I was misunderstood."

2. *Confront* – One of the easiest methods to impeach a witness with an inconsistent statement is simply to ask the witness whether it was made. It is permissible to literally read the passage out loud to the witness. Example:

Counsel: "Do you recall telling the officer at the scene that you *thought* the light was green, but you weren't sure?"
Witness: "I was in shock and he seemed in a hurry."
Counsel: "Thank you. But, my question was, did you say to him, quote, 'that you weren't sure whether the light was green?'"
Witness: "I might have. It's been a long time."
Counsel: "But you do remember speaking with an officer, correct?"
Witness: "Yes. I guess."
Counsel: "Well, did you or did you not say to him, that you weren't sure the light was green?"
Witness: "I guess. Yes."

The objective here is to force the witness to either admit or deny making the prior statement. Some witnesses will try not to answer, but the examiner needs to be firm. Typically, if a witness has made a clearly inconsistent and damaging statement, the witness will respond in some predictable ways:

Scenario A –The witness admits to making the statement, but attempts to qualify it with an explanation. "I said that, but…" "I didn't understand the question" or "I was confused." However, as the cross-examiner, you generally would like to prevent the witness from giving a non-responsive explanation. Thus, be prepared to cut off the explanation using witness control techniques (discussed supra, at p. 104.) and confirm again, with just an affirmation or denial, that the statement was made to drive the point home.

Counsel: "Well, did you or did you not say to him that you weren't sure the light was green?"
Witness: "Yes, I did, but I really didn't understand what he was asking. I was in shock and…
Counsel: "Objection, unresponsive. Move to strike after her answer, "yes."

While it is true that on re-direct, opposing counsel will likely ask her to explain why she said it, which is permissible, during the cross-examination, the cross-examiner should maintain control and not allow the witness to go beyond the leading questions. You point out the inconsistencies and let them clean it up, if they can.

Scenario B – Complete denial. "No, I never said that!" ... "That's not true." The witness denies making the prior statement. Here, the claim is usually that the reporter (the officer) misunderstood what the witness said, twisted her words, or did not accurately record the statement. Confirm the answer.

Counsel: "So, is it your testimony that you *never* made such a statement to the officer?"
Witness: "No, I didn't."
Counsel: "You don't denying talking with him, do you?"
Witness: "No. I just didn't say what's in his report. He obviously made a mistake."
Counsel: "Well, whatever you told him, were you truthful?"
Witness: "Yes."

In this situation, the next step is to call the officer/witness to testify regarding the inconsistent statement to establish that the reporter (officer) accurately recorded the witness's statement and to rebut her claim.

Scenario C – Lack of memory. The witness will claim he or she is unable to remember what was said previously. "I don't remember [making the statement]." This response is one of the easiest and most common avenues of escape because there is nothing for the witness to explain. The witness simply testifies that she cannot remember what she told the officer. "It was a long time ago." The question then becomes how to get her prior statement before the jury.

3. *Closing Argument* – The final "C" is perhaps the most important. The process of impeachment is not always very exciting, and the jurors may not have understood the significance of what you were doing or the nuances of how the witness's story has changed. This is especially true if you are questioning the witness at length regarding prior testimony from a deposition. Small differences in verbiage can be important, but the differences or inconsistencies likely went right over the juror's heads. Your argument is where the inconsistencies and the importance thereof should be fully explained. If there are multiple inconsistencies, use a chart to compare and contrast the witness's statement.

Trial Tip: In some cases where there any numerous inconsistencies, during argument it can be helpful to create a chart or a PowerPoint slide which highlight the passages and conflicts. Visual aids are persuasive.

10. WITNESS REHABILITATION

The preceding chapters have discussed the use of cross-examination and related techniques to impeach a witness. However, if it is *your* witness who has been impeached, it is equally as important to know the rules and techniques for rehabilitating the witness. During cross-examination, uncertainty or confusion may have been created in the minds of the jurors that needs to be cleared up. For example, the witness may not have been permitted to fully explain an answer or words may have been taken out of context. The opposing party may have planted the seed that your witness's testimony is corrupt due to an improper motive, bias, or inconsistent statement. In this situation, as the proponent of the testimony, you may need to employ counter measures to rebut the claims and shore up the witness's credibility.

Trial Tip: To keep opposing counsel honest, so to speak, whenever a witness is questioned concerning a prior statement, request to "inspect" the writing or document before questioning resumes. (See CA Evid. Code 768(b) [" If a writing is shown to a witness, all parties to the action must be given an opportunity to inspect it before any question concerning it may be asked of the witness." (FRE Rule 613)

Protect Your Witness

Before having to rehabilitate a witness, the first objective is to be proactive and prevent the need for it in the first place. This can be accomplished by being vigilant during cross-examination, ensuring that the questions being asked are proper and fair. Some questions propounded to the witness by your opponent may be objectionable. However, because the questioning under cross-examination can come quickly and in rapid succession, you must be prepared to respond at a moment's notice. Although the court allows "wide latitude" for cross-examination, the questions must still be properly framed. An example of the types of questions that are objectional include compound questions, vague or ambiguous questions, or irrelevant questions. (See Trial Objections, infra, at p. 226.) One other type of objectionable question to be alert for is when misinformation or irrelevant information is woven into the context of the question. For example, it is not uncommon that during cross-examination, the examiner will preface the question with a statement of fact.

Counsel: "Sir, do you recall stating to an officer at the scene that you weren't sure whether a car ran the red light?"

In this example, the issue is whether the witness said those words to the officer or has counsel misquoted or summarized them inaccurately? Some attorneys will put their own interpretation or spin on the witness's prior statements or testimony. For instance, in the above, if the witness actually said he was not sure which car ran the red light, then counsel has misquoted the witness. Words can matter; therefore; an objection would be appropriate.

Opp. Counsel: "Objection, Your Honor, misstates the evidence. That's not what my client's statement to the officer."

Similarly, it is also not uncommon that the cross-examiner will reference the witness's prior testimony, even from earlier in the day. Often, opposing counsel will attempt to paraphrase the witness's prior testimony. Again, be vigilant that the question accurately recites the prior testimony and is not a misleading summary or a slanted version.

Counsel: "Yesterday you testified during direct examination that you were having a hard time seeing just before your vehicle struck the plaintiff. My question is, when did you first realize you had hit someone?"

Opp. Counsel: "Objection, Your Honor. Misstates the evidence. That misstates my client's prior testimony."

Generally, if an attorney is going to be referring to a witness's prior testimony, that attorney should have a transcript or at a minimum be able to accurately quote the witness. In addition, as framed, the question is also arguably improper because counsel's recitation of the witness's prior testimony as a lead-in is not necessary to form the question, which related to when the witness first realized she had hit someone. Counsel's statement about the witness having a hard time seeing is basically surplusage. On the other hand, it is not improper per se for the examiner to reference previous testimony if it is quoted correctly *and* necessary to set-up the question to provide some context for the answer. Keep in mind that if counsel is misstating or misquoting testimony and there is no objection, the jurors will assume that what counsel said must be true.

Some lawyers will also preface a question with a statement of purported fact that is not necessarily required for the witness to answer the question. Unless certain facts are necessary to set up the question, attorney statements of facts are not evidence and they are not permitted to simply declare facts, as if true.

Counsel: "Sir, three witnesses have testified already that the light was green. But, according to you, the light had turned yellow before the car entered the intersection. Is that your testimony, sir?"

Opp. Counsel: Objection, Your Honor. Argumentative. Counsel's testifying."

In the above, the attorney's comment regarding the testimony of other witnesses is essentially just argument and improper. On the other hand, if a summary of other evidence is necessary to put the question into proper context, it is generally permissible, especially if it is not highly contested.

The bottom line is that, as the proponent, you must be vigilant that the questions being propounded to your witness are fair and proper. As discussed, one of the most common issues is when opposing counsel is misstating the evidence or misquoting a witness's prior statement. You must be prepared to object quickly when that happens. On the other hand, keep in mind that although the cross-examiner may not misstate evidence, it is generally *not* improper for the cross-examiner to pick and choose which words or phrases to inquire about. Again, wide latitude is accorded and this generally includes highlighting only specific statements, passages, or facts, and not others. If you object merely because you feel counsel has focused only on certain words or phrases and not others, the court will likely overrule your objection. Your remedy is re-direct examination or perhaps introducing the entirety of the statement, as discussed below.

Trial Tip: Be particularly alert when opposing counsel is referring to a witness's prior testimony from earlier in the trial or at a deposition. If counsel is quoting from a transcript, request to know the page number and confirm what was said. If counsel is paraphrasing, then you really need to be alert that the summary is accurate.

Redirect Examination

A relatively easy method to rehabilitate a witness is simply to use redirect examination (or re-cross-examination) to clear up whatever issues or possible confusion were raised during the cross-examination. "Redirect examination" is an examination of a witness by the direct examiner subsequent to the cross-examination of the witness." (Evid. Code § 762.)

Trial Tip: During cross-examination, take notes re: any areas where you feel clarification or amplification is needed. If you don't keep notes, you may forget. If opposing counsel has impugned the witness, go back and request the witness respond in a narrative fashion. In other words, don't leave anything unsettled or unanswered hanging out there by the time the witness steps off the stand.

During cross-examination, be sure to listen carefully to the content of your opponent's questions and the witness's answers to ensure the jury is not becoming confused. If there is any doubt about this during the redirect, walk the witness methodically back over the area in controversy to clear up any confusion or misunderstanding. If an inconsistency was suggested during the cross-examination, a good tactic is just to be blunt about it and ask the witness to explain, in his or her own words, why there is a difference, if any. You want the jury to feel confident you have nothing to hide. If only certain portions of a witness's prior statement(s) were elicited, consider having the witness describe the entirety of the statement for proper context, discussed infra.

Counsel: "During cross-examination, counsel asked you about a statement you made to the police right after the accident where it was reported that you said that you 'thought' the light was green. How were you feeling when he was speaking with you?"

Witness: "I was very upset and still kind of in shock."

Counsel: "Did you talk with the same officer a few hours later, after the accident?"

Witness: "Yes, he came to the hospital to interview me."

Counsel: "How were you feeling then?"

Witness: "Much calmer."

Counsel: "What did you tell him about the light at that time?"

Witness: "That my light was green, for sure."

Counsel: "Any doubt?"

Witness: "No."

Often, during cross-examination, accusations or insinuations are made of bias or improper motive by the witness. The redirect is the opportunity to dispel those claims. It pays to be direct and confront the witness yourself with the accusations.

Counsel: "You're my client's sister, correct?"

Witness: "Yes."

Counsel: "During cross-examination, opposing counsel implied that you were trying to help your sister avoid responsibility. Are you doing that?"

Witness: "No. I'm not."

Counsel: "Has she ever tried to influence your testimony or told you what to say?"

Witness: "No."

Counsel: "Is your testimony designed to help her in any way?"

Witness: "No"

Counsel: "Have you told us the truth?"

Witness: "Yes."

Counsel: "Did she run a red light?"

Witness: "Absolutely not."

Trial Tip: The redirect may be the last time the witness speaks to the jury. Thus, if the witness's credibility was attacked, use redirect to permit the witness to respond in his or her own words. Thereafter, have the witness re-confirm the substance of the critical testimony.

Rule of Completeness

As discussed above, it is not an uncommon tactic for the cross-examiner to focus on particular passages or specific words the witness may have said in a prior statement, i.e., in a deposition or a statement to a police officer. As the proponent of the witness, you may feel that by counsel's selectively picking and choosing various passages or words, the meanings have been taken out of context. In this circumstance, the "Rule of Completeness" (Evid. Code § 356) is your tool to rehabilitate the witness.

CA Evid. Code § 356. Entire act, declaration, conversation, or writing to elucidate part offered (FRE Rule 106)

Where part of an act, declaration, conversation, or writing is given in evidence by one party, the whole on the same subject may be inquired into by an adverse party; when a letter is read, the answer may be given; and when a detached act, declaration, conversation, or writing is given in evidence, any other act, declaration, conversation, or writing which is necessary to make it understood may also be given in evidence." (See also FRE 107 [similar].)

C.C.P.2025.620(e) Depositions

Subject to the requirements of this chapter, a party may offer in evidence all or any part of a deposition, and if the party introduces only part of the deposition, any other party may introduce any other parts that are relevant to the parts introduced.

The redirect examination is typically the time when counsel may wish to introduce the entire statement of a witness to put everything into proper context. "When one party puts into evidence one part of a conversation or statement, the balance of the conversation or statement is admissible under section 356, provided the other statements have some bearing upon, or connection with, the admission or declaration in evidence." (*People v. Zapien* (1993) 4 Cal.4th 929, 959.) "Section 356 is founded not on reliability, but on fairness, so that one party may not use selected aspects of a conversation, act, declaration, or writing, so as to create a misleading impression on the subjects addressed. In other words, reliability of the evidence is not a factor in determining admissibility under the rule of completeness—indeed, the evidence proffered by the defendant and the prosecution may both be unreliable." (*People v Parrish* (2007) supra, 152 Cal.App.4th at p. 273-274.) "Section 356 applies when the balance of a conversation is necessary to make it understood." (*People v. Johnson* (1989) 47 Cal.3d 1194, 1237.) "Further, the jury is entitled to know the context in which the statements on direct [or cross-]examination were made." (*People v. Harris* (2005) 37 Cal.4th 310, 334-335.) In effect, Evidence Code section 356 operates as an exception to the hearsay rule. (See also *People v. Williams* (1975) 13 Cal.3d 559, 565 [suggesting that hearsay rules do not apply to statements admitted under section 356].)

If a only certain words or phrases from a witness's prior statement(s) have been singled out during opposing counsel's questioning, consider whether it would be helpful to introduce the entire statement, or at least larger portions of it, to put the witness's words in proper context. For example, if, at a certain point in a deposition, the witness did say she was having a hard time seeing just before the accident, the cross-examiner may focus only on those specific words and not allow the witness to explain or reference any other statements she may have made later in the deposition. As the proponent, you may feel it is important for the jury to learn her entire statement on the topic to put her earlier statements in proper context. This would typically be accomplished with the witness during the direct examination.

Counsel: "During his examination, counsel asked you about the portion of your deposition testimony where you said you were having a hard time seeing. Correct?"

Witness: "Yes."

Counsel: "Now, later in the same deposition, did you further explain what you meant by that?"

Witness: "Yes."

Counsel: "Do you have a copy of your deposition transcript in front of you?

Witness: "Yes."

Counsel: "At page 105, line one, were you asked to elaborate on your ability to see?"

Witness: "Yes."

Counsel: "Can you read into the record the answer and explanation you gave at the deposition, beginning at line one."

In practice, redirect examination is generally the time to introduce the witness's entire statement under the Rule of Completeness. Some attorneys merely have the witness testify as to the remainder of the conversation, while others will move to have the written form admitted. As discussed above, the Rule of Completeness may not allow the entire deposition transcript, but only those portions necessary for proper context. The Court is the final arbitrator if the parties disagree.

Trial Tip: It is important that the witness's prior statements are accurately recited and not taken out of context. By picking and choosing selected passages, the jury may be left with the wrong impression regarding the witness's credibility. To clear this up, consider having the witness relate more fully the entirety of the statement on redirect or introduce the remaining portion of the statement.

Prior Consistent Statement

Another method to rehabilitate a witness is to introduce the witness's prior consistent statement. The use of a prior consistent statement is useful when it is suggested that the witness's trial testimony is motivated by some improper motive or purpose and the earlier consistent statement would show that the witness was saying the same thing before the alleged improper motive arose. In other words, the witness's story has not changed. For example, in a criminal case, the prosecution may seek to admit a witness's prior consistent statement to show that the witness's testimony has not been influenced or motivated by a plea deal the witness entered into with the prosecution. CA Evid. Code § 1236 (below) sets forth the requirements to admit a Prior Consistent Statement, which is not hearsay.

Evid. Code § 1236. Prior consistent statements (FRE Rule 801(d)(1)(B))

Evidence of a statement previously made by a witness is not made inadmissible by the hearsay rule if the statement is consistent with his testimony at the hearing and is offered in compliance with Section 791.

Evid. Code 791. Prior consistent statement of witness

Evidence of a statement previously made by a witness that is consistent with his testimony at the hearing is inadmissible to support his credibility unless it is offered after:

(a) Evidence of a statement made by him that is inconsistent with any part of his testimony at the hearing has been admitted for the purpose of attacking his credibility, and the statement was made before the alleged inconsistent statement; or

(b) An express or implied charge has been made that his testimony at the hearing is recently fabricated or is influenced by bias or other improper motive, and the statement was made before the bias, motive for fabrication, or other improper motive is alleged to have arisen.

Initial Consistent Statement
"To be admissible as an exception to the hearsay rule, a prior consistent statement must be offered (1) after an inconsistent statement is admitted to attack the testifying witness's credibility, where the consistent statement was made before the inconsistent statement or (2) where there is an express or implied charge that the witness's testimony recently was fabricated or influenced by bias or improper motive, and the statement was made prior to the fabrication, bias, or improper motive. (*People v. Riccardi* (2012) 54 Cal.4th 758, 801.)

Subdivision 791(a) permits the introduction of a witness's prior consistent statement if evidence of an inconsistent statement of the witness has been admitted for the purpose of attacking his credibility and if the consistent statement was made *before* the alleged inconsistent statement. (*People v. Kennedy* (2005) 36 Cal.4th 595, 614.) This section presumes the witness gave an initial (consistent) statement, followed by a subsequent (inconsistent) statement, and then the (consistent) trial testimony. If at trial the witness is impeached with the inconsistent statement, then the original consistent statement is admissible to rehabilitate the witness. Thus, for example, if the witness told a police officer at the scene of the accident the light was green and testifies the light was green, but is impeached with a statement allegedly made to an investigator that the light was red, the initial statement is admissible to shore up her credibility that she has not changed her original story.

Express or Implied Charge

Evidence Code section 791(b) permits the admission of a prior consistent statement when there is a charge that the testimony given is fabricated or biased, not just when a particular statement at trial is challenged. (*People v. Andrews* (1989) 49 Cal.3d 200, 210-211; *People v. Bunyard* (1988) 45 Cal.3d 1189, 1208-1209.) In evaluating the admissibility of prior consistent statements, the focus is on "the specific agreement or other inducement suggested by cross-examination as supporting the witness's improper motive." (*People v. Noguera* (1992) 4 Cal.4th 599, 630; *People v. Crew* (2003) 31 Cal.4th 822, 843.) The prior consistent statement is used in this circumstance to show that nothing has improperly influenced the witness to change the story, e.g., a deal with the prosecution; the theory being the witness made the statement before any deal or promise was struck, therefore it is truthful.

The most difficult question to answer under section (b) is when did the alleged "improper motive" arise? A prior consistent statement is admissible if it was made before the existence of any one or more of the biases or motives that, according to the opposing party's express or implied charge, may have influenced the witness's testimony. (*People v. Cannady* (1972) 8 Cal.3d 379, 388; *People v. Duvall* (1968) 262 Cal.App.2d 417, 421; *People v. Hayes* (1990) 52 Cal.3d 577, 609.) A prior consistent statement logically bolsters a witness's credibility whenever it predates any motive to lie, not just when it predates all possible motives. Accordingly, under Evidence Code section 791, "a prior consistent statement is admissible as long as the statement is made before the existence of any one of the motives that the opposing party expressly or impliedly suggests may have influenced the witness's testimony." (*People v. Noguera,* supra*; People v. Hillhouse* (2002) 27 Cal.4th 469, 492.) In *People v. Kennedy* (2005) 36 Cal.4th 595, 614, the court held that "Evidence Code section 791 permits the admission of a prior consistent statement when there is a charge that the testimony given is fabricated or biased, not just when a particular statement at trial is challenged." (*People v. Kennedy* (2005) 36 Cal.4th 595, 614; See also *United States v. Simonelli*, 237 F.3d 19, 25-29 (1st Cir.2001) ["When prior consistent statements are admitted to rehabilitate a witness, admissibility is "determined by the interplay between the rule of completeness and the common law doctrine about prior consistent statements... There is no rule admitting all prior consistent statements simply to bolster the credibility of a witness who has been impeached by particulars."].)

Silence is Inconsistent

In *People v. Lopez* (2013) 56 Cal.4th 1028, the victim testified at the preliminary hearing that the defendant kidnapped and assault her. At trial, the defendant presented testimony from family members that the victim's actions were consensual and she never complained of the assault. In rebuttal, the prosecution sought to introduce excerpts from the victim's diary and a statement to a teacher that were consistent with her preliminary hearing testimony. The court in *Lopez* held the evidence was admissible as a consistent statement under sections 1236 and 791 because the defendant attacked the victim's apparent silence of not speaking about the assault to family members. The court held that when "a witness's silence is presented as inconsistent with his or her later testimony, a statement made at the earliest opportunity after the silence that is consistent with the witness's later testimony may be admissible as a prior consistent statement under section 791(b)." (*Lopez*, at p. 1067.)

It has long been recognized that when a witness's silence is presented as inconsistent with his or her later testimony, a statement made at the earliest opportunity after the silence that is consistent with the witness's later testimony may be admissible as a prior consistent statement under section 791(b). (*People v. Gentry* (1969) 270 Cal.App.2d 462, 474.) This situation arises when the witness does not initially report a crime, but later provides the information and testifies.

If a cross-examiner suggests that the witness "did not speak of the matter when it would have been natural to speak" and the witness's silence is alleged to be inconsistent with trial testimony, "then the prior consistent statement can be introduced to disprove the alleged prior silence." (*People v. Williams* (2002) 102 Cal.App. 4th 995, 1011–1012.)For example, the plaintiff testifies during direct examination that her light was green and the other car ran the red light. During cross-examination, however, she is questioned regarding why she did not report that fact at the hospital afterwards when asked by a doctor what happened. In this situation, plaintiff's counsel would move to admit the plaintiff's earlier statement to a police officer at the scene, which is consistent with her trial testimony. The court would likely admit this as a consistent statement under *Williams*, supra.

Trial Tip: Whenever your witness is impeached regarding an alleged improper motivation *and* the witness made an early consistent statement, consider whether the requirements for admissibility for a prior consistent statement have been met. Jurors tend to put more stock in statements made closest in time to the event before any motives or other reasons to change the story or shade the truth arise.

Impeach and Rehabilitate Your Own Witness

You take your witnesses as you find them, and quite often it is necessary to impeach your own witness, which is permitted. "The credibility of a witness may be attacked or supported by any party, including the party calling him." (Evid. Code § 785.) The situation frequently arises when your cooperative witness makes a mistake, gets confused, or misremembers. In this circumstance you must be able to impeach your own witness coolly and seamlessly, possibly with an inconsistency, and then work to rehabilitate the witness's credibility in the eyes of the jury. It is important to get the witness straightened out before cross-examination. You want to steal your opponent's thunder, so to speak. An easy method to do this is simply to have the witness review his or her prior statement, e.g., deposition testimony or a police report, to "refresh" his or her recollection, and then permit the witness to correct the oversight or explain any discrepancy.

Own It

Furthermore, if your witness has made a mistake, an inconsistency, or has otherwise done something untoward, one of the best methods to neutralize it is to get it out there first and have the witness own up to it and explain it away, *before* cross-examination.

Counsel: "Have you reviewed the police reports in this case before testifying here today?"

Witness: "Yes."

Counsel: "And did you read a statement you allegedly made to a police officer on the morning of the accident?"

Witness: "Yes, I read that."

Counsel: "The officer wrote in his report that you told him that you were *pretty sure* you had the green light. Did you see that in his report?"

Witness: "Yes, I read that portion."

Counsel: "Did you say that to him?"

Witness: "Yes, I did."

Counsel: "Why?"

Witness: "The way he was asking questions was very confusing. I was in the back of the ambulance and in shock."

Counsel: "Is there any doubt in your mind now that your light was green?"

Witness: "Absolutely none."

If the witness has a potentially serious credibility flaw that you anticipate opposing counsel will use for impeachment, for example, a prior criminal conviction, the best course is generally to tackle it head on. During jury selection, for example, inform the jury about the conviction and inquire whether it would prevent any juror from being impartial. Mention it again during the opening statement. And, during the direct examination of your client, bring it up and allow your client to explain it. When precisely to bring it up during the examination is a tactical consideration. You probably do not want to start out the testimony by talking about the conviction or conclude the testimony on a sour note. Find some place in the middle to work it in when it would have the least impact. During your argument, you can confidently state that your client has openly and candidly admitted her past transgressions and remind the jurors that during jury selection they promised not to hold it against her. If opposing counsel harps on it during their closing, during your rebuttal you can argue that opposing counsel would rather dwell on irrelevant matters, than on the important facts of the case.

> **Trial Tip:** Jurors tend to accord more credibility to witnesses who atone for their mistake or inconsistencies, rather than denying or minimizing them. Steal your opponent's thunder by addressing issues *prior* to cross-examination.

Counsel: "Mrs. Jones, did you have a few drinks before the accident?"

Witness: "Yes."

Counsel: "Can you tell us about that?"

Witness: "I had two glasses of wine before I left the restaurant."

Counsel: "What time?"

Witness: "A glass before and then one during dinner."

Cousnel: "Did you feel the effects of the wine at the time of the accident?"

Witness: "Oh, no. When I left about an hour after dinner, I felt fine."

Counsel: "Now, while at the scent of the accident that evening, did you say to a police officer that you hadn't had anything to drink that evening?"

Witness: "Yes. Yes, I did."

Counsel: "Why did you say that to him if it wasn't true?"

Witness: "It was stupid. I was scared and shaken up from the accident."

Counsel: "Were you trying to hide the fact you had two glasses of wine from him?"

Witness: "No, I just wasn't thinking. I should have told him the truth."

Character for Truthfulness

If your witness's credibility has been attacked, even with an implied assertion of untruthfulness, another means to rehabilitate the witness is to present evidence of the witness's good character for truthfulness. In practice, this type of evidence typically relates mainly to a party/witness. Recall that under Evidence Code § 790 "evidence of the good character of a witness is inadmissible to support his credibility *unless* evidence of his bad character has been admitted for the purpose of attacking his credibility." (See discussion re: Impeachment of Character, supra, at p. 125.) Thus, you could call to testify people who know the witness/party to express their opinion or the witness's reputation for truthfulness.

Witness: "I've known the plaintiff for 30 years, and, in my opinion, she's the most honest and trustworthy person I know."

Keep in mind, however, that by introducing good character evidence, you are always running the risk of potentially "opening the door" to other bad character evidence in rebuttal, for example, if the plaintiff once falsified a job application.

> **Trial Tip:**   In any case where you are considering introducing evidence of a witness's "good" character, your concern is always whether that may open the door to your opponent's attempt to counter with "bad" character. This is particularly true if the witness is your client.

"Have you Heard?"

Another consideration if you are planning to introduce good character via reputation or opinion evidence is opposing party's cross-examination.   During cross-examination, the opposing party would be permitted to delve into the extent to which the character witness knows, or is familiar with, the party/witness's reputation or background. If permitted by the court, the witness might be asked whether she "had heard" or knew about the plaintiff's untruthful act, namely, the falsifying of the job application, and whether that would have any effect on the character witness's opinion. (*People v. Hempstead* (1983) 148 Cal.App.3d 949, 953.) Once a witness testifies, on direct, to the defendant's good character, it is a common and accepted method of cross-examination to ask whether the witness is aware of instances of the defendant's bad character. A variant of this is to ask, as here, whether the witness's opinion would change if the witness became aware of instances of the defendant's bad character. (*People v. Hawara* (2021) 61 Cal.App.5th 704, 713.) Specifically, when the witness has testified to the defendant's reputation, based on what the witness has heard, the proper form is to ask, "if you heard." However, when the witness has testified to the witness's own opinion, based on the witness's perceptions, it is perfectly proper to ask, "if you knew." (*Hawara*, supra; 1 McCormick on Evid. (8th ed.) § 48.)

11. NON-TESTIMONIAL EVIDENCE

The preceding chapters have discussed the rules, procedures, and strategies related to witness testimony. However, in a trial, there are other important types of "non-testimonial" evidence which can be helpful, if not necessary, to prove or defend a case. The more common types include documentary evidence, photographs, maps, audio and video recordings, and tangible items, sometime referred to as "real evidence." "Demonstrative evidence" is another form, where the purpose is to help illustrate or explain a witness's testimony, such as a chart or a computer animation.

Regardless of form, all non-testimonial evidence must comport with the foundational requirements necessary for its admission which the proponent generally has the burden of showing. The evidence must: (1) be relevant; (2) be properly authenticated; (3) not in violation of an exclusionary rule, i.e., Hearsay or Best Evidence; and (4) be such that the probative value is not substantially outweighed by the danger of undue prejudice. (Evid. Code § 352.) If you can get past these hurdles, then there is really no restriction on the type of evidence that can be potentially admitted and creative lawyers are always thinking of new approaches and ideas, e.g., advanced computer animations. Often, the issue of admissibility is determined at the front end in a motion in limine, however, it can also be considered at the time a party moves to have the evidence admitted during the trial itself.

Writings

In California, the rules regarding the admissibility of non-testimonial evidence often relates to "writings." Generally, we tend to think of a writing as a document, however, the definition of a writing, as set forth in Evidence Code § 250 (below), is much broader and includes virtually any form of recorded communication

> **Evid. Code § 250. Writings**
>
> Writing means handwriting, typewriting, printing, photostatting, photographing, photocopying, transmitting by electronic mail or facsimile, and every other means of recording upon any tangible thing, any form of communication or representation, including letters, words, pictures, sounds, or symbols, or combinations thereof, and any record thereby created, regardless of the manner in which the record has been stored.

Authentication

To be admissible, evidence must be properly "authenticated." To satisfy the requirement of authenticating or identifying an item of evidence, the proponent must produce evidence sufficient to support a finding that the item is what the proponent claims it is. (FRE Rule 901(a); CA Evid. Code § 1400.) This burden "is not to establish validity or negate falsity in a categorical fashion, but rather to make a showing on which the trier of fact reasonably could find by a preponderance of the evidence the proffered writing is authentic." (*People v. Valdez* (2011) 201 Cal.App.4th 1429, 1437.) In California, the rules for authentication are mostly codified and begin with the general rules at sections 1400 thru 1402 (Below), followed by more specific methods in sections 1403-1421. (See Appendix) Similarly, FRE Rule 901 provides examples of how to authenticate certain forms of evidence. (See Appendix at p. 275.)

Evid. Code § 1400   (FRE Rule 901)

Authentication of a writing means (a) the introduction of evidence sufficient to sustain a finding that it is the writing that the proponent of the evidence claims it is or (b) the establishment of such facts by any other means provided by law.

Evid. Code § 1401. Authentication required (FRE Rule 901)

(a) Authentication of a writing is required before it may be received in evidence.
(b) Authentication of a writing is required before secondary evidence of its content may be received in evidence.

Evid. Code § 1402. Authentication of altered writings

The party producing a writing as genuine which has been altered, or appears to have been altered, after its execution, in a part material to the question in dispute, must account for the alteration or appearance thereof. He may show that the alteration was made by another, without his concurrence, or was made with the consent of the parties affected by it, or otherwise properly or innocently made, or that the alteration did not change the meaning or language of the instrument. If he does that, he may give the writing in evidence, but not otherwise.

The California Evidence code also provide more specific rules and examples for authenticating and proving a writing, depending upon the circumstance. For example, the testimony of the subscribing witness is not required (§1411). A writing can be authenticated by anyone who saw the writing made (§1413); a party admitted to its authenticity or has been acted upon as authentic (1414); by handwriting evidence (§§1415-1418); that the writing was received in response to a communication sent to the person who is claimed by the proponent of the evidence to be the author of the writing (§1420); that the writing refers to or states matters that are unlikely to be known to anyone other than the person who is claimed by the proponent of the evidence to be the author of the writing (§1421).

Section 1410 states that "nothing in this article shall be construed to limit the means by which a writing may be authenticated or proved," meaning, the examples given are not exclusive and authentication can be proved via other means as well. It is important to keep in mind that a "writing" can also refer to such evidence as electronic communications, recordings, and photographs. FRE Rule 901 is similar and a good reference in that it provides examples of how to authenticate various forms of evidence. (See Appendix.)

Standard for Authentication – Weight versus Admissibility

The burden is on the proponent to prove authenticity. Although the court is required to make a preliminary finding regarding authenticity, it is a relatively low standard. "To establish authenticity, the proponent need not rule out all possibilities inconsistent with authenticity, or ... prove beyond any doubt that the evidence is what it purports to be. Rather, the standard for authentication, and hence for admissibility, is one of reasonable likelihood." (*United States v. Alicea–Cardoza*, 132 F.3d 1, 4 (1st Cir.1997) (quoting *United States v. Holmquist*, 36 F.3d 154, 168 (1st Cir.1994)). This requirement is satisfied if sufficient proof has been introduced so that a reasonable juror could find in favor of authenticity or identification." (*United States v. Pluta*, 176 F.3d 43, 49 (2d Cir.1999).) This burden "is not to establish validity or negate falsity in a categorical fashion, but rather to make a showing on which the trier of fact reasonably could find by a *preponderance of the evidence* the proffered writing is authentic." (*People v. Valdez* (2011) 201 Cal.App.4th 1429, 1437 [emphasis added].) The fact that conflicting inferences can be drawn regarding authenticity goes to the weight as evidence, not its admissibility." (*People v. Goldsmith* (2014) 59 Cal.4th 258, 267; *Jazayeri v. Mao* (2009) 174 Cal.App.4th 301, 321; see *Thorstrom v Thorstrom* (2011) 196 Cal.App.4th 1406, 1418 [despite conflicting evidence, testimony of persons who recognized testator's signature on trust sufficient to admit]; See also *Islas v. D & G Mfg. Co., Inc.*(2004) 120 Cal.App.4th 571, 577 ["The trial court's role here is to assess whether there is sufficient evidence to present these matters to the jury. If there is, the matter is submitted to the jury for a final determination; if not, the matter is inadmissible."])

As can be seen from sections Evidence Code sections 1400 thru 1422, , there can be many different ways to authenticate evidence, and the examples listed are not exhaustive. In courtroom parlance, to establish authenticity means to "lay the foundation" for admissibility. The failure to properly authenticate evidence is a proper trial objection, to wit: "Lack of foundation." (See Trial Objections, infra, at p. 235.) In the typical case, the proponent party will call a witness to the stand who will be shown the exhibit and asked to describe what it is, where it came from, and how it is relevant.

Counsel: "Sir, showing you what has been marked for identification as Exhibit number 37, do you recognize this document?"
Witness: "Yes. This is a copy of the contract I entered into with the defendant when I purchased the car."
Counsel: "How can you tell?"

Witness: "I recognize my signature at the bottom and the dealer's name on the top."

In many cases, there is no real dispute regarding authenticity and the process goes quickly, or sometimes opposing counsel will stipulate or not object to any deficiencies. Evidence can also be "self-authenticating," meaning, the evidence speaks for itself. For example, a letter where the contents makes it clear who the author was and perhaps even when it was written. In this circumstance, the only witness needed might be someone to explain where the letter came from.

Trial Tip: You probably have spent thousands of dollars getting the case to trial, so don't scrimp now on the presentation. The use of demonstrative evidence to capture and hold the juror's attention is important. In today's high-tech era, juror' may expect high tech and to be entertained. For example, computer animation, photographs, satellite, imagery, can all bring an event to life. Computer programs, such as Power Point and others specifically designed for courtroom presentations, can make your case seem very professional and impactful.

Documents

Documents are one of the most common forms of non-testamentary evidence, and, as you might expect, there are many different varieties. Some examples include contracts, business records, medical records, deposition transcripts, reports, logs, ledgers, receipts, memorandums, notes, letters, emails, etc. Normally, we think of documents as being written or typed on paper; however, in today's electronic era, documents or communications can also be in an electronic format, such as an email or a Facebook post. However, in most courts, even electronic communications will still need to be printed on paper for courtroom use and marked as an exhibit, otherwise it can be difficult to keep a good record. However, it may not be long before courts go fully digital, where instead of binders full of documents, the parties bring thumb drives or other storage devices.

If planning to introduce documents of any kind, your initial concern should be having them organized in such a manner that they are easy to handle and use during the trial. For instance, related documents, such as a multi-page contract, are usually stapled or fastened together in some fashion and marked as just one exhibit. If there are multiple documents, consider putting them all in a three-holed binder, separated and tabbed for each document and in the order you plan to introduce them. Commonly, when binders are used for exhibits, duplicate binders with the same materials are also prepared for the witness, opposing counsel, and the court. If recordings are going to be played, some attorneys will have transcripts for each juror in binders.

Also consider how the documents will be displayed as testimony progresses. The courtroom might be equipped with an overhead projector-type device and/or hard wired such that you can connect your laptop to courtroom TV monitors. When a witness is referring to a particularly important passage in a document, for instance, you may be able to display that passage on the projector/monitors for the jury and court to see. Although technically the exhibit has not been formally "admitted" as evidence yet, many courts will permit it to be "published" to the jury at this point, unless the admission of the document is highly contested. This process saves time and avoids having to move and admit each exhibit one at a time, especially when there are many such exhibits. The court may direct that the parties make their motions to admit evidence en masse and outside the presence of the jury at a break or the close of a party's case. (See Exhibits and Evidence, supra, at p. 8 et seq.)

> **Trial Tip:** Organizing and preparing documents for trial is important. If there are many documentary exhibits, consider placing them in binders and tabbed according to the order of presentation or their exhibit numbers. Duplicate binders for opposing counsel, the court, and the witness are typical.

Authentication of Documents

In some cases, a witness will come to court to authentic the writing. However, authentication might also be established via a declaration by the custodian of records if they were produced via subpoena and there is compliance with the requirement of Evidence Code sections 1560-1562 (See Appendix), or they might be self- authenticating just by their very nature. Although writings must be authenticated before they are received into evidence or before secondary evidence of their contents may be received (§ 1401), a document is authenticated when sufficient evidence has been produced to sustain a finding that the document is what it purports to be (§ 1400). As long as the evidence would support a finding of authenticity, the writing is admissible. The fact conflicting inferences can be drawn regarding authenticity goes to the document's weight as evidence, not its admissibility. (*Jazayeri v. Mao* (2009) 174 Cal.App.4th 301, 321; See also *People v. Martinez* (2000) 22 Cal.4th 106, 128 [An objection that a computerized record is 'incomplete' generally 'goes to the weight of the evidence and not its admissibility.]; *McAllister v. George* (1977) 73 Cal.App.3d 258, 263 [where invoice for dental services was authenticated by its contents, "contrary inferences flowing from the facts that the bill was handwritten, not on official stationery, and signed by a student were issues going to the weight of the evidence ..."].)

Hearsay- Business Record exception

In addition to authentication, documents are often the subject of a hearsay objection. The most commonly cited exception at trial is "business records," under CA Evid. Code § 1271 (FRE Rule 803(6).) See Appendix; "Section 1271 permits admission of business records to establish the truth of the matters contained therein if: "(a) The writing was made in the regular course of a business; (b) The writing was made at or near the time of the act, condition, or event; (c) The custodian or other qualified witness testifies to its identity and the mode of its preparation; and (d) The sources of information and method and time of preparation were such as to indicate its trustworthiness." (*Jazayeri v. Mao* (2009) 174 Cal.App.4th 301, 321; *People v. Hovarter* (2008) 44 Cal.4th 983, 1011.) "The key to establishing the admissibility of a document made in the regular course of business is proof that the person who wrote the information or provided it had knowledge of the facts from personal observation. So long as 'the person who originally feeds the information into the process has firsthand knowledge, the evidence can ... qualify as a business record. It is not necessary that the person making the entry on a business record have personal knowledge of the transaction. Nor need the individual with personal knowledge testify; the rule permits any "qualified witness" to establish to the conditions of admissibility It is the object of the business records statutes to eliminate the necessity of calling each witness, and to substitute the record of the transaction or event. The witness need not have been present at every transaction to establish the business records exception; he or she need only be familiar with the procedures followed." (See *Jazayeri*, supra [internal quotes/citations omitted.]; *Hovarter*, supra.) For example, hospital records and similar documents are often admissible as business records, assuming a custodian of records or other duly qualified witness provides proper authentication to meet the foundational requirements of the hearsay exception. (*In re R.R.* (2010) 187 Cal.App.4th 1264, 1280; *People v. Landau* (2016) 246 Cal.App.4th 850, 872, fn. 7.)

In some cases, the if the document is a public record, it might qualify as an Official Record, under California Evidence Code Section 1280. This section makes admissible a writing that records an act, condition, or event if (a) The writing was made by and within the scope of duty of a public employee; (b) The writing was made at or near the time of the act, condition, or event; and (c) The sources of information and method and time of preparation were such as to indicate its trustworthiness." This exception to the hearsay rule is based on the presumption that public officers properly perform their official duties. (*Jazayeri v. Mao* (2009) 174 Cal.App.4th 301, 321 [USDA inspection report admissible as Official Record.].)

Photographs, Videos, and Audio Recordings

"A picture is worth a thousand words" is a phrase particularly applicable in the courtroom. A photograph or a video depicting a place or a scene, e.g., an intersection or a damaged vehicle, is truly the best evidence. Photographs and video recordings are considered as "writings" in California. (Evid. Code § 250) To be admissible in evidence, they must be authenticated. (Evid. Code § 1401, subd. (a).) That is, there must be evidence that they are accurate depictions of what they purport to show. (Evid. Code § 1400; see *People v. Mayfield* (1997) 14 Cal.4th 668, 747.) The proponent of the evidence has the burden of producing evidence to establish authenticity. (Evid. Code § 403, subd. (a)(3); *People v. Marshall* (1996) 13 Cal.4th 799, 832.)

A photograph or video recording is typically authenticated by showing it is a fair and accurate representation of the scene depicted. (*People v. Gonzalez* (2006) 38 Cal.4th 932.) However, it is not necessary to call to testify the person who took the picture. The foundation can be supplied by the person taking the photograph or by a person who witnessed the event being recorded. It may be supplied by other witness testimony, circumstantial evidence, content, and/or location. Once properly authenticated and admitted into evidence, a photograph may be used as demonstrative evidence to support a witness's testimony or as probative evidence of what is shown. (Id.)

"In making the initial authenticity determination, the court need only conclude that a prima facie showing has been made that the photograph is an accurate representation of what it purports to depict. The ultimate determination of the authenticity of the evidence is for the trier of fact, who must consider any rebuttal evidence and balance it against the authenticating evidence in order to arrive at a final determination on whether the photograph, in fact, is authentic. The fact conflicting inferences can be drawn regarding authenticity goes to the document's weight as evidence, not its admissibility." (*Goldsmith*, supra, 59 Cal.4th at p. 267; *In re K.B.* (2015) 238 Cal.App.4th 989, 997.)

. Once properly authenticated and admitted into evidence, a photograph may be used as demonstrative evidence to support a witness's testimony or as probative evidence of what is shown. (*People v. Goldsmith* (2014) 59 Cal.4th 258, 267; *In re K.B.* (2015) 238 Cal.App.4th 989, 997.)

In the typical case, the witness is permitted to view the photograph or video and then asked to describe what it is, when it was made, and who or what is depicted.

Counsel: "Sir, on the monitor, I am showing you what has been previously marked for identification as Exhibit 14, do you recognize what is depicted in this photograph?"
Witness: "Yes."
Counsel: "What is it?"
Witness: "It appears to be the intersection where the accident happened."
Counsel: "Does this picture fairly and accurately depict the intersection?"
Witness: "Well, yes, but this photograph appears to have been taken in the evening. The accident happened in the afternoon."
Counsel: "Okay. Otherwise, does the photograph appear to accurately show the layout of the intersection?"
Witness: "Yes, it does."
Counsel: "Your Honor, I move to have Exhibit 14 admitted."

In the above example, whether the photograph will be admitted may depend upon whether the lighting conditions are in issue. If the purpose of the photograph is to illustrate the lighting conditions, opposing counsel might object that the scene depicted in the photograph is not substantially similar, to wit: afternoon versus evening. Generally, when a photograph or video is meant to represent an environmental or other condition as it was at the time of the event, there is a requirement of *substantial similarity*. Thus, in the above example, if the lighting conditions are an issue, it might be difficult for a photograph or a video taken at a later time to accurately recreate or duplicate those conditions. For this reason, the court might exclude the evidence under Evidence Code section 352. On the other hand, if the photograph or video is meant to only depict an environmental condition that is relatively static, for example, a bend in the roadway, a tree, or the configuration of the streets, etc., similarity is easier to establish.

Obviously, a photograph or a video taken at the time of the event is the easiest to authenticate, assuming a witness can confirm this is how the scene looked at that exact moment, including the lighting conditions. Even so, there could still be an issue whether the photograph or video accurately captured the lighting conditions, as there are many variables regarding how cameras operate that can affect the final image. However, recall that for the purpose of a finding by the court of authentication, the standard is relatively low. If the parties dispute whether a photograph or video is similar enough, the court may admit the evidence, noting that the issue is one of weight, rather than admissibility.

When considering the admissibility of photographs, some courts have considered the following factors: (1) the photograph's subject (i.e., its focal point); (2) the view of the subject (e.g., close-up, distant, isolated, in context); (3) the photograph's perspective (e.g., eye-level, overhead, ground-level); (4) the use of any plain-view altering devices (e.g., camera color filter, fish-eye lens, computer-manipulation); (5) the characteristics of the photograph (e.g., sharp and clear, blurry, grainy, color or black and white); (6) whether the photograph was taken under identical or substantially similar conditions (e.g., timing, lighting, weather); and (7) any other relevant circumstances (e.g., addition of extrinsic aids, such as a ruler or pointer). (See e.g., *Kasparian v. AvalonBay Communities, Inc.* (2007) 156 Cal.App.4th 11, at p. 25.)

Video Recordings

Perhaps even better than a still photograph is a video recording. For example, a well-shot video of an intersection or a walk around a wrecked vehicle can be impactful for jurors who are accustomed to watching video and reality TV shows. Video might also be helpful for other purposes, for instance, in *Jones v. City of Los Angeles* (1993) 20 Cal.App.4th 436, 440, the court upheld the use of a 20-minute 'day in the life' video of a woman (plaintiff) confined to a wheelchair. The woman narrated the video as it played. The video depicted the difficulties she experienced each day and even showed her facial expressions while in pain. The court noted that "photographic material, including films, can uniquely demonstrate the nature and extent of an accident victim's injuries." (Id.) The court held the videotape was relevant on the issue of the extent of the plaintiff's medical needs and the extent of her pain and suffering. The videotape was also probative to aid the jurors in determining the quantum of compensation required based on the extent of her needs. Moreover, because there was an opportunity to cross-examine, the risk of any prejudice was greatly reduced. (Ibid.) In determining whether the probative value of such a video outweighs the possibility of prejudice, a key factor is whether the video "fairly represents the facts with respect to the impact of injuries on the plaintiff's daily activities." (Id. at p. 444, citing *Bannister v. Town of Noble* (10th Cir.1987) 812 F.2d 1265, 1270.)

Like a photograph, to authenticate a video, typically a witness will testify that he or she is familiar with the content of the recording, e.g., can recognize the voices talking and/or the scenes depicted. A video recording is authenticated by showing it is a fair and accurate representation of the scene depicted. This foundation may, but need not, be supplied by a person who witnessed the event being recorded. It may be supplied by other witness testimony, circumstantial evidence, content, and/or location. (*People v. Goldsmith* (2014) 59 Cal.4th 258, at p. 267-268.) A videotape is the equivalent of a writing under the Evidence Code and thus must comply with the requirements of Evidence Code sections 1400 and 1401. (*Jones v. City of Los Angeles* (1993) 20 Cal.App.4th 436, 440, fn. 5; *McGarry v. Sax* (2008) 158 Cal.App.4th 983.) Under Evidence Code section 1400, a video recording is authenticated by testimony or other evidence that it depicts what it purports to show. (*People v. Mayfield* (1997) 14 Cal.4th 668, 747, 60 Cal.Rptr.2d 1, 928 P.2d 485.) An authenticated video may be "a silent witness" and serve as evidence of the facts depicted independent of testimony to those facts by a witness. (See, *Bowley*, supra, 59 Cal.2d at p. 859; accord, *Fashion 21 v. Coalition for Humane Immigrant Rights of Los Angeles* (2004) 117 Cal.App.4th 1138, 1146 [holding that silent witness theory applies not only to pictures but also to videos].) "A court's main concern in admitting a videotape as substantive evidence of an event is making sure the tape accurately depicts what occurred." (Ibid.)

Trial Tip: An important consideration when preparing for the use of photographs and/or recordings is how will they be presented in the courtroom and/or the jury room. How is the courtroom equipped, e.g., TV monitors, document projector, compatibility with your own equipment? Prepare for Murphy's Law of inevitable equipment failure moments before the jurors are seated. The bailiff and the clerk are often your best sources of information.

Video/Photograph Enhancement

With the increasing popularity of video cameras or "cams" in many public and private places, the use of captured video or photographs in the courtroom will only become more prevalent. For example, in *People v. Hung Tran* (2020) 50 Cal.App.5th 171, an assault was captured on multiple video surveillance cameras surrounding the scene. A "certified forensic video analyst" was retained by the prosecution who performed a "video synchronization" to essentially stitch together the videos in chronological order. He also enhanced the quality of the videos and added colored arrows to show the movements of specific actors depicted in the various scenes. In upholding its admission, the court in *Hung Tran* held that no *Kelly-Frye* (Daubert) analysis was required and the evidence was admissible as a form of "demonstrative evidence." The court reasoned, "Although jurors ordinarily may be capable of watching a surveillance video and understanding what they see without expert help, the scene captured by the multiple videos was especially challenging. As such, Fredericks's (expert) assistance in this case was critical because multiple surveillance videos depicted a moving melee, at night, with at least a dozen bodies interacting on a crowded street. Fredericks's testimony and sequenced videos were necessary to aid the jury's understanding of how the different videos captured the same action from different angles, thus minimizing confusion that can result from contrasting video perspectives, contradictory descriptions, or unreliable eyewitnesses." (Id. at p. 189.)

Handling Digital Evidence

More recently, photographic/recording evidence comes in digital formats (and different ones too) and are electronically stored on computers, CDs, thumb drives, the "cloud," or similar storage devices. How to handle and use this digital evidence in the courtroom presents some unique challenges. For example, how will the digital images or recordings be marked as exhibits, displayed in the courtroom, and maintained as evidence? How will the jurors have access to it in the jury room? How will it be maintained for the appellate record? Some jurisdictions have developed rules and procedures for electronic evidence that you would be wise to research prior to trial.

Regarding photographs and images, many attorneys still prefer to have an actual printed "hard" copy available for the witnesses to review on the witness stand and for the jurors to handle and examine in the jury room. Jurors like to hold and see evidence, and having enlarged photographs in the jury room can be invaluable. During testimony, some attorneys will have the digital images or recordings stored on their laptop computers which are connected to the courtroom monitors. There is commercial software available that is specifically designed for courtroom presentations, which assigns a bar code to an image or item of evidence, permitting it to be displayed on the courtroom monitors with the click of the mouse. Very slick. Of concern to the court is maintaining a good record. Some courts may require a "hard copy" of each electronic image be maintained, which is given an exhibit number. If, during the testimony, counsel is displaying only a digital image, care must be taken that counsel is creating a good record by referring to the proper exhibit number, to wit: "May the record reflect, I am now displaying Exhibit 35." For deliberation, the jurors are typically provided the hard copies or a laptop to view the images.

Trial Tip: 'A picture is worth a thousand words' is a phrase trial lawyers should strongly consider when preparing their presentations.

Authentication of Digital Evidence

Some courts have expressed concern regarding the ease at which digital evidence can be altered or manipulated. For example, in *People v. Beckley* (2010) 185 Cal.App.4th 509, 515, the court held that *without expert testimony*, photographs downloaded from the internet (Myspace) allegedly depicting the defendant flashing a gang sign were not properly authenticated because of the danger that digital images can be faked. The court held that with the advent of computer software programs such as Adobe Photoshop, "it does not always take skill, experience, or even cognizance to alter a digital photo." (*Beckley*, supra, at p. 515.) Other courts have disagreed with *Beckley* and admitted photographs from the internet without expert testimony. For example, in *People v. Valdez* (2011) 201 Cal.App.4th 1429, 1436-1437, the court cautioned that "...Hacking may occur and ... documents and other material on the internet may not be what they seem. But the proponent's threshold authentication burden for admissibility is not to establish validity or negate falsity in a categorical fashion, but rather to make a showing on which the trier of fact reasonably could conclude the proffered writing is authentic." (Id. at p. 1436-1437; see also *People v. Goldsmith* (2014) 59 Cal.4th 258, 267 [only a "prima facie" case needed for admissibility]) "The fact conflicting inferences can be drawn regarding authenticity goes to the document's weight as evidence, not its admissibility." (*Valdez*, supra, at p. 1435.) The court in *Valdez*, supra, found Myspace pages were properly authenticated when there was a matching profile picture and greetings addressed to the defendant (including by a relative) which included details matching information known about defendant. (Ibid.) Valdez could argue that the profile belonged to someone else, but that was not a decision for the court as gatekeeper of the evidence. (See also *United States v. Vazquez-Soto*, 939 F3d 365, (1st Cir. 2019) [upholding admission of internet photographs from Facebook. "...what is at issue is only the authenticity of the photographs, not the Facebook page].)

Digital images might also be authenticated via presumption. Evidence Code section 1553, subdivision (a), establishes a rebuttable presumption that a printed representation of images stored on a video or digital medium is presumed to be an accurate representation of the images it purports to represent. The presumption affects the burden of proof and is rebutted by a showing that the "printed representation of images stored on [the] video or digital medium is inaccurate or unreliable. The burden then shifts to the proponent of the printed representation to prove by a preponderance of evidence that it accurately represents the existence and content of the images on the video or digital medium. (Ibid.) If the proponent of the evidence fails to carry his burden of showing the printed representation accurately depicts what it purportedly shows, the evidence is inadmissible for lack of adequate foundation. (*Bowley*, supra, 59 Cal.2d at pp. 860-861; see also *People v. Goldsmith* (2014) 59 Cal.4th 258 [upholding the authentication of red light cameras by presumption].)

> **Trial Tip:** For video and audio recordings, rather than playing a short segment and then stopping to authenticate it with witness testimony, which seems cumbersome, consider requesting permission from the court to play the entirety without interruption, even before it is technically admitted. In most cases, unless the recording is contested, opposing counsel will not object and the court will allow it.

Audio Recordings

The use of audio recordings in court is common and authentication is very similar to photographs and videos. The proponent generally has a CD or some other digital audio recording, usually of a conversation. Authentication generally requires some evidence regarding who is doing the speaking and the circumstances, e.g. when and where. In the typical case, a party to the conversation or the person who made the recording is called to testify, who will first describe his or her familiarity with the speaker's voices and then identify the voices speaking on the recording.

[Portion of recording is played long enough for the witness to hear the voices.]
Counsel: "Officer, I have just played a short segment of Exhibit 34. Do you recognize the persons speaking on the recording?"
Witness: "Yes. One person is me. The other is the defendant."
Counsel: "Is this from the recorded interview you conducted with the defendant at the stationhouse on July 3rd?"
Witness: "Yes."
Counsel: "Your Honor, permission to play the full recording?"
[Each juror has a copy of the transcript of the interview in a binder.]
Court: "Yes. Ladies and gentleman of the jury, you are about to hear a recording and you have been provided a transcript of that recording. The transcript is merely an aid to assist you in listening to the recording. The actual evidence is the recording itself."

"The identity of the person may be established by proof of recognition of his voice, or by other circumstances which satisfactorily indicate the identity of the individual." (*People v. Hawkins* (1968) 268 Cal.App.2d 99.) Further, a writing can be self-authenticated if there is something in the recording that makes it clear who the speaker is. The content of the writing itself may be considered. (*People v. Gibson* (2001) 90 Cal.App.4th 371, 383; *People v. Olguin* (1994) 31 Cal.App.4th 1355, 1373; see also Evid. Code § 1421.) "If there are matters in the conversation that are unlikely to have been known by anyone other than the alleged speaker, in effect, the conversation proves itself." (*People v. Fonville* (1973) 35 Cal.App.3d 693, at p. 709.)

To be admissible, recordings need not be completely intelligible for the entire conversation as long as enough is intelligible to be relevant without creating an inference of speculation or unfairness. (*People v. Polk* (1996) 47 Cal.App.4th 944, 952.) Thus, a partially unintelligible tape is admissible unless the audible portions of the tape are so incomplete the tape's relevance is destroyed. The fact a tape recording "may not be clear in its entirety does not of itself require its exclusion from evidence since a witness may testify to part of a conversation if that is all he heard and it appears to be intelligible. Because a live witness may testify as to so much of a conversation as he heard, a partially audible tape recording is equally admissible." (*Polk,* supra.)

Transcription

In most jurisdictions, if a video or audio recording includes dialogue, a verbatim transcript of that dialogue must also be prepared and submitted. The purpose is to have a record of what is said in the recording, as often the court reporter will not report from a recording. (See e.g., California Rule of Court 2.1040(b)(c)(d)) When a recording with dialogue is played in the courtroom, the court, jury, and opposing counsel are generally also provided with copies of the prepared transcript. The court will admonish the jurors that the transcript is merely an aid to assist them in hearing the recording. Some courts require that the transcript should be marked for identification as an exhibit, for example, the video is marked as Exhibit #14 and the transcript is marked #14A. If the recording is admitted, there is the question of whether the transcript is also admitted and, therefore, goes into the jury room? Some courts have held that the transcript is admissible, while others have held that the transcript is merely an aid for the jury. (See *People v. Polk* (1996) 47 Cal. App. 4th 944, 954 [recording and transcript properly admitted]; "When an audio recording is in English, the common practice is to play the recording, make a transcript available, mark the transcript as an exhibit, and use it as an aid. Our court, and many others, have approved such use of transcripts as aids to the jury, provided the court makes clear to the jury that the tape rather than the transcript constitutes the best evidence. In ordinary circumstances, the district court does not abuse its discretion in allowing the jury to use the transcripts during deliberations." (*U.S. v. Morales-Madera,* 352 F.3d 1, 7 (1st Cirt. 2003).) In some instances, an issue can arise as to whether the transcription is accurate. Some portions of the recording might be inaudible. If a proper foundation is laid, both an audio recording and a written transcript of a conversation are admissible. (*People v. Siripongs* (1988) 45 Cal.3d 548, 574; *People v. Wojahn* (1959) 169 Cal.App.2d 135, 146.) However, the party seeking to introduce a recording must establish that it is an accurate representation of what it purports to be. (See *People v. Mayfield* (1997) 14 Cal.4th 668, 747; *People v. Spencer* (1963) 60 Cal.2d 64, 77-78.)

Trial Tip: If you intend to present a recording with a transcript, prepare a copy for each juror, opposing counsel, and the court. If it is more than a few pages, consider providing each juror a binder with the transcript(s) for their convenience.

Other Recording Issues

In some instances, sections of the recording might be unintelligible or missing for some reason. However, recordings need not be completely intelligible for the entire conversation, as long as enough is intelligible to be relevant without creating an inference of speculation or unfairness. (See *People v. Polk* (1996) 47 Cal.App.4th 944, 952.) Thus, a partially unintelligible recording is admissible unless the audible portions of the tape are so incomplete the tape's relevance is destroyed. The fact that a tape recording "may not be clear in its entirety does not of itself require its exclusion from evidence since a witness may testify to part of a conversation if that is all he heard and it appears to be intelligible. Because a live witness may testify as to so much of a conversation as he heard, a partially audible tape recording is equally admissible." (*Polk,* supra.)

Language can also create issues. If the recording includes people speaking in languages other than English, those conversations will generally have to be translated into English. Many jurisdictions have guidelines and procedures for the use of courtroom interpreters, particularly in criminal cases. For recordings, typically before trial, the conversation is translated into English and a verbatim transcript prepared. If a party seeks to introduce the recording with the translation into evidence, courts have different approaches. For example, in *U.S. v. Morales-Madera*, 352 F.3d 1, 7 (1st Cirt. 2003), the prosecution sought to admit transcripts prepared in English that had been translated from undercover wire conversations which were all in Spanish. The Court explained, "Once translation and transcription disputes have been addressed and the transcripts have been submitted to the jury for its use, parties using audio recordings in other languages should ensure that the English transcripts become part of the record by introducing them in evidence. The English transcripts should be marked and admitted in evidence in addition to the wiretaps themselves."

If the recording is clear and if it is important for the court and/or jurors to observe the demeanor of the speakers (even though speaking in a different language), the court might permit a video recording to be played in open court and direct the interpreter(s) to simultaneously translate the conversations into English. The jurors might also be provided with the translated transcript to assist them.

It can get even more complicated if the parties disagree over whether the translation is accurate. Some languages have dialects, words, or phrases that do not translate exactly to English and vice versa. Thus, there is a subjective component to translation and there could be a difference of opinion regarding what the speaker meant or heard. Generally, when this dispute occurs, the court will hold an evidentiary hearing in order to determine if the translation is reasonably accurate. In *United States v. Le, 256 F.3d 1229, 1238 (11th Cir.2001),* the court adopted one possible procedure: "Initially, the district court and the parties should make an effort to produce an "official" or "stipulated" transcript, one which satisfies all sides. If such an "official" transcript cannot be produced, then each side should produce its own version of a transcript or its own version of the disputed portions. In addition, each side may put on evidence supporting the accuracy of its version or challenging the accuracy of the other side's version." The jury would then resolve the dispute as to which translation was more accurate.

Trial Tip: Choreographing your presentation is important and takes some practice. The timing of when and how an image is displayed in relation to the witness's testimony, can help make the testimony more interesting. For example, some attorneys can skillfully use the document camera or their laptops to zoom in or out on an image as the witness is simultaneously narrating an event.

Satellite Imagery

Satellite imagery deserves special mention because the technology and accuracy surrounding it have become so advanced that its use in the courtroom should be considered for *every* case where the scene or a location matters. An aerial image or a satellite map of a location is one of the best forms of evidence available to make a location or a scene clear for the jury. For example, Google Earth has some amazing features, including the ability to determine very accurate distances and measurements between points. Additionally, these resources are low cost and easy to access. With a little practice, some attorneys become experts at projecting a satellite or aerial image using the courtroom projection equipment and manipulating it as the witness testifies. Thus, when a witness refers to a particular location or feature, the attorney can zoom in and magnify that precise area showing extreme detail. In this respect, courtroom technology has come a long way since just a few years ago when the jury had to strain to see a grainy blow-up photograph on an easel next to the witness stand.

Regarding authentication, satellite imagery has become so accurate and reliable that today a court would likely take *judicial notice* of the accuracy and reliability, thereby not requiring any further evidence to establish that requirement. (*See* e.g.,

United States v. Perea-Rey (9th Cir.2012) 680 F.3d 1179, 1182, fn. 1 [finding "Google map" to be a source "'whose accuracy cannot reasonably be questioned'"].) "When faced with an authentication objection, the proponent of Google–Earth–generated evidence would have to establish Google Earth's reliability and accuracy. That burden could be met, for example, with testimony from a Google Earth programmer or a witness who frequently works with and relies on the program. *It could also be met through judicial notice of the program's reliability."* (U.S. v. Lizarraga 789 F.3d 1107, 1110 (9th Cir. 2015) [emphasis added.]; see Judicial Notice, supra at p. 23.)

> **Trial Tip:** Satellite images and/or aerial photography of a scene or location can be very helpful and informative for the factfinder. Google Earth, for instance, can very accurately show distances between two points down to the centimeter. Moreover, it is easy to acquire and display in the courtroom. And it's inexpensive. To authenticate, request the court to take Judicial Notice of the accuracy. Often, opposing counsel will not object.

Maps, Graphs, and Diagrams

Charts, maps, graphs, diagrams, and the like, are often used in conjunction with the witness's testimony. Typically, the evidence is displayed for the jury in some manner, for example, on the courtroom monitor tied into counsel's laptop or on a poster board set up on an easel where the jurors can see it. During the testimony, the examiner requests the witness to refer to the exhibit. It takes some coordination between the examiner and the witness to have the process go seamlessly. In a case where the physical layout of the scene is important, for example, the witness might use a laser pointer to indicate locations or even mark on the exhibit with a Sharpe. Software programs are available that can create very professional looking diagrams of a scene, e.g., an intersection.

> **Trial Tip:** If a witness is referring to a diagram or a photograph to help describe an event, the use of markings on the exhibit can be helpful. However, ensure the markings are clear and logical. If more than one marking is required, consider having the witness number them to coincide with the sequence of events. Use arrows or lines to show direction or motion. Consider using different colored markers or pre-made tabs. Lastly, to keep the marking coherent and logical, nothing prevents counsel from doing the actual marking at the direction of the witness and then the witness confirms they are accurate. To be avoided is an exhibit with confusing or unintelligible markings that will be meaningless later in the jury room.

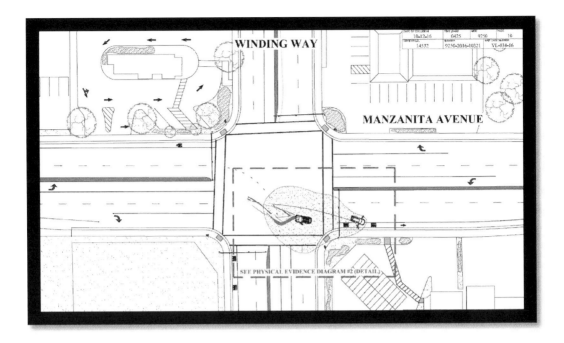

Diagram of Intersection

Counsel: "Sir, on Exhibit 14 [enlarged diagram of intersection], can you point to where your car came to rest immediately after the collision?"

Witness: "Right here." [Witness points to location.]

Counsel: "For the record, you're pointing on the diagram to the top right-hand corner of the intersection where there is a light pole. Is that correct?"

Witness: "Yes."

Counsel: "Using the red marker, can you draw a rectangle on Exhibit 14 to represent your vehicle and where it came to rest? Could you also place your initials inside the rectangle?"

[Witness complies.]

Counsel: "Let the record reflect the witness has drawn a rectangle on the upper right hand corner of the intersection and has initialed it, MSC."

Note: In this example, counsel also recreated a good record by describing where and what the witness marked. In some jurisdictions, the court might require counsel to ask permission to have the record reflect something. For example, "Your Honor, may the record reflect the witness has drawn an X near the top of Exhibit 14?"

If a witness is referring to a diagram or a photograph to help describe an event, the use of markings on the exhibit can be helpful. However, ensure the markings are clear and logical. If more than one marking is required, consider having the witness number them to coincide with the sequence of events. Use arrows or lines to show direction or motion. Consider using different colored markers or pre-made tabs. Lastly, to keep the marking coherent and logical, nothing prevents counsel from doing the actual marking at the direction of the witness and the witness confirms they are accurate. To be avoided is an exhibit with confusing or unintelligible markings that will be meaningless later in the jury room.

Trial Tip: Despite modern technology, having a photograph or a diagram mounted on poster board and set on a easel in the courtroom is still a good method to display this form of evidence because the jurors will have access to it later in the jury room to review more closely at their leisure.

Other Common Charts and Diagrams

Financial Information- Charts showing financial information, such as spread sheets or itemized dollar amounts. The jury can see how the numbers add up. Excellent to show damages.

Scene Diagram – To-scale diagrams or drawings of a scene, such as an intersection. Include a legend. The witness can mark on the exhibit to help explain the testimony.

Documents – If the case involves documents, an enlargement of the document in questions helps the jury to see what the witness is talking about.

Pictorial Drawings – A drawing or an illustration of something in issue, e.g., a drawing depicting the internal muscles or bones of the neck to illustrate an injury. This can greatly amplify an expert's testimony.

Aerial Photograph/Map – Aerial photographs, such as Google Earth images, are very illustrative, accurate, and easy to procure. The use of Google Maps or imagery is so accurate and widely used that a court may be willing to take "judicial notice" of that fact, if requested. (*See United States v. Perea-Rey* (9th Cir.2012) 680 F.3d 1179, 1182, fn. 1 [finding "Google map" to be a source "'whose accuracy cannot reasonably be questioned'"]; Evid. Code 452, subds. (g), (h).)

Timeline Chart – A chart showing a timeline or the sequence of events. One type of such a chart is in the form of a large calendar. As each witness testifies concerning an event, an entry is made on that particular date. The entry is a summary of the witness's testimony. Some enterprising trial attorneys have the witness place a pre-printed note with an adhesive backing on the chart for that date, for example, "date of accident." The chart remains up on an easel throughout all the testimony and permits the jurors to see how the evidence fits.

Tangible (Real) Evidence

In some trials, the evidence is more tangible, such as an object of some type. Some courts refer to this type of evidence as "real evidence." No amount of oral testimony can replace the fact finder's ability to actually see, examine, and sometimes hold something. In criminal cases, for example, this type of evidence can include items of contraband, firearms, bullets, and materials or items of evidence collected from a crime scene. In a murder trial presided over by the author, the victim's actual skull was displayed in the courtroom and used in conjunction with expert testimony to illustrate the location of a bullet hole and cause of death. In another murder trial, bloody river rocks were admitted (sealed in clear plastic bags) to prove the instrumentality of the killing. In civil cases, tangible items can include car parts, defective tools, a piece of concrete, or even a stop sign. There is really no limitation to the types of tangible evidence that might be admitted, as long as it can fit into the courtroom or perhaps even be made available for a jury view in the courthouse parking lot, e.g., a wrecked vehicle.

Trial Tip: If you're going to introduce tangible evidence, plan ahead regarding how it will be marked, handled, and displayed for the jury. Some evidence, such as controlled substances or blood, are biohazards requiring special precautions. Many courts have local rules regarding the handling of hazardous objects. Consideration must also be given re: how the jurors will safely view the item in the jury room, e.g., a firearm.

As with other forms of evidence, tangible items are generally marked for identification as an exhibit with an exhibit tag. The storing and handling of the exhibit is an issue that should be discussed with the court and courtroom staff, particularly for items that may constitute a safety hazard. Often the evidence is brought to court packaged and sealed. Consideration should be given to how the evidence will be unpackaged or unsealed in preparation for testimony. In some criminal prosecutions, for example, the prosecutor will have an evidence tech or an officer unseal the evidence right there on the witness stand in front of the jury to show the evidence has not been tampered with and the chain of custody has been preserved. (Discussed infra, below). If the item is going into the jury room, thought must be given as to how the jurors will be able to view and manipulate the item.

As a side note, if the jurors are allowed to have tangible items of evidence in the jury room, one concern could be whether they (the jury) will be tempted to conduct an improper "experiment" with the evidence, which could constitute juror misconduct. Generally, however, unless specifically instructed otherwise, jurors are permitted to examine the evidence and even manipulate and touch it. (See e.g., *People v. Bogle* (1995) 41 Cal.App.4th 770, 778 [not misconduct for jurors to manipulate a safe and keys in the jury room]; see also *People v. Cumpian* (1991) 1 Cal.App.4th 307, 313-315 [*not* misconduct for the jurors to use a duffle bag submitted as evidence and attempt to reenact in the jury room the manner in which defendant was carrying duffel bag as described by testimony.])

Authentication and Chain of Custody

Like other forms of evidence, proper authentication is required for tangible evidence too. Typically, this is accomplished with a witness who is shown the item and requested to identify it and explain the circumstances of how it relates to the case. An additional requirement, mainly related to tangible evidence, is proof of an adequate "chain of custody." Evidence can pass through a number of hands between the time it was initially obtained until the time it arrives at the courtroom, which can be months, if not years later. For example, in the case of suspected narcotics found during a criminal investigation, that evidence will be collected at the scene, packaged, and booked as evidence at the stationhouse. Later, that same evidence will be transported to the lab, examined by a lab tech, and then returned to the storage locker. Eventually, someone will retrieve the item from the locker and bring it to court for the trial During this process, numerous people may have handled or transported the evidence. The concern with this type of evidence is the possibility that somewhere along the line, the evidence might have been mishandled, lost, tampered with, or contaminated.

To prove an adequate "chain of custody," the proponent need only demonstrate that, as a matter of reasonable probability, possibilities of misidentification and adulteration have been eliminated. Once the evidence is admitted, a gap in the chain of custody goes only to the weight given to the evidence by the trier of fact. (*U.S. v. Mitchell,* 816 F.3d 865, 871 [citations/quotes omitted; see also *Melendez–Diaz v. Massachusetts,* 557 U.S. 305, 311 n. 1, 129 S.Ct. 2527, 174 L.Ed.2d 314 (2009) ["Gaps in the chain ... normally go to the weight of the evidence rather than its admissibility."].) In California, the court in *People v. Catlin* (2001) 26 Cal.4th 81, 134, set forth a good analysis: "In a chain of custody claim, the burden on the party offering the evidence is to show to the satisfaction of the trial court that, taking all the circumstances into account including the ease or difficulty with which the particular evidence could have been altered, it is reasonably certain that there was no alteration. The requirement of reasonable certainty is not met when some vital link in the chain of possession is not accounted for, because then it is as likely as not that the evidence analyzed was not the evidence originally received. Left to such speculation the court must exclude the evidence. Conversely, when it is the barest speculation that there was tampering, it is proper to admit the evidence and let what doubt remains go to its weight. While a perfect chain of custody is desirable, gaps will not result in the exclusion of the evidence, so long as the links offered connect the evidence with the case and raise no serious questions of tampering. The trial court's exercise of discretion in admitting the evidence is reviewed on appeal for abuse of discretion." (*Catlin,* at p. 134.) Of note: The chain of custody analysis has been applied in civil cases too. (See *Edgerton v. State Personnel Bd.* (2000) 83 Cal.App.4th 1350 [failure to maintain chain of custody of urine sample in employment termination action].)

Counsel: "Officer, showing you what has been marked for identification as Exhibit number 15. Do you recognize this object?"

Witness: "Yes, sir. This is the evidence envelope I booked into the department's evidence locker on the day I found the contraband."

Counsel: "How do know it's the same envelope?"

Witness: "I marked the envelope with my badge number, case number, and date. I also recognize my handwriting on the envelope."

Counsel: "Please open the envelope if you would, officer." [Witness opens envelope and retrieves smaller plastic bag with substance.]

Counsel: "Your Honor, may the record reflect that the witness has opened the envelope and retrieved a smaller clear plastic bag?"

Court: "Yes, it may."

[Sometimes, the clerk will mark an object inside an exhibit with a corresponding exhibit number, e.g., 15A]

Counsel: "Officer, do you recognize what's inside?"

Witness: "Yes. This is the small plastic envelope that it I put the pills in after I retrieved them from his pocket. I recognize my initials on the envelope."

Counsel: "Do the pills appear to be the same pills you found on the defendant?"

Witness: "Yes."

Counsel: "Same condition?"

Witness: "Appears so."

In the above example, the prosecution may also call a second witness, such as the criminalist who examined the evidence or an evidence clerk, to explain the chain of custody, often by referring to an evidence log or other records. The records typically show where the item has been and who has handled it, since collection. If there is a hearsay objection, the business record exception may apply. In practice, "chain of custody" only really becomes an issue when the evidence is susceptible of mishandling or contamination, such as fragile DNA swabs or contraband. If the evidence is larger or unique, such as a machine part or a handgun, the fact that every step of its journey from collection to the courtroom cannot be accounted for is generally not a bar to admission, as long as some witness is able to authenticate it. Generally, unless there is something seriously amiss, the court will admit the evidence noting that any deficiency goes to weight, rather than admissibility.

Demonstrative Evidence

When preparing a case for trial, one important consideration is whether there is anything that can be prepared or used to supplement or enhance a witness's testimony. Dry, monotonous oral testimony can be difficult for jurors to absorb and it is well documented that people tend to retain and process information better when they have visual stimuli and memory aids. The use of demonstrative-type evidence is one strategy to consider.

Although there has been some disagreement in the courts regarding what precisely "demonstrative evidence" means, it generally denotes evidence that is used in conjunction with a witness's testimony to help "demonstrate" a point. In this regard, some courts draw a distinction between *substantive* evidence, which is admitted and goes to the jury room, versus *demonstrative* evidence, which is used for illustration purposes only during the witness's testimony, but is not admitted. "Demonstrative evidence is designed for the purpose of illustrating and clarifying a witness's testimony so long as a proper foundation is laid." (*Carson v. Polley*, 689 F.2d 562, 579 (5th Cir.1982); *People v. Roldan* (2005) 35 Cal.4th 646, 708; *People v. Vasquez (*2017) 14 Cal. App. 5th 1019, 1036.) "Demonstrative evidence is generally a pedagogical device used to aid the jury in its understanding of the evidence that has already been admitted. Pedagogical charts or summaries may include witnesses' conclusions or opinions, or they may reveal inferences drawn in a way that would assist the jury. But ... in the end, they are not admitted as evidence." (*Baugh ex rel. Baugh v. Cuprum S.A. de C.V.* 730 F.3d 701 (7th Cir. 2013); *United States v. Janati*, 374 F.3d 263, 273 (4th Cir.2004).) Demonstrative exhibits are meant to "illustrate or clarify a party's position," and they are by definition "less neutral in [their] presentation" and thus are not properly considered evidence. (*United States v. Milkiewicz*, 470 F.3d 390, 396–98 (1st Cir.2006; see also *People v. Duenas* (2012) 55 Cal. 4th 1, 20 ["a computer animation is not substantive evidence used to prove the facts of a case; rather it is demonstrative evidence used to help a jury to understand substantive evidence"].)

Whether the proposed "demonstrative" evidence will be admitted as substantive evidence can be an important issue to take up with the court beforehand, perhaps in a motion in limine. Suppose, for example, that during the testimony of an expert witness (accountant), the expert uses a chart to demonstrate how she calculated the plaintiff's damages, including a grand total. On the chart is written the various numbers and calculations for the jury to see. However, to arrive at the numbers, she may have used complicated formulas for determining future or present values. The plaintiff would like to admit the chart as substantive evidence, meaning, it goes to the jury room. If the defendant objects, the court would likely conduct a Rule 403-type analysis to access whether it is misleading, prejudicial, or argumentative in some fashion. If the chart is neutral and merely lays out the numbers and calculations performed by the expert, who was subjected to cross-examination about it, the court may admit it.

Trial Tip: The use of "demonstrative" evidence to help illustrate or clarify testimony can be important. Whether it is also admitted as substantive evidence is a matter you should take up with the court beforehand. Some forms of "demonstrative" evidence are also admitted as substantive evidence.

Computer Animation

A computer animation is an attempt to recreate some action or event using computer software so the jurors and/or the court can better appreciate what transpired. Typically, the animation is introduced via an expert witness who describes how the animation was created and authenticates the scenes depicted. It is usually designed based on the known facts. The animation can be designed to demonstrate the sequence of events from a particular point of view, for example, from the perspective of a driver in a motor vehicle accident. The same animation might also show the accident from a birds-eye reference point. In criminal cases, animations are often used to recreate the positions of the people at the time of the crime or to show crime scene evidence, such as how blood was spattered. There are commercial animation software applications available and numerous companies that specialize in preparing animations for attorneys. A motion in limine to exclude or admit animation evidence is generally how the issue comes to the court's attention. To determine admissibility, the court may hold an evidentiary hearing requiring testimony.

"Animation is merely used to illustrate an expert's testimony while simulations contain scientific or physical principles requiring validation. Animations do not draw conclusions; they attempt to re-create a scene or process, thus they are treated like demonstrative aids." (*People v. Duenas* (2012) 255 Cal.4th 1, 20.) "We allow the admission of a computer animation as demonstrative evidence of expert testimony, but only if certain conditions are met. The animation must accurately depict an expert opinion, the expert opinion must fairly represent the evidence, the trial court must provide a proper limiting instruction, and the animation must be otherwise admissible under Evidence Code section 352 [FRE 403]." (*People v. Caro* (2019) 7 Cal.5th 463, 509 [crime scene animation that featured three-dimensional, mannequin-like recreations designed with relevant details, such as clothing and hair – upheld].) For an animation, the designer uses facts proven during the trial to illustrate the positions and motions of people or objects. In other words, a computer animation is demonstrative evidence offered to help a jury understand expert testimony or other substantive evidence. (*People v. Hood* (1997) 53 Cal.App.4th 965, 969.) Courts have compared computer animations to classic forms of demonstrative evidence such as charts or diagrams that illustrate expert testimony. A computer animation is admissible if it is a fair and accurate representation of the evidence to which it relates... (*Duenas*, supra.; see also *Robinson v. Missouri Pacific R. Co.*, 16 F.3d 1083, 1088 (10th Cir.1994) [concluding that it was not abuse of discretion for district court to admit video animation depicting collision between train and automobile, but stressing that, because of its dramatic power, trial judges should carefully and meticulously examine proposed animation evidence for proper foundation, relevancy and the potential for undue prejudice.]) "At a minimum, the animation's proponent must show the computer simulation fairly and accurately depicts what it represents, whether the computer expert who prepared it or some other witness who is qualified to so testify, and the opposing party must be afforded an opportunity for cross-examination." (*Byrd v. Guess,* 137 F.3d 1126 (9th Cir. 1998)).

Trial Tip: A computer animation brings an event to life. In criminal cases, for example, it can be used to show movement and trajectories in a crime scene. In civil cases, traffic accidents are the most common form of animation, typically showing the vehicles in motion and various positions prior to, during, and after the collision.

3D Scene Recreation

One of the newest technologies for scene recordation uses precise laser measurements and a computer to recreate a 3D-like view of a scene. For example, if the layout of a house is important, a laser device is placed in each room and also outside which takes precise measurements. The measurements are then uploaded to a computer which stitches it all together to create a very accurate 3-D animation of the scene. Using the computer's mouse, the vantage point of the scene can be moved in practically any direction, allowing the viewer to see any portion of the house from any location, very similar to Google Earth where the vantage points can be manipulated for a 3D view of the earth from practically any viewpoint and elevation. Typically, the animation is introduced with an expert or some other witness who can authenticate the scene depicted. Unlike an animation, this method generally does not show movement.

Computer Simulation

Courts and commentators draw a distinction between computer animations and computer simulations. (*People v. Duenas* (2012) 55 Cal. 4th 1, 20.) "Animation is merely used to illustrate an expert's testimony while simulations contain scientific or physical principles requiring validation. Animations do not draw conclusions; they attempt to recreate a scene or process, thus they are treated like demonstrative aids. Computer simulations are created by entering data into computer models which analyze the data and reach a conclusion. In other words, a computer animation is demonstrative evidence offered to help a jury understand expert testimony or other substantive evidence; a computer simulation, by contrast, is itself substantive evidence." (*Id.* at p. 20 [internal citations deleted].)

Simulations are created by entering known data into a computer program, which analyzes that data according to the rules by which the program operates (e.g., the laws of physics or mathematics) to draw conclusions about what happened and to recreate an event at issue. The program itself, rather than witness testimony, is the source of the visual images depicted and may actually serve as the basis for opinion testimony. Simulations are, therefore, usually classified as substantive evidence and require a much more rigorous foundation, because the jury is being asked to accept the simulation, which may go beyond anything a witness observed, as evidence of what actually happened. "A simulation normally must be authenticated by showing: (1) the qualifications of the expert who prepared the simulation; (2) the capability and reliability of the computer hardware and software used; (3) the calculations and processing of data were done on the basis of principles meeting the standards for scientific evidence under Fed.R.Evid. 702; (4) the data used to make the calculations were reliable, relevant, complete, and properly inputted; and (5) the process produced an accurate result. Simulations which are not properly authenticated are excluded." (See *Bullock v. Daimler Trucks N. Am., LLC*, 819 F. Supp. 2d 1172, 1175 (D. Colo. 2011) (quoting 5 Federal Evidence § 9:26 (3d ed. 2010).)

In practice, because a computer *simulation* is much more difficult to get admitted than a computer animation under the above standards, they are not commonly used in trials. Looking forward, however, with the rapid advancement in computer technology, one can only imagine how far it may some day extend to the courtroom.

Reconstruction/Reenactment

Attempting to reenact or reconstruct an event without relying as much on a computer is the more traditional method of demonstrative evidence and is still very effective. In the typical case, a party will attempt to recreate the same conditions that existed at the time of the event and then conduct an experiment to see how objects react. For example, in an experiment, a vehicle will be driven at the same speed and under the same road conditions as the time of the accident to measure the stopping distances. The proponent will generally videotape the experiment and later seek to admit the video in conjunction with the testimony of an accident reconstruction expert.

For admission, it must be shown that the experiment is relevant and was conducted under substantially similar conditions as those of the actual occurrence. (*Culpepper v. Volkswagen of America, Inc.* (1973) 33 Cal.App.3d 510, 521.) "Evidence of experiments is most commonly used in the context of products liability law, where recreations of accidents, explosions, and product malfunctions are now common. Because this type of evidence can be quite persuasive, in order to avoid unfair prejudice, the conditions under which an experiment is performed must be "substantially similar" to those surrounding the simulated event. This is a flexible requirement: "substantially similar" does not mean "identical," and dissimilarities can be explored on cross-examination. In other words, as a general matter, "dissimilarities between experimental and actual conditions affect the weight, not the admissibility of the evidence." (*U.S. v. Jackson* 479 F.3d 485, 489 (7th Cir. 2007) [internal citations omitted]; *Jodoin v. Toyota Motor Corp.*, 284 F.3d 272, 278 (1st Cir. 2002) See also *Dirosario v. Havens* (1987) 196 Cal.App.3d 1224, 1231 [videotaped reenactment of traffic accident properly admitted].) Within these limits, the physical conditions, which existed at the time the event in question occurred, need not be duplicated with precision, nor is it required that no change has occurred between the occurrence of the event and the time the [videotape] is taken. (*People v. Rodrigues* (1994) 8 Cal.4th 1060, 1113; *People v. Boyd* (1990) 222 Cal.App.3d 541, 565-566; *People v. Jones* (2011) 51 Cal.4th 346, 375; see also *Ehrhardt v. Brunswick, Inc.* (1986) 186 Cal.App.3d 734 [videotaped reenactment of water-skiing accident excluded for lack of similarity]; *Nachtsheim v. Beech Aircraft Corp.*, 847 F.2d 1261, 1278 (7th Cir.1998). [video showing experiments with icing on airplane wing properly admitted.].)

Trial Tip: If there is a dispute regarding how objects or things reacted when in motion, a videotaped experiment or recreation can be persuasive evidence and is generally not too expensive.

Replicas

Jurors like to see evidence and presenting a replica of some disputed object can help bring an event to life. A replica is generally used when the actual evidence is missing or unavailable for some reason. A witness will be called who has personal knowledge of the original item and confirms that the replica in the courtroom looks nearly the same as the original. Of course, there must be some relevance to the use of a replica, for example, to illustrate that a firearm that same size could or could not be easily concealed.

Courts have repeatedly "approved the use of replica evidence, more specifically guns, for demonstrative purposes." (See e.g., *United States v. Park*, 364 F.3d 902, 907 (8th Cir. 2004); *United States v. McIntosh*, 23 F.3d 1454, 1456 (8th Cir. 1994); *United States v. Aldaco*, 201 F.3d 979, 986 (7th Cir. 2000); *United States v. Russell*, 971 F.2d 1098, 1105 (4th Cir. 1992); *United States v. Adkins*, 196 F.3d 1112, 1116-17 (10th Cir. 1999) [affirming district court's admission into evidence of a rifle similar to the firearm charged in the indictment, even though a bayonet not seen with the charged firearm was attached to the replica rifle]; *United States v. Howe*, 538 F.3d 842, 848-49 (8th Cir. 2008) [affirming admission into evidence of a photograph of a pistol similar to the one used by the defendant]; *United States v. Baggett*, 284 Fed. Appx. 341, 344, 2008 (7th Cir. July 7, 2008) [stating that "we have frequently approved the use of demonstrative evidence to establish that a similar object was used in the commission of a crime."]; *United States v. Goodson*, 198 F.3d 238, (4th Cir. Oct. 18, 1999) [finding no abuse of discretion in permitting brief demonstrative use of a shotgun with the same make and model as the firearm charged.]) "It is entirely proper to use objects similar to those connected with the commission of a crime for purposes of illustration." (*People v. Barnett* (1998) 17 Cal.4th 1044, at p. 1135 [no abuse of discretion in allowing prosecution to show jury demonstrative fishing lure and knife, even though items were not identical to those used in crime, where no attempt was made to mislead the jury that the objects were anything other than demonstrative exhibits].)

Props and Models

Prop and models are fairly common at trial and generally used in conjunction with an expert witness's testimony. For example, an anatomically correct skeleton or a model of the spine or neck region might be used by an expert witness (doctor) during testimony to help describe the plaintiff's injuries. In a criminal case, the pathologist might use a mannequin with dowels to illustrate gunshot trajectories. A to-scale model of an intersection or a residence might be prepared to help explain a scene tp make it more clear for the jury. Generally, this is considered "demonstrative" evidence, and thus, not admitted as evidence, but not always. The primary objection to this type of evidence is the complaint that it does not accurately depict the facts or is misleading and prejudicial. (FRE Rule 403) (See e.g., People v. Medina (1995) 11 Cal.4th 694, 754; People v. Riel (2000) 22 Cal.4th 1153, 1194 [use of mannequin to illustrate stab wounds upheld]; *People v. Cummings* (1993) 4 Cal.4th 1233, 1291 ["Mannequins may be used as illustrative evidence to assist the jury in understanding the testimony of witnesses or to clarify the circumstances of a crime."]; Colgan Air, Inc. v. Raytheon Aircraft Co., 535 F. Supp. 2d 580 (E.D. Va. 2008) [Use of aircraft mock-up as a demonstrative evidence approved.]; *People v. Gonzales* (2012) 54 Cal.4th 1234, 1273 [Use of foam doll by pathologist to illustrate how victim was grabbed from behind - upheld.])

Trial Tip: The use of a prop, model, or replica can greatly enhance the force of testimony. However, alert opposing counsel and the court beforehand to avoid getting an objection during testimony.

Courtroom Demonstrations

In some instances, a witness might be requested to reenact an event or to do something *in the courtroom* while the court and/or jury look on. For example, the plaintiff might be asked to demonstrate how she was holding the steering wheel or sitting at the time of the collision; a witness might be requested to stand up or move around in the well in order for the jury to access the witness's physical attributes or limitations, assuming it is relevant. In criminal cases, witnesses are often asked to demonstrate, using their own hands and arms, how a person was holding or pointing a firearm; a firearms expert might manipulate a weapon's action to show how the weapon operates. (See *People v. Buttles* (1990) 223 Cal.App.3d 1631, 1639 [witness was allowed to demonstrate the manner in which the accused had pointed his pistol out of his car before firing the weapon].)

In *Rubert-Torres v. Hospital San Pablo, Inc.* 205 F.3d 472 (1st Cir. 2000), a medical malpractice case, the court held it was error for the trial court to exclude from the courtroom the plaintiff, who suffered from cerebral palsy, for the purpose of a physical demonstration during a doctor's testimony. The court held, "the clearest evidence on her physical appearance would have been for the jury to see her, which is usually favored over mere description." (*Id.* at p. 479, citing 4 Wigmore on Evidence § 1158 (Chadbourn rev.1972); *Rich v. Ellerman & Bucknall S.S. Co.*, 278 F.2d 704, 708 (2d Cir.1960) ["Limitation of proof of the nature of the injuries to a description by a doctor was unduly restrictive. Autopathic preference is always proper, unless reasons of policy apply to exclude it."].)

Things can become more problematic, however, if a witness is asked to recreate an event or perform some "experiment" right there in the courtroom. The burden is on the party offering this type of evidence to establish a similarity of circumstances and conditions. Although the conditions of the demonstration need not be identical to the event at issue, "they must be so nearly the same in substantial particulars as to afford a fair comparison in respect to the particular issue to which the test is directed. Further, experimental or demonstrative evidence, like any evidence offered at trial, should be excluded "if its probative value is substantially outweighed by the danger of unfair prejudice, confusion of the issues, or misleading the jury." (*U.S. v. Gaskell* 985 F.2d 105 (11th Cir. 1993) [experts demonstration of shaking rubber doll in courtroom to simulate shaken baby, not sufficiently similar and prejudicial. Conviction reversed.].)

In practice, judges are generally wary of courtroom demonstrations where the witness is attempting to reenact a potentially complex scenario with many variables over the concern that the conditions cannot be adequately reproduced in the courtroom. Of course, one of the most infamous courtroom demonstrations occurred when O.J. Simpson was asked by the prosecution, over the defense objection, to try on a glove found at the scene of the murders. It didn't fit. Lesson learned.

Trial Tip: Requesting a witness to demonstrate something in the courtroom can be an effective method to help illustrate the testimony. For example, the witness might show the jury a scar from an injury, or in a criminal case, demonstrate how the defendant was holding or pointing a weapon.

12. HEARSAY, SECONDARY EVIDENCE, PRIVILEGE

As discussed previously, the court is the "Gatekeeper" of evidence in a trial, and when there is an objection, it is the court's duty to determine admissibility of that evidence. (Supra, at p. 15.) The four principal requirements for the admissibility of any type of evidence are: (1) The evidence must relevant; (2) the evidence must be properly authenticated; (3) the evidence must not violate a rule prohibiting admission; and (4), the probative value must not be substantially outweighed by the prejudicial effect; (Section 352; supra at p. 19.) The previous chapters have discussed relevance, authentication, and the court's authority to exclude relevant evidence. This chapter, therefore, relates solely to the question of whether admission of the proposed evidence violates an evidentiary exclusionary rule. In the trial setting, the three most commonly cited exclusionary rules are hearsay, best evidence, and privilege. As you can imagine, the law related to these areas is quite expansive and entire treatises have been written on each. Thus, the discussions below are meant to provide only an overview of the most important basic requirements and issues related to these rules; those that, as a trial lawyer, you should know and understand well.

Hearsay

Hearsay is an issue which crops up fairly often at trial. It can come to the court's attention either in a motion in limine at the beginning or rather unexpectedly during the midst of testimony. Despite the fact that the rule and its exceptions have been around for a while, some attorneys object when a statement is clearly not hearsay, while others fail to object when obvious and damaging hearsay is elicited. The basic rule is simple enough.

Evidence Code section 1200, subdivision (a) defines hearsay as "evidence of a statement that was made other than by a witness while testifying at the hearing and that is offered to prove the truth of the matter stated." Thus, a hearsay statement is one in which a person makes a factual assertion out of court and the proponent seeks to rely on the statement to prove that assertion is true. Hearsay is generally inadmissible unless it falls under an exception. (Evid. Code § 1200, subd. (b).; *People v. Sanchez* (2016) 63 Cal.4th 665.)

When attempting to determine whether something is or is not hearsay, consider the underlying rationale behind the rule. "The essence of the hearsay rule is a requirement that testimonial assertions shall be subjected to the test of cross-examination. The basic theory is that the many possible deficiencies, suppressions, sources of error, and untrustworthiness, which lie underneath the bare untested assertion of a witness, may be best brought to light and exposed by the test of cross-examination." (*Buchanan v. Nye* (1954) 128 Cal.App.2d 582, 585; *Target Nat. Bank v. Rocha* (2013) 216 Cal.App.4th Supp. 1.) Thus, if it would be important to cross-examine the declarant of an out-of-court statement, then the statement is probably hearsay.

The Analysis

Because a trial is a fluid and fast-moving environment, the trial lawyer must be able to quickly identify what is hearsay, whether there is an applicable exception, and whether to object. The admissibility can be determined using a quick five-step analysis:

1. Is there a "statement" by a *person* which makes an *assertion*?
2. Is the statement being offered to prove the *truth of the matter* asserted in the statement?
3. If it is not hearsay, then what is the *relevance* of the non-hearsay purpose?
4. If it is hearsay, is there an applicable *hearsay exception*? The various statutory exceptions are set forth between Evidence Code sections 1220 and 1390. (Appendix.)
5. In a criminal case, does admission of the statement violate the defendant's Sixth Amendment right to confrontation?

CA Rule of Evid. § 1200. The hearsay rule (FRE Rule 801-802)

(a) "Hearsay evidence" is evidence of a statement that was made other than by a witness while testifying at the hearing and that is offered to prove the truth of the matter stated.
(b) Except as provided by law, hearsay evidence is inadmissible.
(c) This section shall be known and may be cited as the hearsay rule.

CA Rule of Evid. § 1201. Multiple hearsay (FRE Rule 805)

A statement within the scope of an exception to the hearsay rule is not inadmissible on the ground that the evidence of such statement is hearsay evidence if such hearsay evidence consists of one or more statements each of which meets the requirements of an exception to the hearsay rule.

Objection and Burden of Proof

As with other types of inadmissible evidence, there must be a *timely* and *specific* objection to the purported hearsay. A failure to object properly generally forfeits the issue on appeal. (See Trial Objections, infra, at p. 221.) In practice, during live testimony, the objection must come quickly to prevent the witness from answering, which requires you to be on your toes, so to speak. If the witness relates inadmissible hearsay and then you object, it will be difficult, if not impossible, to "unring the bell," even if the court sustains the objection and strikes the answer from the record. Further, if you wait until later to make the objection, even one or two more questions, the court will likely overrule the objection as "untimely."

Opp. Counsel: "What did the officer tell you?"
Counsel: "Objection, Your Honor, calls for hearsay."

Once an objection is raised, the burden of showing admissibility is on the proponent which must convince the court that either the statement is not hearsay or that an exception applies. (*U.S. v Arnold* 486 F. 3d. 177, 195 (6th Cir. 2007); *People v. Blacksher* (2011) 52 Cal.4th 769, 819 ["The proponent of proffered testimony has the burden of establishing its relevance, and if the testimony is comprised of hearsay, the foundational requirements for its admissibility under an exception to the hearsay rule. Evidence is properly excluded when the proponent fails to make an adequate offer of proof regarding the relevance or admissibility of the evidence."].)

Counsel: "Did you talk with Mrs. Jones?"
Opp. Counsel: "Objection, Your Honor, hearsay."

The court should overrule this objection because, technically, the question does not ask the witness to recite what Mrs. Jones said. It can be answered with either a "yes" or "no" response. It is not uncommon for attorneys to object prematurely.

Witness: "Yes."
Counsel: "What did she say?"
Opp. Counsel: "Objection. Hearsay." [Objection proper]
Court: "Counsel, your response?"
Counsel: "It qualifies as an excited utterance, Your Honor." ...or... "It's
                not offered for the truth. It goes to her state of mind."

Regarding an excited utterance, how the court rules will depend on whether the proponent has established the requirements for that exception; namely, that it is "...was made spontaneously while the declarant was under the stress of excitement caused by such perception.." (See Evid. Code § 1240. Spontaneous statement, infra at p. 264.) If the proponent claims a non-hearsay purpose, i.e., state of mind, then the next question is whether the declarant's state of mind is relevant. Some attorneys will claim there is a non-hearsay purpose, but then have a difficult time articulating the relevance of that purpose. (See discussion below re: hearsay vs. non-hearsay.)

Trial Tip: If there is an important hearsay issue to be resolved, raise the issue in a motion in limine. Judges really do not like being confronted with complex hearsay issues in the midst of testimony.

Is there a statement made by a person?

The first question in the hearsay analysis is whether a "statement" was made by a "person." The term "statement" means (a) oral or written verbal expression, or (b) nonverbal conduct *of a person* intended by him as a substitute for oral or written verbal expression. (Evid. Code § 225.) "A 'person' includes a natural person, firm, association, organization, partnership, business trust, corporation, limited liability company, or public entity." (Evid. Code § 175.) If there is no "statement," then there is no hearsay, and the only remaining issue is relevance.

Nonverbal/ Non-Assertive Conduct

Evidence of a person's conduct out of court is not inadmissible under the hearsay rule expressed in Section 1200 unless that conduct is clearly assertive in character. Nonassertive conduct is not hearsay. Put differently, "for purposes of the hearsay rule, conduct is assertive if the actor at the time intended the conduct to convey a particular meaning to another person. For example, a nod of the head in response to a question calling for a yes-or-no answer, or a gesture pointing to a particular person when asked to identify a perpetrator, are examples of assertive conduct." (*People v. Jurado* (2006) 38 Cal.4th 72, 129.) Nonverbal conduct may or may not be a "statement," depending upon the intent of the person doing the acting. Running away or hiding evidence is probably not hearsay. If there is an issue of whether nonverbal conduct is hearsay, it will be up to the court to make a preliminary determination of the person's intent.

For example, in *People v. Rogers* (2009) 46 Cal.4th 1136, 1161, the defendant was asked "Who are you going to kill next?" The defendant did not say anything, but got real "bug-eyed" and nervous and started pacing. Held: The defendant's reaction was not hearsay because it merely described nonverbal, nonassertive, emotional behavior. It was relevant to show the defendant knew a killing had occurred and had a consciousness of guilt. Because the reaction was not hearsay, no finding that it qualified as an Adoptive Admission (Evid. Code § 1221) was required. (*Rogers*, supra, at p. 1162; See also *People v. Jurado* (2006) 38 Cal.4th 72, 129 ["defendant's emotional displays were nonassertive conduct, and thus not within the hearsay rule"]; *People v. Snow* (1987) 44 Cal.3d 216, 227 [defendant's silence upon learning of the victim's death was not a statement under the hearsay rule and was admissible to show his prior knowledge of the killing].)

In *People v. Myers* (2014) 227 Cal.App.4th 1219, the court considered whether a robbery victim's act of putting his hands up during a robbery, as described by a detective who observed the act on a surveillance video, was hearsay. Finding the act was not hearsay, the court explained: "We recognize that the universal meaning of Hurst's act in human communication—as a sign of surrender—supports a conclusion that his use of that gesture was an intentional (if reflexive) communicative act. But it is equally indisputable that Officer Donnel's and the Inn's owner's account of the clerk raising his hands in the surveillance video was not offered to prove that Hurst actually surrendered to Myers. Thus, the testimony was not offered to prove the matter asserted—a surrender. The same would be true if Hurst had uttered the words "I surrender." Such proof of actual surrender—oral or gestural—would be of no relevance or materiality in the case at issue. What was at issue was that Myers used fear to effect the robbery. The clerk's raised hands reflected his state of mind of surrender and thus tended to support a contention that Myers used fear to effect his crime. So, we have no hearsay." (*Myers*, supra, at p. 1227.)

Machines

Only people can generate hearsay. Machines, animals, chemical reactions cannot. (*People v. Dungo* (2012) 55 Cal. 4th 608, at pp. 646-647 (dis. opn. of Corrigan, J.).) "The Evidence Code does not contemplate that a machine can make a statement." (*People v. Goldsmith* (2014) 59 Cal.4th 258, 274.) Machine-generated data is not a hearsay statement. (*People v. Lopez* (2012) 55 Cal.4th 569.) In *Lopez*, the court held that data generated by a gas chromatography machine were not "statements" of the analyst. The issue, therefore, was only whether the internal operations of the machine were working properly. (Id. at p. 583; See also *People v. Nazary* (2010) 191 Cal.App.4th 727, 754 [gas station computer receipt showing date, time, and total of purchase not hearsay].) Evidentiary issues concerning machine-generated evidence are foundational and the test of admissibility is whether the machine was operating properly at the time of the reading, and that the mechanical recordings of information are subject to impeachment through evidence of machine imperfections or by cross-examination of the expert who explained or interpreted the information in the device. (*People v. Hawkins* (2002) 98 Cal.App.4th 1428, 1449-1450.)

Computers

Computers are also machines. Are printouts from a computer hearsay? The answer depends on what is being printed out. In *People v. Hawkins* (2002) 98 Cal.App.4th 1428, the court held that a printout of the results of when the computer was last accessed were part the computer's *internal operations* and not hearsay evidence. "It does not represent the output of statements placed into the computer by out-of-court declarants. Nor can we say that this printout itself is a 'statement' constituting hearsay evidence. The underlying rationale of the hearsay rule is that such statements are made without an oath and their truth cannot be tested by cross-examination. Of concern is the possibility that a witness may consciously or unconsciously misrepresent what the declarant told him or that the declarant may consciously or unconsciously misrepresent a fact or occurrence. With a machine, however, there is no possibility of a conscious misrepresentation, and the possibility of inaccurate or misleading data only materializes if the machine is not functioning properly." (*Hawkins*, at p. 1449.)

However, if the computer is merely a storage device for other hearsay declarations, e.g., stored documents, then a printout of those documents would still be subject to the hearsay rule. The mere fact they were stored in and printed from a computer does not make them immune to the hearsay rule. As one court explained, "A computer can be used to store documents and information entered by human operators, but a computer can also be programmed to generate information on its own, such as a record of its internal operations. The latter type of computer-generated information is not hearsay because it is not a statement by a person." (*Hawkins*, supra, 98 Cal.App.4th at p. 1449; accord, *People v. Nazary* (2010) 191 Cal.App.4th 727, 754.) Even if printouts from a computer are hearsay, California cases have held generally that computer printouts are admissible when they fit within a hearsay exception, such as a business record under Evidence Code section 1271. (*People v. Lugashi* (1988) 205 Cal.App.3d 632, 641-642; see also *People v. Zavala* (2013) 216 Cal.App.4th 242 [computer-generated cell-phone records admissible as business record].)

To prove the truth of the matter asserted?

The question of whether a statement is being offered to prove the truth of the matter asserted in the statement *or* whether there is a valid non-hearsay reason to admit it is probably the most common issue when an objection is raised. Often, the proponent will argue that the statement is not hearsay because it is being offered for some other reason than the truth.

Witness:	"I was on routine patrol when I received a call from dispatch regarding a traffic collision."
Counsel:	"What did the dispatcher inform you?"
Witness:	"That a motor vehicle accident had just occurred at the intersection of Elm and Lincoln. A blue minivan had run the red light, hit a pedestrian, and there were injuries."
Opp. Counsel:	"Objection, Your Honor. Hearsay. Move to strike."
Court:	"Your response, counsel?"
Counsel:	"Your Honor, it's not being offered for the truth, but to explain why the officer then proceeded to the intersection of Elm and Lincoln. To explain his conduct."

There are legitimate non-hearsay reasons why a statement might be admissible; for example, if the hearer's reaction to the statement is a relevant fact sought to be proved. (*People v. Livingston* (2012) 53 Cal.4th 1145, 1162; *People v. Armendariz* (1984) 37 Cal.3d 573, 585; see also *People v. Samuels* (2005) 36 Cal.4th 96, 122 [out-of-court statement properly admitted to explain witness's subsequent actions]; See also *United States v. Reed*, 908 F.3d 102, 120 (5th Cir. 2018) ["Ordinarily, a statement is not hearsay if it is offered to prove the statement's effect on the listener."]) However, the proffered non-hearsay purpose must also be *relevant* to the contested issues. In the above example, the court would likely find there is no relevance to the stated non-hearsay purpose. The details of the accident are not relevant to explain why the officer proceeded to the intersection. At a minimum, the court would likely strike the portion of the answer regarding the blue mini-van running the red light and hitting a pedestrian. It should also be noted that opposing counsel failed in one respect, and that was by not objecting sooner, before the witness answered.

Trial Tip: One of the most common issues at trial is whether there is some non-hearsay purpose of the statement, and if so, the relevance of that purported non-hearsay purpose.

Evidence of a declarant's statement that is offered to prove that the statement imparted certain information to the hearer and that the hearer, believing such information to be true, acted in conformity with that belief. The statement is not hearsay because it is the hearer's reaction to the statement that is the relevant fact sought to be proved, not the truth of the matter asserted in the statement. (*People v. Turner* (1994) 8 Cal.4th 137, 189, disapproved on other grounds in *People v. Griffin* (2004) 33 Cal.4th 536, 555, fn. 5.)

Counsel: "Why did you leave your house so early on the morning of the accident?"

Witness: "Well, the evening before, my daughter informed me that her teacher was requesting to meet with me at the classroom a few minutes before class started to discuss my daughter's grades."

Opp. Counsel: "Objection, Your Honor, hearsay.

In the above, does the *truth* of what the defendant's daughter or the teacher said matter, when the issue is whether she ran a red light on the way to the school that morning? The information received by the witness is relevant for the non-hearsay purpose of explaining why the witness was in a hurry that morning, which in turn, may have contributed to her inattentiveness, possibly a contributing factor in the accident. Thus, the court would likely overrule the objection simply because the statements by the daughter or the teacher are not hearsay.

Operative Facts

A statement is also not hearsay if the words spoken or stated are themselves important, regardless of whether or not they are true. This non-hearsay purpose often arises in cases where the issue is breach of contract or contract interpretation, a will contest, prior notice or knowledge, or fraud and deceit. A verbal act is an utterance of an operative fact that gives rise to legal consequences. Verbal acts, also known as verbal statements, are not hearsay because the statement is admitted merely to show that it was actually made, not to prove the truth of what was asserted. For example, the hearsay rule does not exclude relevant evidence as to what the contracting parties said or wrote with respect to the making or terms of an agreement. (*United States v. Tann,* 425 F. Supp. 2d 26, 36 (D.D.C. 2006); see also *United States v. Porter,* 482 F.2d 933, 934 n. 5 (5th Cir. 1973) ["The hearsay rule does not apply to utterances introduced as operative facts."].) An out-of-court statement is properly admitted for a relevant non-hearsay purpose, such as to show a warning, admonition, or notice, "since the hearsay rule does not forbid the introduction of evidence that a request has been made when the making of the request is significant irrespective of the truth or falsity of its content." (*Caro v. Smith* (1997) 59 Cal.App.4th 725, 733.) "Where the very fact in controversy is whether certain things were said or done and not ... whether these things were true or false ... in these cases the words or acts are admissible not as hearsay, but as original evidence." (*Jazayeri v. Mao* (2009) 174 Cal.App.4th 301, 316.)

Multiple Layers

The rules can get a little more complicated when there are potentially multiple layers of hearsay. Generally, when a party seeks to introduce a document that contains hearsay within hearsay, any double hearsay statements are inadmissible unless a hearsay exception applies to each level of hearsay. (*United States v. Habteyes,* 356 F. Supp. 3d 573 (E.D. Va. 2018); *People v. Arias* (1996) 13 Cal.4th 92, 149; *People v. Perez* (1978) 83 Cal.App.3d 718, 730; CA Evid. Code § 1201 (See above).)

In practice, the multiple layer issue arises most often concerning records. For example, a party may move to admit the plaintiff's hospital records under the Business Record exception. However, those records may include the statements of many different declarants, for instance, first responder notes, statements of third-party witnesses, treating physician's notes or diagnosis, nurse's notes, laboratory or radiological tests and results, or the opinions or statements from other non-testifying experts.

Ordinarily, when a party seeks to introduce a statement containing multiple layers of hearsay, "each link in the chain must be admissible, either because it is an admission and thus not hearsay or under some other hearsay exception." (*Vazquez v. Lopez-Rosario,* 134 F.3d 28, 34 (1st Cir. 1998).) Under this logic, courts refuse to admit portions of a business's records because they were originally created by outsiders to that business, unless the underlying statements themselves qualify under an exception. (*United States v. Patrick,* 248 F.3d 11, 22 (1st Cir. 2001).)

> **Trial Tip:** Be alert for multiple layers of hearsay, particularly within documents, such as business records. Simply because the writing itself qualifies for an exception, e.g., a business record, does not necessarily mean that every statement contained within that writing is admissible. The same principle also applies to court records.

Experts and Hearsay

It is well accepted that an expert can rely on inadmissible evidence to form an opinion, such as hearsay. However, recently courts have begun to examine the extent to which an expert can recite hearsay to the factfinder as the basis of the opinion. For example, in *People v. Sanchez* (2016) 63 Cal.4th 665, 676, the court held that it was improper for the expert to relate "case-specific" hearsay versus general-knowledge hearsay. (See full discussion re Experts and hearsay, infra, at p. 204.)

Is there an applicable hearsay exception?

If the out-of-court statement is hearsay, the next question is whether it falls within a hearsay exception? As mentioned, upon objection, it is the proponent's burden to prove the statement falls within an exception. (*People v. Blacksher* (2011) 52 Cal.4th 769, 819 ["The proponent of proffered testimony has the burden of establishing its relevance, and if the testimony is comprised of hearsay, the foundational requirements for its admissibility under an exception to the hearsay rule."].) If there is an objection, be prepared to cite the applicable exception and how the requirements have been fulfilled. California Evidence Code sections 1220 thru 1390 (See Appendix), set forth the statutory exceptions to the Hearsay Rule.

> **Trial Tip:** Having a "cheat sheet" available during trial for a quick review of the hearsay rules and exceptions can be helpful.

Is there a Confrontation Clause (*Crawford*) Issue?

In criminal cases, there is an additional analysis. The issue relates to the defendant's inability to cross-examine a hearsay declarant. In *Crawford v. Washington*, 541 U.S. 36, 51–52, 124 S. Ct. 1354, 158 L. Ed. 2d 177 (2004), the United States Supreme Court concluded that an out-of-court "testimonial" statement made by a witness to law enforcement officials is barred by the Sixth Amendment's Confrontation Clause, even if there has been a judicial determination that the statement bears particularized guarantees of trustworthiness, unless the defendant had a prior opportunity to cross-examine the witness and the witness is unavailable to testify at trial. Thus, even if a statement is admissible under a hearsay exception, the rule still applies that admission of a "testimonial" hearsay statement by a declarant who does not appear for cross-examination at trial violates the Confrontation Clause, unless the defendant had a prior opportunity to cross-examine the witness. In contrast, the Confrontation Clause does not bar admission of hearsay statements that are "nontestimonial." Thus, in criminal cases, there has been extensive litigation regarding the precise meaning of "testimonial" versus "nontestimonial" hearsay.

Secondary Evidence Rule

Some older attorneys may remember the "Best Evidence Rule," however, in California, that rule was repealed by the Legislature in 1998 and replaced with the "Secondary Evidence Rule," as set forth in Evidence Code sections 1520 and1521.

Evid. Code § 1520.

The content of a writing may be proved by an otherwise admissible original.

Evid. Code § 1521. Secondary evidence rule (FRE Rule 1002 -1008)

(a) The content of a writing may be proved by otherwise admissible secondary evidence. The court shall exclude secondary evidence of the content of writing if the court determines either of the following:
(1) A genuine dispute exists concerning material terms of the writing and justice requires the exclusion.
(2) Admission of the secondary evidence would be unfair.

(b) Nothing in this section makes admissible oral testimony to prove the content of a writing if the testimony is inadmissible under Section 1523 (oral testimony of the content of a writing).

(c) Nothing in this section excuses compliance with Section 1401 (authentication).

Generally, issues of "Secondary Evidence" arise in trials when the original "writing" is not available for some reason. It is very common at trial that copies of originals are used, e.g., faxed or photocopied copies. If the authenticity of the copies is not contested, Section 1521 permits the introduction of "otherwise admissible secondary evidence" to prove the contents of a writing. The rule does not excuse, however, the proponent from complying with other rules of evidence, most notably the hearsay rule. (*Dart Industries, Inc. v. Commercial Union Ins. Co.* (2002) 28 Cal.4th 1059, 1070, fn. 2.) The Secondary Evidence Rule does not "excuse compliance with Section 1401" (authentication). Thus, to be "otherwise admissible," secondary evidence must be authenticated. (*People v. Skiles* (2012) 51 Cal.4th 1178, 1187 [upholding admission of copies of certified records.].) Once the proponent of the evidence establishes its authenticity, section 1521 requires exclusion of secondary evidence only if the court determines: (1) a genuine dispute exists concerning material terms of the writing and justice requires the exclusion or (2) admission of the secondary evidence would be unfair. (§ 1521, subd. (a) (1) & (2); *Skiles,* supra, at p. 1188.)

Lost Documents
Sometimes an issue can arise if the original writing is lost or not available. The admission of oral testimony regarding the contents of a writing is specifically

governed by section 1523, which provides, in pertinent part, that such testimony is admissible "if the proponent does not have possession or control of the original or a copy of the writing and ... [¶] ... neither the writing nor a copy of the writing was reasonably procurable by the proponent by use of the court's process or by other available means..." (See Evid. Code § 1523, Appendix at p. 265.)

These statutes are codifications of the venerable common law rule that lost documents may be proved by secondary evidence. "The rule ... for the admission of secondary evidence of a lost paper requires 'that a bona fide and diligent search has been unsuccessfully made for it in the place where it was most likely to be found;' and further, 'the party is expected to show that he has in good faith exhausted in a reasonable degree all the sources of information and means of discovery which the nature of the case would naturally suggest, and which were accessible to him." (*Dart Industries, Inc. v. Commercial Union Ins. Co.* (2002) 28 Cal.4th 1059, 1068-1069 [contents of a lost insurance policy may be proved by secondary evidence].) A corollary of the rule that the contents of lost documents may be proved by secondary evidence is that the law does not require the contents of such documents be proved verbatim. (Ibid.)

While section 1505 permits secondary evidence of the contents of a writing, it does not permit a party who has never seen the writing to testify to its contents. As one commentator has stated, "The witness must have personal knowledge of the original, whether he authenticates a copy or gives oral testimony of its contents. (2 Witkin, Cal. Evidence (3d ed. 1986) § 942, p. 898.)

Privilege

Another set of exclusionary rules are referred to as "privilege," where for policy reasons, the law excludes or prohibits certain forms of evidence in a trial or hearing, even if highly relevant. However, the court in *Trammel v. U.S.*, 445 U.S. 40, 50, 100 S. Ct. 906, 912, 63 L. Ed. 2d 186 (1980), cautioned: "Testimonial exclusionary rules and privileges contravene the fundamental principle that the public has a right to every man's evidence. As such, they must be strictly construed and accepted only to the very limited extent that permitting a refusal to testify or excluding relevant evidence has a public good transcending the normally predominant principle of utilizing all rational means for ascertaining truth." (Id. at p. 50

Under California law, privileges are strictly statutory. Courts have no power to "create" an evidentiary privilege as a matter of judicial policy. (Ev.C. § 911); *Roberts v. City of Palmdale* (1993) 5 C4th 363, 373.) On the other hand, FRE Rule 501 authorizes federal courts to define privileges by interpreting common law principles and stare decisis. Rather than statutorily define privileges, as they did with the Hearsay Rule and its exceptions, Congress left it up to the courts and common law to determine privilege on a case- by-case basis. (*Jaffee v. Redmond*, 518 U.S. 1, 18, 116 S.Ct. 1923, 135 L.Ed.2d 337 (1996).) However, in civil cases involving state claims, the Federal court looks to the relevant state law regarding privilege.

In California, there are numerous statutory "privileges" which have developed into an extensive body of law, beyond the scope of this handbook. (See Evid. Code §§ 900 thru 1070.) However, for the practicing attorney, a review of the most commonly cited privileges applicable in a trial is helpful. The issue is typically brought to the court's attention in a motion in limine where a party will seek to exclude certain evidence, e.g., records or testimony, on the ground that it is "privileged." The issue can also arise mid-trial and unexpectedly, for example, when a witness asserts the Fifth Amendment. To resolve the issue, the court will generally need to hold a hearing outside the presence of the jury.

Attorney Client

The attorney-client privilege is contained in Evidence Code section 950 et seq., and in general allows the client "to refuse to disclose, and to prevent another from disclosing, a confidential communication between client and lawyer...." (CA Evid.Code, § 954; *Wellpoint Health Networks, Inc. v. Superior Court* (1997) 59 Cal.App.4th 110, 120.) Under the Evidence Code, the attorney-client privilege applies to confidential communications within the scope of the attorney-client relationship even if the communication does not relate to pending litigation; the privilege applies not only to communications made in anticipation of litigation, but also to legal advice when no litigation is threatened. (*Wellpoint Health*, supra; *Roberts v. City of Palmdale* (1993) 5 Cal.4th 363, 371.) For the communication to be privileged where a corporate entity is the client, "the dominant purpose must be for transmittal to an attorney in the course of professional employment." (*Holm v. Superior Court* (1954) 42 Cal.2d 500, 507.) "The privilege is absolute and disclosure may not be ordered, without regard to relevance, necessity or any particular circumstances peculiar to the case." *(Gordon v. Superior Court* (1997) 55 Cal.App.4th 1546, 1557; *Costco Wholesale Corp. v. Superior Court* (2009) 47 Cal.4th 725, 763 [opinion letter from attorney to client – protected].) At the same time, documents prepared independently by a party, including witness statements, do not become privileged communications or work product merely because they are turned over to counsel. (See *Nacht & Lewis Architects, Inc. v. Superior Court* (1996) 47 Cal.App.4th 214.)

The party claiming the privilege has the burden of establishing the preliminary facts necessary to support its exercise, i.e., a communication made in the course of an attorney-client relationship. (*Wellpoint Health Networks, supra.*) Once that party establishes facts necessary to support a prima facie claim of privilege, the communication is presumed to have been made in confidence and the opponent of the claim of privilege has the burden of proof to establish the communication was not confidential or that the privilege does not for other reasons apply. (Evid.Code, § 917, subd. (a); *Wellpoint Health Networks, Inc.*, at pp. 123–124; *Costco Wholesale Corp*, supra.)

Work Product Doctrine

The work product rule in California creates for the attorney a *qualified privilege* against discovery of general work product and an absolute privilege against disclosure of writings containing the attorney's impressions, conclusions, opinions or legal theories. (*BP Alaska Exploration, Inc. v. Superior Court* (1988) 199 Cal.App.3d 1240, 1249.) The attorney work product doctrine is codified in section 2018 of the Code of Civil Procedure which provides in relevant part: "(a) It is the policy of the state to: (1) preserve the rights of attorneys to prepare cases for trial with that degree of privacy necessary to encourage them to prepare their cases thoroughly and to investigate not only the favorable but the unfavorable aspects of those cases; and (2) to prevent attorneys from taking undue advantage of their adversary's industry and efforts. [¶] (b) Subject to subdivision (c), the work product of an attorney is not discoverable unless the court determines that denial of discovery will unfairly prejudice the party seeking discovery in preparing that party's claim or defense or will result in an injustice. [¶] (c) Any writing that reflects an attorney's impressions, conclusions, opinions, or legal research or theories shall not be discoverable under any circumstances." (*Wellpoint Health Networks, Inc.,* at p. 120.)

Self Incrimination

It is not uncommon that a witness may potentially have some criminal liability, meaning, the witness's testimony could expose the witness to criminal prosecution. For example, a party in a family law trial who is also currently charged in a criminal case with domestic abuse against the other party. "When a trial court has reason to believe that a witness may be charged with a crime arising out of events to which he might testify, it has a duty to insure that the witness is fully advised of his privilege against self-incrimination." (*People v. Schroeder* (1991) 227 Cal.App.3d 784, 787–788.) The court may advise the witness or appoint counsel to advise the witness. If the court chooses to advise the witness, it must do so in such a way as to fully advise the witness of the risks of testifying and the right not to testify, but not to coerce the witness not to testify. The coerciveness of an advisement is evaluated in light of all of the circumstances. (Id. at p. 793.)

In some cases, a witness might refuse to testify, citing the Fifth Amendment. When this occurs, the court will generally hold a hearing outside the presence of the jury to determine whether the witness has a valid claim. The claim could have merit or it could be a ploy to avoid testifying. "To invoke the privilege, a witness need not be guilty of any offense; rather, the privilege is properly invoked whenever the witness's answers would furnish a link in the chain of evidence needed to prosecute the witness for a criminal offense.... A trial court may compel the witness to answer only if it clearly appears to the court that the proposed testimony cannot possibly have a tendency to incriminate the person claiming the privilege." (*People v. Cudjo* (1993) 6 Cal.4th 585, 617.) "The privilege can be asserted in any proceeding, civil or criminal, administrative or judicial, investigatory or adjudicatory...." *(Segretti v. State Bar* (1976) 15 Cal.3d 878, 886.) "However, a blanket refusal to testify is unacceptable; a person claiming the Fifth Amendment privilege must do so with specific reference to particular questions asked or other evidence sought.... Once this is done, the trial court must undertake a particularized inquiry with respect to each specific claim of privilege to determine whether the claimant has ... established that the testimony or other evidence sought might tend to incriminate him." (*Warford v. Medeiros* (1984) 160 Cal.App.3d 1035, 1045, citations and italics omitted; accord, *Fisher v. Gibson* (2001) 90 Cal.App.4th 275, 286.) [The burden is on the party or witness invoking the privilege to show that the testimony or other evidence could tend to incriminate him or her.].)

A related issue can be whether the invocation of the Fifth Amendment by a witness is considered as admissible evidence, permitting the jury (or court) to draw inferences? The general rule in civil cases is that a non-party's invocation of the Fifth Amendment privilege against self-incrimination is admissible evidence so long as it does not unduly prejudice a party to the case. (See *LiButti v. United States*, 107 F.3d 110, 124 (2d Cir.1997); *Federal Deposit Ins. Corp. v. Fidelity & Deposit Co. of Maryland*, 45 F.3d 969, 977 (5th Cir.1995).)

Trial Tip: If you believe a witness may have self-incrimination issues, it is prudent to raise that issue to the court and opposing counsel beforehand. It the witness is not your client, it can be perilous to give that witness legal any advice whether or not the testimony might be incriminating.

Psychotherapist/Patient

"A privilege protecting confidential communications between a psychotherapist and her patient 'promotes sufficiently important interests to outweigh the need for probative evidence." (*Jaffee*, 518 U.S. at 9–10, 116 S.Ct. 1923 (citing Trammel, 445 U.S. at 51, 100 S.Ct. 906; CA Evid. Code § 1012 et al.) The patient ... has a privilege to refuse to disclose, and to prevent another from disclosing, a confidential communication between patient and psychotherapist. (*Menendez v. Superior Court* (1992) 3 Cal.4th 435, 447–448.)

Doctor/Patient

Federal common law has not historically recognized a privilege between patients and physicians. (*Northwestern Mem'l Hosp. v. Ashcroft*, 362 F.3d 923, 926 (7th Cir.2004); *Whalen v. Roe*, 429 U.S. 589, 602 n. 28, 97 S.Ct. 869, 51 L.Ed.2d 64 (1977) ["The physician-patient evidentiary privilege is unknown to the common law."].) However, most state jurisdictions do have such a privilege. (See CA Evidence Code § 992 et al. In addition, statutory restrictions on patient information, e.g., HIPAA, may be applicable, although not considered a "privilege." (See *U.S. v. Bek,* 493 F.3d 790, 802, (7th Cir. 2007).)

Under the California Evidence Code the physician-patient privileges grants a patient the right to decline to disclose, or prohibit a third party from disclosing, any "confidential communications" with a medical professional. (Evid.Code, § 994.) Evidence Code section 994 limits the right to claim the physician-patient privilege to the holder of the privilege (i.e., the patient); a person authorized to claim the privilege by the holder of the privilege; or the physician who received the confidential communication. The privilege serves two purposes: (1) to prevent humiliation that might follow disclosure of his or her ailments, and (2) to encourage the patients' full disclosure to his or her physician. (*Los Angeles Gay & Lesbian Center v. Superior Court* (2011) 194 Cal.App.4th 288, 309; *Binder v. Superior Court* (1987) 196 Cal.App.3d 893, 898.)

Marital Privileges

There are two related privilege concerning married persons. The first is that generally, a married person cannot be called to testify against his or her spouse. Under § 970, a spouse has the privilege not to testify against the other spouse, subject to some exceptions. Section 971 provides "…a married person whose spouse is a party to a proceeding has a privilege not to be called as a witness by an adverse party to that proceeding without the prior express consent of the spouse having the privilege under this section…" Section 972 sets forth some exceptions to the rules, including where a spouse is the adverse party, e.g., a divorce proceeding, or when a spouse is the victim of a crime alleged to have been perpetrated by the other spouse.

The second privilege for married persons concerns confidential communications made during marriage. "A spouse, whether or not a party, has a privilege during the marital or domestic partnership relationship and afterwards to refuse to disclose, and to prevent another from disclosing, a communication if he or she claims the privilege and the communication was made in confidence between him or her and the other spouse while they were spouses." (CA Evid. Code § 980.) Sections 981 thru 987 provide exceptions to the rule, such as when the proceedings involve litigation between spouses (§ 984), or where one spouse is charged with committing certain crimes (§ 985), or if one spouse is a defendant in a criminal prosecution (§ 987.)

Waiver of Privilege

To invoke a privilege, one must be the "holder" of the privilege. However, most privileges can also be waived by the actions or conduct of the holder of the privilege, e.g., by consent. Since privileges are personal to the "holder," they may be waived only by one who is the holder of the particular privilege. (*Rittenhouse v. Sup.Ct. (Board of Trustees of Leland Stanford Junior Univ.)* (1991) 235 CA3d 1584, 1588.) A privilege predicated on confidential communications in a protected relationship, e.g., lawyer-client, lawyer referral service-client, physician-patient, psychotherapist-patient, clergy-penitent, sexual assault/domestic violence victim-counselor, or spouses, may be waived by voluntarily abandoning the secrecy that the privilege protects. (See Evid. Code § 912.)

13. EXPERT WITNESS

The use of an expert witness at trial is very common. An "expert" can provide testimony and opinions in a wide variety of subject matters. For example, in criminal cases, expert opinion can include intoxication, pathology, fingerprints, crime scene reconstruction, DNA, gangs, medical conditions, false confessions, psychology, mental state, insanity, firearms, eyewitness identification, and battered woman syndrome. For civil cases, expert opinion can include accident reconstruction, causation, defective products, medical treatment and diagnosis, damages, accounting, biomechanics, design, auto repair, real estate valuation, and even child custody.

Expert testimony can provide informative and persuasive evidence for the jury but, on the other hand, because the threshold for the admissibility of "expert testimony" is relatively low, there is also the concern that jurors may give "expert" opinion too much weight and credence. Especially, in the realm of science, expert testimony "is apt to be given considerable, perhaps undue, weight by lay jurors impressed with the 'posture of mystic infallibility.'" (*People v. Kelly* (1976) 37 Cal.3d 24, 31-32; *People v. McDonald* (1984) 37 Cal.3d 351, 372-373.) One of the benefits, but also one of the dangers, of expert testimony is that the witness can rely on hearsay, which can be difficult to challenge. Because expert testimony can be so persuasive and also so damaging, it is vital that trial lawyers know not only how to present this type of evidence, but also how to effectively counter it.

Trial Tip: If the admissibility of expert testimony is disputed, it is generally best to reduce the objection to a written motion in limine. In response, the court may order an evidentiary "402" hearing outside the presence of the jury *or* require a detailed offer of proof by the proponent.

Preparation

Perhaps no other part of a trial requires more preparation than that which is required for expert witness testimony. If you are considering calling an expert witness as part of your case, first you have to find a suitable expert and then prepare to effectively present that expert's testimony in the courtroom. The use of an expert may be desirable in some cases, but absolutely critical in others, such as medical opinion, damages, and accident reconstruction. When choosing an expert, remember that many jurors are often distrustful of so-called "experts," believing they will say anything a party desires because they are being paid. An important consideration is the expert's qualifications and background. Jurors will note whether the expert has received a degree or training from a reputable source versus the self-educated or "experts" who received degrees online. Another important factor is how well the expert communicates. Some extremely bright and highly qualified experts have no jury appeal due to their inability to express themselves clearly in a public forum. Cost may also be a factor. However, in the end, the guiding factor should always be how the expert will be received by the jury.

Defending against expert testimony arguably requires even more preparation. The first step is to assemble and review all the known discovery concerning the expert. The expert's CV, reports (oral or written), and even raw notes should be sought using the discovery process. The expert should be deposed prior to trial, if possible. Perhaps one of the most valuable methods of preparation is to obtain and review any *prior* testimony of the expert. Knowing what the witness has said before on this topic is invaluable and having the transcripts will help keep the witness honest, so to speak.

Understanding the subject matter itself is also a great advantage because it helps you know what questions to ask and helps you to understand the answers. You do not necessarily need to become an expert yourself, but you should be conversant with at least the basic terms and understand the principals involved. Lastly, doing a little background investigation might pay dividends, such as carefully reviewing the expert's testimony from other cases or confirming that the accolades set forth in the witness's 10-page resume are true. Some experts may embellish or exaggerate their credentials both on the stand and in their CV. This is particularly true regarding alleged writings and/or publications, as some experts will take credit for publications and/or accomplishments where they had marginal involvement. Bringing that to the jury's attention may cast a little pall over the testimony.

Trial Tip: You might be surprised what you can dig up about an "expert" simply by doing a little background investigation yourself, i.e., an online search. For example, experts will often list in the CV "publications" and teaching experience. However, upon deeper inquiry it may turn out that the "expert" was only tangentially involved, such as on a review board or an editor. Some experts may appear on paper to have impressive degrees; however, a little research may reveal it was all obtained "on-line." If you have prior testimony, take a good look at what the expert has said before re: his or her credentials. If you can show the expert's qualifications and CV have been exaggerated by such "fluff," it may cause the jury to be a bit more skeptical.

Discovery and Notice Requirements

Most jurisdictions have fairly strict rules and discovery procedures for experts, including the identity of the expert and the substance of the testimony, see e.g., Fed. R. Civ. P. 26(a)(2)(B)(v); C.C.P. 2034 et seq.) A compliant at trial that one party or the other has not complied with the rules is not uncommon. The ultimate sanction could be evidence exclusion. (*Cottini v. Enloe Medical Center* (2014) 226 Cal.App.4th 401 [expert testimony properly excluded for not complying with discovery statutes].) "The California statutes governing expert witness discovery are part of the Civil Discovery Act (C.C.P. § 2016.010 et seq.). The purposes of the discovery statutes are 'to assist the parties and the trier of fact in ascertaining the truth; to encourage settlement by educating the parties as to the strengths of their claims and defenses; to expedite and facilitate preparation and trial; to prevent delay; and to safeguard against surprise." (*Boston v. Penny Lane Centers, Inc.* (2009) 170 Cal.App.4th 936, 950.) The expert witness discovery statutes are to "give fair notice of what an expert will say at trial. This allows the parties to assess whether to take the expert's deposition, to fully explore the relevant subject area at any such deposition, and to select an expert who can respond with a competing opinion on that subject area." (*Bonds v. Roy* (1999) 20 Cal.4th 140, 146-147.)

Court as "Gate Keeper"

The court is often referred to as the "gatekeeper" of expert testimony. A court permits an expert witness "wide latitude" to offer opinions, so long as the opinion has a reliable basis in the knowledge and experience of the expert's discipline. A court's responsibility as gatekeeper should not replace the adversary system or the jury's role in assigning weight, as "vigorous cross-examination, presentation of contrary evidence, and careful instruction on the burden of proof are the traditional and appropriate means of attacking shaky but admissible evidence." (*Daubert v. Merrell Dow Pharmaceuticals, Inc.*, 509 U.S. 579, 113 S.Ct. 2786, 125 L.Ed.2d 469 (1993))

Under California Evidence Code sections 801, subdivision (b), and 802, the trial court acts as a gatekeeper to exclude expert opinion testimony that is (1) based on matter of a type on which an expert may not reasonably rely, (2) based on reasons unsupported by the material on which the expert relies, or (3) based on speculation. Other provisions of law, including decisional law, may also provide reasons for excluding expert opinion testimony. But courts must also be cautious in excluding expert testimony. The trial court's gatekeeping role does not involve choosing between competing expert opinions. (*Sargon Enterprises, Inc. v. University of Southern Cal.* (2012) 55 Cal.4th 747, 771.) In elaborating upon the court's "gatekeeper" role, the court in *Sargon Enterprises* explained: "The court must not weigh an opinion's probative value or substitute its own opinion for the expert's opinion. Rather, the court must simply determine whether the matter relied on can provide a reasonable basis for the opinion or whether that opinion is based on a leap of logic or conjecture. The court does not resolve scientific controversies. Rather, it conducts a 'circumscribed inquiry' to 'determine whether, as a matter of logic, the studies and other information cited by experts adequately support the conclusion that the expert's general theory or technique is valid...'"

Subject Matter – Beyond Common Experience

The first issue for expert testimony is whether the subject matter is proper for expert opinion. Expert opinion is admissible only if the subject matter of the testimony is "sufficiently beyond common experience that the opinion of an expert would assist the trier of fact." (Evid. Code § 801(a).) The subject matter does not necessarily have to be scientific or overly complex. More common topics can also be appropriate for expert testimony; for example, "a witness who through knowledge and experience possesses the means to form an intelligent judgment as to the value of land beyond that possessed by persons generally is competent to give an opinion on fair market value even though he is not a real estate appraiser or broker." (*San Bernardino County Flood Control Dist. v. Sweet* (1967) 225 Cal.App.2d 889, 898.) "The admissibility of expert opinion is a question of degree. The jury need not be wholly ignorant of the subject matter of the opinion in order to justify its admission; if that were the test, little expert opinion testimony would ever be heard. Instead, the statute declares that even if the jury has some knowledge of the matter, expert opinion may be admitted whenever it would 'assist' the jury. It will be excluded only when it would add nothing at all to the jury's common fund of information, e.g., when the subject of inquiry is one of such common knowledge that men of ordinary education could reach a conclusion as intelligently as the witness." (*Summers v. A.L. Gilbert Co.* (1999) 69 Cal.App.4th 1155, 1168-1169.) The pertinent question is whether, even if jurors have some knowledge of the subject matter, expert opinion testimony would assist the jury. (*People v. Prince* (2007) 40 Cal.4th 1179, at p. 1222.) An "expert must not usurp the function of the jury." (*People v. Humphrey* (1996) 13 Cal.4th 1073, 1099.) "Where the jury is just as competent as the expert to consider and weigh the evidence and draw the necessary conclusions, then the need for expert testimony evaporates." (*People v. Vang* (2011) 52 Cal.4th 1038, 1046; *PM Group, Inc. v. Stewart* (2007) 154 Cal.App.4th 55, 63.)

Evid. Code § 801 Expert witnesses; opinion testimony (FRE Rule 703)

If a witness is testifying as an expert, his testimony in the form of an opinion is limited to such an opinion as is:

(a) Related to a subject that is sufficiently beyond common experience that the opinion of an expert would assist the trier of fact; and

(b) Based on matter (including his special knowledge, skill, experience, training, and education) perceived by or personally known to the witness or made known to him at or before the hearing, whether or not admissible, that is of a type that reasonably may be relied upon by an expert in forming an opinion upon the subject to which his testimony relates, unless an expert is precluded by law from using such matter as a basis for his opinion.

Qualifications

Assuming the subject matter is one where expert opinion may be helpful, the next question is whether the witness is *qualified* to make the opinions proffered. The proponent of an expert witness has the burden to establish the proper qualifications. A witness is qualified if the witness has special knowledge, skill, experience, or education pertaining to the matter on which the testimony is offered. (Evid. Code § 720; *People v. Mendoza* (2000) 24 Cal.4th 130, 177.) The threshold to be designated as an "expert" is relatively low and does not require the witness be a doctor or a scientist. Virtually anyone who has some knowledge about a subject matter that is sufficiently beyond the common experience of the average juror can be considered an "expert," e.g., a mechanic or a collector regarding value.

Against the objection of a party, such special knowledge, skill, experience, training, or education must be shown before the witness may testify as an expert. (Evid. Code § 720; *People v. Bolin* (1998) 18 Cal.4th 297, 321.) An expert is permitted to offer an opinion on a subject that is sufficiently beyond common experience so that the opinion of an expert would assist the trier of fact. (*People v. Mayfield* (1997) 14 Cal.4th 668, 766.) To be competent to testify as an expert, one may have acquired specialized knowledge of the subject matter either by study or by practical experience. (*People v. Brown* (1991) 234 Cal.App.3d 918, 938.)

The qualification of expert witnesses, including foundational requirements, rests in the sound discretion of the trial court. That discretion is necessarily broad: The competency of an expert "is in every case a relative one, e.g., relative to the topic about which the person is asked to make his statement." Absent a manifest abuse, the court's determination will not be disturbed on appeal. (*People v. Ramos* (1997) 15 Cal.4th 1133, 1175.)

Evid. Code § 720 Qualification as an expert witness (FRE Rule 702)

(a) A person is qualified to testify as an expert if he has special knowledge, skill, experience, training, or education sufficient to qualify him as an expert on the subject to which his testimony relates. Against the objection of a party, such special knowledge, skill, experience, training, or education must be shown before the witness may testify as an expert.

(b) A witness' special knowledge, skill, experience, training, or education may be shown by any otherwise admissible evidence, including his own testimony.

Weight vs. Admissibility

Where a witness has disclosed sufficient knowledge of the subject to entitle his opinion to go to the jury, the question of the degree of his knowledge goes more to the weight of the evidence than its admissibility. (*People v. Bolin*, supra, 18 Cal.4th at p. 322, quoting *Seneris v. Haas* (1955) 45 Cal.2d 811, 833.) The witness's qualifications may be established by his or her own testimony. (Evid. Code § 720, subd. (b).) "A person may be qualified as an expert on one subject and yet be unqualified to render an opinion on matters beyond the scope of that subject." (*People v. Williams* (1992) 3 Cal.App.4th 1326, 1334; *People v. Hill* (2011) 191 Cal.App.4th 1104, 1120.)

Court Recognition

After the witness's background and expertise have been established, some courts require the judge to recognize the witness as an expert in the proffered field of expertise. (See *People v. Jablonski* (2006) 37 Cal.4th 774, 823-824 [Without court approval, a witness does not become a de facto expert simply because his or her personal observations may be partially informed by some professional training.].) The process is somewhat theatrical because presumably, if there had been an objection to the expert's testimony (qualifications), that objection would have been handled outside the presence of the jury. However, the court's acknowledgement before the jury that the witness is qualified to make an "expert" opinion helps to emphasize that fact for the jury.

Counsel: "Your Honor, at this time, I would offer Mr. Smith as an expert in the field of toxicology."

Before the court acknowledges the witness as an "expert" and further direct examination continues, the court may permit opposing counsel an opportunity to voir dire the witness regarding the qualifications. For opposing counsel, if there is a weakness in the expert's qualifications, even if you sense or know the judge is going to allow the testimony, `do not pass up the opportunity to at least briefly highlight the deficiency before direct examination commences.

Counsel: "Your Honor, at this time, I would offer Mr. Smith as an expert in the field of toxicology."
Court: "Does counsel wish to voir dire the witness?"
Opp. Counsel: "Yes, Your Honor, thank you. Sir, you're not a member of the National Forensic Board of Examiners, are you?"
Witness: "No."
Opp. Counsel: "You're not certified by that organization, are you?"
Witness: "No."
Opp. Counsel: "In fact, you've only been a criminalist for two years, correct?"
Witness: "Yes."
Opp. Counsel: "And, this is only the second time you've testified as an expert?"
Witness: "That's true."
Opp. Counsel: "Your Honor, I submit on his expertise."
Court: "All right. The Court will permit the witness to testify as an expert in the field proposed."

If the judge does not offer voir dire, and if it would be helpful, respectfully make the request. On the other hand, if the expert is very clearly qualified, conducting additional questioning about the witness's impressive credentials will only serve to bolster the witness's credibility. In this situation, it is probably better to simply announce, "We submit it, Your Honor." However, keep in mind that if you did not formally object previously, i.e., in limine, and you want to preserve the issue for an appeal, you must lodge an objection, otherwise, the appellate court may find the issue was forfeited. (See Trial Objects, infra, at p.226.)

Trial Tip: When requesting the expert to describe his or her qualifications, be careful not to overdo it. Remember that jurors have limited attention spans. Your precious time is probably better spent having the witness discuss the substantive issues, rather than the first 20 minutes talking only about background. Initially, hit the highlights of the expert's qualifications and move on to the substantive issues. If necessary, during re-direct, you can always shore up the expert's qualifications.

Once the expert's qualifications have been established, the direct examination generally progresses from the general to the specific. Meaning, the witness will begin by explaining the general principals of the field. Remember, the jurors are not experts and may know literally nothing about the field. Thus, the expert has to essentially educate the jury, as though teaching a class at about a sixth-grade level. For example, a DNA expert will provide the jury with an overview of the basic science and principles of DNA, often by using a prepared slide show to assist. The examiner will utilize more opened-ended questions and permit the witness to answer in the narrative without much interruption. Unlike the direct examination of an ordinary witnesses, courts tend to allow lengthier answers and even leading questions for experts. Next, the expert will be asked to describe in greater detail specific information related to the case, such as the actual testing performed and the reliability of the scientific instruments used. Finally, the expert will be asked to express the "ultimate opinion," in the case of DNA, the statistical probability that the DNA matches the defendant's DNA. At some point during the process, the witness may also be asked to describe the bases of the opinion and the information the witness relied on in the formation the opinion. Whether this comes before the witness makes the ultimate opinion or after is really a tactic decision.

Use of Exhibits and Demonstrative Evidence

The use of exhibits and/or demonstrative evidence during the direct examination of an expert can be particularly helpful. For example, some experts will have a prepared PowerPoint-like slideshow to help explain the testimony. Photographs, diagrams, models, or other forms of demonstrative evidence are also common. Before the trial, it is important that you and the expert coordinate on how the examination will go and what demonstrative evidence will be used and when. (For further discussion re: the use of demonstrative evidence in the courtroom, see Non-Testimonial Evidence, supra, at p. 154.)

Trial Tip: Before the trial, it is important that you and the expert coordinate on how the examination will go and what demonstrative evidence will be used and when. A common occurrence is when counsel and the expert don't appear to be on the same page (and the jurors notice it too).

Basis of the Opinion

Evid. Code § 802 Statement of basis of opinion (FRE Rule 703)

A witness testifying in the form of an opinion may state on direct examination the reasons for his opinion and the matter (including, in the case of an expert, his special knowledge, skill, experience, training, and education) upon which it is based, unless he is precluded by law from using such reasons or matter as a basis for his opinion. The court in its discretion may require that a witness before testifying in the form of an opinion be first examined concerning the matter upon which his opinion is based.

Evid. Code § 803 Opinion based on improper matter

The court may, and upon objection shall, exclude testimony in the form of an opinion that is based in whole or in significant part on matter that is not a proper basis for such an opinion. In such case, the witness may, if there remains a proper basis for his opinion, then state his opinion after excluding from consideration the matter determined to be improper.

One of the advantages of utilizing expert testimony is that the expert is not required to have personal knowledge. (Evid. Code § 702(a).) An expert is permitted to testify about matters to which they were not a percipient witness. The expert is permitted to opine based upon his or her fund of knowledge drawn from experience, training, education, or extraneous sources, such as hearsay. However, there are limitations on how far the opinion can go. The scope and breadth of an expert's opinion is an issue that is commonly litigated and one that should be raised via motion in limine at the beginning of the trial.

Experts and Hearsay

As the party opposing an expert, a concern often is the extent to which the expert will relate to the jury the specifics of information reviewed or relied upon to reach the opinion. For example, a physician called to make a medical opinion, may have reviewed medical records, that in turn may include statements from a party, nursing notes, test results, or the diagnosis and conclusions from other doctors. The obvious concern is that if the expert informs the jury of the details or findings of those materials, you will have no means to cross-examine the originators to confirm or contradict its reliability and accuracy. In other words, it's hearsay.

Traditionally, experts have been permitted to consider and rely upon hearsay in the formation of their opinion, and later at trial, even during the direct examination, relate some or all of that information to the jury as the basis for opinions. The courts got around the hearsay objection by finding that the information is not hearsay because it is not being received for the truth, but rather for the non-hearsay purpose of permitting the jurors to determine the weight to give to the opinion. (See *People v. Coleman* (1985) 38 Cal.3d 69, 92; *Williams v. Illinois* (2012) 567 U.S. 50, 78 132 S.Ct. 2221, 183 L.Ed.2d 89 (Williams) ["Under that rule (703), 'basis evidence' that is not admissible for its truth may be disclosed even in a jury trial under appropriate circumstances. The purpose for allowing this disclosure is that it may assist the jury to evaluate the expert's opinion…The Rule 703 is based on the idea that the disclosure of basis evidence can help the factfinder understand the expert's thought process and determine what weight to give to the expert's opinion."]) (Id. at p. 78.) Some courts allow the expert to relate this type of (hearsay) information, but then instruct the jury that they may consider out-of-court statements only to evaluate the expert's opinion and not as proof that the information contained in the statements is true. (CALCRIM 360.)

Although some inadmissible evidence, e.g., hearsay, may be proper for the jury to hear as the basis of the opinion, the tension is how much and how specific? In *U.S. v. Mejia* 545 F.3d 179, 197 (2nd Cir. 2008), for example, a criminal case, the court explained: "The expert may not, however, simply transmit that hearsay to the jury. Instead, the expert must form his own opinions by "applying his extensive experience and a reliable methodology" to the inadmissible materials. Otherwise, the expert is simply "repeating hearsay evidence without applying any expertise whatsoever," a practice that allows the Government "to circumvent the rules prohibiting hearsay." In California, the general rule has been that during *direct examination*, the expert may explain the reasons for his opinions, including the matters he considered in forming them; however, prejudice may arise if, under the guise of reasons, the expert's detailed explanation brings before the jury incompetent hearsay evidence. (*People v. Catlin* (2001) 26 Cal.4th 81, 137.)

More recently, however, the California Supreme Court in *People v. Sanchez* (2016) 63 Cal.4th 665, attempted to clarify the law regarding the use of hearsay by experts. The court held that when any expert relates to the jury *case-specific* out-of-court statements, and treats the content of those statements as true and accurate to support the expert's opinion, the statements are hearsay. It cannot logically be maintained that the statements are not being admitted for their truth. Because the information is hearsay, there must be an applicable hearsay exception that applies before case-specific information can be related to the jury. (Ibid at p. 676.)

The court in *Sanchez* was careful to draw a distinction between "*case-specific*" hearsay and general-knowledge hearsay. "The hearsay rule has traditionally not barred an expert's testimony regarding his general knowledge in his field of expertise. The common law recognized that experts frequently acquired their knowledge from hearsay, and that to reject a professional physician or mathematician because the fact or some facts to which he testifies are known to him only upon the authority of others would be to ignore the accepted methods of professional work and to insist on ... impossible standards. Thus, the common law accepted that an expert's general knowledge often came from inadmissible evidence. Knowledge in a specialized area is what differentiates the expert from a lay witness, and makes his testimony uniquely valuable to the jury in explaining matters beyond the common experience of an ordinary juror." As such, an expert's testimony concerning his general knowledge, even if technically hearsay, has not been subject to exclusion on hearsay grounds." (*Sanchez,* supra, at p. 676.)

"By contrast, an expert has traditionally been precluded from relating case-specific facts about which the expert has no independent knowledge. Case-specific facts are those relating to the particular events and participants alleged to have been involved in the case being tried. Generally, parties try to establish the facts on which their theory of the case depends by calling witnesses with personal knowledge of those case-specific facts. An expert may then testify about more generalized information to help jurors understand the significance of those case-specific facts. An expert is also allowed to give an opinion about what those facts may mean. The expert is generally not permitted, however, to supply case-specific facts about which he has no personal knowledge." (Ibid. at p. 676.)

The court in *Sanchez* explained: "Any expert may still rely on hearsay in forming an opinion, and may tell the jury in general terms that he did so. Because the jury must independently evaluate the probative value of an expert's testimony, Evidence Code section 802 properly allows an expert to relate generally the kind and source of the 'matter' upon which his opinion rests. A jury may repose greater confidence in an expert who relies upon well-established scientific principles. It may accord less weight to the views of an expert who relies on a single article from an obscure journal or on a lone experiment whose results cannot be replicated. There is a distinction to be made between allowing an expert to describe the type or source of the matter relied upon as opposed to presenting, as fact, case-specific hearsay that does not otherwise fall under a statutory exception. What an expert cannot do is relate as true case-specific facts asserted in hearsay statements, unless they are independently proven by competent evidence or are covered by a hearsay exception." (*Sanchez*, supra, at pp. 685-686.) The court in *Sanchez* also held that in criminal cases, if hearsay is introduced via expert testimony and used against the defendant, the trial court must determine whether it violates the defendant's Sixth Amendment right to confrontation. This, in turn, requires an analysis of whether the hearsay is "testimonial." (See *Crawford v. Washington* (2004) 541 U.S. 36, 124 S.Ct. 1354, 158 L.Ed.2d 177.)

> **Trial Tip:** Be alert for possible Sanchez issues. It is worth noting that in California, the Sanchez analysis has been applied in civil cases. Other jurisdictions might be inclined to adopt the Sanchez reasoning.

In light of the above and referencing the above example of the expert's opinion regarding the plaintiff's neck pain, the court would likely rule that the expert could recite for the jury, in general, all the materials and evidence reviewed and considered, including how they support his opinion, but may not relate the specifics of the hearsay, for example, the opinion of the non-testifying expert. However, keep in mind that if the expert's opinion is attacked during cross-examination, the court may permit further explanation by the expert to rebut the attack on his credibility.

> **Trial Tip:** During the direct it probably better not to have the expert delve too much into the complicated details and studies. Too much information is only likely to overwhelm and possibly confuse the jurors. You still have re-direct to shore up the testimony, if necessary.

Direct Examination – No Details

Similar to the holding in *Sanchez*, the courts have generally held that, while an expert may rely on inadmissible hearsay in forming his or her opinion, and may state *on direct examination* the matters on which he or she relied, the expert may not testify as to the *details* of those matters if they are otherwise inadmissible. This rule is based in part upon the rationale that by allowing an expert to testify as to the details of inadmissible hearsay reports, the jury might improperly consider such testimony as independent proof of the facts described in the reports and the adverse party is denied the opportunity to cross-examine the person who made the statements. (*People v. Dean* (2009) 174 Cal.App.4th 186, 197-198; *People v. Coleman* (1985) 38 Cal.3d 69, 92.) In other words, "the court in *Coleman* was attempting to balance the desirability of allowing an expert to explain the basis for an opinion and the need to prevent the jury from considering inadmissible matter for an improper purpose." (*People v. Martin* (2005) 127 Cal.App.4th 970, 977.)

For example, in a civil trial regarding the alleged negligent design of an intersection where a fatal car accident occurred, the expert may have reviewed eyewitness accounts, police reports, and perhaps even the reports of other experts. During direct examination, he can, of course, render his opinion that the intersection is poorly designed and dangerous, and he may also describe generally the nature of the information he reviewed in forming the opinion. However, he cannot reveal the detail of the information (hearsay), for example, what the eyewitnesses said or what other experts who are not testifying also concluded. During cross-examination, the opponent *is* permitted to fully question the expert about the content of the materials reviewed. Once that door has been opened on cross, counsel on redirect examination may be permitted to flesh out more detail from the information relied on by the expert. (See infra, re: cross-examination of experts.)

Opinions – Ultimate Issue

Even when the expert is qualified and the subject matter is within the realm of expert testimony, there may still be an issue regarding the scope of the expert's testimony. In other words, how far can the expert go?

Evid. Code § 805 Opinion on ultimate issue (FRE Rule 704)

Expert opinion testimony is not inadmissible merely because it embraces the ultimate issue to be determined by the trier of fact.

Perhaps contrary to what some lawyers may believe, an expert can make an opinion regarding the "ultimate" issue. (Evid. Code § 805.) Or can they? Despite the seemingly clear edict of Section 805, the courts have nonetheless put limits on the scope of expert opinions concerning the ultimate issue. As the California Supreme Court explained: "There is no hard and fast rule that the expert cannot be asked a question that coincides with the ultimate issue in the case. We think the true rule is that admissibility depends on the nature of the issue and the circumstances of the case, there being a large element of judicial discretion involved ... Oftentimes an opinion may be received on a simple ultimate issue, even when it is the sole one, as for example where the issue is the value of an article, or the sanity of a person; because it cannot be further simplified and cannot be fully tried without hearing opinions from those in better position to form them than the jury can be placed in." (*People v. Wilson* (1944) 25 Cal.2d 341, 349; see also *People v. Lowe* (2012) 211 Cal.App.4th 678, 684; see also *People v. Olguin* (1994) 31 Cal.App.4th 1355, 1371 [opinion evidence is admissible even though it encompasses the ultimate issue in the case].) Opinions embracing ultimate issues "are expressly contemplated by Evidence Code section 805." (*People v. Doss* (1992) 4 Cal.App.4th 1585, 1596 [expert may testify ultimate issue possession for sale].) On the other hand, "Expert opinion is not admissible if it consists of inferences and conclusions which can be drawn as easily and intelligently by the trier of fact as by the witness." (*People v. Valdez* (1997) 58 Cal.App.4th 494, 506.) Expert opinion testimony may not invade the province of the jury to decide a case. Thus, expert opinion testimony that merely expresses a general belief as to how the jury should decide the case is not permissible. (*Lowe* at p. 684.) Such evidence is "wholly without value" to the trier of fact. The determination of whether an expert witness's opinion bears upon or decides an ultimate issue in the case is sometimes a difficult decision, and "a large element of judicial discretion is involved." (*People v. Wilson* (1944) 25 Cal.2d 341, 349; *People v. Frederick* (2006) 142 Cal.App.4th 400, 412.) In criminal cases, an expert is prohibited from expressing certain opinions regarding the defendant's mental state. (See Penal Code § 28-29; *People v. Coddington* (2000) 23 Cal.4th 529, 582.)

Opinion of Law Prohibited

The admissibility of opinion evidence that embraces an ultimate issue in a case does not bestow upon an expert carte blanche to express any opinion he or she wishes. There are limits to expert testimony, not the least of which is the prohibition against admission of an expert's opinion on a question of law. An expert witness cannot testify to conclusions of law. Thus, an expert cannot opine whether the defendant violated the law. (*Summers v. A.L. Gilbert Co.* (1999) 69 Cal.App.4th 1155, 1178 [error for the court to permit an attorney to testify as an expert and opine whether there was a duty or negligence]; see also *Ferreira v. Workmen's Comp. Appeals Bd.* (1974) 38 Cal.App.3d 120 [error to permit a doctor to state legal conclusions rather than medical opinions]; *Downer v. Bramet* (1984) 152 Cal.App.3d 837 [court concluded expert opinions on legal questions are not admissible regardless of whether the opinion embraces an ultimate issue]; *Burton v. Sanner* (2012) 207 Cal.App.4th 12, 21 [error to permit expert to opine whether self-defense in wrongful death case was reasonable].) For example, in the trial concerning an alleged dangerous intersection, the expert can opine concerning what is wrong with the intersection and the dangerous condition it created. However, the expert cannot opine that the state was negligent or at fault, or the cause of the accident.

Speculative Opinions Prohibited

"Where the jury is just as competent as the expert to consider and weigh the evidence and draw the necessary conclusions, then the need for expert testimony evaporates." (*PM Group, Inc. v. Stewart* (2007) 154 Cal.App.4th 55, 63; Evid. Code § 801, subd. (a).) Expert testimony will be excluded "when it would add nothing at all to the jury's common fund of information, e.g., when 'the subject of inquiry is one of such common knowledge that men of ordinary education could reach a conclusion as intelligently as the witness." (*Summers*, supra, 69 Cal.App.4th at p. 1169.) "An expert opinion has no value if its basis is unsound. Matter that provides a reasonable basis for one opinion does not necessarily provide a reasonable basis for another opinion. Evidence Code section 801, subdivision (b), states that a court must determine whether the matter that the expert relies on is of a type that an expert reasonably can rely on 'in forming an opinion upon the subject to which his testimony relates.' We construe this to mean that the matter relied on must provide a reasonable basis for the particular opinion offered, and that an expert opinion based on speculation or conjecture is inadmissible." (*Sargon Enterprises, Inc. v. University of Southern Cal* (2012) 55 Cal.4th 747, 769.) "Thus, under Evidence Code section 801, the trial court acts as a gatekeeper to exclude speculative or irrelevant expert opinion. As we recently explained, the expert's opinion may not be based 'on assumptions of fact without evidentiary support, or on speculative or conjectural factors ... Exclusion of expert opinions that rest on guess, surmise, or conjecture is an inherent corollary to the foundational predicate for admission of the expert testimony: Will the testimony assist the trier of fact to evaluate the issues it must decide?" (*Sargon,* supra.)

Trial Tip: If the field of expertise is scientific or complex, try not to talk over the jurors' heads. A complicated explanation or a conversation between counsel and the expert where the jurors are lost benefits no one. Assume the jury is about on par with a group of sixth graders and keep it simple and concise. Monitor the jurors' apparent attentiveness. Do they appear to be following or are their eyes beginning to glaze over?

Kelly Analysis

If the expert opinion includes some novel or new scientific theory, upon request, the court may be required to hold a "Kelly/Frye" hearing. In *People v. Kelly* (1976) 17 Cal.3d 24, the court held that evidence obtained through a new scientific technique may be admitted only after its reliability has been established under a three-pronged test. The first prong requires proof that the technique is generally accepted as reliable in the relevant scientific community. The second prong requires proof that the witness testifying about the technique and its application is a properly qualified expert on the subject. The third prong requires proof that the person performing the test in the particular case used correct scientific procedures.

However, generally, expert opinion, no matter how novel or new, is not subject to the *Kelly* analysis. Under California law, the predicate for application of the *Kelly* rule is that the expert testimony is based, at least in some part, on a new scientific technique, device, procedure, or method that is not generally accepted in the relevant scientific community. The predicate is not that the opinion or underlying theory asserted by the expert is itself not generally accepted in the relevant scientific community or is faulty. "Absent some special feature which effectively blindsides the jury, expert opinion testimony is not subject to Kelly-Frye." (*Roberti v. Andy's Termite & Pest Control, Inc.* (2003) 113 Cal.App.4th 893, 902; *People v. McDonald* (1984) 37 Cal.3d 351, 372-373; *Frye v. U.S.,* 293 F. 1013 [overruled in *Daubert v. Merrell Dow Pharmaceuticals, Inc.,* 509 U.S. 579, 113 S. Ct. 2786, 125 L. Ed. 2d 469, 37 Fed. R. Evid. Serv. 1 (1993).)

Trial Tip: Whether you are presenting or opposing an expert, a few questions to the jury during voir dire about their attitudes or feelings concerning expert testimony might be worthwhile. Some people distrust any form of expert testimony no matter what the field. Others may treat an expert opinion as though it were gospel.

Experts and Causation

Experts are sometimes called upon to express an opinion that some act or condition caused an injury. However, there must be some evidence to support the expert's conclusion. Issues arise when there is minimal or no evidence. A party "cannot manufacture a triable issue of fact through use of an expert opinion with self-serving conclusions devoid of any basis, explanation, or reasoning." (*Nardizzi v. Harbor Chrysler Plymouth Sales, Inc.* (2006) 136 Cal.App.4th 1409, 1415.) "The value of opinion evidence rests not in the conclusion reached, but in the factors considered and the reasoning employed. Where an expert bases his conclusions upon assumptions which are not supported by the record, upon matters which are not reasonably relied upon by other experts, or upon factors which are speculative, remote, or conjectural, then his conclusion has no evidentiary value." (*Lockheed Litigation Cases* (2004) 115 Cal.App.4th 558, 563 [court excluded expert testimony regarding link between chemicals and cancer]; see also *Geffcken v. D'Andrea* (2006) 137 Cal.App.4th 1298, 1311-1312 [mold causing health issues—expert testimony excluded]; *Dee v.PCS Property Management, Inc.* (2009) 174 Cal.App. 4th 390.)

Medical Causation

The law is well settled that in a personal injury action, causation must be proven within a reasonable medical probability based upon competent expert testimony. Mere possibility alone is insufficient to establish a prima facie case. Proffering an expert opinion that there is some theoretical possibility the negligent act could have been a cause-in-fact of a particular injury is insufficient to establish causation. (*Saelzler v. Advanced Group 400* (2001) 25 Cal.4th 763, 775-776 [expert testimony positing a "mere possibility of such causation is not enough; and when the matter remains one of pure speculation or conjecture, or the probabilities are at best evenly balanced, it becomes the duty of the court to direct a verdict for the defendant"]; accord, *Leslie G. v. Perry & Associates* (1996) 43 Cal.App.4th 472, 487.) Instead, the plaintiff must offer an expert opinion that contains a reasoned explanation illuminating why the facts have convinced the expert, and therefore should convince the jury, that it is more probable than not the negligent act was a cause-in-fact of the plaintiff's injury. (*Jennings v. Palomar Pomerado Health Systems, Inc.* (2003) 114 Cal.App.4th 1108, 1117; *Cooper v. Takeda Pharmaceuticals America, Inc.* (2015) 239 Cal.App. 4th 555, 578.)

The Hypothetical Question

An expert witness may be asked a hypothetical question which asks the expert to "assume" certain facts or theories are true. The expert is then requested to make an opinion based on the assumed facts. The hypothetical question is normally propounded by counsel and is often rather lengthy in that it may incorporate a series of facts related to the case. The hypo can include facts from the present case and need not be "disguised." (*People v. Xue Vang* (2011) 52 Cal. 4th 1038, 1045-1046.) In *Xue Vang,* supra, the California Supreme Court discussed the use of hypotheticals, stating, "It is not necessary that the question include a statement of all the evidence in the case. The statement may assume facts within the limits of the evidence, not unfairly assembled, upon which the opinion of the expert is required, and considerable latitude must be allowed in the choice of facts as to the basis upon which to frame a hypothetical question. On the other hand, the expert's opinion may not be based 'on assumptions of fact without evidentiary support or on speculative or conjectural factors ... The traditional method of taking the opinion evidence of an expert is the hypothetical question. This may be framed on any theory that can be deduced from the evidence, and the questioner may assume any facts within the limits of the evidence and omit any facts not deemed material. But, however much latitude a party has to frame hypothetical questions, the questions must be rooted in the evidence of the case being tried, not some other case." (*People v. Xue Vang,* supra, at pp. 1045-1046; see also *People v. Gardeley* (1996) 14 Cal.4th 605, 618.) The use of a hypothetical was also approved recently in *People v. Sanchez* (2016) 63 Cal.4th 665, with the caveat that hearsay recited in the hypothetical must be proven independent of the expert's opinion. "If an expert testifies to case-specific out-of-court statements to explain the basis for his opinion, those statements are necessarily considered by the jury for their truth, thus rendering them hearsay. Like any other hearsay evidence, it must be properly admitted through an applicable hearsay exception. Alternatively, the evidence can be admitted through an appropriate witness and the expert may assume its truth in a properly worded hypothetical question in the traditional manner." (Id. at p. 677.)

Counsel: "Dr. Jones, I would ask you to assume the following facts: That there was 150 feet of friction skid marks on the pavement starting at the limit line and extending into the intersection 125 feet, as shown in this diagram; that the weight of the Ford 150 is 3,600 pounds; and that the pavement was dry. Based on these factors, do you have an estimate of the minimum speed of the pickup truck when it entered into the intersection?"

Witness: "Yes, based on those criteria, it is my opinion the vehicle was traveling in excess of 45 miles per hour when it crossed over the limit line into the intersection."

> **Trial Tip:** A good hypothetical question summarizes the evidence that forms the backbone of your case and then asks the expert to make an opinion based on those "assumed" facts. The hypothetical is not unlike the closing argument in that the jurors can see the big picture and how the facts relate to your theory.

Expert Cross-examination – "Wide Latitude"

The cross-examination of an expert witness can be especially difficult because they are often professional witnesses who may have been subjected to cross-examination many times before, know what to expect, and come prepared. Some are also "experts" at the art of dodging and weaving and not being pinned down. What is also daunting is the very fact that they are "experts" and presumably possess more knowledge about the field than you do, making it difficult to challenge them without making yourself look uninformed or even foolish. Furthermore, those who attempt to cross-examine an expert witness without a clear objective or a plan in mind stand a very real chance of impaling themselves on their own proverbial sword.

When contemplating a strategy, a good place to start is California Evidence Code § 721 (below), which codifies the law most jurisdictions follow concerning the cross of experts. Just about every aspect of an expert's testimony can be attacked from the qualifications to the basis of the opinion. The key to good preparation is to determine where the potential weaknesses lie as well as a strategy. The next several pages discuss areas where cross-examination might be effective, depending upon the nature of the case. Keep in mind, however, that especially for experts, the mere rehash of the direct-examination is generally not good cross-examination. Focused and concise questions are the key.

Evid. Code § 721 Cross-examination of expert witness (FRE Rule 705)

(a) Subject to subdivision (b), a witness testifying as an expert may be cross-examined to the same extent as any other witness and, in addition, may be fully cross-examined as to (1) his or her qualifications, (2) the subject to which his or her expert testimony relates, and (3) the matter upon which his or her opinion is based and the reasons for his or her opinion.

(b) If a witness testifying as an expert testifies in the form of an opinion, he or she may not be cross-examined in regard to the content or tenor of any scientific, technical, or professional text, treatise, journal, or similar publication unless any of the following occurs:

(1) The witness referred to, considered, or relied upon such publication in arriving at or forming his or her opinion.

(2) The publication has been admitted in evidence.

(3) The publication has been established as a reliable authority by the testimony or admission of the witness or by other expert testimony or by judicial notice.

If admitted, relevant portions of the publication may be read into evidence but may not be received as exhibits.

"Generally, parties are given wide latitude when cross-examining an expert witness to test the credibility of the expert. Accordingly, a broader range of evidence may be properly used on cross-examination to test and diminish the weight to be given the expert opinion than is admissible on direct examination to fortify the opinion. For example, a party seeking to attack the credibility of the expert may bring to the attention of the jury material relevant to the issue on which the expert has offered an opinion of which the expert was unaware or which he did not consider. The purpose and permissible scope of impeachment of an expert is to call into question the truthfulness of the witness's testimony." (*San Diego Gas & Electric Company v. Schmidt* (2014) 228 Cal.App.4th 1280, 1301.)

Once an expert witness offers an opinion, "he exposes himself to the kind of inquiry which ordinarily would have no place in the cross-examination of a factual witness. The expert invites investigation into the extent of his knowledge, the reasons for his opinion including facts and other matters upon which it is based, and which he took into consideration; and he may be 'subjected to the most rigid cross examination' concerning his qualifications, and his opinion and its sources." (*Hope v. Arrowhead & Puritas Waters, Inc.* (1959) 174 Cal.App.2d 222, 230; see People v. Nye (1969) 71 Cal.2d 356, 374-375.)

"If the threshold test of general testimonial qualifications is found to be met and the witness is permitted to testify on direct examination, he is subject to as penetrating a cross-examination as the ingenuity and intellect of opposing counsel can devise. This inquiry may challenge not only the knowledge of the witness on the specific subject at issue, but also the reasons for his opinion and his evaluation of any written material upon which he relied in preparation for his testimony. Further, a defendant is free to argue that the witness's testimony is not entitled to acceptance or credibility because he lacks personal acquaintance with the subject at the time the alleged negligent act occurred, and defendant may produce his own witnesses in rebuttal." (*Brown v. Colm* (1974) 11 Cal.3d 639, at p. 646.)

> **Trial Tip:** Before cross-examining an expert, create a written outline and checklist of the objectives and questions planned. Consider consulting with another "expert" in the field to provide you with guidance on how and where to attack. It is also important that you have at least some working knowledge regarding the subject matter.

Materials Considered

It is generally good cross-examination to question the expert concerning the basis of the opinion, including what information or facts the expert did or did not consider. Particularly important is to highlight facts or information that the expert did *not* consider, the theory being that the expert reviewed only favorable information and disregarded or did not consider facts or information contrary to the opinion. This would demonstrate the expert's bias towards one party, if true.

The general rule is that "a party seeking to attack the credibility of the expert *may* bring to the attention of the jury material relevant to the issue on which the expert has offered an opinion of which the expert was unaware or which he did not consider. The purpose and permissible scope of impeachment of an expert is to call into question the truthfulness of the witness's testimony." (*San Diego Gas & Electric Company v. Schmidt* (2014) 228 Cal.App.4th 1280, 1301.) "It is common practice to challenge an expert by inquiring in good faith about relevant information, including hearsay, which he may have overlooked or ignored." (*People v. Montiel* (1993) 5 Cal.4th 877, 924.)

An expert may be cross-examined about the content and detail of any materials he or she considered in forming the opinion, e.g., research papers or studies. (Evid. Code § 721(b).) Thus, if during the direct examination the expert referenced some finding or a particular study, the cross-examiner is permitted to delve into the specifics of that study. Recall that on direct examination, the witness is *not* permitted to provide the details of the study. (*People v. Catlin* (2001) 26 Cal.4th 81, 137.)

> **Trial Tip:** Some experts are expert at not answering the question or quite willing to launch into further explanation regarding why your theory is wrong. Thus, the key is to keep control by using tight, leading questions and control techniques. (Discussed, supra, at p. 104 et. seq.) A few well-placed ""non-responsive" objections at the beginning may help to keep the witness in check.

One problem the cross-examiner may face is when the expert claims to have *not* considered certain information contrary to his opinion—for example, when, through research and good trial preparation, the cross-examiner finds certain studies or information contrary to the expert's opinion which the expert claims to have no knowledge of. Of course, the examiner would like to confront the expert with that information to discredit the expert in the eyes of the jury. However, the rule is that an expert may *not* be cross-examined about the *contents* of materials unless the witness *referred to, considered, or relied upon* such publication in arriving at or forming his or her opinion. (Evid. Code § 721(b)(1), emphasis added.) "The purpose of section 721(b) is to prevent an adverse party from getting before the trier of fact the inadmissible hearsay views of an absent expert, which may be contrary to the expert witness's opinion, through the device of cross-examining the expert witness regarding the absent expert's publication or report even though the testifying expert had not used or considered that publication or report in any way in arriving at or forming his opinion testimony. Permitting such cross-examination would bring before the jury the opinions of absentee authors without the safeguard of cross-examination." (*McGarity v. Department of Transportation* (1992) 8 Cal.App.4th 677, 683 (McGarity), quoting 2 Jefferson, Evidence Benchbook (2d ed. 1982) § 29.8, p. 1036, original italics.; Id. at p. 683.) "It is error to permit the use of professional studies not relied upon by an expert in the formulation of his opinion. (Evid. Code § 721, subd. (b).) To allow their use would be to circumvent the hearsay rule." (*People v. Visciotti* (1992) 2 Cal.4th 1, 80.)

Considering this rule, for the cross-examiner, the key is to get the expert to concede that, at the very least, the contrary information was "considered," even if discounted. If the expert *"in any way"* used or considered the contrary information, cross-examination about the contents is permitted. (*McGarity v. Department of Transportation* (1992) 8 Cal.App.4th 677, at p. 683 citing 2 Jefferson, Evidence Benchbook (2d. ed. 1982) § 29.8, p. 1036, original emphasis.) For example, if a medical expert opines that a certain chemical causes cancer, the expert can be cross-examined about whether he considered other studies that found no link. If the expert concedes he considered those studies, then the cross-examiner is permitted to go into more detail regarding those contrary studies and their findings and explore why this expert disagrees. In essence, the jury will hear about the specifics of those contrary studies. However, if the expert claims to have no knowledge of those studies and represents that they were never "considered" or "relied upon," then the cross-examiner is forbidden to elicit the details and specifics of those studies in the form of a question.

Note, however, that under § 721(b)(3) (above), even if the expert did not "consider" the inconsistent materials, if you can convince the court to take judicial notice that the materials you are referencing are from a "reliable authority," e.g., well-recognized treatises, publications, or standard works, cross-examination regarding the findings of those materials may be permitted.

Trial Tip: A good strategy for cross-examination is to point out the information or evidence the expert did *not* consider or rely upon. A failure to consider *all* the evidence, or an important piece of evidence, may show the witness's opinion is unsupported or one-sided. Often experts may not have reviewed materials favorable to the other party, performed any actual examinations or tests, or visited the scene.

Production of Materials

If your opponent's expert reviewed materials prior to trial, you may have the right to demand production and inspection of those materials. During your cross-examination, consider asking what material the expert has reviewed prior to testimony and double-check that you have seen those materials too. Evidence Code section 771, subdivision (a), provides: "If a witness, either while testifying or prior thereto, uses a writing to refresh his memory with respect to any matter about which he testifies, such writing must be produced at the hearing at the request of an adverse party and, unless the writing is so produced, the testimony of the witness concerning such matter shall be stricken." The "adverse party may ... inspect the writing, cross-examine the witness concerning it, and introduce in evidence such portion of it as may be pertinent to the testimony of the witness." (Evid. Code § 771, subd. (b); see supra at p. 82 for text.)

If an expert reviewed or relied upon arguably privileged information, e.g., attorney-client or psychotherapist-patient records, an issue can arise regarding whether the opposing party is entitled to that information. However, cross-examination properly includes documents and records examined by an expert witness in preparing his or her testimony. (*People v. Osband* (1996) 13 Cal.4th 622, 712.) Once a party calls an expert to the stand, the expert loses his status as a consulting agent of the attorney, and neither the attorney-client privilege nor the work-product doctrine applies to matters relied on or considered in the formation of his opinion. (*People v. Milner* (1988) 45 Cal.3d 227 at p. 241.) The moral of the story for the proponent of an expert witness is to be careful what materials the expert reviews prior to trial because you may have to turn it over to your opponent.

Bias

Highlight the expert's relationship or affiliation to a party, the expert's *compensation*, and any other facts suggesting the witness may have bias or some other motive to put a spin on the evidence. Some experts are professional experts, meaning, they make their living only from providing opinions and conclusions for attorneys to use in court. Some experts also tend to work only for one type of attorney, e.g.. personal injury versus insurance defense. Some attorneys use the same expert over and over again. An expert's testimony in prior cases involving similar issues is a legitimate subject of cross-examination when it is relevant to the bias of the witness. (*People v. Zambrano* (2007) 41 Cal.4th 1082, 1165, 63 Cal.Rptr.3d 297, 163 P.3d 4.) Pointing out these types of relationships, particularly financial incentives, may help show the witness is not impartial.

Counsel: "You were hired by Mr. Smith (counsel) to review this case and to provide an opinion, correct?"

Counsel: "How much money have you been paid to review this case, to date?"

Counsel: "You also charge for your courtroom time, correct? What are you being paid for today's testimony?"

[Notes: Some experts, such as physicians, can charge up to $10,000 for one day of testimony!]

Counsel; "In addition to your regular practice, doctor, you also earn income from consulting with attorneys and providing opinions, right?"

Counsel: "And, isn't it true, that you do most of your work primarily with plaintiff personal injury lawyers?"

Counsel: "In fact, you've performed other evaluations for Mr. Smith on other cases and gotten paid, correct?"

Note regarding payment: Be aware that some "experts" do not collect their fees up front, but may put a lien on any settlement or judgment proceeds. This payment arrangement should be explored.

Qualifications

Highlighting any deficiencies or unflattering facts about the witness's background may also cast the expert in a different light. For example, does the expert only have minimal experience in the field? Does the expert have the appropriate degrees, training, or certificates, or something less impressive, i.e. on-line degrees. Do a thorough review and double-check, if you can, on the expert's CV. Experts often have impressive looking resumes, but a little probing may show a lot of it is "fluff" and/or embellished. In particular, some experts like to take credit for "publications" when in actuality they really only had a minor role in its preparation. A little internet background search may yield interesting results. Showing that an "expert" has embellished their credentials, even just a little, may take the expert down a notch in the eyes of the jurors; for example, boasting regarding an advanced degree without noting that it was obtained via some fly-by-night on-line school. On the other hand, if the expert is clearly qualified, inquiring about the expert's impressive credentials may (will) only serve to reinforce the expert's qualification and credibility. In that circumstance, move on to the substantive questioning.

Counsel: "Now, on your CV it says you have a graduate degree in holistic medicine, is that correct?"
Counsel: "However, that degree was received through an online school, true?"
Counsel: "And, you're not board certified in orthopedic surgery or any field of medicine are you?"
Counsel: "In fact, your main field of practice has been weight loss and pain management, correct?"
Counsel: "In your CV, under the heading of publications, you listed a study entitled, 'Treating Neck Pain with Alternative Medicine.' That was not a scientific, peer-reviewed paper, was it?"
Counsel: "In fact, it was published in High Times Magazine, wasn't it?"
Counsel: "And, you did not write that article yourself, did you?"
Counsel: "You only helped to edit it, correct?"
Counsel: "Yet, you've included it here on your CV, isn't that true?"

Trial Tip: Experts often come to court with an impressive looking 15-page CV, however, a little research to double-check may prove worth the effort.

Materials or Investigation not Reviewed or Considered

During direct examination, the expert witness is generally asked to provide the "bases" for the opinion. As part of that testimony, the witness will often relate the facts or evidence upon which the expert relied on to reach the opinion or conclusion. Depending upon the type of case, this might include a review of records, reports, and many other potential forms of hearsay, such as the opinions and findings of other experts or test results. In addition, the expert may have reviewed and relied on scientific studies, papers, journals, or other publications.

For the purposes of cross-examination, it is generally helpful to know what information, facts, or evidence the expert considered. Thus, if during direct-examination, it was not established clearly what the expert considered as the basis of the opinion, it may be helpful to inquire yourself and have the witness list off the sources or types of information and evidence considered. The reason you want to know what the expert has considered is twofold: First, you may want to cross-examine the expert more thoroughly about the content and specifics of those materials. Recall that, generally, an expert can rely on inadmissible evidence as the basis of the opinion. During direct examination, the expert may have discussed or mentioned that evidence, such as records or other forms of hearsay. Also recall that during direct-examination, an expert is generally precluded from revealing the fact specific contents of that hearsay. During cross-examination, however, you are permitted to delve into the details and specifics of everything the expert reviewed or considered to come up with the opinion.

For example, during the direct examination of a traffic accident reconstruction expert, the expert may have opined regarding the speed of a vehicle based on the skid marks. During his testimony, he may have referenced several scientific studies on tire friction coefficient, which he felt supported his calculations and opinion. During direct examination, he could mention those studies and that their findings helped him reach his ultimate conclusion; however, he would be precluded from going into the specific facts and findings from them. During cross-examination, however, you could confront and challenge the expert regarding the specific finding and facts in those publications, including any contradictions or errors. In other words, you can take him to task and require the expert to relate the specifics and even quote from those same studies. This illustrates the importance of deposing an expert before trial such that you will know the basis of the opinion well before trial to allow you time to do your own research.

> **Trial Tip:** Taking on an expert in his or her own field of expertise can be perilous. For example, if you confront the expert with contrary data or a study, you can easily be "schooled" and corrected by the expert *if* you get it wrong, e.g., the study you cited is outdated. Thus, you must know the subject material well before you embark on this risky strategy.

A party seeking to attack the credibility of the expert *may* bring to the attention of the jury material relevant to the issue on which the expert has offered an opinion of which the expert was unaware or which he did not consider. The purpose and permissible scope of impeachment of an expert is to call into question the truthfulness of the witness's testimony. (*San Diego Gas & Electric Company v. Schmidt* (2014) 228 Cal.App.4th 1280, 1301.) "It is common practice to challenge an expert by inquiring in good faith about relevant information, including hearsay, which he may have overlooked or ignored." (*People v. Montiel* (1993) 5 Cal.4th

877, 924.) "As a general rule, there is certainly nothing problematic about asking an expert about materials he has read that relate to an issue at trial." (*Wipf v. Kowalski,* 519 F.3d 380, 386 *(7th Cir. 2008).)*

The second reason you would like to know what the expert has considered is to point out facts or evidence the expert did *not* consider or take into account. The expert may not have reviewed or even known about all the evidence in the case. For example, some experts may base their opinion only on the information provided to them by counsel. They may not have conducted their own investigation, visited the scene, examined a party, or reviewed or considered other evidence that might have been available. Pointing out how the expert's review has not been thorough may make the witness's opinion seem more one-sided and unsupported.

Counsel: "Doctor, in arriving at your opinion, you only reviewed the materials provided to by counsel for the plaintiff, correct?"

Witness: "Yes."

Counsel: "You did not review or consider any of the neurological reports prepared by the doctors we sent her to, have you?"

Witness: "No, I was not provided those to review."

Counsel: "And, you have never visited the scene of the accident, have you?"

Witness: "No, I haven't."

Counsel: "You've never spoken with my client or attempted to interview her, have you?"

Witness: "No."

Counsel: "And, you've never conducted your own physical exam of her either, have you?"

Witness: "That's right."

Counsel: "So, your entire opinion is *essentially* based only on the information plaintiff's counsel provided, just her medical records from the hospital, is that correct?"

Witness: "Well, that and also my expertise with these types of injuries."

Inconsistency

It is quite common in civil cases that an expert witness will be deposed prior to trial. The great advantage to deposing an expert prior to trial, in conjunction with the information collected related to the rules of discovery, is that you can prepare by determining whether to object as well as construct your cross-examination. When an expert is deposed, one issue at trial you will need to be concerned with is whether there are any inconsistencies between the deposition testimony and the trial testimony. (See e.g., Federal Rules of Civil Procedure Rule 32(a)(2) ["Any party may use a deposition to contradict or impeach the testimony given by the deponent as a witness, or for any other purpose allowed by the Federal Rules of Evidence."]) In order to do that effectively, however, the expert's deposition testimony transcript must be organized and summarized, such that you can quickly discern an inconsistency if one occurs during the trial testimony. Additionally, if the expert has provided testimony previously in another case, it might be worth it to obtain those transcripts and review them prior to trial. Even if the subject matter of the former testimony is not exactly the same as here, the prior testimony may still give you some good information regarding the expert's qualifications.

> **Trial Tip:** Knowing exactly what the expert has said before, e.g., by reviewing transcripts of prior testimony, is a great advantage for cross-examination.

Evidence Helpful to Your Case

Another strategy is to use the expert to highlight any facts or evidence helpful to your case. This is an area of cross-examination that is often overlooked. Even if the expert's opinion is seemingly unassailable, there still might be facts or evidence you can draw out, which are helpful. For example, no rule prohibits an attorney during cross-examination from giving the opposing expert a hypothetical that incorporates *your* theory of the facts. Request the expert make an opinion based upon *your* assumed facts. The key is to demand the expert "assume" your facts are true.

Counsel: "Doctor, you've reviewed all the medical records in this case, haven't you?"

Witness: "Yes."

Counsel: "And, my client was complaining of severe neck pain and stiffness when she arrived at the emergency room that night, correct?"

Witness: "That's what the medical records reflects, yes."

Counsel: "Three months later, at a follow-up appointment, she was also complaining about pretty bad neck pain and numbness, wasn't she?"

Witness: "Yes."

Counsel: "Now, doctor, assuming, hypothetically, that she didn't have *any* neck pain for years after the first accident, and then had severe neck pain after this accident, wouldn't that indicate that some new injury occurred from this accident?"

Witness: "I suppose, hypothetically if that were true."

Counsel: "And, assume, hypothetically, if her neck pain continues until today, wouldn't that indicate that this accident is the cause of her pain and not the prior accident?"

Witness: "Assuming she had no pain leading up to the injury, I would agree."

In the above, the defense expert's testimony during direct testimony was that because the plaintiff was reporting fairly severe pain even shortly before the accident in question, her current neck and spinal pain is likely the result of the prior serious accident and not from this low speed fender bender. Note: causation is a common issue in many personal injury trials where the plaintiff is requesting compensatory and/or non-compensatory damages for "pain and suffering" *caused* by the defendant's tortious act.

Limitations on Materials not Considered

Although "wide latitude" is accorded for cross-examination, there are limitations. One of the more significant restrictions is the rule that an expert may not be cross-examined in detail regarding publications or studies the expert did *not* refer to, consider, or rely on in forming the opinion. (See CA Evid. § 721(b) (above).) "The purpose of section 721(b) is to prevent an adverse party from getting before the trier of fact the inadmissible hearsay views of an absent expert, which may be contrary to the expert witness's opinion, through the device of cross-examining the expert witness regarding the absent expert's publication or report even though the testifying expert had not used or considered that publication or report in any way in arriving at or forming his opinion testimony. Permitting such cross-examination would bring before the jury the opinions of absentee authors without the safeguard of cross-examination." (*McGarity v. Department of Transportation* (1992) 8 Cal.App.4th 677, 683 (McGarity), quoting 2 Jefferson, Evidence Benchbook (2d ed. 1982) § 29.8, p. 1036, original italics.; Id. at p. 683.) "It is error to permit the use of professional studies not relied upon by an expert in the formulation of his opinion. To allow their use would be to circumvent the hearsay rule." (*People v. Visciotti* (1992) 2 Cal.4th 1, 80.)

Although not codified, as in California, Federal law and other jurisdictions are essentially in accord with this principle. "Cross-examination which attempts to impeach by slipping hearsay evidence into the trial will not be permitted. Until defendant establishes that plaintiff (expert) had relied on the report of the other doctor, it was improper for the defendant to read from that report in cross-examining plaintiff's witness." *(Bobb v. Modern Products, Inc.,* 648 F.2d 1051, 1056 (5th Cir. 1981), [improper to cross-examine an expert from deposition of another expert which had not been admitted in evidence and not relied on by expert].) A party is not allowed to impeach an opposing party's expert witness with hearsay statements from another expert witness (unless the party can show that the witness relied on those statements in forming his opinion). (See *Ochoa–Valenzuela v. Ford Motor Co.,* 685 Fed.Appx. 551, 554 (9th Cir. 2017) [error to permit an expert witness to be cross-examined about an opinion given by his business partner in deposition in a different case; absent reliance by the expert on the out-of-court statement to form his opinion, "the use of testimony from another expert who did not testify in this trial constitutes admission of inadmissible hearsay"]; *In re Hanford Nuclear Reservation Litig.,* 534 F.3d at 1012 ["Reports of other experts cannot be admitted even as impeachment evidence, unless the testifying expert based his opinion on the hearsay in the examined report or testified directly from the report."].)

A further example, if an expert provides a scientific opinion at trial and bases that opinion partly on certain scientific literature or publications he is familiar with and has reviewed, he can be thoroughly cross-examined about those specific studies, including the details. The cross-examiner may also question the expert about any similar studies or publications the expert considered and perhaps ignored or discounted. Further, the expert can be confronted with any publications or studies that the cross-examiner feels conflict with the expert's opinion and/or support the examiner's theories. The cross-examiner would also naturally like to further cross-examine the expert on the details or specifics of those publications or studies which purportedly conflict with the expert's sources or theories. Whether this is permitted, however, is really one of degree.

Assuming the expert has literally never heard of nor considered the publications or studies, the court would most likely not permit cross-examination about the substance of those publications. The cross-examiner would need to call their own expert witness to render a different opinion based on those publications. On the other hand, if the expert concedes he is familiar with and "considered" the studies, but found them inapplicable to this case, the Court would probably allow deeper cross-examination into those studies.

Note, however, that under Rule 721, if the studies or publications were admitted as evidence, e.g., via another expert, or if the publication can be established as a "reliable authority" by the testimony or admission of the witness or by other expert testimony or by judicial notice, the cross-examination regarding those sources would be proper. This might apply, for example, if the publication was a well-known and commonly used resource for experts in the same field. In that regard, the expert might even concede that point.

Counsel: "Doctor, you've heard of Hansen's Comprehensive Handbook on Drug Interactions, Third Edition have you not?"

Witness: "Yes."

Counsel: "That's a respected and reliable publication in your field of expertise, correct?"

Witness: "Yes."

Counsel: "Did you review that handbook when coming up with your diagnosis and conclusions here?"

Witness: "No. I did not."

Counsel: "Are you aware that in the handbook at Chapter 7, page 19, it states that, quote, the use of non-steroidal anti-inflammatory drugs *are* an appropriate treatment for soft tissue nerve damage, unquote, contrary to your opinion here."

Witness: "Well, I am aware that reasonable minds may differ. There are other studies I am aware of that find otherwise. I don't think it is appropriate."

Counsel: "But, you would agree, would you not, that Hansen's is a publication many physicians refer to and follow?"

Witness: "Yes. That's true."

> **Trial Tip:** Getting the expert to concede that there is controversy in the field; that other experts have contrary opinions or viewpoints, may help to illustrate that the issue is not as cut-and-dry as the opposing party suggests.

Witness Control (Expert)

Any attorney who has ever attempted to cross-examine an expert witness knows how frustrating it can be because some experts are good at their job. After all, they are getting paid to impress the jurors, so they are often good speakers, know what to expect, and generally rehearsed. Some have egos and do not like being challenged and will be resistant to any concession. Many like to talk and, therefore, are more than happy to repeat and even expand on their conclusions and opinions during *your* cross-examination, if given a chance. Thus, one key element of good cross-examination is not to give them that opportunity. One of the most challenging aspects, therefore, is trying to rein in and control the expert, such that the witness answers just your question, and does not go past your question and into a narrative response. The use of witness control techniques is particularly important for experts. (See cross-examination witness control techniques, supra, at p. 104.)

Counsel: "Doctor, there have been other published studies that have concluded there is no link between airborne mold and lung cancer, isn't that true?"

Witness: "Those studies have been largely discounted by the scientific community, and the Rosenthal study found a 90 percent correlation rate, something the other studies did not consider."

[Repeat and admonish]

Counsel: "The question was, doctor, there have been other *published* studies that have concluded there is no link between airborne mold and lung cancer, isn't that true? Yes or no."

Witness: "Yes, but the Rosenthal study is probably the most famous."

Counsel: "Objection, your honor, unresponsive, move to strike."

[Some judges may sustain the objection. Other judges may take a more hands-off approach with experts. In that case then, it is important that you attempt to keep the witness in check. If anything, the jury is observing how non-compliant the witness.]

Counsel: "And, one of those studies was performed at the University of California, led by Doctor Andrews. You've heard of that study, correct?"

Witness: "I'm familiar with it."

Counsel: "Well, in forming your opinion in this case, surely you at least considered it, didn't you?"

Witness: "As I said, I'm familiar with it."

Counsel: "Now, the University of California study was completed about 2012, wasn't it?"

Witness: "About then. I'm not sure exactly."

Counsel: "And, doctor, you are aware, are you not, that that study found no correlation between mold and lung cancer? That was the finding wasn't it?"

Witness: "There have been two other studies since then, including the Rosenthal study."

Counsel: "That wasn't my question, doctor. My question *was,* the University of California study found no correlation between mold and lung cancer, correct? True or false, doctor?"

Witness: "True, but the Rosenthal study was much more thorough and involved."

Counsel: "Objection, Your Honor, unresponsive. I move to strike the answer after 'true.'"

10 Steps to Successful Cross-examination of Expert

The battle of the experts is sometimes the lynchpin of a case. Thus, cross-examination becomes critically important. Overall, the key to success is preparation and having a strategy. In that regard, below are ten strategies to consider as you prepare for trial:

1. Depose the expert prior to trial, if possible;
2. Obtain transcripts of other prior testimony;
3. Research and familiarize yourself with the subject matter. Consult with similar experts;
4. Formulate a strategy and plan of attack;
5. File a motion in limine to exclude or limit expert testimony, if appropriate;
6. Prepare an outline for cross-examination;
7. Raise the topic during voir dire to access juror receptiveness;
8. Use, short, concise leading questions during cross-examination;
9. Maintain witness control during cross-examination;
10. Save key points made for closing argument.

14. TRIAL OBJECTIONS

An "objection" is a procedural device used to notify the court that a party has an issue or a complaint. Objections at trial are commonplace and knowing how to properly make and respond to an objection is an important trial skill. Typically, objections are registered either at the beginning of a trial in the form of a motion in limine, where the parties have the luxury of time to respond, or mid-trial, often during testimony, when there is little time.

Overall, trial objections serve two main purposes: (1) to keep your opponent in line and playing by the rules, and (2) to preserve the issue for later appellate review. More specifically, the objection may seek a ruling by the court to limit or exclude inadmissible evidence, for example, evidence that is not relevant or considered hearsay. Or it may be to complain about a rule violation; for instance, that your opponent used an improper leading question during direct examination. A review of appellate opinions, both published and unpublished, reveal that *many* potential meritorious grounds for appeal are forfeited due to either no objection or improper objection.

"It is, of course, a familiar rule that appellate courts will not review errors to which an objection could have been, but was not, made in the trial court." (*People v. Scott* (2012) 203 Cal.App.4th 1303, 1309.) As a general rule, a claim of error will be deemed to have been forfeited when a party fails to bring the error to the trial court's attention by timely motion or objection. (*People v. Simon* (2001) 25 Cal.4th 1082, 1103; *Keener v. Jeld-Wen, Inc.* (2009) 46 Cal.4th 247, 265-266.).)

Evid. Code § 353 Erroneous admission of evidence; effect (FRE Rule 103)

A verdict or finding shall not be set aside, nor shall the judgment or decision based thereon be reversed, by reason of the erroneous admission of evidence unless:

(a) There appears of record an objection to or a motion to exclude or to strike the evidence that was timely made and so stated as to make clear the specific ground of the objection or motion; and

(b) The court which passes upon the effect of the error or errors is of the opinion that the admitted evidence should have been excluded on the ground stated and that the error or errors complained of resulted in a miscarriage of justice.

Trial Tip: At counsel table, have a cheat sheet with a list of the common objections available at your fingertips for quick reference, including the hearsay exceptions.

Timely *and* Specific

Evidence Code section 353(a) codifies the general rule that the objection or motion must specify the ground for objection, a general objection being insufficient. An objection must be timely, specific, *and* state the legal ground for the objection. An objection is sufficient if it fairly apprises the trial court of the issue it is being called upon to decide. (*People v. Frank* (1978) 21 Cal. 3d. 284,290; CA Evid. Code § 353; FRE 103(a) [objecting party must make a timely objection or move to strike *and* state the specific ground].) A failure to make a recognized specific objection forfeits review on appeal. If an objection is not timely, e.g., at the point of the transgression, the objection is untimely. When the nature of a question indicates that the evidence sought is inadmissible, there must be an objection to the question; a subsequent motion to strike is not sufficient. (*People v. Demetrulias* (2006) 39 Cal.4th 1, 21; see also *People v. Champion* (1995) 9 Cal.4th 879, 918-919.) [reviewing courts will not consider a challenge to the admissibility of evidence absent a specific and timely objection in the trial court on the ground sought to be urged on appeal].)

This means that the objection must be made as soon as practical. The flow of a trial can move quickly and you may only have seconds to react. If the question asked by opposing counsel requests inadmissible evidence, an objection should be lodged *before* the witness answers, if possible. However, this requires you to be paying attention and listening carefully. Some lawyers fail to object quickly simply because they were not paying attention or were distracted. If the witness answers, it is difficult, if not impossible, to "unring" the proverbial bell in the minds of the jurors, even if the court strikes the testimony and directs them to disregard the answer.

Counsel: "What did the officer tell you?"
Opp.Counsel: "Objection, Your Honor, hearsay." [Before witness answers.]

If you wait to object, even a few questions later, the court may overrule the objection as "untimely." Even worse, if you wait until the end of the examination and then complain that the witness introduced inadmissible evidence, the court will almost certainly overrule the objection. The bottom line, therefore, is that when something objectionable occurs, you may literally only have seconds to react. Often, however, an objectionable area or question can be anticipated; for example, when you observe that the focus of opposing counsel's questions are moving towards an objectionable area. In addition, if the witness begins to answer, be prepared to assertively interrupt the witness mid-sentence, if necessary.

Counsel: "What did the officer tell you?"
Witness: "The officer told me that..."
Opp Counsel: "Objection, Your Honor, hearsay!"

> **Trial Tip:** The objection must be loud and clear enough for the judge, opposing counsel, and even the witness to hear in order to stop the action and to permit the court to rule. If you timidly or quietly object, it may not be clear to the judge that you are objecting and you can get left behind in the dust. However, worse than objecting timidly is objecting and then changing your mind by announcing "Withdrawn," which is not very impressive to the jury or to the court.

In addition to being "timely," the objection must also state a "specific ground," unless it is obvious from the context. This means that counsel must clearly set forth a cognizable *legal* basis for the objection, e.g., relevance, hearsay, vague and ambiguous, speculation, etc. Merely stating, "I object!" without any reference to the legal ground is insufficient and some judges may summarily deny the motion without further comment and the testimony continues. Some attorneys who do not know the legal ground will object and try to state some reason, although incorrect. "I object, Your Honor, the witness can't say that..." or "...that's an improper question." Again, failing to state the correct legal basis could result in the court overruling the failed objection without further comment. Kindlier judges may gave a prompt and allow counsel an opportunity to state the legal ground.

In addition, even if counsel does state a legal basis, it must be the *correct* legal basis. For example, if the question calls for a hearsay response and counsel objects "relevance," the objection will be overruled. Furthermore, if there are multiple basis to object to, for example, the question or answer contains hearsay and is irrelevant, to preserve the issue for appeal, counsel must state *all* the applicable grounds. (See [holding that objection based on "relevance" did not preserve Rule 403 error]).The judge, and the appellate court, will only consider the grounds stated and the failure to object waives the issue on appeal. (*People v. Demetrulias* (2006) 39 Cal.4th 1, 21; see also *People v. Champion* (1995) 9 Cal.4th 879, 918-919. (See *People v. Dykes* (2009) 46 Cal.4th 731, 766 [defense counsel objected on the grounds of relevance rather than prosecutor misconduct; claim forfeited].) One example where two different objections are similar in nature, but different, is *relevance* versus *undue prejudice* under FRE Rule 403 (Discussed below). Some attorneys lump the two together or do not understand the difference.

Counsel: "Objection, Your Honor. Hearsay. Vague and ambiguous. Relevance."

Moreover, proper court etiquette is generally to first notice an objection properly, to wit: "I object, Your Honor,..." followed by the legal basis. Some attorneys get lazy and simply say, "Relevance!" or "Hearsay!" without the preceding words. Judges have different requirements for formality, but the better practice is to keep your trial performance more formal. It looks professional and more impressive to the jury and the court. In that same vein, although you must state the correct legal basis, it is generally *not* required that you also recite the specific rule number or code section. Again, if there are multiple reasons to object, the objection should state all grounds, otherwise, the appellate court may consider the issue forfeited.

Trial Tip: If you object and the judge responds, "Overruled, on *that* ground," it could be a hint that you have missed the correct objection.

Continuing (Standing) Objection

If you have objected and the court has overruled the objection, rather than continuing to object repeatedly on the same issue, notify the court you would like to make a "standing objection." A standing objection can preserve an issue for appellate review. (*People v. Gurule* (2002) 28 Cal.4th 557, 621.) If you do make a standing objection, request the court to recognize the objection and concur *on the record* that no further objections are necessary on that issue. However, make sure the standing objection relates to the *same* issue and *same* topic as the court's previous ruling; otherwise, you risk an argument on appeal that the failure to make a specific objection forfeited the issue. If it is not clear, it is better to err on the side of caution and make another objection. In addition, if an objection was made during a motion in limine that the court overruled, the safest course is to confirm with the court *on the record* that you do not have to object again during the actual testimony. However, again, if it could be argued that the issue is different in some way than the issue litigated in limine, there could be an issue of forfeiture. Better to object in this circumstance than risk forfeiting the issue on appeal. (See supra, at p. 15, re: rulings on limine motions.)

Trial Tip: If you lodge a "continuing" or "standing" objection, request the court to acknowledge on the record that you do not have to object again.

Motion to Strike

If the objection is sustained and inadmissible evidence was nonetheless set forth on the record, e.g., the witness answered, the party making the motion must also make a motion to "strike" the evidence (testimony) from the record. Failure to make the motion is a common mistake and could result in forfeiture on appeal. (See *People v. Demetrulias* (2006) 39 Cal.4th 1, 19-20) Even though the objection was "sustained," technically, without a motion to strike, the evidence is still on the record. The best practice is to move to have the testimony "stricken" *and* request the court give a curative admonishment to disregard the evidence. However, consider whether the court's admonishment might only "ring the bell" one more time. In the typical jury instructions, the jurors are directed to disregard any evidence stricken from the record by the court.

Witness: "The officer told me the other car ran the red light."
Counsel: "Objection, Your Honor, hearsay. Move to strike."
Court: "Sustained. The answer is stricken."

Trial Tip: The failure to include a motion to strike is a common mistake. Whether or not to request the court to also admonish the jury to disregard the answer is a tactical consideration.

Responding to an Objection

Nearly as important as making a proper objection, is how to respond when one is made. For basic procedural-type objections, such as "leading," "narrative," or "speculation," the trial court may rule summarily without permitting any response. For the proponent, these types of adverse rulings can be easily cured by re-formatting the question, i.e., ask the question again in a non-leading or less-vague manner. For more complex objections, however, such as "hearsay," it may require counsel to respond. Most judges do not permit "speaking objections" where the attorneys are allowed to "argue" their respective positions in the presence of the jurors. Rather, most judges want only a concise legal objection and a similarly concise legal response, without a lot of argument.

Counsel: "Objection, Your Honor, hearsay."
Opp. Counsel: "Your Honor, the statement qualifies as a spontaneous
                      statement."

In the above circumstance, the court might also permit both counsel to briefly argue how they have or have not met the elements for an exception or whether the statement is being offered for the truth. If the issue is important and if the court appears ready to rule or does rule without permitting you an opportunity to respond, politely request permission "to be heard" at the side-bar or otherwise out of juror earshot.

Counsel: "Your Honor, may I be heard?" or "Your Honor, may I be heard at
              the side-bar regarding this matter?"

Sidebar Conferences

As discussed, many courts prohibit speaking objections. If the issue is important, a request for a sidebar conference may be appropriate. The court's procedures or preferences regarding objections and sidebars should be a topic of the pre-trial conference.

Counsel: "What did the victim tell you at the scene?"
Opp. Counsel: " Objection, calls for hearsay."
Court: "Counsel, your response?"
Counsel: "Your honor, it qualifies as an excited utterance."
Court: "Counsel?" [to opposing counsel]
Opp. Counsel: "Your Honor, we don't believe it qualifies under that exception
                      due to the passage of time. If necessary, Your Honor, may I be
                      heard at the sidebar on this issue?"
Court: "Yes. Counsel may approach."

The purpose of the sidebar is to permit argument by counsel out of jury earshot. However, keep in mind that for many procedural-like objections, such as "leading" or "vague and ambiguous," the court may simply sustain or overrule the objection without eliciting *any* response by opposing counsel. If the court does rule summarily against you, and you think the issue is important enough, a request "to be heard" may be appropriate.

Court: "Objection sustained."
Counsel: "Thank you, Your Honor. But, may I be heard briefly at the side bar on
               this issue?"

Generally, if the court senses the issue is, in fact, material and important to a party, the court may allow a sidebar. When permitted, the attorneys will typically approach the bench and have a quiet conversation with the court where the court allows each side to argue their respective positions. Keep in mind that often sidebar conversation is not reported; however, some courtrooms may have microphones at the bench which permit the court reporter to hear and report the argument. If the sidebar argument is not reported, it is incumbent on counsel to later make a record of what was argued and the court's ultimate ruling. If the issue requires more substantial argument, the court also has the option to temporarily excuse the jury from the courtroom, e.g., put them on a break, or hold the conference in chambers. Keep in mind that sidebar conferences usually occur in the presence of the jurors and they will be very curious as to what the judge and the attorneys are talking about. If the attorneys are animated or talking loudly, the jurors will pick up on it.

Protect the record – An important rule for an appeal is that generally the appealing party has the burden to produce a record of the alleged error. Thus, during trial, be conscious of any argument or ruling made by the court that was not reported, e.g., during a sidebar or in chambers. To save costs, many trials are not reported, thus making an appeal more difficult. In some cases, the court will conference with the attorney in chambers and may even make substantive rulings or findings, often related to a motion in limine. If the issue is important, politely request to make a record of the court's findings and/or ruling at some later time, e.g., during a break when the jurors are out. In some cases where an objection is made and argument heard, rather than ruling summarily, the court will take the matter "under submission" with the intention to render a ruling later. However, if, for whatever reason, the court does not rule or seems to have forgotten, it is incumbent upon the objecting party to request a ruling. Otherwise, the issue may be considered forfeited as it is incumbent on the moving party to seek a ruling. (See *People v. Rowland* (1992) 4 Cal. 4th 238, at p. 259; *People v. Bolden* (2002) 29 Cal. 4th 515, 543.)

Speaking Objections

Many courts have a rule prohibiting "speaking objections." Objections during trial should be more formalistic and should state only the legal basis for the objection and, if requested by the court, only the legal basis to oppose the objection. A speaking objection is when the attorney essentially wants to argue the merits of the objection or the response in the presence of the trier of fact. If allowed, the argument by the attorneys has the potential to introduce irrelevant or prejudicial information to the jury. If the court's ruling is important and requires additional argument, one solution is to make a request "to be heard at the sidebar" such that the issued can be addressed out of jury earshot. (See below.)

> **Trial Tip:** Judges (and juries) quickly perceive whether an attorney is the type who objects repeatedly regarding relatively trivial issues, or one who reserves objections for only important matters. If you continually object and request "to be heard" and "approach" regarding minor issues, the court may begin to rule summarily and deny such requests without comment.

Reasons Not to Object

Just because you may have a legal ground to object does not necessarily mean that you should. There may be valid tactical reasons why you may wish to forego an objection. One of the primary concerns should be how the jurors perceive your objections. If the jury forms the impression you are objecting repeatedly simply to be an obstructionist or to hide evidence, it does not help your cause. Furthermore, repeated objections, sidebar conferences, and interruptions are irritating to jurors who are anxious to keep the case moving forward. The best rule of thumb is *no harm, no foul*. If the objectionable evidence will not have any negative impact on your case, consider not objecting. On the other hand, an objection might be necessary just to keep opposing counsel in line, for example, when leading questions are used continually. Sometimes, a few well-placed objections at the beginning sends the message that you are "on guard," so to speak, and opposing counsel may be more apt to play by the rules knowing you are prepared to object.

Common Trial Objections

A trial can be a fast moving, changing environment truly requiring counsel to think on their feet. Trial objections generally relate to either the form of the question or the nature of the answer given by the witness. Every trial lawyer should know by heart the most common objections and their requirements. Below are 18 of the most common trial objections, in relative order of frequency.

"Objection, Your Honor, _____!"

1. **"Relevance"** – This is unquestionably the most common trial objection. Only relevant evidence is admissible. (Evid. Code § 350.) Unless prohibited by statute, all relevant evidence is admissible. (Evid. Code § 351; See discussion re: relevant evidence, supra, at p. 19.) The "relevance" objection is one of those objections that you "know it when you see it," so to speak. It is generally appropriate when your opponent's question, or the answer given, seems to have no connection or relationship to the contested issues. The objection often occurs when one party is attempting to introduce evidence that is collateral. Tactically, if you sense opposing counsel is moving down the path towards irrelevant information, a few well-placed objections at the beginning may help cut short the inquiry.

2. **"Vague and Ambiguous"** – This is also a very common trial objection and one that trial counsel should be particularly alert for because it is meant to head-off confusing information from reaching the trier of fact. The cause is generally that the question is too long, compound, or poorly worded, e.g., a double-negative. Some attorneys make their question unclear by starting to formulate a question, then changing course mid-sentence, and asking something different, a fact every court reporter can attest to.

Counsel: "As you approached the intersection, I mean, how well could you see if there was oncoming traffic?"
Counsel: "Was the light green when you applied your breaks as you stopped?"
Counsel: "Is it not true, that the light was green when you approached the intersection, correct?"

Counsel: "The light was green as you approached the intersection, then it turned red, and that is when you applied your brakes, correct?"

Shorter, more concise questions generally avoids the issue. The objection can apply during both direct and cross-examination, and frequently, even the witness does not understand precisely what is being requested. If the objection is sustained, simply rephrase or reword the question to make it clearer. A confusing question can often be cured by backing up a few steps and simply breaking down the subject matter into smaller segments with several questions, rather than just one. In addition, an unclear question often results in an equally unclear answer. Repeated poor questions is generally the hallmark of an attorney who is not very prepared and "winging" it without an outline. Keeping the questions short and in some logical sequence is the key.

3. "Speculation" or "Calls for Speculation/Conjecture" – This is a very common objection and appropriate whenever a question asks the witness to essentially guess, or when the answer is based on a guess, a hunch, or "speculation." It often means the witness has no "personal knowledge," also a valid ground for an objection. (See discussion re: personal knowledge, supra, at p. 60.)

Counsel: "What was your impression of who ran the light?"
Opp. Counsel: "Objection, Your Honor, calls for speculation."

If the witness did not actually see who ran the light, then her answer lacks personal knowledge and is speculative. In addition, her "impression" is irrelevant, unless somehow her state of mind is at issue.

Witness: "I think the red car ran the red light."
Opp. Counsel: "Objection, Your Honor, speculation. Move to strike."

If the witness did not actually observe the accident, then the answer is speculation and the answer should be stricken. However, if the witness did see the accident and her equivocation "I think…" merely demonstrates her uncertainty of what she saw, the court might overrule the objection and allow the jurors to give it the appropriate weight. Recall that if there is some evidence to believe the witness may have observed the accident, but her recollection or memory is questionable, the court will likely rule that it is a question of weight, rather than admissibility.

Counsel: "How was the defendant acting right after the accident?"
Witness: "Oh, he was very irate and angry, as if he didn't think he did anything wrong."
Opp. Counsel: "Objection, Your Honor, speculation. Move to strike."

Witnesses are permitted to make lay opinions, if rationally based on the witness's perception and if helpful. (See Evid. Code § 800; supra at p. 65.) In this circumstance, the court would likely permit the witness's opinion regarding the defendant's anger and irritation to stand, but strike the later half of the answer as speculation.

Witness: "He was obviously feeling guilty for causing the accident."

In the above, the court would likely sustain an objection to speculation and improper lay opinion, as the witness is speculating about the defendant's state of mind.

4. "Leading" – As discussed previously, leading questions are generally prohibited during direct-examination. (See discussion re: direct testimony, supra, at p. 81 et seq..) However, there are exceptions and not every leading question is improper. One key to this objection is to object quickly before the witness answers. Objecting to an improper leading question also helps to keep opposing counsel in check, so to speak.

Counsel on direct: "You observed the blue car run the light, didn't you?"
Opp. Counsel: "Objection, Your Honor, leading."
Court: "Sustained."

Trial Tip: Anticipate when opposing counsel may be tempted to use leading questions and object at the first instance to set the tone. If opposing counsel knows you are willing and able to object, they tend to police themselves better.

5. "Lack of Foundation" – This catchall objection is generally applicable when some foundational requirement for the admission of evidence or testimony has not been established by the proponent, e.g., a failure to authenticate a writing. As the name implies, the objection is appropriate if the proponent has not established the necessary preliminary facts (foundation) for the admissibility of the evidence. However, a generic objection of "lack of foundation" without more specificity regarding what exactly is deficient, could be overruled as being too non-specific. (*U.S. v. York*, 572 F.3d 415, 421 (7th Cir. 2009) [treating objection to "foundation" as a general objection]; see also *People v. Moore* (1970) 13 Cal.App.3d 424, 434, fn. 8 [as a general rule, "where the objection is lack of proper foundation, counsel must point out specifically in what respect the foundation is deficient"]; *People v. Modell* (1956) 143 Cal.App.2d 724, 728–729 [objection on the ground that proper foundation has not been laid in this did not preserve appellate claim]; but see *People v. Cowan* (2010) 50 Cal.4th 401, 502, fn. 36 [hearsay claim was preserved for review where trial court had apparently understood objections to testimony, which included lack of foundation, as encompassing a hearsay objection].) Therefore, the best practice is to not only state "lack of foundation," but also the missing foundational requirement, e.g., personal knowledge.

Counsel: "Which car ran the red light?"
Opp Counsel: "Objection, Your Honor, lack of foundation; personal knowledge."

The court might sustain the objection if there is no preliminary testimony or evidence that the witness actually observed the accident. A few more questions might clear up the ambiguity.

> **Trial Tip:** The "lack of foundation" objection is often made incorrectly by not stating the specific foundational element that is lacking, e.g., personal knowledge or proper authentication.

6. "Lack of Personal Knowledge" – This objection is appropriate whenever it has not been established that the witness observed or otherwise perceived the subject matter of the testimony. The burden is on the proponent to establish the witness's personal knowledge. (See discussion re: personal knowledge, supra, at p. 60.) Often, a witness will testify concerning an event, such as a traffic collision, but it may not be clear initially how the witness came about that information. For example, it may not have been established yet whether the witness was present and saw it happen, or learned or heard about it via another source, i.e., hearsay, or is making an opinion based on speculation. Typically, the problem is that the proponent counsel failed to "lay the foundation," for example, by establishing that the witness was present and observed the collision. If the objection is sustained, the cure is to go simply back a few steps and elicit more information. Recall, however, that if the issue is one of credibility or there is conflicting evidence whether the witness has the requisite personal knowledge, the court will likely overrule the objection and find it is a matter of weight, rather than admissibility.

7. "Nonresponsive" – This objection is appropriate whenever the witness has not properly responded to the question. If the court sustains the objection, then a motion to "strike" the testimony is generally also appropriate. (See discussion re: nonresponsive/narrative answers, supra, at p. 63.)

Counsel: "You never applied your brakes before the collision, correct?"
Witness: "How could I? The other car came out of nowhere and broadsided me!"
Opp. Counsel: "Objection, Your Honor, nonresponsive. Move to strike."

> **Trial Tip:** The "nonresponsive" objection is a good method to keep the witness in check during cross-examination, with one caveat: ensure the question only calls for a "yes" or "no" answer. If the question is poorly phrased or cannot be answered without explanation, the court may overrule the objection, making you look like the bad guy.

8. "Compound Question" – This objection is appropriate whenever a question consists of two or more questions rolled into one—where an answer by the witness could apply to either question. This form of objectionable question usually occurs when the examiner's question is too long. A shorter, more concise question normally cures the problem.

Counsel: "So, if I understand your testimony, as you approached the intersection you applied your brakes and looked in your rearview mirror, is that correct?"
Counsel: "Objection, Your Honor, compound question."

In the above, a "yes" or "no" answer could technically apply to either proposition. Be particularly alert for compound questions when *your* witness is being cross-examined. Often, during poor cross-examination, the examiner weaves in to the question more than one factual statement to be answered.

> **Trial Tip:** Be particularly alert whenever opposing counsel propounds a *long-winded* question, because there is a good chance it is vague and ambiguous and probably also compound.

9. "Hearsay" – Hearsay objections are common. The best method to spot and analyze hearsay issues is to follow a step-by-step approach. (See discussion re: hearsay, supra, at p. 182.) The objection can be appropriate if the question requests a hearsay response or if the answer given is inadmissible hearsay. Of course, the best course is to object before the answer if given. Recall that if there is an objection, the proponent has the burden to show either that the statement is not hearsay or that an exception applies. (See hearsay exceptions, Appendix.)

Witness: "While at the scene, the officer said the other car ran the red light."
Counsel: "Objection, Your Honor. Hearsay. Move to strike the answer."

Counsel: "Did you talk to the witness at the scene?"
Opp. Counsel: "Objection, Your Honor, calls for hearsay."

The court should overrule the objection at this point, because technically, the question does not ask what the witness said. It can be answered with either a "yes" or "no" response.

Witness: "Yes."
Counsel: "What did the witness tell you?"
Opp. Counsel: "Objection, Your Honor. Calls for hearsay."
Court: "Counsel, your response?"
Counsel: "Yes, Your Honor, it qualifies as a party admission and also an excited utterance."

10. "Improper Lay Opinion" – As discussed previously, lay witnesses are permitted to make some opinions; however, if an opinion strays more into the realm of expert opinion or speculation, the court may sustain an objection. (See discussion re: lay opinion, supra, at p. 65.) The objection is generally appropriate whenever the witness is making an opinion regarding a substantive issue at the trial, for example, that a party was negligent or caused the accident. On the other hand, estimates of distance, time, or descriptions of mental states, e.g., sad or angry, are generally permitted.

Counsel: "How fast would you estimate the other car was traveling when it entered the intersection?"
Objection: "Objection. Improper lay opinion."

Unless the witness has been qualified as a traffic expert, the court would likely sustain the objection if the witness were requested to estimate a specific MPH. On the other hand, the witness could properly make an opinion that the car was traveling "fast" or "speeding."

11. "Assumes Facts Not in Evidence" – This objection is appropriate whenever the question, as worded, assumes preliminary facts not yet established. "A common vice is for the examiner to couch a question so that it assumes as true matters to which the witness has not testified, and which are disputed between the parties.... Whether the witness is friendly or hostile, the answer can be misleading. If the witness answers the question without separating out the assumption, it is impossible to determine whether the assumption was ignored or affirmed.'" (*U.S. v. Smith*, 354 F.3d 390, fn 5 (5th Cir. 2003), citing McCormick on Evidence § 7 (5th ed.1999).) In some instances, the problem is merely that counsel is putting the cart before the horse, so to speak.

Counsel: "Immediately after the minivan ran the red light, what did you see happen?"
Opp. Counsel: "Objection, Your Honor, assumes facts not in evidence."

In this example, the court would likely sustain the objection if there has been no testimony or evidence established that the minivan in fact ran the light, let alone without braking. For the proponent, a simple cure is to direct the witness back in time in order to establish the missing assumption. Obviously, if the witness did not actually observe the minivan run the light, then the witness would have no personal knowledge.

12. "Misstates the Evidence" – This objection is appropriate whenever counsel misstates evidence. For example, during cross-examination, counsel may preface a leading question with a factual statement that is inaccurate or misleading. This occurs sometimes because counsel is attempting to paraphrase or summarize the status of the evidence, in particular, a witness's prior statement or testimony.

Counsel: "Now, you were present in court, were you not, when the defense
            expert testified?"
Witness: "Yes."
Counsel: "And, you heard him testify that it would have been impossible
            for your vehicle to have caused that much damage to my client's
            vehicle, if you were only traveling 20 miles-per-hour, as
            you claimed in your deposition. Are you still certain that was your
            speed?"
Opp. Counsel: "Objection, Your Honor, misstates the evidence."

In this example, the court might sustain the objection if counsel's summary of the expert's testimony was inaccurate or misleading. Further, counsel might have also misstated the witness's deposition testimony. Opposing counsel might also complain that the question is argumentative. (See below.) This type of objection can be difficult for the court, if the assumed facts are not patently incorrect. The cross-examiner is generally permitted to confront a witness with contradictory evidence. Given the wide latitude allowed for cross-examination, if the court felt that counsel's statements were fair, the court would likely overrule the objection. The objection can also apply during closing argument if counsel misstates or misrepresents the trial evidence; however, the parties are permitted to argue their interpretation of the facts and inferences to be drawn from them. (See discussion re: misconduct during argument, supra, at p. 259.)

13. "Argumentative" – This objection is typically made during cross-examination when the examiner makes a statement in the guise of a question—when the question is designed to engage a witness in argument rather than elicit facts within the witness's knowledge. (*People v. Mayfield* (1997) 14 Cal.4th 668, 755.) "An argumentative question that essentially talks past the witness, and makes an argument to the jury, is improper because it does not seek to elicit relevant, competent testimony, or often any testimony at all." (*People v. Chatman* (2006) 38 Cal.4th 344, at p. 384 [prosecutor's question to the defendant whether the safe was lying when his fingerprints were found on a safe was argumentative].) Counsel's statement to a witness, "Sir, are you going to pick and choose what you feel like telling us today and what you don't feel like telling us? Is that what you're saying?" was held argumentative. (*People v Johnson* (2003) 109 Cal. App. 4th 1230, 1235.) Other examples might include, "So, you just happened to be at the wrong place at the wrong time?"…"So, you're the *victim* here and everyone else is at fault, is that what you're saying?"

Questions become argumentative when it becomes clear to the court that the examiner's intent is not to elicit relevant information, but rather, to make an editorial or insulting comment just to make a point. How the judge rules may also depend on the counsel's demeanor and the witness's vulnerability, e.g., a little old lady versus a convicted felon.

On the other hand, because courts generally accord wide latitude for cross-examination, the fact that the questioning is done in a vigorous, confrontational manner or includes accusations or insinuation of bad behavior, does not necessarily make the question improperly "argumentative." Thus, in the first two examples below, the court would probably overrule an "argumentative" objection.

Counsel: "Isn't it true, that you lied to the officer at the scene when you claimed the light was green?"
Counsel: "And, you're lying now just to avoid liability, aren't you?"
Counsel: "You don't expect these jurors to believe that, do you?" [This question is more argumentative and the court could sustain the objection.]

Trial Tip: A question is generally *not* "argumentative" merely because the cross-examiner turns up the heat and confronts the witness with inconsistencies or suggests an improper motive.

14. "Narrative" –Witness examination is generally required to proceed in a question-and-answer format. As such, the witness is not permitted to take the stand and simply say whatever they want without any direction or guidance from counsel. (See discussion re: narrative responses, supra, at p. 64.) The "narrative" objection can pertain either to the form of the question which might request a narrative response or a run-on answer given by the witness. For example, if the question is merely, "Tell us what happened?" the objection, "Calls for a narrative response," would be appropriate because the witness was provided with literally no direction regarding the subject matter or a time and place to reference. The objection is also appropriate when the witness proceeds to relate a long-winded answer that strays from the subject matter of the original question. When this occurs, at some point you must interrupt the testimony with the objection.

Counsel: "Objection, Your Honor, narrative."

Most courts will allow a witness leeway to answer questions with some narration and explanation, but may sustain the objection when it appears the witness is clearly going off-topic or the explanation has become too lengthy. If the court sustains the objection, the proponent should simply re-frame the questions in a more question-and-answer format. However, for expert witnesses, courts will generally permit longer answers and explanations. For instance, it is not unusual for an expert to give a five or ten minute explanation without interruption on a complicated subject matter.

15. "Asked and Answered" – This objection is appropriate whenever a witness has been previously asked the same question by the same examiner and is requested to basically repeat the same answer. On direct examination, a witness is generally permitted to give the answer only once. However, trial lawyers will often attempt to have the witness describe important information more than one time to drive home the point. Asking for the same basic information, but using a slightly different format or question, might avoid the objection.

Counsel:	"Moments before you entered the intersection, what color was the traffic light in your direction?"
Witness:	"It was green."
Counsel:	"Any doubt in your mind?"
Witness:	"No."
Counsel:	"You saw it was green?"
Witness:	"Yes."
Counsel:	"So, to be clear then, it's your testimony that the light was green before you entered into the intersection?"
Opp Counsel:	"Objection, Your Honor. Asked and answered. Leading."

The "asked and answered" objection is less likely to be sustained during cross-examination because of the "wide latitude" given. For example, in *People v. Riel* (2000) 22 Cal.4th 1153, at p. 1197, the court explained: "Although a court should not, over objection, permit an attorney to [question] witnesses with ceaseless reiteration through endless matters concerning which they had testified that they knew nothing, often some amount of repetition is the essence of effective cross-examination. More latitude should be granted to a cross-examiner asking the same question more than once than is permitted the direct examiner. One major purpose of cross-examination is to continue probing the same subject matter in an effort to get a witness possibly to modify his or her testimony. There is good reason, therefore, to permit the cross-examiner to ask a witness the same question more than once."

In practice, most courts will consider sustaining the objection when it becomes clear that the second or third asking of the same general question has no purpose, other than to make a point. However, if the witness's credibility has been attacked during the cross-examination, on the re-direct examination, the court may permit the witness to reiterate important testimony as a means of rebuttal. (See discussion re: rehabilitating the witness, supra, at p. 142.)

16. "352" Undue Prejudice (FRE Rule 403) – This objection is typically made by a party seeking to exclude evidence on the grounds that it is prejudicial or harmful to the case. However, this motion is not too common during actual testimony, rather, it is more commonly made in a pre-trial motion in limine. (See motions in limine, supra, at p. 20.) Essentially, the motion requires the court to conduct a weighing analysis of the prejudice versus the probative value of the evidence. CA Evid. Code § 352 states: "The court in its discretion may exclude evidence if its probative value is substantially outweighed by the probability that its admission will (a) necessitate undue consumption of time, or (b) create substantial danger of undue prejudice, of confusing the issues, or of misleading the jury."

> **Trial Tip:** If a 352 (403) issue crops up during testimony, it is a good time to request a sidebar or an evidentiary hearing outside the presence of the jury. One common 352-type issue is when one party seeks to introduce bad character evidence regarding the opposing party or a witness.

17. "Improper Character Evidence" – This objection is appropriate whenever a party seeks to introduce inadmissible "character evidence" of a party or witness. It generally applies when a party is seeking to admit evidence of some prior act or conduct by a party. If the character evidence is being offered as a form of circumstantial evidence to prove the current complaint or charge, it is normally litigated in a motion in limine. (See discussion re: Character Evidence, infra, at p. 244.) Character evidence can also be admissible related to a witness's character for truthfulness or untruthfulness. (See discussion re: Impeachment of Character, supra, at p. 125.)

18. "Beyond the Scope" – "Cross-examination should not go beyond the subject matter of the direct examination and matters affecting the witness's credibility. The court may allow inquiry into additional matters as if on direct examination." (FRE Rule 711(b); CA Evid. Code § 772(c).) The objection, "Beyond the scope," generally applies when the cross-examiner goes into a wholly different area than covered during direct examination. How the judge rules will depend upon on how related the question is to the issues and facts elicited during direct examination. However, as discussed previously, the cross-examiner is given "wide latitude," thus if the subject matter has at least some tangential relationship to the areas covered on direct-examination *or* relates to witness credibility, the court will likely allow it. Similarly, if, during direct-examination, the witness said something which may have "opened the door" to more collateral areas of questioning, the court may permit the questioning on that topic. However, the further afield the questions get from the main contested issues the more likely it is that the court will invoke FRE Rule 403 at some point to cut it off and prevent the trial from "degenerating into nitpicking wars of attrition over collateral credibility issues." (*People v. Wheeler* (1992) 4 Cal.4th 284, 296; see discussion re: "Is the Door Open?" supra, at p. 109.)

Counsel: "On the morning of the collision, were you in any way distracted or not paying attention as you approached the intersection?"

Witness: "Oh, no. I was very aware of my surroundings. I've always been a very careful driver."

In this situation, opposing counsel may seek to impeach the witness with the fact that nine years earlier she was involved in another traffic accident where she was determined to have been at fault. Counsel for the plaintiff would argue that the line of inquiry is "beyond the scope" of direct examination because the witness was never asked about that prior incident during direct examination. The court may have even excluded this evidence at the beginning of the trial following a motion in limine brought by the plaintiff. Opposing counsel would counter, of course, that the witness "opened the door," by stating she has *always* been a very careful driver.

To resolve the issue, the Court would likely consider the prejudice to the opposing party if the court were to prevent cross-examination, the similarity of the current accident to the prior accident, the age of the prior incident, and how much time would be consumed if the witness disputed the facts of the prior accident. In this case, because the plaintiff went beyond what the question initially asked for, namely, whether she was paying attention *that* morning, and essentially injected her own good character evidence as a careful driver, in fairness, the court could very well permit the cross-examination to prevent the witness from having the false aura of credibility.

Trial Tip: Jurors (and the court) do not like contentious trials where the attorneys are constantly objecting and bickering. It can be distracting and it slows down the pace of the trial. Save your objections for infractions that are material or prejudicial to your case. Don't let opposing counsel get under your skin. Stay professional. The jury will take note of it.

---

15. CHARACTER EVIDENCE

The use of character or "propensity" evidence is fairly common at trial, especially criminal cases. Because its admission can be very prejudicial to a party, typically there are motions in limine to either admit or exclude it. The issue arises when one party seeks to introduce evidence that another party has acted a certain way or done something improper in the past. The character evidence can take the form of a past condition, act, or event. For example, in criminal cases, the prosecution often wants to introduce evidence of a prior uncharged crime or bad act committed by the defendant to help prove the defendant committed the currently charged offense. Similarly, in civil cases, a party may wish to introduce evidence of prior accidents, complaints, employment history, or other prior misconduct to prove a party is at fault. In some cases, character evidence can also include subsequent acts. The general rule is that character evidence is *inadmissible* unless an exception to the rule applies. (Evid. Code § 1101.)

"Character evidence" can also be relevant regarding a witness's credibility. e.g., the witness has done something in the past that makes her less believable. Some attorneys (and courts) confuse the two purposes of character evidence: to prove conduct versus witness credibility. However, each theory has its own separate rules for admissibility. Evidence Code section 1101 et seq., and this chapter, relate to the former, while Evidence Code sections 786-790 concern witness credibility and are discussed supra, at p. 125, Impeachment.

Evid. Code § 1101. Evidence of character to prove conduct (FRE Rule 404)

(a) Except as provided in this section and in Sections 1102, 1103, 1108, and 1109, evidence of a person's character or a trait of his or her character (whether in the form of an opinion, evidence of reputation, or evidence of specific instances of his or her conduct) is inadmissible when offered to prove his or her conduct on a specified occasion.

(b) Nothing in this section prohibits the admission of evidence that a person committed a crime, civil wrong, or other act when relevant to prove some fact (such as motive, opportunity, intent, preparation, plan, knowledge, identity, absence of mistake or accident, or whether a defendant in a prosecution for an unlawful sexual act or attempted unlawful sexual act did not reasonably and in good faith believe that the victim consented) other than his or her disposition to commit such an act.

(c) Nothing in this section affects the admissibility of evidence offered to support or attack the credibility of a witness.

"Section 1101 excludes evidence of character to prove conduct in a civil case for the following reasons. First, character evidence is of slight probative value and may be very prejudicial. Second, character evidence tends to distract the trier of fact from the main question of what actually happened on the particular occasion and permits the trier of fact to reward the good man and to punish the bad man because of their respective characters. Third, introduction of character evidence may result in confusion of issues and require extended collateral inquiry." (*Bowen v. Ryan* (2008) 163 Cal.App.4th 916, 924 [evidence of dentist's treatment of other patients held inadmissible].) In negligence cases, for example, it has been held that "evidence that a person is a competent or skilled professional or the inverse, whether proven by reputation, opinion, or specific acts, is not admissible to prove the defendant was negligent on a particular occasion." *(Boyen, supra; Hinson v. Clairemont Community Hospital* (1990) 218 Cal.App.3d 1110, 1120, disapproved on other grounds in *Alexander v. Superior Court* (1993) 5 Cal.4th 1218, 1228, fn. 10.) A trial centers on a specific incident, not the defendant's general behavior. "A doctor's reputation for skill and ability will not exonerate him where gross negligence and want of the application of skill is alleged and proved. Nor can the fact that a doctor is reputed to be negligent or unskillful be allowed as proof to establish negligence or unskillful treatment in a particular case, because he may have treated that case with unusual skill and care." (*Hinson*, supra, at p. 1121.) For that reason, evidence of a defendant's prior negligence in medical treatment is inadmissible to prove negligence in a particular instance. (Id. at p. 1122; see also § 1104 ["evidence of a trait of a person's character with respect to care or skill is inadmissible to prove the quality of his conduct on a specified occasion"].)

1101(b) Exceptions

Section 1101(b) provides exceptions to the general rule prohibiting character evidence. The purported relevance of the character evidence must relate to something other than character, such as "motive, opportunity, intent, preparation, plan, knowledge, identity, absence of mistake, or accident." (1101(b)) However, these areas must be *relevant* to the contested issues. Whether character evidence is admissible generally turns upon its similarity to the contested issue.

For example, in *Bowen v Ryan*, supra, a civil suit against a dentist for inappropriately touching a child patient, the trial court allowed testimony of nine other patients about unrelated treatment by the defendant dentist. The plaintiff contended it was relevant to prove a common plan or design, and thus an exception to prohibit character evidence. The court in *Bowen* ruled the admission of the other patients' testimony was reversible error. To establish a common design or plan, "evidence of uncharged misconduct must demonstrate not merely a similarity in the results, but such a concurrence of common features that the various acts are naturally to be explained as caused by a general plan of which they are the individual manifestations. The common features must indicate the existence of a plan rather than a series of similar spontaneous acts, but the plan thus revealed need not be distinctive or unusual ... It need only exist to support the inference that the defendant employed that plan in committing the charged [act]." The court in *Bowen* held none of the dentist's other acts were sufficiently similar to the acts complained of in the lawsuit and therefore should not have been admitted.

In *People v. Ewoldt* (1994) 7 Cal.4th 380, 396-402, the California Supreme Court set forth the different standards for the admission of character evidence under 1101(b), depending upon the reason for its use. Although *Ewoldt* was a criminal case, the principles announced have also been applied to civil cases. (See *Bowen*, supra.) The *Ewoldt* court explained the "subtle, but significant" distinction between the use of evidence of uncharged acts to establish the existence of a common design or plan as opposed to the use of such evidence to prove intent or identity.

"Evidence of *intent* is admissible to prove that, if the defendant committed the act alleged, he or she did so with the intent that comprises an element of the charged offense. In proving intent, the act is conceded or assumed; what is sought is the state of mind that accompanied it. For example, in a prosecution for shoplifting in which it was conceded or assumed that the defendant left the store without paying for certain merchandise, the defendant's uncharged similar acts of theft might be admitted to demonstrate that he or she did not inadvertently neglect to pay for the merchandise, but rather harbored the intent to steal it." (*Ewoldt*, supra.)

"Evidence of a *common design or plan* is admissible to establish that the defendant committed the act alleged. Unlike evidence used to prove intent, where the act is conceded or assumed, in proving design, the act is still undetermined ... For example, in a prosecution for shoplifting in which it was conceded or assumed that the defendant was present at the scene of the alleged theft, evidence that the defendant had committed uncharged acts of shoplifting in a markedly similar manner to the charged offense might be admitted to demonstrate that he or she took the merchandise in the manner alleged by the prosecution." (*Ewoldt*, supra.)

"Evidence of *identity* is admissible where it is conceded or assumed that the charged offense was committed by someone, in order to prove that the defendant was the perpetrator. For example, in a prosecution for shoplifting in which it was conceded or assumed that a theft was committed by an unidentified person, evidence that the defendant had committed uncharged acts of shoplifting in the same unusual and distinctive manner as the charged offense might be admitted to establish that the defendant was the perpetrator of the charged offense." (*Ewoldt*, surpa, at p. 394, fn.2, citing 2 Wigmore (Chadbourn rev. ed. 1979) § 300, p. 238).)

Once the purported use of character evidence has been identified, the next inquiry is the similarity between the uncharged offense to the present offense, depending on the purpose:

Intent

Intent may be relevant in some cases, such as fraud. "The least degree of similarity between the uncharged act and the charged offense is required in order to prove intent. The recurrence of a similar result tends increasingly with each instance to negative accident or inadvertence or self-defense or good faith or other innocent mental state, and tends to establish (provisionally, at least, though not certainly) the presence of the normal, e.g., criminal, intent accompanying such an act ... In order to be admissible to prove intent, the uncharged misconduct must be sufficiently similar to support the inference that the defendant probably harbored the same intent in each instance." (*Ewoldt*, supra, at p. 402.)

Common Design or Plan

A greater degree of similarity is required to prove the existence of a common design or plan. As noted above, in establishing a common design or plan, evidence of uncharged misconduct must demonstrate not merely a similarity in the results, but such a concurrence of common features that the various acts are naturally to be explained as caused by a general plan of which they are the individual manifestations The difference between requiring similarity, for acts negating innocent intent, and requiring common features indicating common design, for acts showing design, is a difference of degree rather than of kind; for to be similar involves having common features, and to have common features is merely to have a high degree of similarity. (*People v. Ewoldt*, supra, 7 Cal.4th at pp. 402-403.)

Knowledge

In civil cases, character evidence is sometimes admitted to prove knowledge; for example, that the owner or manufacturer knew of a dangerous condition before the accident in question. "Evidence of prior accidents is admissible to prove a defective condition, knowledge, or the cause of an accident, provided that the circumstances of the other accidents are similar and not too remote." (*Elsworth v. Beech Aircraft Corp.* (1984) 37 Cal.3d 540, 555.) In *Elsworth*, the accident in question was a fatal airplane crash that occurred after the plane, built by the defendant, went into a spin and crashed seven minutes after takeoff. At trial, the plaintiffs presented evidence of twenty other stall-and-spin accidents involving the defendant's airplanes, fifteen of which involved a model other than the one at issue in the trial, but all of which had the same wing design that the plaintiffs claimed was defective. On appeal, the Supreme Court upheld the admission of the evidence and rejected the defendant's claim that the accidents were not sufficiently similar to prove causation. (*Elsworth*, at p. 555.)

Identity

The "greatest degree of similarity is required for evidence of uncharged misconduct to be relevant to prove identity. For identity to be established, the uncharged misconduct and the charged offense must share common features that are sufficiently distinctive so as to support the inference that the same person committed both acts. The pattern and characteristics of the crimes must be so unusual and distinctive as to be like a signature." (*People v. Ewoldt*, supra, 7 Cal.4th at p. 403; see also *People v. Balcom* (1994) 7 Cal.4th 414, 425.) In order to be admissible on the issue of identity, evidence underlying an uncharged offense must share with the charged offense characteristics that are so unusual and distinctive as to be like a signature and virtually eliminate the possibility that anyone other than the defendant committed the charged offense. (*Balcom*, supra.)

Criminal Cases – Defendant's character

In criminal cases, Evidence Code section 1102 (below) carves out a specific exception for a criminal defendant. This exception allows a criminal defendant to introduce evidence, either by opinion or reputation, of his character or a trait of his character that is "relevant to the charge made against him. Such evidence is relevant if it is inconsistent with the offense charged—e.g., honesty, when the charge is theft—and hence may support an inference that the defendant is unlikely to have committed the offense. (People v. McAlpin (1991) 53 Cal.3d 1289, 1305 [error to exclude opinion that defendant is of "high moral character" when charged with sex offenses.].)

Evid. Code § 1102. Opinion and reputation evidence of character of criminal defendant to prove conduct

In a criminal action, evidence of the defendant's character or a trait of his character in the form of an opinion or evidence of his reputation is not made inadmissible by Section 1101 if such evidence is:

(a) Offered by the defendant to prove his conduct in conformity with such character or trait of character.

(b) Offered by the prosecution to rebut evidence adduced by the defendant under subdivision (a).

A defendant who elicits character or reputation testimony opens the door to the prosecution's introduction of hearsay evidence that undermines testimony of his good reputation or of character inconsistent with the charged offense. "When a defendant elects to initiate inquiry into his own character, presumably to establish that one with his lofty traits would be unlikely to commit the offense charged, an anomalous rule comes into effect. Opinion based upon hearsay is permitted. (Evid.Code, § 1324; *People v. Tuggles* (2009) 179 Cal.App.4th 339, 357.) But the price a defendant must pay for attempting to prove his good name is to throw open a vast subject which the law has kept closed to shield him. The prosecution may pursue the inquiry with cross-examination as to the contents and extent of the hearsay upon which the opinion was based, and may disclose rumors, talk, and reports circulating in the community. The prosecution may explore, in good faith, opinion-based hearsay by asking whether the witness has heard of statements at odds with the asserted good character or reputation. "The rationale allowing the prosecution to ask such questions (in a 'have you heard' form) is that they test the witness's knowledge of the defendant's reputation." (Id. at p. 357.)

Trial Tip: In any case where you are considering introducing some type of "good" character, the concern is always whether that will open the door to your opponent's attempt to counter with "bad" character.

Previous Accidents

In lawsuits involving alleged dangerous conditions, one party may wish to introduce evidence of previous accidents. It is well settled that before evidence of previous accidents may be admitted to prove the existence of a dangerous condition, it must first be shown that the conditions under which the alleged previous accidents occurred were the same or substantially similar to the one in question. The question of admissibility of other accidents is primarily one for the trial court and is confined to its sound discretion. While there must be substantial similarity to offer other accident evidence for any purpose, a stricter degree of substantial similarity is required when other accident evidence is offered to show a dangerous condition; the other accident must be connected in some way with that thing. (*Salas v. Department of Transportation* (2011) 198 Cal.App.4th 1058, citing *Sambrano v. City of San Diego* (2001) 94 Cal.App.4th 225, 237 [exclusion due to lack of similarity upheld].)

Care and Skill

In civil trials involving negligence or malfeasance, an issue may arise whether a party's prior behavior is relevant. "A trial centers on a specific incident, not the defendant's general behavior." (*Bowen v. Ryan* (2008) 163 Cal.App.4th 916, 924.)

Evid. Code § 1104 Character trait for care or skill, states:

Except as provided in Sections 1102 and 1103, evidence of a trait of a person's character with respect to care or skill is inadmissible to prove the quality of his conduct on a specified occasion. (Note: §§ 1102/1103 relate only to criminal cases.)

The legislative comments for this section explain that the purpose of the rule is to prevent collateral issues from consuming too much time and distracting the attention of the trier of fact from what happened on the instant occasion. "It is a fundamental rule of evidence that you cannot prove the commission of an act by showing the commission of similar acts by the same person at other times and under other circumstances. Such evidence is simply not relevant..." (*Brokopp v. Ford Motor Co.* (1977) 71 Cal.App.3d 841, 851, quoting *Larson v. Larsen* (1925) 72 Cal.App. 169, 172; see also *Hinson v. Clairemont Community Hospital* (1990) 218 Cal.App.3d 1110, 1120-1122 [physician's performance in medical school and his termination from two hospitals was inadmissible character evidence under Evidence Code sections 1101, subd. (a) and 1104, and irrelevant to the question of his negligence on a specific occasion], disapproved on other grounds in *Alexander v. Superior Court* (1993) 5 Cal.4th 1218, 1228.)

Habit and Custom

In some cases, a party may try to avoid the prohibitions of section 1101 by arguing the prior acts are "habit or custom."

> **Evid. Code § 1105 Habit or custom to prove specific behavior**
>
> Any otherwise admissible evidence of habit or custom is admissible to prove conduct on a specified occasion in conformity with the habit or custom.

In reality, 1105 is essentially a codified exception to the rule prohibiting character evidence, the theory being that if the person has repeatedly and routinely performed an act in the past, it is more likely he or she performed it again in the present case. "Custom or habit involves a consistent, semi-automatic response to a repeated situation." (*Bowen v. Ryan* (2008) 163 Cal.App.4th 916, 924 ["Defendant's (dentist) conduct, occurring in different circumstances, toward nine of some 45,000 patients, does not qualify as custom or habit. Improper character evidence does not become admissible simply by citing to section 1105 and claiming actions in accordance with a custom or habit."]; *Webb v. Van Noort* (1966) 239 Cal.App.2d 472, 478, 48 Cal.Rptr. 823.) Character evidence "is clearly distinguishable from that establishing a custom or habit of doing some particular thing in a particular way. Because one is a skillful workman in a given occupation does not tend to disprove negligence in some specific act, but, if the question in controversy is whether he did the thing at all or his manner of doing it, his custom or habit regarding that particular matter would be significant." (*Wallis v. Southern Pacific Co.* (1921) 184 Cal. 662, 666.)

Subsequent Conduct

Most character evidence issues involve the use of prior acts, conditions, or events, however, in some cases *subsequent* conduct may be relevant. Section 1101(b) does not distinguish between prior or subsequent conduct. "As Wigmore astutely observed ... a man's trait or disposition a month or a year after a certain date is as evidential of his trait on that date as his nature a month or a year before that date; because character is a more or less permanent quality and we may make inferences from it either forward or backward." (*People v. Medina* (2003) 114 Cal.App.4th 897, 903; *People v. Griffin* (1967) 66 Cal.2d 459.) In civil cases, a plaintiff may seek to introduce evidence that the defendant has subsequently corrected the alleged dangerous condition or circumstances that led to the lawsuit, e.g., changed the design or redrafted a poorly written contract. The plaintiff will generally seek to use the correction as evidence of an admission by the defendant that the condition was in fact dangerous or wrongful, however, evidence of subsequent remedial conduct is generally not admissible.

Evid. Code § 1151. Subsequent remedial conduct

When, after the occurrence of an event, remedial or precautionary measures are taken, which, if taken previously, would have tended to make the event less likely to occur, evidence of such subsequent measures is inadmissible to prove negligence or culpable conduct.

The policy behind the rule precluding the use of subsequent remedial conduct was set forth in *Helling v. Schindler* (1904) 145 Cal. 303, which held: "The fact that an accident has happened, and some person has been injured, immediately puts a party on a higher plane of diligence and duty, from which he acts with a view of preventing the possibility of a similar accident, which should operate to commend rather than to condemn the person so acting. If the subsequent act is made to reflect back upon the prior one, although it is done upon the theory that it is a mere admission, it virtually introduces into the transaction a new element and test of negligence, which has no business there, not being in existence at the time. Further, to hold that an act of repairing affords evidence tending to show that a previous injury was the result of a defect in the appliances would deter a prudent person from making repairs." (See also *McIntyre v. Colonies-Pacific, LLC*, (2014) 228 Cal.App.4th 664 [quoting *Helling* and holding that subsequent hiring of security guard following alleged negligent failure to maintain safe conditions was properly excluded].)

However, section 1151 does not require exclusion if the evidence is offered for some other purpose, such as proving ownership, control, or feasibility of precautionary measures, if controverted, or impeachment. (*McIntyre*, supra, at p. 673; *Alcaraz v. Vece* (1997) 14 Cal.4th 1149, 1169.)

352 Analysis Required

It is important to keep in mind that even if the evidence qualifies as an exception to the general rule excluding character evidence, the trial court always has the discretion to exclude it pursuant to Evidence Code § 352. In fact, the court in *Ewoldt*, supra, mandated the trial court to conduct a 352 analysis when considering the admissibility of character evidence.

16. ARGUMENT

The closing argument is the essence of trial lawyering, and arguably, *the* single most important phase of a trial. After months, if not years, of trial preparation and days or weeks of trial, the closing argument is the one opportunity where trial counsel for both sides are permitted to stand before the jury (or the court), and using their powers of persuasion and skills as an orator, argue the case. Close cases can be won or lost depending on which attorney delivers the most persuasive argument, and sometimes, seemingly strong cases are lost due to poor argument.

Preparing, building, and then delivering a *good* closing argument can be a daunting task even for experienced lawyers. It is more than merely reciting a canned speech. Even for straightforward cases it requires thoughtful analysis of many factors, such as how to structure the argument, what points to cover and/or omit, and what visual aids or exhibits to use. During the course of the trial, evidence was introduced in piecemeal fashion with interruptions and juror fatigue taking its toll. Subtle, yet important, points may have been established on direct or cross-examination that need explanation or amplification, points "saved for closing." The closing argument is where it should all come together—where the facts are illuminated and the law is explained.

Wide Latitude

"In conducting closing argument, attorneys for both sides have wide latitude to discuss the case." (*Garcia v. ConMed Corp.* (2012) 204 Cal.App.4th 144, 148.) "The right of counsel to discuss the merits of a case, both as to the law and facts, is very wide, and counsel has the right to state fully his or her views as to what the evidence shows, and as to the conclusions to be fairly drawn therefrom. The adverse party cannot complain if the reasoning be faulty and the deductions illogical, as such matters are ultimately for the consideration of the jury." (Id.) "Counsel may vigorously argue his case and is not limited to 'Chesterfieldian politeness.' An attorney is permitted to argue all reasonable inferences from the evidence ... and only the most persuasive reasons justify handcuffing attorneys in the exercise of their advocacy within the bounds of propriety." (*Garcia*, supra, *Cassim v. Allstate Ins. Co.* (2004) 33 Cal.4th 780, 795–796.) Unlike the other phases of a trial, which are guided for the most part by stringent evidentiary rules, the closing argument is less structured and there is no one specific way to deliver an effective argument. Over time and with experience, every trial lawyer will develop his or her own style for argument, and the beauty of the argument is that there are no hard and fast rules. As such, you can format your argument pretty much any way you see fit and, as you gain experience, you should not hesitate to experiment a little and try various techniques and tactics to see what works best for you. However, there are a few general principles concerning the closing argument that you may wish to consider, which are described for you in greater detail below.

> **Trial Tip:** When preparing your argument, you should *always* assume that during the trial at least one or more of the jurors was not paying attention, were confused, or were doubting your theory of the case. The argument is the time to distill the issues and simplify the facts, such that every juror (and the court) is onboard. A common mistake is when trial counsel wrongly assumes a point was obvious. Your closing argument should be designed and delivered with doubting jurors in mind.

Preparation

Preparation for the closing argument should not begin the night before. Rather, it should have begun practically from the inception of the case as you were contemplating your strategies or defenses. During the weeks and months leading up to trial, start thinking about how the closing argument might look and creating a rough outline. What will be the contested issues? What are the strong points? What are the weak points? What will the opposition probably argue?

Preparation also continues *during* the trial. Keep good notes of those "gems" that were elicited during testimony and points you may wish to revisit during the argument. As the trial is unfolding, start putting together a written outline for the argument. The entire case, from pre-trial preparation through examination of the last witness, should be constructed with the closing argument in mind. In other words, build your case around your closing argument.

> **Trial Tip:** Some lawyers miss important points for argument simply because they did not keep good trial notes. Keep a notepad handy at counsel table to jot down points you want to cover later during argument; otherwise, you might forget.

Bench Trial

Many cases are tried before the court without a jury. In these bench trials, some attorneys opt to waive or make an abbreviated argument based on the assumption the court fully understands the issues and the facts better than a jury would. This is a mistake. Although the court may understand the legal theories better, how all the facts line up may not be entirely clear to the judge, especially if the trial had breaks and interruptions, which is common in bench trials. In addition, judges are often handling multiple cases and calendars simultaneously and have a lot on their plate. Some attorneys in a bench trial prefer to submit "written" argument, filed with the court weeks, if not longer, afterwards. Consider suggesting a hybrid, where there is some oral argument, followed by written argument, submitted subsequently on a schedule agreed to by everyone. One advantage to written argument is that you can also include case law and legal authorities. Keep in mind that once the judge takes the matter "under submission," it might be weeks or even months before the judge finally has time to review the matter. If there are many exhibits and days of testimony, it can take a substantial amount of time for the court to digest everything *and* prepare a written decision.

> **Trial Tip:** Don't short-change the closing argument in a bench trial just because it's before the court and not a jury.

Visual Aids/Stimuli

One primary objective of your argument is to help the jury (and the court) *remember* the important points. Therefore, it is important to incorporate into the argument as much stimuli as possible to have the maximum impact. If exhibits, such as photographs or diagrams were admitted, revisit each and explain the importance and relevance to the jury. To assist, there are some commercial courtroom software programs and technologies available to enhance courtroom presentations. One of the most powerful tools for any lecture is the use of a PowerPoint-like slide presentation. It is proven effective, easy to use, and looks professional. For example, you can prepare an abbreviated version of your argument outline and permit the jurors to follow along, point by point, as your argument progresses; you can display key points of law and dim or highlight important passages; and video or photographic evidence can be embedded into the presentation and presented with a click of the mouse. Some 'old school' lawyers may scoff at the "bells and whistles," but today's jurors expect it.

> **Trial Tip:** When you are displaying your PowerPoint slides, politely remind the jury that they are not permitted to have your notes in the jury room; therefore, they might consider taking their own notes. You will be surprised how many jurors will take heed and scribble down info from your slides. Note that it is not an uncommon request from a deliberating jury to get a transcript of one party's closing argument, which obviously is not allowed.

The Delivery

How you say something is sometimes nearly as important as *what* you say. Consider, for example, the captivating speakers you have observed in your lifetime and ask yourself what it was about their mode or style of delivery that captured your attention. It was likely the cadence, the inflections in their voice, and the emotion or passion they projected. Some busy trial lawyers try case after case without ever really paying much attention to the *art* of delivery. However, this is what separates the run-of-the-mill trial lawyer from the truly accomplished. You do not need to have been the captain of the college debate team, but you do need to effectively communicate your message. One of *the* most important factors for creating a good delivery is the extent of preplanning. If you have a good outline to follow, you will find the delivery will flow more smoothly and you will feel much less nervous. The following techniques may help improve your delivery:

- **Pace** – The pace or speed at which you talk is important. Nervousness naturally causes people to speak more rapidly. I have witnessed many closing arguments where the attorney speaks so rapidly that even the court reporter has trouble keeping up. For most people, it requires some conscious thought to slow down. Good speakers use pace and rhythm to their advantage. They talk at a medium to slow pace and pause when important points are made. The impact of a few moments of actual silence in the courtroom, the type where you can hear a pin drop, before or after making an important point, is a very powerful tool to let the point sink in. Bottom line: Slow it down.

- **A Little Emotion** – Jurors respond to attorney emotion and passion, if sincere. A dry, monotone voice will put the jury to sleep no matter how strong the evidence. Likewise, simply reading from a script is dry and boring. The use of voice inflection and emotion can capture the jurors' attention. However, a little goes a long way. Use an amount of emotion that fits the facts and evidence, somewhere between a flat monotone and an overly theatrical or melodramatic delivery.

- **Flow** – A good closing argument is one that has a beginning, a middle, and an end. It should flow naturally and follow some logical progression. Thus, avoid digressing or jumping from point to point and out of sequence. This only tends to confuse the jurors. In addition, every trial has certain key issues that are controverted. Discussing the contested issues is where the majority of your time should be spent. If you waste too much time talking about the minutia or facts surrounding uncontested matters, you risk losing the jury's attention. Lastly, at the very beginning, consider giving the jurors a very brief overview of the order of your closing so they will know what to expect.

- **Simplicity and Time** – Keep in mind that a jury is a compilation of people from all walks of life. A juror with a PhD might be sitting next to a gas station attendant with a GED, if that. With such a wide variety of backgrounds and intellects, your argument has to be presented at a level that everyone can follow. At the risk of offending past or future jurors, the presentation has to be made at about a sixth-grade level. Keep it simple, logical, and concise. In addition, avoid the temptation for overkill or argument that lasts for hours. Time is of the essence regarding the jurors' attention span. An argument that gets right to the heart of the matter and covers just the contested facts and issues is obviously much more effective than one that drones on for hours and puts the jurors to sleep.

Trial Tip: Use a detailed, written outline for the argument that you can refer to periodically as the argument proceeds. This will help you remember important points and stay on task. On the other hand, avoid reading from it like a script, or the argument will seem canned and prevent you from having some spontaneity.

Help the Jury

Unless a juror has served before, most will have no idea what to expect or what to do when they first enter the jury room to begin deliberations. Typically, they will be provided with copies of the court's instructions and the evidence. If the trial took more than a few days, there could be literally hundreds of exhibits piled on the deliberation room table. From the court's instructions, the jurors probably understand they are supposed to first select a foreperson, but beyond that, there are really no instructions or rules provided to them regarding *how* to deliberate; no directions are given on how to organize themselves, which issues to tackle first, or how to take votes. Given the importance placed on the sanctity and secrecy of the jury process, by design, the jurors are left to their own devices to figure out a method.

The astute trial lawyer, however, will provide them with a method by suggesting how they might organize and evaluate the evidence. And, of course, the approach suggested by you will be the one that best highlights your evidence. In other words, give them a method or a process of how they can get from point A to point B in the jury room. In addition, make it easy for the jury to find the important information by referring them to specific exhibit numbers or page numbers of documents or passages from the testimony. If a witness said something critically important, encourage the jury to request "read back" of that passage in the jury room, if there is any doubt. Regarding the law, refer them to the particular page numbers in the court's instructions. If you give the jury a little guidance on how to deliberate and where to find the evidence, you will be surprised how often juries actually follow your "suggestions."

Trial Tip: During closing, assist the jury by suggesting to them an approach or method for organizing and then analyzing the evidence. In addition, direct them where to find important evidence, e.g., specific exhibit numbers or page numbers in documents.

A Closing Format

Persuasive arguments tend to follow the same basic format, to one degree or another. Jurors will process and understand arguments better if they are logical and flow, rather than being disorganized and scattered. Half the battle is presenting an argument they will *remember* later in the jury room. In that regard, it can be helpful to break your argument into sections or building blocks. Below are the basic components (building blocks) of a typical closing argument.

Introductory Comments – Define the Issues

Due to the incremental and slow nature of a trial, by the close of the evidence, some jurors may still not be entirely clear what the contested issues are or the cause of actions or defenses involved. Some jurors will have paid close attention and get it, while others may be completely befuddled and lost. The beginning of your summation, therefore, should be devoted to clarifying and defining the issues. Distill for the jurors the key issues in dispute. Summarize *briefly* the facts proven and your legal theories in a narrative format, weaving the facts and the law together. Think of it as describing for someone who was not at the trial, *in 10 minutes or less*, the key facts and theories of the case. The introductory comments are designed to ensure that *all* the jurors are operating on the same page *before* you move on to a more detailed discussion about the facts and the law. Again, you must *assume* that at least one or more of the jurors is confused, was not paying attention during the trial, or is doubtful of your theory of the case. Your entire argument, and particularly the introductory comments, should be designed with these people in mind. In addition, recall that the first 10 or 15 minutes of any lecture is the time when the audience is typically most attentive. Play the odds. Try to avoid getting too bogged down in the minutia during the introductory comments.

> **Trial Tip:** Most trials boil down to only one or two key contested issues or facts. Identifying for the jury these key issues will help them to stay focused on what is important and prevent them from going off the track in the jury room, which happens.

Your Evidence

This segment is where you will discuss in some detail the key facts and evidence—what was either proven or disproven. If it was a long trial, you may prefer to review the testimony of each witness by summarizing and highlighting the key facts that were established. Important photographs, documents, or other *key* pieces of evidence should be highlighted and shown again to the jury. The use of PowerPoint slides to summarize the evidence by providing bullet points of key testimony is very effective here. Notice, however, that the emphasis is on "important" and "key" evidence. Remember, time is of the essence regarding the jurors' attention span, so hit only the disputed facts and issues. Talking at length about inconsequential or uncontested matters is a waste of precious time and you risk losing the jury.

Your Opponent's Evidence

At some point during the argument, you will likely want to comment on your opponent's evidence, or the lack thereof. However, when and how to do so is obviously a tactical matter. It may depend on whether you are the plaintiff and thus have a rebuttal argument remaining. One tactic is to steal your opponent's thunder by predicting their arguments or theories and tearing them down before opposing counsel even has the opportunity to speak. Attacking your opponent's case before their argument tends to put the defense on the defensive and sometimes forces them to deviate from their planned comments in order to respond to your criticisms. Another similar tactic is to pose to the jury hypothetical questions or problems associated with the opponent's case, challenging the opposition to respond, if they care to. This puts the opposing counsel in the position of having to make a tactical decision of whether or not to respond. For example:

Counsel: "Three credible eyewitnesses testified that the defendant ran the red light; their testimony was corroborated by the physical evidence. How can all three witnesses and the physical evidence be wrong? Were all three witnesses lying? That's what they'll have to argue to prevail."

Witness Credibility

Many trials, whether tried before the court or a jury, boil down to the question of witness credibility and, sometimes, just one witness. Which witnesses were truthful and believable; which witnesses were not? How the jury comes down on this single question is often determinative of the entire case, whether it is a murder trial, a multi-million dollar civil case, or a family law trial over child custody. As a practical matter, "the law" really has no answer for this question, other than to provide the jurors with some basic, common sense factors to apply, the very same factors most people apply in their everyday lives when deciding whether they should believe someone or not. Your role, as the trial lawyer, is to bring to light for the fact finders all the various factors and conditions that will help them make the determination.

During your argument, therefore, focus on the evidence that either supports or undermines the witness's testimony, some of which may be more subtle and not readily apparent, such as inconsistencies. Consider using a chart or a graphic to illustrate these points. As discussed previously, recall that impeaching a witness's credibility does not always mean you are calling them a liar, rather it could be as simple as an honest mistake due to the passage of time, poor lighting conditions, or an unconscious bias to favor one side over the other. In practice, some lawyers fail to recognize what is important and spend a great deal of their precious time arguing facts not really in issue. If the case hinges on the credibility of only a few key witnesses, that is where most or your time should be spent in the argument.

A Dollar Amount

For the plaintiff seeking monetary damages, at some point during argument, you are going to want to broach the subject of what dollar amount you are requesting. If it is economic damages, consider using a chart or a diagram to show how the numbers add up. However, requesting a sum for non-economic damages, such as for pain and suffering or punitive, can be more challenging because you certainly do not want to undersell your case by suggesting a number that is actually lower than some jurors might have been thinking. On the other hand, you do not want to request an outrageously high amount as it might offend some jurors and weaken your credibility. Your request has to seem reasonable. One tactic for non-economic damages might be to suggest a range, a high and a low, and to provide some explanation regarding how you arrived at those numbers. In other words, don't just pick a number out of the blue without giving the jurors at least some rational basis of how you came up with the amount. In addition, consider explaining how to properly fill out the jury verdict forms with your suggested numbers. The same holds true for the defense.

The Law

Typically, some portion of your argument must be devoted to the law, depending on the nature of the case. Some attorneys like to start out with an explanation of the applicable law. Regardless, it is critical that you clearly explain the applicable elements of the causes of actions and/or defenses. A discussion regarding the burden of proof or the use of circumstantial evidence may also be in order. Once again, the use of PowerPoint-type slides is particularly useful when explaining the law by going element by element. An effective argument not only highlights the law, but also incorporates the facts simultaneously to show how either an element or requirement of law has been proven or not proven.

Trial Tip: The art of persuasively weaving together the facts and the law is a skill that separates good lawyers from great ones.

Concluding

Nearly as important as the first ten minutes of your argument are the last ten. To wake up the jurors, so to speak, let them know the conclusion is drawing near. People tend to pay the most attention at the very beginning and at the very end of a lecture. By this point, you will have described the big picture during the introductory comments, gone through the evidence in some detail, and explained the law. Now is the opportunity to wrap it all up. At the risk of being redundant (which can be a good thing), remind the jurors again of the basic key facts, the law, and how they intersect. Summarize, one last time, in five minutes or less (like you did at the beginning), the contested issues and what has been proven or not proven.

> **Trial Tip:** A good argument is one that is redundant without seeming redundant, e.g., saying the same thing a slightly different way to make the point. This might help with jurors who didn't make the connection the first time.

Misconduct during Argument

As discussed above, "wide latitude" is given counsel to argue their views of the facts and theories, however, there are limits and misconduct by counsel can occur during argument requiring an objection. "For example, while a counsel in summing up may indulge in all fair arguments in favor of his client's case, he may not assume facts not in evidence or invite the jury to speculate as to unsupported inferences. Nor may counsel properly make personally insulting or derogatory remarks directed at opposing counsel or impugn counsel's motives or character." (*Garcia v. ConMed Corp., supra.*) Other forms of misconduct can occur if counsel appeals to the emotions of the jury or suggests they should make their decision based on something other than the facts, e.g., to send a message. "An attorney's appeal in closing argument to the jurors' self-interest is improper and thus is misconduct because such arguments tend to undermine the jury's impartiality." (*Cassim*, supra, at p. 796.) "Furthermore, the appeal to a juror to exercise his subjective judgment, rather than an impartial judgment predicated on the evidence cannot be condoned. It tends to denigrate the jurors' oath to well and truly try the issue and render a true verdict according to the evidence. Moreover, it in effect asks each juror to become a personal partisan advocate for the injured party, rather than an unbiased and unprejudiced weigher of the evidence." (Id. at p. 797.)

Personal attacks on opposing counsel, referring to a party's wealth, the existence of insurance, or suggesting that a party's case has some form of judicial approval, have been held improper argument. (*Cassim*, supra.) Referred to as the "Golden Rule," it is also improper for counsel to ask the jurors to step into the shoes of party or a victim. (*Learmonth v. Sears, Roebuck and C*o., 631 F.3d 724, 732-33, 84 Fed. R. Evid. Serv. 698 (5th Cir. 2011) [holding counsel's argument that jury should "place themselves in the plaintiff's position and do unto him as they would have him do unto them" was an improper Golden Rule argument, but that court's instructions mitigated prejudice].)

In practice, one of the most common forms of attorney misconduct during argument is when counsel misstates either the evidence or the law, and/or both. Although attorneys are permitted to argue their interpretation of the evidence, in some cases, whether intentionally or unintentionally, they may recite facts or evidence purportedly from the trial that is simply not true or materially inaccurate. A misstatement of a key point of law is also problematic. In addition, watch for attorneys who refer to evidence or facts that were *not* received at trial, for example, antidotal stories of other similar cases. Some attorneys will push the envelope by discussing their own personal beliefs or background. Some more aggressive attorneys will make snide or disparaging comments concerning opposing counsel; however, this is a real turn-off for jurors and generally has the opposite effect. In the final analysis, during argument, you may literally only have seconds to react to a statement by opposing counsel that could be misconduct. In making that snap decision, it helps to have contemplated beforehand what types of comments might trigger you to object; the main concern generally being whether the comment will prejudice your client.

Whether or not to object during your opponent's closing argument is obviously a tactical matter. Some jurors may frown upon one attorney interrupting another's argument. There is also somewhat of an unspoken rule amongst trial lawyers not to interrupt during argument. Further, since "wide latitude" is permitted, you run the risk that if you do object, the court may overrule the objection with the stern comment, "It's argument, counsel." On the other hand, if there is serious misconduct, a timely objection may be necessary to set the record straight, so to speak; for example, where counsel has blatantly misstated the evidence. Keep in mind, however, that in most cases the objection has to be made immediately at the time of the misconduct. It is *not* timely to wait until the argument is concluded and then object. Also, if the court sustains the objection, to preserve the issue for appeal, some courts require that you also request a curative instruction. (See *Cassim v. Allstate Ins*. Co., supra.) The federal courts erect a "high threshold" to claims of improper closing arguments in civil cases raised for the first time *after* trial. A "high threshold" is warranted, in part, because allowing a party to wait to raise the error until after the negative verdict encourages that party to sit silent in the face of claimed error. (*Hemmings v. Tidyman's Inc*., 285 F.3d 1174, 1193 (9th Cir. 2002).)

Trial Tip: Whether to object during your opponent's argument is a tactical decision and depends upon the severity of the transgression. If counsel has blatantly misstated some fact, an objection might be in order. On the other hand, if it is relatively minor, repeatedly objecting may not sit well with the jury. Whether or not you have a rebuttal argument to respond is also a factor.

Criminal Cases

Most of the case law related to closing argument in criminal cases concerns limitations on the prosecution's argument and prosecutorial misconduct. It is important not only for prosecutors to know these guidelines, but also for the defense. This is critical because a failure to properly object, forfeits the issue on appeal. To avoid forfeiture or waiver on appeal of a claim of prosecutorial misconduct, a defendant generally must make a timely objection, make known the basis of his or her objection, *and* ask the trial court to admonish the jury. (*People v. Brown* (2003) 31 Cal.4th 518 at p. 553 [emphasis added].) Absent a timely objection and request for a curative admonition, an appellate contention of prosecutorial misconduct is reviewable only if an admonition would not have cured the harm caused by the misconduct or if either a timely objection or request for admonition would have been futile. (*People v. Brown,* supra).

Argument in General

During argument the parties are given wide latitude to discuss their respective cases and reasonable inferences drawn from the evidence. (*People v. Dennis* (1998) 17 Cal.4th 468, 522.)   A party is entitled both to discuss the evidence and to comment on reasonable inferences that may be drawn therefrom. (*People v. Morales* (2001) 25 Cal.4th 34 at p. 44.) "The argument may be vigorous as long as it amounts to fair comment on the evidence, which can include reasonable inferences or deductions to be drawn therefrom." (*People v. Hill* (1998) 17 Cal.4th 800 at p. 819.)

Misconduct in General

"A prosecutor commits reversible misconduct under California law if he or she makes use of 'deceptive or reprehensible methods' in attempting to persuade either the trial court or the jury, and there is a reasonable possibility that without such misconduct, an outcome more favorable to the defendant would have resulted. Under the federal Constitution, conduct by a prosecutor that does not result in the denial of the defendant's specific constitutional rights—such as the denial that ensues from a comment upon the defendant's invocation of the right to remain silent—but is otherwise worthy of condemnation, is not a constitutional violation unless the challenged action so infected the trial with unfairness as to make the resulting conviction a denial of due process." (*People v. Rundle* (2008) 43 Cal.4th 76, 190.)

Griffin Error – Comment on Defendant Not Testifying

It is error for a prosecutor to comment directly or indirectly upon a defendant's failure to testify in his own defense. (*Griffin v. California* (1965) 380 U.S. 609, 615; *People v. Medina* (1995) 11 Cal.4th 694, 755.) The prosecutor's argument cannot refer to the absence of evidence that only the defendant's testimony could provide. (*People v. Carter* (2005) 36 Cal.4th 1215, 1266.) The rule, however, does not extend to comments on the state of the evidence or on the failure of the defense to introduce material evidence or to call logical witnesses. (*People v. Lewis* (2009) 46 Cal.4th 1255, 1304.)

"There is a distinction between the permissible comment that a defendant has not produced any evidence, and on the other hand, an improper statement that a defendant has a duty or burden to produce evidence, or a duty or burden to prove his or her innocence." (*People v. Thomas* (2012) 54 Cal.4th 908, 939; *People v. Jasso* (2012) 211 Cal.App.4th 1354, 1370.) "The former is permissible because a prosecutor generally is permitted to remark on the state of the evidence at closing argument. The prosecutor may comment 'on the state of the evidence, or on the failure of the defense to introduce material evidence or call logical witnesses ...." (*People v. Carter*, supra, 36 Cal.4th at p. 1277; *Jasso*, supra.)

Under these principles, the Supreme Court in *People v. Redd* (2010) 48 Cal.4th 691, rejected a claim where the prosecutor made reference to blanks on a chart. There, the prosecutor repeatedly challenged the basis for the defense theory. He remarked: "I have a blank paper because I'm not sure exactly what the defense is yet. I'm going to sit here like you and listen to [defense counsel]. I don't know what he's going to say." (Id. at p. 739.) Later, the prosecutor jibed that he was " 'waiting to hear what the defense was.' " (Ibid.) *Redd* rejected a claim that the foregoing remarks shifted the burden of proof to the defendant. "[T]he prosecutor's comments merely highlighted his observation that there seemed to be no coherent defense to the charges" (*People v. Redd*, supra, 48 Cal.4th at p. 740), which, although Redd did not say so explicitly, was a permissible comment on the state of the evidence. (*Jasso*, supra, at 1370-1371.)

Doyle Error – Comment on Post Miranda Silence

Both federal and state courts have held that the prosecution's use of a defendant's post- Miranda silence is a violation of federal due process. (*Doyle v. Ohio* (1976) 426 U.S. 610, 96 S.Ct. 2240, 49 L.Ed.2d 91; 1448 *Wainwright v. Greenfield* (1986) 474 U.S. 284, 295, 106 S.Ct. 634, 88 L.Ed.2d 623; *People v. Crandell* (1988) 46 Cal.3d 833, 878, 251 Cal.Rptr. 227, 760 P.2d 423.) "The defendant's silence may not be used to impeach his credibility. An assessment of whether the prosecutor made inappropriate use of defendant's post arrest silence requires consideration of the context of the prosecutor's inquiry or argument. A violation of due process does not occur where the prosecutor's reference to defendant's post arrest silence constitutes a fair response to defendant's claim or a fair comment on the evidence. *Griffin* and *Doyle*'s protection of the right to remain silent is a 'shield,' not a 'sword' that can be used to 'cut off the prosecution's "fair response" to the evidence or argument of the defendant.' Questions or argument suggesting that the defendant did not have a fair opportunity to explain his innocence can open the door to evidence and comment on his silence. (*People v. Champion* (2005) 134 Cal.App.4th 1440, 1447-1448.)

Hard Blows

"Although the prosecutor must prosecute with earnestness and vigor and may strike hard blows, he is not at liberty to strike foul ones." (*Berger v. United States* (1935) 295 U.S. 78, 88, 55 S.Ct. 629, 79 L.Ed. 1314; see also ABA Model Code Prof. Responsibility, EC 7–13 ["The responsibility of a public prosecutor differs from that of the usual advocate; his duty is to seek justice, not merely to convict"]; *People v. Daggett* (1990) 225 Cal.App.3d 751, 759.)

Vouching

It is settled that "a prosecutor is prohibited from vouching for the credibility of witnesses or otherwise bolstering the veracity of their testimony by referring to evidence outside the record. Nor is a prosecutor permitted to place the prestige of [his or her] office behind a witness by offering the impression that [he or she] has taken steps to assure a witness's truthfulness at trial. However, so long as a prosecutor's assurances regarding the apparent honesty or reliability of prosecution witnesses are based on the 'facts of [the] record and the inferences reasonably drawn therefrom, rather than any purported personal knowledge or belief,' her comments cannot be characterized as improper vouching." (*People v. Frye* (1998) 18 Cal.4th 894, 971.)

A prosecutor is free to give his opinion on the state of the evidence, and in arguing his case to the jury, has wide latitude to comment on both its quality and the credibility of witnesses. (See, e.g., *People v. Green*, (1980) 27 Cal.3d 1 at p. 35, fn. 20; *People v. Heishman* (1988) 45 Cal.3d 147, 195.) It is misconduct, however, to suggest to the jury in arguing the veracity of a witness that the prosecutor has information undisclosed to the trier of fact bearing on the issue of credibility, veracity, or guilt. The danger in such remarks is that the jury will believe that inculpatory evidence, known only to the prosecution, has been withheld from them. (*People v. Padilla* (1995) 11 Cal.4th 891, 945.)

"It is misconduct for prosecutors to bolster their case 'by invoking their personal prestige, reputation, or depth of experience, or the prestige or reputation of their office, in support of it.' Similarly, it is misconduct 'to suggest that evidence available to the government, but not before the jury, corroborates the testimony of a witness." (*People v. Bonilla* (2007) 41 Cal.4th 313, 336.) Prosecutors can run afoul of this rule when they appear to interject their own personal opinion or viewpoint into the argument, for instance, "I believe the evidence proves...." or "I know for a fact that ...." An easy fix is to simply to refer to yourself or your theories as, "the prosecution(s)."

Comments on the Evidence

A prosecutor may fairly comment on and argue any reasonable inferences from the evidence. (*People v. Wharton* (1991) 53 Cal.3d 522, 567.) Comments on the state of the evidence or on the defense's failure to call logical witnesses, introduce material evidence, or rebut the People's case are generally permissible. (*People v. Medina* (1995) 11 Cal.4th 694, 755.) However, a prosecutor may not suggest that "a defendant has a duty or burden to produce evidence, or a duty or burden to prove his or her innocence." (*People v. Bradford* (1997) 15 Cal.4th 1229, 1340; see also *People v. Young* (2005) 34 Cal.4th 1149, 1195–1196.)

A prosecutor may not suggest the existence of "facts" outside of the record by arguing matters not in evidence. (*People v. Benson*, supra, 52 Cal.3d at pp. 794–795.) Nor may a prosecutor suggest that matters outside the record establish the veracity of a witness; however, the prosecutor may assure the jury of a witness's apparent honesty or reliability based on matters in the record. (*People v. Padilla* (1995) 11 Cal.4th 891, 946.)

Counsel may argue to the jury matters which are not in evidence, but which is common knowledge or illustrations drawn from common experience, history, or literature. (*People v. Sassounian* (1986) 182 Cal.App.3d 361, 396.) "A prosecutor may vigorously argue his case, marshalling the facts and arguing inferences to be drawn therefrom. We have held he may not express a personal belief in defendant's guilt, in part because of the danger that jurors may assume there is other evidence at his command on which he bases this conclusion." (Ibid.)

Prosecution argument that the defendant has an "obligation" to present evidence is misconduct. (*People v. Woods* (2006) 146 Cal.App.4th 106, 114) While the prosecutor may not misstate the record, "in general, he may comment on the record as it actually stands." (*People v. Keenan* (1988) 46 Cal.3d 478, 509.)

The prosecutor may not invite the jury to abrogate their personal responsibility to determine the appropriate verdicts based on the evidence. *(People v. Zambrano* (2007) 41 Cal.4th 1082, 1177-1178 [no misconduct in describing jury as the conscience of the community or by noting the jury's important role in the criminal justice system].) Prosecutors should not purport to rely in jury argument on their outside experience or personal beliefs based on facts not in evidence." (*People v. Medina* (1995) 11 Cal.4th 694, 776.)

Attacks on Counsel

It is improper for a prosecutor to resort to personal attacks on the integrity of opposing counsel. (*People v. Bell* (1989) 49 Cal.3d 502, 538.) "A prosecutor commits misconduct if he or she attacks the integrity of defense counsel, or casts aspersions on defense counsel." (*People v Hill* (1998) 17 Cal.4th 800 at p. 832.) It is misconduct when a prosecutor in closing argument "denigrates counsel instead of the evidence" because "personal attacks on opposing counsel are improper and irrelevant to the issues." (*People v. Sandoval* (1992) 4 Cal.4th 155, 184.) "An attack on the defendant's attorney can be seriously prejudicial as an attack on the defendant himself, and, in view of the accepted doctrines of legal ethics and decorum, it is never excusable." (*Hill*, supra, at p. 832.)

"We have also held it improper for the prosecutor to imply that defense counsel has fabricated evidence or otherwise to portray defense counsel as the villain in the case. It is not necessary to find that such implication impinges upon defendant's constitutional right to counsel. Instead it is sufficient to note that defendant's conviction should rest on the evidence, not on derelictions of his counsel. Casting uncalled for aspersions on defense counsel directs attention to largely irrelevant matters and does not constitute comment on the evidence or argument as to inferences to be drawn therefrom." (*People v. Pitts* (1990) 223 Cal.App.3d 606, 707.)

While a prosecutor may properly sympathetically portray a victim, he may not include defense counsel as a villain who was attacking the victim. (*People v. Turner* (1983) 145 Cal.App.3d 658, 673-674 .) By so doing, he casts aspersions on the defendant's right to defend himself and to be represented by counsel. (Id. at p. 674.) Moreover, such misconduct cannot be justified even though the prosecutor's remarks may be in reply to those made by defense counsel. (*People v. Perry* (1972) 7 Cal.3d 756, 789; *People v. Pitts* (1990) 223 Cal.App.3d 606, 707.)

Epithets

Prosecutors should exercise caution when using strong epithets. Most cases finding no misconduct are in the setting of the penalty phase of a capital case. "Where they are so supported, we have condoned a wide range of epithets to describe the egregious nature of the defendant's conduct." (*People v Farnam* (2002) 28 Cal.4th 107, 168 [defendant is "monstrous," "cold-blooded," vicious, and a "predator"; evidence is "horrifying" and "more horrifying than your worst nightmare"]; *People v. Thomas* (1992) 2 Cal.4th 489, 537 [defendant is "mass murderer, rapist," "perverted murderous cancer," and "walking depraved cancer"]; *People v. Sully* (1991) 53 Cal.3d 1195, 1249 [based on facts of crime, defendant is "human monster" and "mutation"]; see also *People v. Zambrano* (2007) 41 Cal.4th 1082, 1172 [No misconduct in referring to the defendant as " 'coiled like a snake,' " or to life imprisonment for the defendant being like " 'putting a rabid dog in the pound' " (overruled in part on other grounds as stated in *People v. Blakeley*(2000) 23 Cal.4th 82, 89.) "A prosecutor is allowed to make vigorous arguments and may even use such epithets as are warranted by the evidence, as long as these arguments are not inflammatory and principally aimed at arousing the passion or prejudice of the jury." *(People v. Young* (2005) 34 Cal.4th 1149, 1195.)

Lies

When a defendant's testimony contradicts the strong evidence of his guilt, it is not improper to call him a liar. (*People v. Edelbacher* (1989) 47 Cal.3d 983, 1030, ["snake in the jungle," "slick," "tricky," a "pathological liar," and "one of the greatest liars in the history of Fresno County"]; *People v. Reyes* (1974) 12 Cal.3d 486, 505.) Calling the defendant a "sociopath" is not misconduct if supported by the evidence. (*People v. Zambrano* (2007) 41 Cal.4th 1082, 1173.)

Emotional Appeals

"It is true that ordinarily a prosecutor may not invite the jury to view the case through the victim's eyes, because to do so appeals to the jury's sympathy for the victim." (P*eople v. Lopez* (2008) 42 Cal.4th 960, 969-970.) A "golden rule" violation refers to asking a juror to "become a personal partisan advocate for a party rather than an unbiased and unprejudiced weigher of the evidence. (*Neumann v. Bishop* (1976) 59 Cal.App.3d 451, 484-485.) A reference to Biblical authority is potentially dangerous. (*People v. Roldan* (2005) 35 Cal.4th 646, 743.)

Reasonable Doubt - Prosecution Charts and Graphs

Prosecutors should use caution when using a charts or graphs to illustrate reasonable doubt standards. Prosecution argument suggesting the reasonable doubt standard is used in daily life to decide such questions as whether to change lanes or marry," are "strongly disapproved" because they tend to "trivialize" the standard and may suggest that it is met by a decision based on reflex or whim, rather than on the requisite abiding conviction and moral certainty. *(People v. Nguyen* (1995) 40 Cal.App.4th 28, 36; see also *People v. Garcia* (1975) 54 Cal.App.3d 61, 69 [cautioning against a " 'watering down' " of the standard by "diverting the jury, in some degree, from their constitutionally prescribed duty not to find guilt unless they 'be reasonably persuaded to a near certainty].)

Experiments,' including mere graphs, lines, charts, or Power Point presentations, may imperil a prosecutor's attempt to establish the concept of guilt beyond a reasonable doubt. "Prosecutors would be wise to avoid such devices. Otherwise a conviction on a closer case may be jeopardized, especially if the trial court does not sustain defense counsel's objection to the argument and fails to advise the jury to disregard the objected to presentation." (*People v. Otero* (2012) 210 Cal.App.4th 865, 873 [error for prosecutor to use mislabeled diagram of California to explain reasonable doubt]; See also *People v. Katzenberger* (2009) 178 Cal.App.4th 1260, 1268 [error for prosecutor to use jigsaw puzzle to explain reasonable doubt.]) Facts supporting proof of each required element must be found in the evidence or the People's burden of proof is unmet. It is thus misleading to analogize a jury's task to solving a picture puzzle depicting an actual and familiar object unrelated to the evidence. (*People v. Centeno* (2014) 60 Cal.4th 659, 669.)

However, charts and graphs used to illustrate *evidence* are proper. "Not all visual aids are suspect. The use of charts, diagrams, lists, and comparisons based on the evidence may be effectively and fairly used in argument to help the jury analyze the case." (*Centeno*, supra, at p. 671)

Misstating the Law

"Although counsel has broad discretion in discussing the legal and factual merits of a case, it is improper to misstate the law. (*People v. Mendoza* (2007) 42 Cal.4th 686, 702.)

APPENDIX

<u>Selected California Evidence Code Sections</u> (Not referenced above) See index for all code sections.

Evid. Code § 1220. Admission of party (FRE 801(d)(2))

Evidence of a statement is not made inadmissible by the hearsay rule when offered against the declarant in an action to which he is a party in either his individual or representative capacity, regardless of whether the statement was made in his individual or representative capacity.

Evid. Code § 1221. Adoptive admission (FRE 801(d)(2))

Evidence of a statement offered against a party is not made inadmissible by the hearsay rule if the statement is one of which the party, with knowledge of the content thereof, has by words or other conduct manifested his adoption or his belief in its truth.

Evid. Code § 1223. Admission of co-conspirator (FRE 801(d)(2)(E))

Evidence of a statement offered against a party is not made inadmissible by the hearsay rule if:

(a) The statement was made by the declarant while participating in a conspiracy to commit a crime or civil wrong and in furtherance of the objective of that conspiracy;

(b) The statement was made prior to or during the time that the party was participating in that conspiracy; and

(c) The evidence is offered either after admission of evidence sufficient to sustain a finding of the facts specified in subdivisions (a) and (b) or, in the court's discretion as to the order of proof, subject to the admission of such evidence.

Evid. Code § 1230. Declarations against interest (FRE 804(b)(3))

Evidence of a statement by a declarant having sufficient knowledge of the subject is not made inadmissible by the hearsay rule if the declarant is unavailable as a witness and the statement, when made, was so far contrary to the declarant's pecuniary or proprietary interest, or so far subjected him to the risk of civil or criminal liability, or so far tended to render invalid a claim by him against another, or created such a risk of making him an object of hatred, ridicule, or social disgrace in the community, that a reasonable man in his position would not have made the statement unless he believed it to be true.

Evid. Code § 1238. Prior identification (FRE 801(d)(1)(C))

Evidence of a statement previously made by a witness is not made inadmissible by the hearsay rule if the statement would have been admissible if made by him while testifying and:

(a) The statement is an identification of a party or another as a person who participated in a crime or other occurrence;

(b) The statement was made at a time when the crime or other occurrence was fresh in the witness' memory; and

(c) The evidence of the statement is offered after the witness testifies that he made the identification and that it was a true reflection of his opinion at that time.

Evid. Code § 1240. Spontaneous statement (FRE 803(2))

Evidence of a statement is not made inadmissible by the hearsay rule if the statement:

(a) Purports to narrate, describe, or explain an act, condition, or event perceived by the declarant; and

(b) Was made spontaneously while the declarant was under the stress of excitement caused by such perception.

Evid. Code § 1241. Contemporaneous statement (FRE 803(3))
Evidence of a statement is not made inadmissible by the hearsay rule if the statement:

(a) Is offered to explain, qualify, or make understandable conduct of the declarant; and

(b) Was made while the declarant was engaged in such conduct.

Evid. Code § 1242. Dying declaration (FRE 804(b)(2))
Evidence of a statement made by a dying person respecting the cause and circumstances of his death is not made inadmissible by the hearsay rule if the statement was made upon his personal knowledge and under a sense of immediately impending death.

Evid. Code § 1250. Statement of declarant's then existing mental or physical state (FRE 803(3))
(a) Subject to Section 1252, evidence of a statement of the declarant's then existing state of mind, emotion, or physical sensation (including a statement of intent, plan, motive, design, mental feeling, pain, or bodily health) is not made inadmissible by the hearsay rule when:

(1) The evidence is offered to prove the declarant's state of mind, emotion, or physical sensation at that time or at any other time when it is itself an issue in the action; or

(2) The evidence is offered to prove or explain acts or conduct of the declarant.

(b) This section does not make admissible evidence of a statement of memory or belief to prove the fact remembered or believed.

Evid. Code § 1251. Statement of declarant's previously existing mental or physical state
Subject to Section 1252, evidence of a statement of the declarant's state of mind, emotion, or physical sensation (including a statement of intent, plan, motive, design, mental feeling, pain, or bodily health) at a time prior to the statement is not made inadmissible by the hearsay rule if:

(a) The declarant is unavailable as a witness; and

(b) The evidence is offered to prove such prior state of mind, emotion, or physical sensation when it is itself an issue in the action and the evidence is not offered to prove any fact other than such state of mind, emotion, or physical sensation.

Evid. Code § 1252. Restriction on admissibility of statement of mental or physical state
Evidence of a statement is inadmissible under this article if the statement was made under circumstances such as to indicate its lack of trustworthiness.

Evid. Code § 1270. A business
As used in this article, "a business" includes every kind of business, governmental activity, profession, occupation, calling, or operation of institutions, whether carried on for profit or not.

Evid. Code § 1271. Admissible writing (FRE 803(6))
Evidence of a writing made as a record of an act, condition, or event is not made inadmissible by the hearsay rule when offered to prove the act, condition, or event if:

(a) The writing was made in the regular course of a business;

(b) The writing was made at or near the time of the act, condition, or event;

(c) The custodian or other qualified witness testifies to its identity and the mode of its preparation; and

(d) The sources of information and method and time of preparation were such as to indicate its trustworthiness.

Evid. Code § 1280. Record by public employee (FRE 803(8))

Evidence of a writing made as a record of an act, condition, or event is not made inadmissible by the hearsay rule when offered in any civil or criminal proceeding to prove the act, condition, or event if all of the following applies:

(a) The writing was made by and within the scope of duty of a public employee.

(b) The writing was made at or near the time of the act, condition, or event.

(c) The sources of information and method and time of preparation were such as to indicate its trustworthiness.

Evid. Code § 1291. Former testimony offered against party to former proceeding (FRE 804(b)(1))

(a) Evidence of former testimony is not made inadmissible by the hearsay rule if the declarant is unavailable as a witness and:

(1) The former testimony is offered against a person who offered it in evidence in his own behalf on the former occasion or against the successor in interest of such person; or

(2) The party against whom the former testimony is offered was a party to the action or proceeding in which the testimony was given and had the right and opportunity to cross-examine the declarant with an interest and motive similar to that which he has at the hearing.

(b) The admissibility of former testimony under this section is subject to the same limitations and objections as though the declarant were testifying at the hearing, except that former testimony offered under this section is not subject to: (1) Objections to the form of the question which were not made at the time the former testimony was given. (2) Objections based on competency or privilege which did not exist at the time the former testimony was given.

Evid. Code § 1340. Publications relied upon as accurate in the course of business

Evidence of a statement, other than an opinion, contained in a tabulation, list, directory, register, or other published compilation is not made inadmissible by the hearsay rule if the compilation is generally used and relied upon as accurate in the course of a business as defined in Section 1270.

Evid. Code § 1341. Publications concerning facts of general notoriety and interests (FRE 803(18))

Historical works, books of science or art, and published maps or charts, made by persons indifferent between the parties, are not made inadmissible by the hearsay rule when offered to prove facts of general notoriety and interest.

Evid. Code § 1520. Content of writing; proof

The content of a writing may be proved by an otherwise admissible original

Evid. Code § 1521. Secondary evidence rule (See supra, at p. 191.)

Evid. Code § 1523. Oral testimony of the content of a writing; admissibility

(a) Except as otherwise provided by statute, oral testimony is not admissible to prove the content of a writing.

(b) Oral testimony of the content of a writing is not made inadmissible by subdivision (a) if the proponent does not have possession or control of a copy of the writing and the original is lost or has been destroyed without fraudulent intent on the part of the proponent of the evidence.

(c) Oral testimony of the content of a writing is not made inadmissible by subdivision (a) if the proponent does not have possession or control of the original or a copy of the writing and either of the following conditions is satisfied:

(1) Neither the writing nor a copy of the writing was reasonably procurable by the proponent by use of the court's process or by other available means.

(2) The writing is not closely related to the controlling issues and it would be inexpedient to require its production.

(d) Oral testimony of the content of a writing is not made inadmissible by subdivision (a) if the writing consists of numerous accounts or other writings that cannot be examined in court without great loss of time, and the evidence sought from them is only the general result of the whole.

Selected Federal Rules of Evidence

FRE Rule 103. Rulings on Evidence   (CA Evid. Code § 353-354)

(a) Preserving a Claim of Error. A party may claim error in a ruling to admit or exclude evidence only if the error affects a substantial right of the party and:

(1) if the ruling admits evidence, a party, on the record:

(A) timely objects or moves to strike; and

(B) states the specific ground, unless it was apparent from the context; or

(2) if the ruling excludes evidence, a party informs the court of its substance by an offer of proof, unless the substance was apparent from the context.

(b) Not Needing to Renew an Objection or Offer of Proof. Once the court rules definitively on the record--either before or at trial--a party need not renew an objection or offer of proof to preserve a claim of error for appeal.

(c) Court's Statement About the Ruling; Directing an Offer of Proof. The court may make any statement about the character or form of the evidence, the objection made, and the ruling. The court may direct that an offer of proof be made in question-and-answer form.

(d) Preventing the Jury from Hearing Inadmissible Evidence. To the extent practicable, the court must conduct a jury trial so that inadmissible evidence is not suggested to the jury by any means.

(e) Taking Notice of Plain Error. A court may take notice of a plain error affecting a substantial right, even if the claim of error was not properly preserved.

FRE Rule 104. Preliminary Questions (CA Evid. Code §§ 402-403)

(a) In General. The court must decide any preliminary question about whether a witness is qualified, a privilege exists, or evidence is admissible. In so deciding, the court is not bound by evidence rules, except those on privilege.

(b) Relevance That Depends on a Fact. When the relevance of evidence depends on whether a fact exists, proof must be introduced sufficient to support a finding that the fact does exist.

The court may admit the proposed evidence on the condition that the proof be introduced later.

(c) Conducting a Hearing So That the Jury Cannot Hear It. The court must conduct any hearing on a preliminary question so that the jury cannot hear it if:

> (1) the hearing involves the admissibility of a confession;

> (2) a defendant in a criminal case is a witness and so requests; or

> (3) justice so requires.

(d) Cross-Examining a Defendant in a Criminal Case. By testifying on a preliminary question, a defendant in a criminal case does not become subject to cross-examination on other issues in the case.

(e) Evidence Relevant to Weight and Credibility. This rule does not limit a party's right to introduce before the jury evidence that is relevant to the weight or credibility of other evidence.

FRE Rule 106. Remainder of or Related Writings or Recorded Statements (CA Evid. Code § 356)

If a party introduces all or part of a writing or recorded statement, an adverse party may require the introduction, at that time, of any other part--or any other writing or recorded statement-- that in fairness ought to be considered at the same time.

FRE Rule 201. Judicial Notice of Adjudicative Facts." (CA Evid. Code §§ 450-458)

(a) Scope. This rule governs judicial notice of an adjudicative fact only, not a legislative fact.

(b) Kinds of Facts That May Be Judicially Noticed. The court may judicially notice a fact that is not subject to reasonable dispute because it:

> (1) is generally known within the trial court's territorial jurisdiction; or

> (2) can be accurately and readily determined from sources whose accuracy cannot reasonably be questioned.

(c) Taking Notice. The court:

> (1) may take judicial notice on its own; or

> (2) must take judicial notice if a party requests it and the court is supplied with the necessary information.

(d) Timing. The court may take judicial notice at any stage of the proceeding.

(e) Opportunity to Be Heard. On timely request, a party is entitled to be heard on the propriety of taking judicial notice and the nature of the fact to be noticed. If the court takes judicial notice before notifying a party, the party, on request, is still entitled to be heard.

(f) Instructing the Jury. In a civil case, the court must instruct the jury to accept the noticed fact as conclusive. In a criminal case, the court must instruct the jury that it may or may not accept the noticed fact as conclusive.

FRE Rule 401. Test for Relevant Evidence   (CA Evid. Code § 210)

Evidence is relevant if:

(a) it has any tendency to make a fact more or less probable than it would be without the evidence; and

(b) the fact is of consequence in determining the action.

FRE Rule 402. General Admissibility of Relevant Evidence (CA Evid. Code § 350 - 351)

Relevant evidence is admissible unless any of the following provides otherwise:

• the United States Constitution;

• a federal statute;

• these rules; or

• other rules prescribed by the Supreme Court.

Irrelevant evidence is not admissible.

FRE Rule 403. Excluding Relevant Evidence for Prejudice, Confusion, Waste of Time, or Other Reasons (CA Evid. Code § 352)

The court may exclude relevant evidence if its probative value is substantially outweighed by a danger of one or more of the following: unfair prejudice, confusing the issues, misleading the jury, undue delay, wasting time, or needlessly presenting cumulative evidence.

FRE Rule 404 Evidence; Other Crimes, Wrongs or Acts (CA Evid. Code 1101)

(a) Character Evidence.

(1) Prohibited Uses. Evidence of a person's character or character trait is not admissible to prove that on a particular occasion the person acted in accordance with the character or trait.

(2) Exceptions for a Defendant or Victim in a Criminal Case. The following exceptions apply in a criminal case:

(A) a defendant may offer evidence of the defendant's pertinent trait, and if the evidence is admitted, the prosecutor may offer evidence to rebut it;

(B) subject to the limitations in Rule 412, a defendant may offer evidence of an alleged victim's pertinent trait, and if the evidence is admitted, the prosecutor may:

(i) offer evidence to rebut it; and

(ii) offer evidence of the defendant's same trait; and

(C) in a homicide case, the prosecutor may offer evidence of the alleged victim's trait of peacefulness to rebut evidence that the victim was the first aggressor.

(3) Exceptions for a Witness. Evidence of a witness's character may be admitted under Rules 607, 608, and 609.

(b) Other Crimes, Wrongs, or Acts.

(1) Prohibited Uses. Evidence of any other crime, wrong, or act is not admissible to prove a person's character in order to show that on a particular occasion the person acted in accordance with the character.

(2) Permitted Uses. This evidence may be admissible for another purpose, such as proving motive, opportunity, intent, preparation, plan, knowledge, identity, absence of mistake, or lack of accident.

(3) Notice in a Criminal Case. In a criminal case, the prosecutor must:

(A) provide reasonable notice of any such evidence that the prosecutor intends to offer at trial, so that the defendant has a fair opportunity to meet it;

(B) articulate in the notice the permitted purpose for which the prosecutor intends to offer the evidence and the reasoning that supports the purpose; and

(C) do so in writing before trial--or in any form during trial if the court, for good cause, excuses lack of pretrial notice.

FRE Rule 405. Methods of Proving Character

(a) By Reputation or Opinion. When evidence of a person's character or character trait is admissible, it may be proved by testimony about the person's reputation or by testimony in the form of an opinion. On cross-examination of the character witness, the court may allow an inquiry into relevant specific instances of the person's conduct.

(b) By Specific Instances of Conduct. When a person's character or character trait is an essential element of a charge, claim, or defense, the character or trait may also be proved by relevant specific instances of the person's conduct.

FRE Rule 501. Privilege in General (CA Evid. Code §§ 900 thru 1070.)
The common law--as interpreted by United States courts in the light of reason and experience--governs a claim of privilege unless any of the following provides otherwise:
• the United States Constitution;
• a federal statute; or
• rules prescribed by the Supreme Court.
But in a civil case, state law governs privilege regarding a claim or defense for which state law supplies the rule of decision.

FRE Rule 601. Competency to Testify in General (CA Evid. Code § 700-701)
Every person is competent to be a witness unless these rules provide otherwise. But in a civil case, state law governs the witness's competency regarding a claim or defense for which state law supplies the rule of decision.

FRE Rule 602   Need for Personal Knowledge   (CA Evid. Code § 702)
A witness may testify to a matter only if evidence is introduced sufficient to support a finding that the witness has personal knowledge of the matter. Evidence to prove personal knowledge may consist of the witness's own testimony. This rule does not apply to a witness's expert testimony under Rule 703.

FRE Rule 603. Oath or Affirmation to Testify Truthfully (CA Evid. Code § 710)
Before testifying, a witness must give an oath or affirmation to testify truthfully. It must be in a form designed to impress that duty on the witness's conscience.

FRE Rule 607. Who May Impeach a Witness   (CA Evid. Code § 785)
Any party, including the party that called the witness, may attack the witness's credibility.

FRE Rule 608. A Witness's Character for Truthfulness or Untruthfulness
(CA Evidence Code §§786-790)
(a) Reputation or Opinion Evidence. A witness's credibility may be attacked or supported by testimony about the witness's reputation for having a character for truthfulness or untruthfulness, or by testimony in the form of an opinion about that character. But evidence of truthful character is admissible only after the witness's character for truthfulness has been attacked.
(b) Specific Instances of Conduct. Except for a criminal conviction under Rule 609, extrinsic evidence is not admissible to prove specific instances of a witness's conduct in order to attack or support the witness's character for truthfulness. But the court may, on cross-examination, allow them to be inquired into if they are probative of the character for truthfulness or untruthfulness of:
    (1) the witness; or
    (2) another witness whose character the witness being cross-examined has testified about.
By testifying on another matter, a witness does not waive any privilege against self-incrimination for testimony that relates only to the witness's character for truthfulness

FRE Rule 611. Mode and Order of Examining Witnesses and Presenting Evidence (CA Evid. Code § 765)

(a) Control by the Court; Purposes. The court should exercise reasonable control over the mode and order of examining witnesses and presenting evidence so as to:

(1) make those procedures effective for determining the truth;

(2) avoid wasting time; and

(3) protect witnesses from harassment or undue embarrassment.

(b) Scope of Cross-Examination. Cross-examination should not go beyond the subject matter of the direct examination and matters affecting the witness's credibility. The court may allow inquiry into additional matters as if on direct examination.

(c) Leading Questions. Leading questions should not be used on direct examination except as necessary to develop the witness's testimony. Ordinarily, the court should allow leading questions:

(1) on cross-examination; and

(2) when a party calls a hostile witness, an adverse party, or a witness identified with an adverse party.

FRE Rule 612. Writing Used to Refresh a Witness's Memory (CA Evid. Code § 771)

(a) Scope. This rule gives an adverse party certain options when a witness uses a writing to refresh memory:

(1) while testifying; or

(2) before testifying, if the court decides that justice requires the party to have those options.

(b) Adverse Party's Options; Deleting Unrelated Matter. Unless 18 U.S.C. § 3500 provides otherwise in a criminal case, an adverse party is entitled to have the writing produced at the hearing, to inspect it, to cross-examine the witness about it, and to introduce in evidence any portion that relates to the witness's testimony. If the producing party claims that the writing includes unrelated matter, the court must examine the writing in camera, delete any unrelated portion, and order that the rest be delivered to the adverse party. Any portion deleted over objection must be preserved for the record.

(c) Failure to Produce or Deliver the Writing. If a writing is not produced or is not delivered as ordered, the court may issue any appropriate order. But if the prosecution does not comply in a criminal case, the court must strike the witness's testimony or--if justice so requires-- declare a mistrial

FRE Rule 613. Witness's Prior Statement (CA Evid. Code § 1235/770)

(a) Showing or Disclosing the Statement During Examination. When examining a witness about the witness's prior statement, a party need not show it or disclose its contents to the witness. But the party must, on request, show it or disclose its contents to an adverse party's attorney.

(b) Extrinsic Evidence of a Prior Inconsistent Statement. Extrinsic evidence of a witness's prior inconsistent statement is admissible only if the witness is given an opportunity to explain or deny the statement and an adverse party is given an opportunity to examine the witness about it, or if justice so requires. This subdivision (b) does not apply to an opposing party's statement under Rule 801(d)(2).

FRE Rule 615. Excluding Witnesses   (CA Evid. Code § 777)

At a party's request, the court must order witnesses excluded so that they cannot hear other witnesses' testimony. Or the court may do so on its own. But this rule does not authorize excluding:

(a) a party who is a natural person;

(b) an officer or employee of a party that is not a natural person, after being designated as the party's representative by its attorney;

(c) a person whose presence a party shows to be essential to presenting the party's claim or defense; or

(d) a person authorized by statute to be present.

FRE Rule 701. Opinion Testimony by Lay Witnesses (CA Evid. Code § 800)

If a witness is not testifying as an expert, testimony in the form of an opinion is limited to one that is:

(a) rationally based on the witness's perception;

(b) helpful to clearly understanding the witness's testimony or to determining a fact in issue; and

(c) not based on scientific, technical, or other specialized knowledge within the scope of Rule 702. (Experts)

FRE Rule 702. Testimony by Expert Witnesses (CA Evid. Code § § 801-802)

A witness who is qualified as an expert by knowledge, skill, experience, training, or education may testify in the form of an opinion or otherwise if:

(a) the expert's scientific, technical, or other specialized knowledge will help the trier of fact to understand the evidence or to determine a fact in issue;

(b) the testimony is based on sufficient facts or data;

(c) the testimony is the product of reliable principles and methods; and

(d) the expert has reliably applied the principles and methods to the facts of the case.

FRE Rule 703. Bases of an Expert's Opinion (CA Evid. Code § 802)

An expert may base an opinion on facts or data in the case that the expert has been made aware of or personally observed. If experts in the particular field would reasonably rely on those kinds of facts or data in forming an opinion on the subject, they need not be admissible for the opinion to be admitted. But if the facts or data would otherwise be inadmissible, the proponent of the opinion may disclose them to the jury only if their probative value in helping the jury evaluate the opinion substantially outweighs their prejudicial effect.

FRE Rule 704. Opinion on an Ultimate Issue (CA Evid. Code §805)

(a) In General--Not Automatically Objectionable. An opinion is not objectionable just because it embraces an ultimate issue.

(b) Exception. In a criminal case, an expert witness must not state an opinion about whether the defendant did or did not have a mental state or condition that constitutes an element of the crime charged or of a defense. Those matters are for the trier of fact alone.

FRE Rule 705. Disclosing the Facts or Data Underlying an Expert's Opinion

Unless the court orders otherwise, an expert may state an opinion--and give the reasons for it--without first testifying to the underlying facts or data. But the expert may be required to disclose those facts or data on cross-examination.

FRE Rule 801. Definitions That Apply to This Article; Exclusions From Hearsay

(a) Statement. "Statement" means a person's oral assertion, written assertion, or nonverbal conduct, if the person intended it as an assertion.

(b) Declarant. "Declarant" means the person who made the statement.

(c) Hearsay. "Hearsay" means a statement that:

(1) the declarant does not make while testifying at the current trial or hearing; and

(2) a party offers in evidence to prove the truth of the matter asserted in the statement.

(d) Statements That Are Not Hearsay. A statement that meets the following conditions is not hearsay:

(1) A Declarant-Witness's Prior Statement. The declarant testifies and is subject to cross-examination about a prior statement, and the statement:

(A) is inconsistent with the declarant's testimony and was given under penalty of perjury at a trial, hearing, or other proceeding or in a deposition;

(B) is consistent with the declarant's testimony and is offered:

(i) to rebut an express or implied charge that the declarant recently fabricated it or acted from a recent improper influence or motive in so testifying; or

(ii) to rehabilitate the declarant's credibility as a witness when attacked on another ground; or

(C) identifies a person as someone the declarant perceived earlier.

(2) An Opposing Party's Statement. The statement is offered against an opposing party and:

(A) was made by the party in an individual or representative capacity;

(B) is one the party manifested that it adopted or believed to be true;

(C) was made by a person whom the party authorized to make a statement on the subject;

(D) was made by the party's agent or employee on a matter within the scope of that relationship and while it existed; or

(E) was made by the party's coconspirator during and in furtherance of the conspiracy.

The statement must be considered but does not by itself establish the declarant's authority under (C); the existence or scope of the relationship under (D); or the existence of the conspiracy or participation in it under (E).

FRE Rule 802. The Rule Against Hearsay (CA Evid. Code § 1200 et seq.)

Hearsay is not admissible unless any of the following provides otherwise:

• a federal statute;

• these rules; or

• other rules prescribed by the Supreme Court.

FRE Rule 803. Exceptions (selected) to the Rule Against Hearsay--Regardless of Whether the Declarant Is Available as a Witness (CA Evid. Code § 1220 et seq.)

The following are not excluded by the rule against hearsay, regardless of whether the declarant is available as a witness:

(1) Present Sense Impression. A statement describing or explaining an event or condition, made while or immediately after the declarant perceived it.

(2) Excited Utterance. A statement relating to a startling event or condition, made while the declarant was under the stress of excitement that it caused.

(3) Then-Existing Mental, Emotional, or Physical Condition. A statement of the declarant's then-existing state of mind (such as motive, intent, or plan) or emotional, sensory, or physical condition (such as mental feeling, pain, or bodily health), but not including a statement of memory or belief to prove the fact remembered or believed unless it relates to the validity or terms of the declarant's will.

(4) Statement Made for Medical Diagnosis or Treatment. A statement that:

(A) is made for--and is reasonably pertinent to--medical diagnosis or treatment; and

(B) describes medical history; past or present symptoms or sensations; their inception; or their general cause.

(5) Recorded Recollection. A record that:

(A) is on a matter the witness once knew about but now cannot recall well enough to testify fully and accurately;

(B) was made or adopted by the witness when the matter was fresh in the witness's memory; and

(C) accurately reflects the witness's knowledge.

If admitted, the record may be read into evidence but may be received as an exhibit only if offered by an adverse party.

(6) Records of a Regularly Conducted Activity. A record of an act, event, condition, opinion, or diagnosis if:

(A) the record was made at or near the time by--or from information transmitted by--someone with knowledge;

(B) the record was kept in the course of a regularly conducted activity of a business, organization, occupation, or calling, whether or not for profit;

(C) making the record was a regular practice of that activity;

(D) all these conditions are shown by the testimony of the custodian or another qualified witness, or by a certification that complies with Rule 902(11) or (12) or with a statute permitting certification; and

(E) the opponent does not show that the source of information or the method or circumstances of preparation indicate a lack of trustworthiness.

(7) Absence of a Record of a Regularly Conducted Activity. Evidence that a matter is not included in a record described in paragraph (6) if:

(A) the evidence is admitted to prove that the matter did not occur or exist;

(B) a record was regularly kept for a matter of that kind; and

(C) the opponent does not show that the possible source of the information or other circumstances indicate a lack of trustworthiness.

(8) Public Records. A record or statement of a public office if:

(A) it sets out:

(i) the office's activities;

(ii) a matter observed while under a legal duty to report, but not including, in a criminal case, a matter observed by law-enforcement personnel; or

(iii) in a civil case or against the government in a criminal case, factual findings from a legally authorized investigation; and

(B) the opponent does not show that the source of information or other circumstances indicate a lack of trustworthiness.

(9) Public Records of Vital Statistics. A record of a birth, death, or marriage, if reported to a public office in accordance with a legal duty.

(16) Statements in Ancient Documents. A statement in a document that was prepared before January 1, 1998, and whose authenticity is established.

(18) Statements in Learned Treatises, Periodicals, or Pamphlets. A statement contained

in a treatise, periodical, or pamphlet if:

(A) the statement is called to the attention of an expert witness on cross-examination or relied on by the expert on direct examination; and

(B) the publication is established as a reliable authority by the expert's admission or testimony, by another expert's testimony, or by judicial notice.

If admitted, the statement may be read into evidence but not received as an exhibit.

(22) Judgment of a Previous Conviction. Evidence of a final judgment of conviction if:

(A) the judgment was entered after a trial or guilty plea, but not a nolo contendere plea;

(B) the conviction was for a crime punishable by death or by imprisonment for more than a year;

(C) the evidence is admitted to prove any fact essential to the judgment; and

(D) when offered by the prosecutor in a criminal case for a purpose other than impeachment, the judgment was against the defendant.

The pendency of an appeal may be shown but does not affect admissibility.

FRE Rule 804. Exceptions to the Rule Against Hearsay--When the Declarant Is Unavailable as a Witness (CA Evid. Code § 1220 et seq.)

(a) Criteria for Being Unavailable. A declarant is considered to be unavailable as a witness if the declarant:

(1) is exempted from testifying about the subject matter of the declarant's statement because the court rules that a privilege applies;

(2) refuses to testify about the subject matter despite a court order to do so;

(3) testifies to not remembering the subject matter;

(4) cannot be present or testify at the trial or hearing because of death or a then-existing infirmity, physical illness, or mental illness; or

(5) is absent from the trial or hearing and the statement's proponent has not been able, by process or other reasonable means, to procure:

(A) the declarant's attendance, in the case of a hearsay exception under Rule 804(b)(1) or (6); or

(B) the declarant's attendance or testimony, in the case of a hearsay exception under Rule 804(b)(2), (3), or (4).

But this subdivision (a) does not apply if the statement's proponent procured or wrongfully caused the declarant's unavailability as a witness in order to prevent the declarant from attending or testifying.

(b) The Exceptions. The following are not excluded by the rule against hearsay if the declarant is unavailable as a witness:

(1) Former Testimony. Testimony that:

(A) was given as a witness at a trial, hearing, or lawful deposition, whether given during the current proceeding or a different one; and

(B) is now offered against a party who had--or, in a civil case, whose predecessor in interest had--an opportunity and similar motive to develop it by direct, cross-, or redirect examination.

(2) Statement Under the Belief of Imminent Death. In a prosecution for homicide or in a civil case, a statement that the declarant, while believing the declarant's death to be imminent, made about its cause or circumstances.

(3) Statement Against Interest. A statement that:

(A) a reasonable person in the declarant's position would have made only if the person believed it to be true because, when made, it was so contrary to the declarant's proprietary or pecuniary interest or had so great a tendency to invalidate the declarant's claim against someone else or to expose the declarant to civil or criminal liability; and

(B) is supported by corroborating circumstances that clearly indicate its trustworthiness, if it is offered in a criminal case as one that tends to expose the declarant to criminal liability.

(4) Statement of Personal or Family History. A statement about:

(A) the declarant's own birth, adoption, legitimacy, ancestry, marriage, divorce, relationship by blood, adoption, or marriage, or similar facts of personal or family history, even though the declarant had no way of acquiring personal knowledge about that fact; or

(B) another person concerning any of these facts, as well as death, if the declarant was related to the person by blood, adoption, or marriage or was so intimately associated with the person's family that the declarant's information is likely to be accurate.

(6) Statement Offered Against a Party That Wrongfully Caused the Declarant's Unavailability. A statement offered against a party that wrongfully caused--or acquiesced in wrongfully causing--the declarant's unavailability as a witness, and did so intending that result.

FRE Rule 805. Hearsay Within Hearsay (CA Evid. Code § 1201)

Hearsay within hearsay is not excluded by the rule against hearsay if each part of the combined statements conforms with an exception to the rule.

FRE Rule 806. Attacking and Supporting the Declarant's Credibility (CA Evid. Code § 1202)

When a hearsay statement--or a statement described been admit in Rule 801(d)(2)(C), (D), or (E)--has ed in evidence, the declarant's credibility may be attacked, and then supported, by any evidence that would be admissible for those purposes if the declarant had testified as a witness. The court may admit evidence of the declarant's inconsistent statement or conduct, regardless of when it occurred or whether the declarant had an opportunity to explain or deny it. If the party against whom the statement was admitted calls the declarant as a witness, the party may examine the declarant on the statement as if on cross-examination.

FRE Rule 807. Residual Exception

(a) In General. Under the following conditions, a hearsay statement is not excluded by the rule against hearsay even if the statement is not admissible under a hearsay exception in Rule 803 or 804:

(1) the statement is supported by sufficient guarantees of trustworthiness--after considering the totality of circumstances under which it was made and evidence, if any, corroborating the statement; and

(2) it is more probative on the point for which it is offered than any other evidence that the proponent can obtain through reasonable efforts.

(b) Notice. The statement is admissible only if the proponent gives an adverse party reasonable notice of the intent to offer the statement--including its substance and the declarant's name--so that the party has a fair opportunity to meet it. The notice must be provided in writing before the trial or hearing--or in any form during the trial or hearing if the court, for good cause, excuses a lack of earlier notice.

FRE Rule 901. Authenticating or Identifying Evidence (CA Evid. §§ Code 1400-1421)

(a) In General. To satisfy the requirement of authenticating or identifying an item of evidence, the proponent must produce evidence sufficient to support a finding that the item is what the proponent claims it is.

(b) Examples. The following are examples only--not a complete list--of evidence that satisfies the requirement:

(1) Testimony of a Witness with Knowledge. Testimony that an item is what it is claimed to be.

(2) Nonexpert Opinion About Handwriting. A nonexpert's opinion that handwriting is genuine, based on a familiarity with it that was not acquired for the current litigation.

(3) Comparison by an Expert Witness or the Trier of Fact. A comparison with an authenticated specimen by an expert witness or the trier of fact.

(4) Distinctive Characteristics and the Like. The appearance, contents, substance, internal patterns, or other distinctive characteristics of the item, taken together with all the circumstances.

(5) Opinion About a Voice. An opinion identifying a person's voice--whether heard firsthand or through mechanical or electronic transmission or recording--based on hearing the voice at any time under circumstances that connect it with the alleged speaker.

(6) Evidence About a Telephone Conversation. For a telephone conversation, evidence that a call was made to the number assigned at the time to:

(A) a particular person, if circumstances, including self-identification, show that the person answering was the one called; or

(B) a particular business, if the call was made to a business and the call related to business reasonably transacted over the telephone.

(7) Evidence About Public Records. Evidence that:

(A) a document was recorded or filed in a public office as authorized by law; or

(B) a purported public record or statement is from the office where items of this kind are kept.

(8) Evidence About Ancient Documents or Data Compilations. For a document or data compilation, evidence that it:

(A) is in a condition that creates no suspicion about its authenticity;

(B) was in a place where, if authentic, it would likely be; and

(C) is at least 20 years old when offered.

(9) Evidence About a Process or System. Evidence describing a process or system and showing that it produces an accurate result.

(10) Methods Provided by a Statute or Rule. Any method of authentication or identification allowed by a federal statute or a rule prescribed by the Supreme Court.

FRE Rule 1002. Requirement of the Original (CA Evid. Code §§ 1520-1521)

An original writing, recording, or photograph is required in order to prove its content unless these rules or a federal statute provides otherwise.

FRE Rule 1003. Admissibility of Duplicates

A duplicate is admissible to the same extent as the original unless a genuine question is raised about the original's authenticity or the circumstances make it unfair to admit the duplicate.

FRE Rule 1004. Admissibility of Other Evidence of Content

An original is not required and other evidence of the content of a writing, recording, or photograph is admissible if:

(a) all the originals are lost or destroyed, and not by the proponent acting in bad faith;

(b) an original cannot be obtained by any available judicial process;

(c) the party against whom the original would be offered had control of the original; was at that time put on notice, by pleadings or otherwise, that the original would be a subject of proof at the trial or hearing; and fails to produce it at the trial or hearing; or (d) the writing, recording, or photograph is not closely related to a controlling issue.

FRE Rule 1007. Testimony or Statement of a Party to Prove Content

The proponent may prove the content of a writing, recording, or photograph by the testimony, deposition, or written statement of the party against whom the evidence is offered. The proponent need not account for the original.

FRE Rule 1008. Functions of Court and Jury

Ordinarily, the court determines whether the proponent has fulfilled the factual conditions for admitting other evidence of the content of a writing, recording, or photograph under Rule 1004 or 1005. But in a jury trial, the jury determines--in accordance with Rule 104(b)--any issue about whether:

(a) an asserted writing, recording, or photograph ever existed;

(b) another one produced at the trial or hearing is the original; or

(c) other evidence of content accurately reflects the content.

Index

California Code Sections

AUTHOR'S NOTE

As mentioned in the Introduction, this handbook took me about five years to complete during my spare time and I did so without the assistance of a research team or a formal publisher. I chose to self-publish because with today's technology it is relatively easy and the author maintains more control. That being said, I welcome any comment or constructive criticism about the handbook such that I can improve and/or update it in the future. Thank you. Mark Curry

trialhandbook@gmail.com

Made in the USA
Las Vegas, NV
06 October 2024

96356130R00166